PRAISE FOR 5/5/2000

D0473057

5/5/2000
ICE: THE ULTIMATE DISASTER

It is 5 P.M. in Boston and the people rushing home from work hardly notice how the setting sun seems to hang on the horizon. They start to wonder why darkness is not coming and start to fear the dull roar they hear. The dull roar gets louder and louder, and the wind blows in gusts up to 100 miles per hour. Trees are plucked from the ground and railroad trains are tumbled over and over. Because of the wind-chill factor, the temperature has plummeted down to just above freezing, even though it is spring. After two days of utter turmoil the winds suddenly subside and material from the sky starts to come crashing down. For a few minutes it seems to be raining automobiles, boats, washing machines, and kitchen sinks. The temperature starts to rise; soon it hits 103°F, just what one would expect for this time of the year—in Africa not Boston. Layers of mud spread for thousands of miles.

— From *We Are The Earthquake Generation*
by Dr. Jeffery Goodman. Adapted from
Chapter One, 5/5/2000.

Colonnade to the temple of Amon-Ra. Drawn by Napoleon's savants in 1798. Aimed like a telescope, the colonnade and the temple's axis oriented to the summer solstice.
From *Secrets of the Great Pyramid,* copyright ©1971 by Peter Tompkins.
Used by Permission.

5/5/2000

ICE: THE ULTIMATE DISASTER

by
RICHARD W. NOONE
Foreword by Richard Kieninger

Three Rivers Press
New York

The author gratefully acknowledges the use of the illustrations reprinted from *Secrets of the Great Pyramid* copyright © 1971, *Mysteries of the Mexican Pyramids* copyright © 1976, and *The Magic of Obelisks* copyright © 1981 by Peter Tompkins, all published by Harper & Row. The author is additionally grateful for the guidance and time Mr. Tompkins spent answering innumerable questions about his landmark book *Secrets of the Great Pyramid*, a structure he considers "the patrimony not only of Egypt but of Humanity."

Published by Three Rivers Press, a division of Crown Publishers, Inc., 201 East 50th Street, New York, New York 10022. Member of the Crown Publishing Group.

Random House, Inc. New York, Toronto, London, Sydney, Auckland
http://www.randomhouse.com/

THREE RIVERS PRESS and colophon are trademarks of Crown Publishers, Inc.

Printed in the United States of America

Library of Congress Cataloging-in-Publication Data
Noone, Richard William, 1944—
    5/5/2000 : Ice, the ultimate disaster.
    Originally published under title: Ice, the ultimate disaster.
    Includes bibliographical references and index.
    1. Prophecies (Occult sciences). 2. Great Pyramids (Egypt)—Miscellanea. 3. Ice—Arctic regions—Miscellanea.
    4. Ice—Antarctic regions—Miscellanea. 5. Natural disasters—Miscellanea. I. Title.
    BF1999.N65   1986   001.9   85-30505

ISBN 0-609-80067-1

10 9 8 7 6 5

PREFACE

When I began this research project in 1973, little did I imagine the lively and entertaining people I would meet along the way. I am indebted to many brilliant teachers who appeared at the proper moment to help me distinguish the authentic from the myth. They made the research an adventure instead of an ordeal. Like witnesses in a courtroom, many of them appear in the book to support my case.

I finished writing this book in 1980, and it was first published in 1982. To date, the body of this text has intentionally remained unchanged. I felt that the evidence presented and the conclusions drawn would have to stand the test of time for the next twenty years. Now, fifteen years later in 1995, much of my research, which seemed preposterous to many scientists in 1980, has been confirmed.

Three months after the initial publication of this book, the *Journal of Climatology* published a report in March 1982 that states that global warming would certainly "cause the Antarctic ice volume to increase." Two years later, the American Geophysical Union published a report in *Eos,* vol. 65, August 1984, that also strengthens my conclusions. Their report supports my evidence that a very advanced worldwide civilization, with both economic motivations and resources, mapped the entire globe 6,000 years ago at a time when Antarctica was not covered with ice!

These recent discoveries in the earth sciences and archaeology sweep away years of calcified ignorance on points of history. For example, the discovery in December 1985 of volcanic ash twenty feet underground in the Nile delta that was found to be identical to the ash from an enormous eruption approximately 3,500 years ago on the Greek island of Santorini. This discovery proves that the effects of the eruption (22,000 times greater than the effects of the atomic bomb dropped on Hiroshima) reached as far as Egypt and supports a theory (presented in chapters two and eight of this book) linking the eruption to the seemingly miraculous events associated with the biblical Exodus of the Israelites from Egypt.

Six years passed, and the November 1991 issue of *Geology* stated that ice growth at the South Pole has "been observed over the past eighty years," which is the entire time that we've had the technology to monitor its growth. They end the report by stating that "Our results suggest strongly that the response of the Antarctic glacial system to future warming would be an increase in mass balance [ice growth]."

v

Nine months later, the August 1992 issue of *Discover* reported that scientists examining sediment cores (also discussed in chapter ten of this book) found that "This sediment record shows that between 7,000 and 4,000 years ago. . .the Antarctic ice sheets were growing again." They state that global warming "may hasten the ice age."

Then in September 1992, Atlanta astronomer James E. Summers computed the planetary alignment for May 5, 2000. He found that in addition to Mercury, Venus, Mars, Jupiter, and Saturn, people on Earth would also see a new moon on the night of May 4, 2000. That new moon, he discovered, will move into alignment with the planets on the night of 5/5/2000.

Smithsonian Magazine, August 1993, states "every 7,000 years" the weight of ice turns the rock under it into a toothpaste consistency providing lubrication and "When this happens, the entire ice sheet over Hudson Bay would slide out into the North Atlantic." Should that event happen today, the resulting tidal wave would be approximately three hundred feet high when it hit New York City.

Then, research by Drs. Barclay Kamb and Hermann Engelhardt at Caltech, in Pasadena, revealed a layer of goo also comprised of water-saturated pulverized rock under the ice at the South Pole. Dr. Engelhardt told me this mixture "has the consistency of toothpaste." Now, neither polar ice sheet is solidly anchored to the underlying strata and both are, at present, resting on a lubricating mixture. It is known that a viscous material will yield easily to a comparatively slight pressure exerted over time.

If a gentle tug or push is exerted horizontally on the earth to shove it in a given direction on 5/5/2000, then the reader will find Drs. Hapgood and Einsteins' research, presented in this book, rather chilling. Einstein knew the rock under the ice would be pulverized forty years ago! In January 1955, he discussed with Hapgood the application of a principle by which the tangential stress proceeding from the icecap was greatly magnified to the point that it would someday pulverize the rock under the icecap. A stress that Einstein wrote, "will, when it has reached a certain point, produce a movement of the earth's crust over the rest of the earth's body, and this will displace the polar regions toward the equator."

Then, by August 1994, research by R. A. Schwaller de Lubïez, John Anthony West, Dr. Thomas L. Dobecki, Frank Domingo and a Boston University geologist, Professor Robert M. Schoch destroyed the theory of orthodox Egyptologists that the Sphinx was built in 2400 B.C. Their evidence (published in *KMT: A Modern Journal of Ancient Egypt*, Vol. 3 No. 2 '92) shows the Sphinx to be thousands of years older than Egyptologists believed and that the body of the Sphinx was eroded by rain when Egypt had a much wetter climate than today. Professor Schoch told me how his facts prove that the Sphinx was probably built between 5000 B.C. and 7000 B.C. Hopefully, Schoch's dating will shock Egyptologists into rethinking their story.

The evidence in this book, in the *Eos* journal above, the new evidence of ice sheet instability, both past and present, the new discovery of the great antiquity of the Sphinx, and the terrestrial effect of Vela X (chapter six) six thousand years ago on the Antarctic ice sheet, when examined collectively give proof of the destruction of a very advanced civilization from which Ancient Egypt inherited her knowledge. The publishing, in 1995, of *Fingerprints of the Gods* by Graham Hancock and *When the Sky Fell* by Rand & Rose Flem-Ath add great validity to the evidence presented and conclusions drawn in *5/5/2000*.

New discoveries like this serve to remind us that the idea of the "progress" of human civilization is a theological doctrine created by early church fathers in their attempt to explain the mystery of the origin of man.

In time, I learned to see ancient astronomy in terms of observational techniques based on measurements of the actual size of Earth, rather than on church-inspired concepts of the universe. A second of time in the motion of the vault of heaven corresponds to a definite length on Earth, and linking time together with length, volume, and weight, the ancients built the Great Pyramid to measure the movement of the planet Earth.

The ancients had a deep concern with cosmic time, that is, the movement of the tilt of Earth's axis in relationship to the movement of the stars they observed. Time occupied and dominated their thoughts as if they were prisoners on an ancient death row. Why? What drove them? What was the motivating force behind it all? Was it something more than just the convenience of an accurate calendar? These ancient astronomers observed and recorded the synodic returns of the planets to four points of a decimal. They knew that Earth rotated on its axis; that it went around the sun; that the planets went around the sun and the relationship between them.

The tilt of the earth today is twenty-three degrees. Has it always been so? Recent scientific research has thoroughly demonstrated that it has not. The evidence suggests that our planet has shifted on its axis more than once and that the tremendous climatic stress of the ice ages coincides with these shifts.

The evidence also indicates that the planet may once again suffer the almost unimaginable results of a shift in its axis on May 5, 2000.

Like a detective mystery, the book ends with a startling commentary on this subject by the late Dr. Albert Einstein. This book should be read in the prepared sequence, for as it unfolds it presents an enlightening look at mankind's past and future.

Richard W. Noone
Atlanta, Georgia
July 5, 1995

CONTENTS

From the library of:

Stelle, Illinois.

In 1963 Mr. Kieninger co-authored with Dr. White a book entitled *The Ultimate Frontier,* a book that foretold and inspired the creation of two technologically advanced, self-sufficient cities in America—Stelle, Illinois (near Chicago), and Adelphi, Texas (near Dallas). Mr. Kieninger's book, the rapid development and significance of these two cities, their impact on the world today, and an internal CIA report confirming, in part, Mr. Kieninger's research are discussed in the book you now hold in your hand.

FOREWORD

Fortunately for the world, there has always been the questioning person who searches for reality and truth in order to avoid being misled by myths, ignorance, and authoritarian lies. Having real facts to deal with, he can make the most appropriate and sane responses to life situations; yet we are all conditioned by traditional values and conventional thinking, so breakthroughs in knowledge proceed slowly in our world. On the individual level, we each have a built-in impulse to fulfill our potential for being human, and we seek happiness, love, beauty, and justice in our everyday lives. The tension between what we could be and the evident failure of our institutions to hasten our attainment of human completeness urges us to seek better ways and the freedom to pursue them.

There are, however, entrenched powers which oppose human yearnings for perfection at almost every turn. During the Renaissance in Europe, for instance, vigorous measures were taken by the Church to suppress scientific discoveries that all too often upset the dogmatic opinions of the authorities and their official interpretations of Holy Scripture. The scientists of those days, in order to survive persecution and to share their discoveries among themselves, gradually formed an underground communication network that transcended national boundaries. This secret society of men of high intelligence wisely defended their work against jealous officialdom and the greed of man. Uplifted by their deeper insights, they endeavored to promote the betterment of the human condition through judicious use of their knowledge and through selective release of their discoveries.

Pressures still exist today which cause men of genius to be very careful about what they share with the world, but they are eager to spread knowledge and seem to recognize their own kind wherever they may be. The formation of Brotherhoods over the ages took place for essentially the same reasons that have forced scientists and other innovators to be on guard in recent centuries. Preservation of scientific and metaphysical knowledge of ancient civilizations has been maintained by the Brotherhoods, and such knowledge has been transmitted continually to those who search for and demand truth. In fact, the prodigious surge of rediscovery during the Renaissance was largely the result of opening ancient archives which were pertinent to the work of certain scientific researchers. The Brotherhoods of scientist-philosophers of the distant past thus passed the truth to their counterparts of the Renaissance. Indeed, the discoveries and history of long-dead cultures are still intact and held by these Brotherhoods for those who can understand.

Richard Kieninger

PART I

Astrophysics indicates that the concept of the universe as orderly and peaceful is startlingly incorrect; if the interest of ancient man in the heavens and their preoccupation with astra determined predictions seems excessive, we need not deduce thereby that they were less intelligent than ourselves — oral tradition may have given them cause for alarm.

Dr. Elizabeth C. Baity
Archaeoastronomy and Ethnoastronomy So Far

CHAPTER ONE
THE ABSOLUTE FIRST WONDER
OF THE WORLD

In 1978 Dr. Jeffery Goodman in his book, *We Are The Earthquake Generation*, wrote the following scenario:

It is 5 P.M. in Boston and the people rushing home from work hardly notice how the setting sun seems to hang on the horizon. After several hours people start to wonder why darkness is not coming and they start to fear the faint dull roar they hear. Some also begin to feel light on their feet whether from the giddiness induced by the prolonged twilight or from subtle gravitational and magnetic changes that the earth's shifting in space is creating. Some have that I-could-jump-over-anything feeling. Animals act skittish and then suddenly all start to move or migrate in the same direction. Then the sky reddens as huge clouds of dust begin to blot out the sun. Next, a steady wind starts to blow. As the wind strengthens, the faint dull roar heard earlier grows even louder as if the source were moving closer. But just then, a temporary stillness sets in and the air seems like it is being sucked up by a giant vacuum cleaner. There is no sign of movement; all the animals are gone. After a few minutes, the winds are back even stronger. There are gusts up to 100 miles an hour. Trees are plucked out of the ground, and railroad trains are tumbled over and over and shuttled along like hockey pucks. As the wind jets up to over 200 miles per hour, buildings and everything above ground are decimated. The air becomes a thick mixture of dirt and debris. Those fortunate enough to be tucked safely away below the ground find the air hard to breathe since it is being drawn by the holocaust above. The wind-chill factor has plummeted the temperature down to just above freezing, even though it is spring. There are almost continuous, grandiose electrical storms. Quakes and volcanoes are set off around the world and a rift opens up as the earth splits in several places to relieve the stress produced by the shift. This holocaust goes on and on as if it is never going to stop: ten hours, fifteen, twenty, forty, forty-eight. Then suddenly the winds subside and material from the sky starts to come crashing down. For a few minutes it seems to be raining automobiles, boats, washing machines, and kitchen sinks. The temperature comes back to normal for this time of year, a pleasant 50° F. But this temperature rise continues. By the next day, the third since the start of the shift, the temperature has hit 103° F, just what one would expect in equatorial Africa for this time of year — not Boston. From Boston to St. Paul to Seattle to Anchorage, out come the Bermuda shorts. Layers of mud spread for thousands of miles as a grim reminder of the holocaust. The decaying bodies of animals of every size and shape are found in caves where they huddled together in their last moments.

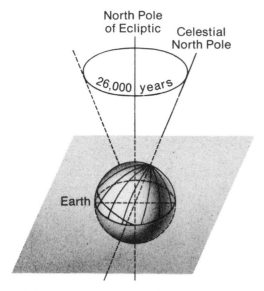

1:1 The precession of the equinoxes.

To discover why Dr. Jeffery Goodman wrote this we must return to a night long ago.

It was almost midnight, and the band of men stood quietly waiting in the dark for an unprecedented event to take place, one that could not happen again for twenty-five thousand eight hundred and ninety years.

These men, what they did, and the subsequent impact of their act on man's history, religions, and development on this planet will be the crux of this book.

The night air was cool to the skin and lungs, refreshing: quite different from a few hours earlier, when their parched lips had been dried and cracked from the blistering winds and sun which torment the dry sands of Northern Africa with an intensity seldom equaled anywhere on this planet.

The countdown had begun. Years of planning, organization, and labor would, in minutes, be completed. The anticipation, anxiety, and tension would have been almost unbearable to an ordinary man.

These were no ordinary men. They were survivors of a civilization destroyed by a sudden shift in the Earth's terrestrial axis triggered by a massive accumulation of ice at the South Pole.

Their eyes calmly scanned the heavens, noting, tracking, and plotting by nocturnal reckoning the various constellations and planets, charting their seemingly minute movements as they had done for so many, many nights before. The clear air of the desert, at that degree of latitude and longitude—the exact center of the greatest land mass on the planet's north-south axis—with its unlimited visibility, had been a carefully calculated asset to their timetable. For tonight, if their efforts were to be successful, their measurements must not only be exact, but so exact and precise that some future generation's attention would eventually be deviated from the normal everyday problems of life and curiously focused on this sublime effort. To make this connection, to communicate across the endless sands of time a message of warning and hope to a generation of men and women in the far distant future, was their purpose. The manner of communication was geometry, indestructibly embodied in stone.

The moment so long anticipated and planned for arrived. It was now midnight—midnight of the autumnal equinox of 4000 B.C. That September 23rd, as always, the daylight of a few hours ago and this night's hours of darkness would be of equal length all over the earth. Conditions were now perfect for these universalists to project their meridian (their imaginary line of sight) out into the heavens to the point in which it would meet and intersect with the ecliptic and celestial equator of the earth. As the full moon rose majestically overhead to govern the night, these ancient astronomers must have smiled as they observed that full

4

moon move into a position equadistant between the two bright stars forming the tips of the horns of the bull in the constellation of Taurus. (See Plate 1:2.)

Exactly one second after midnight the earth, because of its almost imperceptible wobble (which causes leap year), precessed out of 4000 B.C. and wobbled into the equinoctial year 3999 B.C. A new "age" had dawned, the Age of Taurus. With the dawning of this new "age" the Egyptian government was quite suddenly changed in both political and religious matters. Habits, customs, and beliefs of the inhabitants of this country were also to change rapidly. Cannibalism was driven back to the frontiers of the country; the practice of strangling servants to accompany their masters in the afterlife was abolished; the custom of tying up the bodies of the dead so they could not walk about at night was stopped; women were treated with more respect and dignity; human sacrifice was restrained. With this sudden cultural shock, the people were to experience a new consciousness, a new awareness of themselves. Ignorance and savagery, by the dispensation of all this new light or knowledge, were driven back into the jungle.

These ancient astronomer-stone masons knew that an enlightened people could never be enslaved, and an ignorant people could never be set free. Following the dawning of this new "age" the Priesthood of Egypt would, in their secret religious dramas, instruct their new candidate or pharoah to have his queen wear a new crown of two horns (symbolizing the horns of the bull Taurus) with a disc (symbolizing the moon) between them. This crown was to commemorate the dawning of the Age of Taurus and to show that there is a female force and a male force. To the ancients, the reflected light of the sun upon the moon

was soft and gentle. Today we see this crown adorning the head of the queens of ancient Egypt almost exclusively (see Plate 1:3).

These ancient gnostics were to communicate to the priesthood that because of the earth's "wobbling effect", the plane of the earth's axis would slowly carve a great circle in the heavens. They explained it would take twenty-five thousand eight hundred and ninety years, (approximately twenty-one hundred years per age) for the plane of the earth's axis to pass slowly through each of the twelve constellations—Taurus, Aries, Pisces, Aquarius, etc. These pictures in the sky, which form a star picture belt or 360° zone around the earth, which we call today the Zodiac, they explained could be used like a road map in the sky. This highly sophisticated system of space and volume, of geometry and astronomy, as well as of other elaborate sciences, were unveiled to the Priesthood of Egypt, who were to veil and reconceal this knowledge in their sacred religious dramas. This was to insure that those who were taught these profound truths of science were at the same time instructed morally, mentally, and physically in how to use this knowledge or force.

Twenty-one hundred years were to pass, the duration of the "Age of Taurus". During these years we know that people living around the Mediterranean Basin made icons and statues of the bull, Apis, which is the basis of the first letter of the English alphabet (see Plate 1:4). At the end of the Age of Taurus, the earth wobbled into the next constellation, the sign of the ram. The "Age of Aries" dawned, and a great exodus in the evolution of mankind took place.

The *inner core* of the Priesthood of Egypt was ready for this new age with another candidate, who, like Joseph before him, had been schooled and instructed from a very

5

PRECESSION OF EQUINOXES.

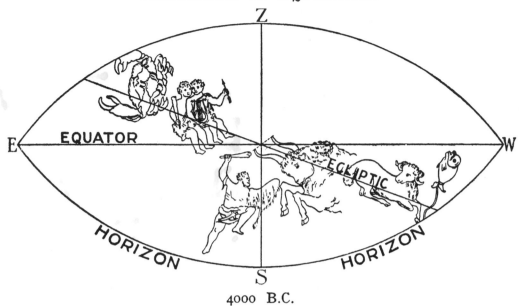

4000 B.C.

Sky above Southern Horizon at Latitude 45° North.
Visible at Midnight, Autumnal Equinox.
Invisible at Noon, Vernal Equinox.

PRECESSION OF EQUINOXES.

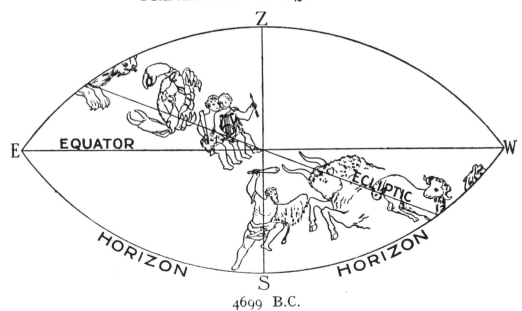

4699 B.C.

Sky above Southern Horizon at Latitude 45° North.
Visible at Midnight, Autumnal Equinox.
Invisible at Noon, Vernal Equinox.

1:2 Precession of Equinoxes.

1:3 Examples of the Horn-and-Moon Symbol Worn by Queens of Egypt.

7

Seirite-Sinaitic	Canaanite-Phoenician-Aramaic	Greek	Latin
	⊬ ⊬	A	A
	9 9	B	B
	⌐	ΓC	CG
	◁ ◁	ΔD	D
	∃ ∃	F E	E
	Y	F Y	FVUWY
	⊥ ⊐	I	Z
	Ⱶ H	H	H
	乙	I	IJ
	Ɣ Ɣ	K	K
	Ɬ ∠	ΛL	L
	ɱ ɱ	M	M
	ɣ ɔ	N	N
	∓Ξ̃	+Ξ	X
	ο ο	O	O
	၅ ၂)	ΠΓ	P
	ɀ Ⱨ ɀ		
	φφφ	Q	Q
	ꝗ	PR	R
	w	Σ ϛ	S
	×	T	T

1:4 Comparison of Alphabets Showing Origins in Pictographs.

people when he came down from the mountain to find that they had lapsed back into worshipping the bull. What Moses did next we find in Exodus 32:20.

> And he took the calf which they had made, and burnt it in the fire, and ground it to powder, and strawed it upon the water, and made the children of Israel drink of it.

Moses had already learned from the High Priest of Midian, his father-in-law, that the Age of Taurus had passed, and that he and his people were living in the Age of Aries, the ram. Moses worked for the priest, married Zipporah, one of his seven symbolic daughters, and studied with him. The High Priest of Midian was the custodian of the Cabbalah—the priceless heritage of Israel, which supplies one of the seven keys to the hidden mysteries of both the Old and New Testaments, *The Book of Seven Seals*,[2] and explains the "Sacred Fruits of the Tree of Sephiroth." The High Priest of Midian instructed Moses in all its mystic and secret teachings until Moses became an "Adept," at which point the custodianship of the Cabbalah was transferred to Moses. Immediately after giving Moses the Cabbalah, the High Priest of Midian changed his name from Ruel to Jethro, a fact usually overlooked by most religious scholars when reading the *Second Book of Moses*, Chapters Two and Three.

early age when he had been drawn from the waters and brought into the royal household. In the Age of Aries, Moses came up out of Egypt and said, "I am the ram, the ram of God."[1] He got awfully mad with his

As our galaxy travelled through the infinite realms of space at approximately one million miles per hour, the earth slowly wobbled through the Age of Aries, and mankind precessed into the "Age of Pisces," the fishes. Christians were to choose the

[1]See Carlo Suares, *Cipher of Genesis*, in the Bibliography for background and explanation of this and all other scriptural interpretations mentioned.

[2]Mentioned in *The Revelation of St. John the Divine*, Chapter Five.

1:5 Romantic nineteenth-century depiction of Moses being found in the bullrushes.

9

fish for their symbol in that new age.

Once again the *inner core* of the Priesthood of Egypt was ready for this new age with another candidate whom they had schooled and instructed. In the first gospel of the New Testament, we read that God said, "Out of Egypt have I called my Son." Jesus, a lion of the tribe of Judah, came up out of Egypt and said, "Come ye after me, and I will make you to become fishers of men." To the ancients, each astronomical age held a special meaning.

Four thousand years before Jesus, a band of men were at work in Egypt under the light of a full moon. Almost sixty centuries before our era, our ancient ancestors patiently stood watching the reflected light of the moon slowly, effortlessly, inch its way across an enormous geometrically arranged and marked pavement of stone. Suddenly men were moving to and fro, marking, measuring, triangulating the reflected light of the moon as it shone down on the exact center of the gigantic shadowbox surrounding their Pyramid.

These measurements of the reflected light of the moon, when coordinated and examined beside their measurements of the sun's shadows and angles (plus a mountain of other important reference material), gave them a date almost six thousand years ahead, in the astronomical "Age of Aquarius," the water bearer. The date that they had was a year date; soon they had the month, then at last the exact day. This new data told them that on that day all the planets of our solar system would align themselves in practically a straight line across space. Within the hour, they knew what effect this would have on the earth's wobble and the accumulation of ice at the earth's South Pole.

These men were to leave Egypt soon, leaving behind for us today one major example of their presence in our past, an example which contains a vast amount of their knowledge and sciences. Today, that example still stands towering over the sands of Egypt, and by its very presence reminds us of a fragment of Man's history almost forgotten today. We may forget these men, but the date they discovered and passed on to us, 5 May 2000 A.D., must weigh heavy on our minds as the planets of our solar system are at this very moment moving into the position predicted by them.

To suggest that Man, almost 6,000 years ago, could have been in possession of such knowledge would cause some academicians of today to cry, "Preposterous! Heretic! Faker and Fraud!"; but, being totally unfamiliar with the building itself and the knowledge afforded by interdisciplinary studies of the building so necessarily needed for a proper evaluation of the problem, they must like men in a bar, in the pulpit, and in the halls of legislation, against their own convictions, and, with what they term "logic", prove to the satisfaction of others that which they do not themselves understand or believe.

Through the study of ancient history, it becomes perfectly obvious that the earth has been innundated by cataclysmic floods, frozen in ice ages, and ripped asunder by earthquakes. Today, as we wobble along in the Age of Aquarius, the water bearer, there is no reason to think that it won't happen again as we count down to May 5, 2000.

Could the designer of the first wonder of the world, the largest geodetic marker ever raised on the face of this planet, the only pyramid that has captured the hearts and minds of Man for almost six thousand years, have been wrong? The answer to this question is still basic to an understanding of our own roots; in the paragraphs ahead, an answer will be found. For today, more than ever before, the geometrical message embodied in the Great Pyramid cries out in silence to be heard.

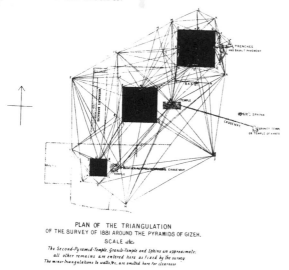

PLAN OF THE TRIANGULATION
OF THE SURVEY OF 1881 AROUND THE PYRAMIDS OF GIZEH.
SCALE ᵇⁱᵈₒ
*The Second-Pyramid-Temple, Granite-Temple and Sphinx are approximate;
all other remains are entered here as fixed by the survey
The minor triangulations to walls,&c, are omitted here for clearness*

1:6 *Some of the Triangulations Around the Pyramids of Giza.*

———————

There must have been some sort of stonecraft guild passing on from generation to generation the precious knowledge about the fabrication and use of tools.

Dr. Carl Sagan
The Dragons of Eden

On this lake it is that the Egyptians represent by night his [Osiris] sufferings whose name I refrain from mentioning, and this representation they call their Mysteries. I know well the whole course of the proceedings in these ceremonies, but they shall not pass my lips.

Herodotus
The History of Herodotus,
Book II
Rawlinson Translation

The Absolute First Wonder of The World

It is a strange, and indeed quite curious, fact that an ancient monument designed and erected thousands and thousands of years ago, in a time that we today term "the dawn of civilization," should be an object of controversy and the main subject of hundreds of books—ranging in size from wafer-thin occult paperbacks claiming to contain a knowledge of occultation to huge encyclopedia-size multivolume scientific sets supposedly written by experts.

Books on the Great Pyramid have been written by everyone from Biblical fanatics to nuclear physicists, covering everything from "prophecies of the future" and "proof of God" to the "outer space influences" theory proposed by some. The first thing that grabs our attention is that both of these theories overlook Man himself, who could be a product of either, neither, or both.

One fact, however, remains constant and unchanging: no other building erected by the hand of Man on the face of this planet can claim for itself the magnetic or mystical attraction on the thought patterns of Man that the Great Pyramid continues to command.

It is well known that certain men today and in the past have forsaken home and family, fame and fortune, to journey by sailing ships, steamers, or jet to the awesome base of that Pyramid—to measure its controversial measurements, to gape in wonder at its stupendous size—and to return humbly homeward, to their own far distant countries, weirdly changed in many instances, to spend the rest of their natural lives writing about what had seduced them, almost psychically, away from home in the first place.

What was it that had attracted these men like a magnet? What was the force that drew these men to the Great Pyramid? What did these men find, to their own satisfaction, that could have effected this strange and dramatic change in their life patterns? What unexplained force surrounds the Great Pyramid and, like a giant cosmic magnet, draws some men to it and repels others? What obviously profound and certainly physical force had come into these men's lives to make them behave in this manner? Did they find something we today may have overlooked? One idea overlooked today is the possibility that these men could have received a message, geometrically encoded and embodied in stone by a band of men waiting patiently in the dark. Could Man, as most of us understand him today, have sent such a message? Is it possible that some men have decoded the message?[3]

Almost six thousand years ago, the Great Pyramid was designed and built. The more one learns about this building, the more obvious it becomes that the building itself has drawn these men to it. They studied it, and each returned to tell to others what he had decoded and learned, to the best of his ability.

For us to understand this strange force, to understand why the power of that force acted only on some men and not on others, can be accomplished only by a careful examination of the facts. Venturing into the area of the unknown into which we are

---

[3]Books written by these men are listed in the Bibliography.

about to plunge, where our conception of the world might be tossed about like so much dust in the wind, we should venture ahead with caution and concrete facts.

André Gide has stated that the new patriotism is to defend the frontiers of the mind, and so indeed we shall. As we begin to explore and understand the seemingly magical passageways and mysterious chambers of the Great Pyramid, as we move up one corridor and down another, passing into and out of its three rooms, as we hear our footsteps echo and reverberate up and down the vast hallway of the Grand Gallery, we shall at the same time begin a tour into the hidden recesses of the minds of the ancient designers of this building, an exploration into the ultimate frontier—the frontier of the human mind.

Citing some evidence and ignoring vast sums of other evidence, Egyptologists espouse their belief that the ambiguous Egyptian Pharoah Khufu (sometimes known by his Greek name "Cheops") built the Great Pyramid as a tomb. New evidence demonstrates this theory untenable. Even Dr. I.E.S. Edwards, a world-renowned Egyptologist, Keeper of Egyptian Antiquities in the British Museum and author of the book *The Pyramids of Egypt*, clouds the issue by saying (emphasis added):

> Cheops, who may have been a megalomaniac, could never, during a reign of about twenty-three years, have erected a building of the size and durability of the Great Pyramid, if *technical advances* had not enabled his masons to handle stones of very considerable weight and dimensions.[4]

As to what these "technical advances" might have been, Dr. Edwards remains silent.

I cannot emphasize strongly enough that this whole tomb theory is nothing more than an unreasonable hypothesis advanced by most Egyptologists, based solely upon the mystic writings of the Greek metaphysician Herodotus (who travelled to Egypt 3,596 years after the Great Pyramid was built). Herodotus learned what he wrote about from the Priesthood of Egypt.

Stranger still is the fact that the tomb theory is based and erected on the rather scant information revealed in the book entitled *A History*[5], written by Herodotus thousands of years after the building was completed. Before he wrote his book, Herodotus had been initiated into the ancient religious mysteries of Egypt; like any member of any secret organization past or present, having been sworn to silence he would not reveal the Great Pyramid's true purpose to non-members or the more-or-less uninitiated. In all ages, even ours, men have formed secret societies, made use of ceremonies of initiation, and employed symbols, emblems, and means of recognition.

The same teachings taught to the Priesthood of Egypt 6,000 years ago by a band of Hyksos (Shepherd Kings who entered Egypt and constructed the Great Pyramid)[6] were also taught to the High Priest of Midian, who was to pass this same teaching to Moses, to be memorized later by Jesus. Sixteen presidents of the United

---

[4] I.E.S. Edwards, *The Pyramids of Egypt* (Baltimore: Penguin Books, 1975). Emphasis added; pp. 167-68.

[5] See the *History* of Herodotus, Rawlinson translation, mentioned in the Bibliography.

[6] Their race bore the genetic name of Hyesos (Hyksos), which means "king shepherds;" for *hyc* in the sacred language denotes "king," and *sos* in the common dialect means "shepherd" or "shepherds." The

States of America, a great "nation of states," were also to learn much of this same teaching.

What psychological effect sixteen Masonic Presidents of the United States have exerted on the world is a field in which there are few ethnologists, few professors.

It is easy to understand that the United States of America was largely founded by members of this ancient order, when one knows that George Washington, the first president of the United States of America, Worshipful Master of a Virginia Lodge of Freemasons (now called The Alexandria Washington Lodge No. 22), and fifteen other presidents of the United States:

THOMAS JEFFERSON, Charlottesville Lodge #90, Charlottesville, Va.

JAMES MADISON, Hiram Lodge, Westmoreland County, Va.

JAMES MONROE, Williamsburg Lodge #6, Williamsburg, Va.

ANDREW JACKSON, Harmony Lodge #1, Nashville, Tenn.

JAMES KNOX POLK, Lodge #31, Columbia, Tenn.

JAMES BUCHANAN, Lodge #43, Lancaster, Pa.

ANDREW JOHNSON, Greenville Lodge #119, Greenville, Tenn.

JAMES A. GARFIELD, Magnolia Lodge #20, Columbus, Ohio

WILLIAM McKINLEY, Hiram Lodge #21, Winchester, Va.

THEODORE ROOSEVELT, Matinecock Lodge #806, Oyster Bay, N.Y.

WILLIAM HOWARD TAFT, Occasional Lodge, Cincinnati, Ohio

WARREN GAMALIEL HARDING, Marion Lodge #70, Marion, Ohio

FRANKLIN DELANO ROOSEVELT, Holland Lodge #8, New York City, N.Y.

HARRY S. TRUMAN, Belton Lodge #450, Belton, Mo.

GERALD R. FORD, Malta Lodge #465, Grand Rapids, Mich.

were all members of the secret brotherhood of Freemasons[7].

The first assembly of the Continental Congress was presided over by Peyton Randolph, a Master Mason, Provincial Grand Master of Virginia. The Revolutionary War, brought about by taxation without representation, was a distinctly Masonic enterprise. The Boston Tea Party was organized in St. Andrews Lodge, at an adjourned meeting, and every member who threw tea into the harbor was a member of that Lodge. Paul Revere, who made his immortal ride, was Junior Warden of that same Lodge. More than fifty of the fifty-six men who risked their lives by signing the *Declaration of Independence* were members of this ancient fraternity. All but one of the five members of the Constitutional Convention were Master Masons. Richard Henry Lee, who moved the resolution for independence in the Continental Congress, was a Mason; the

combined word form is "Hyesos." At present the preferred etymology sees in the Hyksos the Egyptian equivalent for "rulers of foreign countries." The name Hyksos as "rulers of foreign countries" is found in the Egyptian text of the *Turina Papyrus* and on a few scarabs.

[7]See *10,000 Famous Freemasons,* 3 Vols., by William R. Denslow, Forward by M∴W∴ Harry S. Truman, P.G.M., Transactions of the Missouri Lodge of Research Vol. No. 14, 1957.

1:8 *George Washington Depicted as a Freemason.*

other members of that committee, Thomas Jefferson, Benjamin Franklin, John Adams, Roger Sherman, and Robert R. Livingston, were all Masons. The American flag was made by the widow of John Ross, a Mason, and was placed in the hands of Washington, who was elected Grand Master of Virginia but did not accept because his duties as Commander-in-Chief of the American Army absorbed all his attention and energies. Washington took the oath of office as President of the United States upon the *Holy Bible* brought from the Masonic St. John's Lodge #1 of New York.

It was Washington, Father of his Country, who in full Masonic regalia laid the cornerstone of the White House. It was also Washington who placed a "certain deposit" under the cornerstone of the White House in the hope that, should the edifice ever be destroyed, the deposit would be found by future generations. Did Washington place a miniature pyramid under the cornerstone, or did he deposit other ancient symbols, relics, and sacred books scarcely known by many today? What is the deposit under the Masonic cornerstone of the nation's capital?

The ritual, consecration, and ceremonies surrounding the laying of the cornerstone just 200 years ago, a sublime ceremony seldom seen today, were also performed almost 6,000 years ago in Egypt by a band of men as the first rays of the morning sun hit the northeast corner of the Great Pyramid.

Today in Central Park, New York City, there stands a huge obelisk brought from Alexandria, Egypt. Although smaller than Washington's Monument in Washington, D.C., it is a splendid piece of work. When the obelisk was moved from its base, a

1:9. The lodge at the "Green Dragon Tavern" (*vide* the two upper-hand windows in illustration), where the Boston Tea Party was planned.

deposit was discovered in the foundations. In the deposit were found a trowel, a lead plummet, a rough rectangular stone, a pure white cubical stone, a stone with a serpent border, a stone trying square, and a stone showing the ancient Egyptian cubical gauge with some hieroglyphs similar to triangles drawn upon Masonic trestleboards: seven symbols, well known to modern Freemasons (see Plates 1:7, 1:10, and 1:11).

The governors of every one of the original thirteen states at the time Washington was inaugurated were Masons. The *Constitution of the United States* was written by Masons. Free speech, free religion, and free schools are the gifts of this ancient fraternity.

Herodotus was a member of one of these so-called secret societies. Herodotus says in Book II of his *History*

> Whoever has been initiated into the *Mysteries of the Cabiri* will understand what I mean. [Emphasis added, p. 99].

Herodotus, the earliest known writer on the Great Pyramid (440 B.C.), certainly could not have expected those who were unfamiliar with the "Mysteries of the Cabiri" to have understood what he meant by that sentence in his book. Herodotus knew a certain percentage of his readers had been initiated into the Mysteries of the Cabiri. He knew these initiates were familiar with the teaching of the Cabbalah (passed to Moses by the High Priest of Midian who had received the same teaching from the Egyptian High Priest in line before him). Could there be a connection between the ancient Egyptian Mysteries, the Cabiric Mysteries of Samothrace, and the modern Mysteries of Freemasonry?

The Cabiric Mysteries of Samothrace were ritualistic dramas centered around four brothers—Aschieros, Achiochersus, Achiochersa, and Cashmala. The mysteries were divided into three parts: (1) the death of Cashmala, murdered by his three brothers; (2) the discovery of his body; and (3) his resurrection. Voltaire said,

> I ask who were these Hierophants, these sacred Freemasons, who celebrated their Ancient Mysteries of Samothrace, and whence came they and their gods Cabiri?

1:14 Francis Marie Arouet, called Voltaire, as a poet, historian and philosopher has few superiors; but as a satirical romanticist, he has not even an equal. A French Freemason, a member of the Lodge of Nine Sisters in Paris, Voltaire used his words like a sword to fight against political and religious despotism.

1:7 *The Obelisk in New York City's Central Park.* It may be moved indoors, as pollutants in the air are eating away at the limestone.

1:10 *The Original Position of the Obelisk.* The New York *Herald*, 13 February 1880, carried the following: "The obelisk and its foundations will be removed and replaced in New York exactly in the positions in which they were found, each piece having been numbered to correspond with numbers on a drawing that was made before the pieces were removed." The monument was erected by Thothmes III at the outer porch of the Temple of Amen at Heliopolis, where it and its twin (now in London) guarded the entrance of the temple for 2,000 years before they were moved to Alexandria. On 12 June 1880, with the assistance of Mr. Zola, Most Worshipful Grand Master of Egypt, the obelisk was entrusted to Lieutenant Commander H. H. Gorringe, U.S.N., a member of Anglo-Saxon Lodge No. 137, for shipment to New York. On 9 October 1880 the obelisk was raised with great Masonic ceremonies in Central Park, New York City. With 8,000 Masons in attendance, the cornerstone of the ancient obelisk was laid by Jesse B. Anthony, Grand Master of Masons in New York State, as 30,000 awe-struck spectators and curiosity-seekers watched, wondering what the strange rites they were seeing performed meant. See *New York World*, 9 October 1880.

1:11 *The Obelisk Lowered Ready for Shipping.* Over 8 feet wide and 69 inches tall, it weighed 224 tons. Masonic emblems are on the foundation stones.

The mysteries of the Cabiri and the ancient Egyptian religious mysteries of Osiris (his murder, hiding of the body, and its recovery by Isis followed by his resurrection to celestial life) are for the most part identical.

Most Egyptologists' interpretations concerning the Great Pyramid as little more than a tomb are of scant use, as we shall soon see.

Antiquated textbooks teach our children the Egyptologists' theory, the tomb theory. The tomb theory has been buried today by an avalanche of new evidence to the contrary—evidence that is being denied our children by the use of antiquated textbooks. Why? An answer to this question is readily apparent, when one realizes that our schools are underfinanced, subject to sectarian infiltration, and forced to use textbooks that in many cases are hopelessly obsolete.

For example, the first skeleton found of a so-called "Neanderthal Man" showed upon examination that the man had walked in a generally bent-over position. Art historians then pictured "Man" in the children's textbooks as a sort of ape-man walking bent over, with stooped shoulders, a hairy back, arms almost touching the ground, as he stomped about dragging a huge club with which he would bash things. Children are taught that their ancestors looked and behaved like this.

As early as 1935 it was discovered that the first skeleton found was that of a man suffering from chronic osteoarthritis, a bone disease which causes stooped shoulders and a generally bent-over posture. When normal skeletons were later found, it was realized that not only did these "Neanderthal Men" walk just as erect as we do, but their average brain capacity was greater than ours today.

Yet our children today are still being deceived by fraudulent pictures drawn over forty years ago, pictures that depict our

20

ancestors, even the ladies, covered with hair like some sort of monkey. It is absolutely impossible, of course, to determine from the skeletal remains of a paleolithic man discovered in Germany in 1856 what amount of body hair he or his mate may have had[8].

Cro-Magnon, the name of a cave near Les Eyzies, France, is the name applied to a group of tall, erect, prehistoric people who lived in southwestern Europe and used various chemical compounds, combined with a vehicle and applied with brushes, to record events and stories for all those who were to follow. Today our modern technology has put men on the moon.

Diamond- and fur-clad women walk their rhinestone-collared poodles down Fifth Avenue, while six stories under their feet winos, outcasts, and derelicts shuffle about in the abandoned steam tunnels of New York City, sometimes stopping to scribble graffiti with pencil, magic marker, or pen, on the walls. Graffiti that is inferior to a Cro-Magnon man's art works on the wall of a natural cave in Les Eyzies, France, twenty-five thousand years ago—inferior in both intellectual content and artistic ability. This ancient artistic ability clearly denotes an exposure to a civilization more advanced than is generally accepted to have existed at that time.

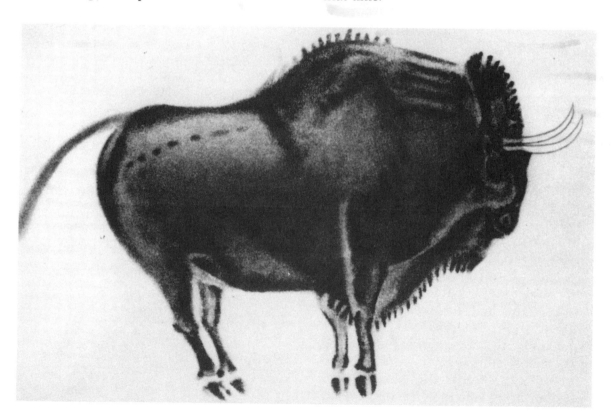

1:15 Examples of Stone Age art. The term "Stone Age" is a term totally devoid of meaning.

---

[8]This is supported by *Omni*, September 1981, p. 30.

What technically advanced civilization could a Cro-Magnon man have turned to for his pencil, magic marker, or pen? What technically advanced civilization could have produced the designers, engineers, and fellow-craftsmen who, by coordinating their talents, erected the Great Pyramid?

The Great Pyramid rises from the man-levelled top of a huge rocky plateau, similar in nature to certain flat-topped mountains in Wyoming. From its apex almost five hundred feet in the air above the plateau's levelled top, it commands a view of the surrounding flat, biscuit-colored, lunar-like wastes of the desolate Egyptian desert.

The next time you are on the fortieth floor of a tall building, look down, and you will see just how tall the remains of the Great Pyramid are. However, to see how tall the Great Pyramid was *originally,* look down from the 45th floor! The base of the Great Pyramid covers thirteen and one-half acres, or approximately *seven* square city blocks.

Anyone who has travelled to Egypt to stand atop the Great Pyramid's truncated apex has found it necessary to make the exhausting one-hour climb up one of the building's rough and ragged faces. The north side of the building is not exposed to the direct rays of the sun until late in the day, making an early-morning climb somewhat cooler, but more dangerous because of the dark shadows.

Standing at the base of the Great Pyramid's north face, ignoring the warning signs against climbing, one—looking up, attempting to count the courses, two hundred three courses of masonry, each course over three feet high, course upon course stacked up like a mountain of stone—wonders if the view from the top will be worth the risk and effort of the climb.

Climbing this gigantic ascending and receding staircase of now-crumbly stone, one arrives perspiring, heart pounding, an hour later at the top of the Great Pyramid, where the north wind quickly evaporates one's perspiration, causing a sudden chill. Anyone who has made this effort and looked down during the past five-and-a-half centuries has seen only the ruined remains of a building once covered with protective blocks of pure white limestone weighing sixteen tons each. These six-sided limestone blocks were smooth-cut in five planes: bottom, top, facing, and two ends. One hundred sixty-eight square feet of precision cutting, per casing stone. The facing stones of the Great Pyramid's four sides—one hundred fifteen thousand casing stones with nineteen million three hundred twenty-six square feet of surface—were polished down to the smoothness of a contact lens. Surface blemishes in the relatively soft limestone casing blocks were carefully chipped out, filled with mortar, sanded, and melted down, to match the surrounding block, furnishing a more highly reflective surface. One hundred fifteen thousand casing stones were then cemented together with an extraordinarily fine film of white cement, no thicker than

1:12 *Reconstruction of the Great Pyramid.* This reconstruction shows the original white po- lished limestone skin that covered it when Al Mamun arrived.

1:16 *An American Tourist Climbing the Great Pyramid.* In this turn-of-the-century photograph it is easy to count the courses of weather-worn core blocks (of which 203 remain).

1:17 *Stopping at the Thirty-Fifth Course.* This turn-of-the-century photograph shows the same American tourist at the 35th course, on his way to the top still 178 courses above.

1:13 Casing blocks still intact at top of Chephren pyramid.

tin foil. Each *joint* was thirty-five square feet in area—yet almost invisible to the naked eye! Such perfection prompted Dr. William Flinders Petrie, the father of modern archaeology, to remark:

> Merely to place such stones in exact contact would be careful work, but to do so with cement in the joint seems almost impossible: it is to be compared to the finest opticians' work on a scale of acres.[9]

1:18 Sir William Flinders Petrie (1853-1942).

Limestone is the only type of stone that, with exposure to the elements, becomes harder and more polished. An answer as to why all this effort was exerted to give the sides of the building such a mirror-like finish was eventually to be discovered by David Davidson, a structural engineer from Leeds, England, in this century. Now the sides of the Great Pyramid are no longer covered with limestone, but are exposed to the elements. The removal of the casing stones of the Great Pyramid is a sad tale, a record of the violence and barbarism practiced by men of later years.

The Great Pyramid's casing stones are truly remarkable when viewed in the proper perspective—casing stones that lay like a

1:19 This photo shows one of the almost invisible joints (35 sq. ft. in area) between two of the remaining casing stones.

slowly-breathing bear in hibernation, expanding and contracting under Egypt's blistering summer sun and 19° winter nights. This building was much more fluid, more capable of movement, than was originally expected. Three-fourths of Man's known history was to pass before he would

[9]Quoted by Peter Tompkins, *Secrets of the Great Pyramid* (New York: Harper & Row, 1971), p. 105.

penetrate its surface and enter its mysterious interior system, only to despoil it. We know this to be a fact, because three thousand five hundred and ninety-six years of darkness were to pass before we find any other mention of the Great Pyramid's exterior.

Herodotus, in 440 B.C., wrote that the building was "built entirely of polished stones, fitted together with the utmost care." Three hundred eighty years later, in 60 B.C., the Greek historian Diodorus Siculus describes the Great Pyramid's sides as "complete and without the least decay." Thirty-six years later, in 24 B.C., the Pontine geographer Strabo wrote:

> High up, approximately midway between the sides, it has a movable stone, and when this is *raised up* there is a sloping passage to the vault. [Emphasis added.]

Eighteen years later, six years before the birth of Christ, the Greek geometry teacher Thales described the facing stones as so smooth that "natives attempting to climb its steep sides rapidly slide back down to its base." After the writings of Thales in 6 B.C., eight hundred twenty-six more years of darkness and mystery were to surround the Great Pyramid. During these centuries the precise location of the entrance described by Strabo in 24 B.C. as a movable stone was forgotten. The door to the Great Pyramid then lay closed, undistinguishable from the surrounding masonry.

PENETRATION

It seems almost impossible that a band of men in 4000 B.C. could have constructed a building so durable that 4,820 years were to drift slowly by before anyone could gather together enough evidence to mount an assault on the north face of the building in search of its entrance, as was done by Prince Abdullah Al Mamun in 820 A.D., four thousand eight hundred twenty years after the building was completed under the light of a full moon.

Abdullah Al Mamun learned from the writings of earlier Arabs that the Great Pyramid contained a secret chamber in which there was a vast treasure. From the writings of Strabo, Al Mamun discovered that one of the huge facing stones on the north face of the Great Pyramid could be *raised up* to gain admission to the interior of the building. He also learned that the entrance was, measuring from side to side, in the exact center of the north face.

Armed with this information, Al Mamun arrived at the base of the Great Pyramid with a large entourage consisting of engineers, architects, builders, and stonemasons. The huge hinged facing stone that served as the secret door to the Great Pyramid's interior lay flush when closed, undetectable among the other perfectly fitted facing stones.

For days, possibly weeks, Al Mamun and his band of men looked, poked, pried, hammered, and picked at the joints of the facing stones of the Great Pyramid's north face in a vain attempt to discover a door fitted and hinged almost five thousand years earlier by another entourage of men. We can easily reconstruct the story of Al Mamun's frustration and success.

Unable to locate the ancient door, Al Mamun decided to gamble by hacking a tunnel directly into the center of this mountain of stone in the hope of finding its interior passage system. Thus he inadvertently revealed to modern historians and laymen alike a remarkable fact concerning the development of Man—the sharpest tools Al Mamun's blacksmiths could produce would do little more than dent the surface of a building precisely cut, fitted, raised and erected *4,820 years earlier*. What a shock it must have been to Prince Abdullah Al Mamun that all his workmen, engineers, architects, and the best of their tools could not make much more than a dent in the surface of this already-ancient man-made mountain! In light of this, one must wonder what kind of tools the *builders* used.

Al Mamun would not give up. He instructed his men to build large fires against the Great Pyramid's facing stones. When the stones were very, very hot, he ordered his men to douse them with cold vinegar. Al Mamun knew that by the application of heat and cold even the hardest stone would crack. Once it did crack, Al Mamun's men used battering rams and the application of brute force to smash through the outer layer of pure white casing stone, which before his attack had protected the Great Pyramid's magnificent interior from intruders for over four thousand years.

What technical advances did a band of men command, thousands of years before Al Mamun? Why were these techniques lost or forgotten in Al Mamun's time?

Once past the harder limestone facing stones, Al Mamun's men were then able to tunnel into and through the softer limestone interior blocks. For over one hundred feet his men tunnelled into this ancient building of stone. The air, illuminated by candle and torch, quickly lost oxygen and became hotter, dustier, and harder to breathe as they dug deeper into the building. Al Mamun, in a frenzy of greed, drove his workmen on until they vomited blood from breathing the foul air in the narrow confines of the tunnel.

Suddenly a cry came from within the tunnel. One of the workmen had heard a sound east of their tunnel, a dull thud—as if a heavy stone had fallen somewhere inside the building. Al Mamun then instructed his men to dig in the direction of the sound. Turning left (toward the east), his men tunnelled twenty-four feet more, where as luck would have it they broke into the Great Pyramid's descending passageway—a passageway 3 feet 5 inches wide and 3 feet 11¹/₂ inches high, built of beautifully polished white limestone.

The entrance, and in fact the whole interior passage system of the Great Pyramid, is offset towards the east from the Great Pyramid's center by 24 feet or 286.1022 inches. (All inches referring to the Pyramid's blueprints are the unit of measure used by the designer, contractor, and builder.)

No gold, no jewels, no mummies, no secret scrolls, no secret maps or tables of the celestial and terrestrial spheres were found by Prince Al Mamun as he tunnelled into an exquisite scale model of the earth's Northern Hemisphere. Al Mamun's tunnel, and his subsequent explorations into the Great Pyramid's interior, are covered in detail in the massive research work *Secrets of the Great Pyramid* (Harper & Row, 1971) by Peter Tompkins, and later in this book. Al Mamun opened the building's interior to Egypt's tremendously destructive humidity. Bats, rodents, snakes, and vandals soon followed.

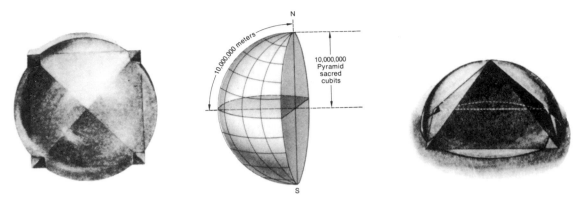

1:20 *The Great Pyramid's Measurements*. These measurements incorporate a value for pi (the constant by which the diameter of a circle may be multipled to give its true circumference); the fundamental proportions of the "golden section" [AB/AC = AC/CB = 1.618]; and the "sacred" 3-4-5 and 2-root 5-3 triangles ($A^2 + B^2 = C^2$) found in its main chamber. These facts are not surprising when one considers that all Masonic Lodges to this day are erected on this geometry.

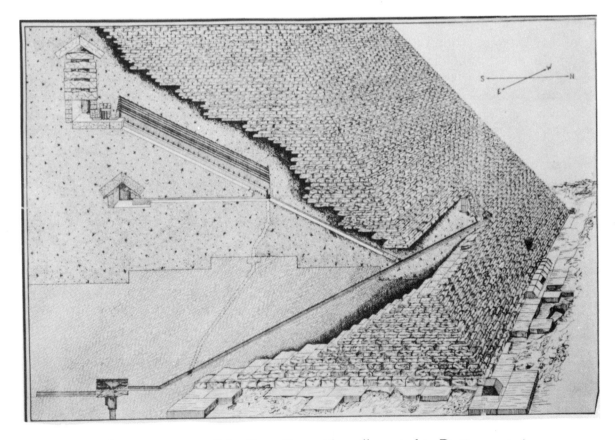

1:21 Interior section of the Great Pyramid, as illustrated in *Destiny* magazine.

CHAPTER TWO
EARTHQUAKES, CATACLYSMS AND VANDALS

EARTHQUAKES

Following Al Mamun's penetration into the Great Pyramid, a series of earthquakes destroyed large parts of Northern Egypt. Men in search of stone to rebuild Cairo turned their eyes toward the Great Pyramid's pure white casing stones.

2:1 *Cairo — Gate of the Metwaleys.* A large part of ancient Cairo was constructed with limestone blocks removed from The Great Pyramid.

These earthquakes were a series of *aftershocks* from an earlier shifting in the earth's crust. A shifting, whose epicenter was located at the Greek island of Santorin in the Aegean Sea. This gigantic volcanic activity wreaked havoc on Upper and Lower Egypt, all cities surrounding the Mediterranean Sea, and other capitals and centers of learning on the other side of the planet in 1486 B.C.

Just ten years ago, most scientists would have discounted even the idea that earthquakes are caused by movement or slippage of gigantic "plates" on which entire continents ride as passive passengers. Today the theory called "plate tectonics" or "continental drift" is universally accepted among geologists. Geophysicists today say 95% of all earthquakes can be explained by the movement of these plates. It is with the triggering of the other 5% of earthquakes that this book will be concerned.

Georgia geologists believe that the Brevard Fault, which runs the length of the state of Georgia in the north of the state, marks the boundary between the North American Plate and the old North African Plate. The movement between these two giant plates, one against another, as pressure built up and one plate slipped over the other, suddenly thrust up the Appalachian Mountain Range thousands of years ago. Geologists fear that should these plates become active again Atlanta, Georgia, would be just as prone as Los Angeles, California, to a massive earthquake. The San Andreas Fault on the west coast of America sepa-

It is the sacrifice of the Lord's passover, who passed over the houses of the children of Israel in Egypt, when he smote the Egyptians and delivered our houses.

Exodus 12:27

The reason why the Israelites were more fortunate in this plague than the Egyptians probably lies in the kind of material of which their dwellings were constructed. Occupying a marshy district and working on clay, the captives must have lived in huts made of clay and reeds, which are more [earthquake] resilient than brick or stone.

Immanuel Velikovsky
Worlds in Collision

31

rates the North American Plate from the Pacific Plate. The Brevard Fault runs parallel with the Appalachian Mountain Range. (Ancient historians described the earth "like a basketball, made of leather and sewn together in pieces."[1]) Could the ancients have had a knowledge of plate tectonics?

The Motagua Fault runs inland from the Gulf of Honduras on the Caribbean coast of Guatemala; it separates the Caribbean Plate—which includes almost the entire floor of the Caribbean Sea, the Central American countries of Guatemala, El Salvador, Honduras, Nicaragua, Costa Rica, and the Isthmus of Panama—from the North American Plate. In 1976, as the North American Plate continued undergrinding the Caribbean Plate, pressure built up between the two until it found a point of release.

The east coast of Guatemala is a lush green tropical region largely uninhabited except for an occasional farm. Gentle green slopes extend from the sea upward to the plateaus just north of the Sierra Madre Mountain Range. In the Sierra Madre and central highlands are more than thirty volcanoes, most no longer active, and three of them attaining heights of 13,000 feet. The Motagua and Polochic Rivers flow down from the mountains to the east coast of Guatemala, having level lengths of 250 and 185 miles respectively. Guatemala is noted for its blue volcanic lakes, including the two largest, Lake Izabal (36 miles long) and Lake Peten (27 miles long), and the more spectacular Atitlan with its apex covered almost year round by snow and ice.

Early in the morning of 4 February 1976, a shiver travelled inland along the Motagua Fault. Carlos Aranja, a language professor, *brujo*, and farmer living on the east coast of Guatemala, had just sat down to breakfast. It was at that moment that he noticed a strange vibration or "rippling action" in his morning bowl of coconut milk. Suddenly *something* told him to leave his house; Kundalini energy ascended his spine, and he jumped from the table. Seconds later a shock wave, travelling like a great fish under water and land, struck miles further inland. The shock wave had found a point of release. Seconds later 23,000 people lay dead; one million men, women and children were left homeless. The earth groaned; volcanic noise, ash and turmoil filled the air.

The epicenter of the earthquake was 17 miles south of Lake Izabal. Dr. Leland T. Long, a geophysicist at the Georgia Institute of Technology, told me "continental drift is what explains the massive destructive quake and aftershocks in Guatemala." Dr. Long said that the initial earthquake caused seismographs at Georgia Tech to go awry: "Even our less sensitive instruments recorded the quake, which tells us it was a massive one."

Carlos Aranja, a human instrument, *sensed* the approach of impending doom. Professor Aranja, leaving his house twenty seconds before it collapsed, noticed out of the corner of his left eye something unusual approaching from the east. Missing the third step of the porch in his mad dash from the house, Professor Aranja fell to the ground, but as his senses returned and his vision cleared he saw that the "something" was his field foreman, Emmanuel, drawing near. Emmanuel had observed the same strange "rippling action" in the water of the irrigation ditches that crisscross the eastern fields of Professor Aranja's farm. Alarmed at the eerie sound of the waves lapping against the bank, amplified by the stillness of the

[1]Plato, *Timeus* (quoted in Zink; see Bibliography).

32

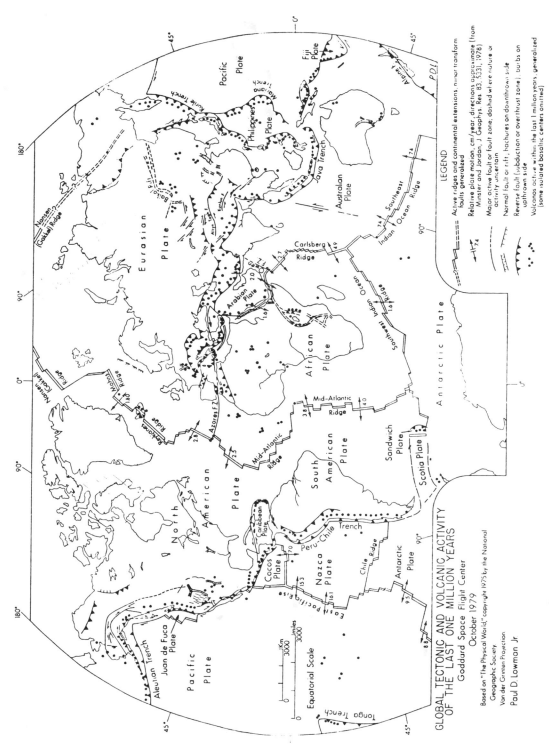

2.2 Map of Global Tectonic and Volcanic Activity.

33

hour, and at the strange manner in which the water trembled, Emmanuel set out across the fields for Professor Aranja. Approaching the house, Emmanuel was once again alarmed as he saw Professor Aranja falling down the steps of his front porch, with his house collapsing behind him. Seconds later and miles further inland, in the Guatemalan town of Joyabaj, coffins were shaken from their graves. Guatemalans were to bury their dead twice. Deep in the earth below Guatemala, rock changed in electrical resistance. Professor Aranja explained to Emmanuel that "when we speak of a major earthquake we are working with a global event. It shakes the entire planet." This massive earthquake was barely recorded at the South Pole where the ice continued to accumulate.

Motion of the earth's plates relative to one another is largely responsible for earthquakes, volcanic activity, and mountain ranges. Ancient scribes, preceding gigantic earthquakes, recorded "strange blisters appear (caused by elastic deformation) swelling the ground."[2] Therefore, it is not unusual that we find the best seismologists of the National Geodetic Survey and the U.S. Geological Survey disturbed by a recent flurry of minor tremors measuring up to 3 on the Richter scale, fanning out across Southern California and measuring the ominous Palmdale Bulge. Pressure between the North American Plate and the Pacific Plate is now building in the San Andreas Fault—building for the superquake expected within the next few years.

According to many writers who have written about the Great Pyramid, the lost continent of Atlantis in the Atlantic Ocean may not be the only lost continent. These writers collectively have spoken of an older civilization, which existed thousands of years before Atlantis in the Pacific Ocean.

This continent is called Mu or Lemuria by various historians; Mu is the correct historical name for the Pacific Plate. The idea that Mankind once had a "golden age" on a huge continent in the Pacific Ocean was considered "Preposterous" until very recently.

On Friday, 3 June 1977, Dr. Amos Nur, a Stanford University geophysicist, announced in a very special press conference that because of his research with Dr. Zvi Ben Avraham of the Israel Oceanographic Institute, he and Dr. Avraham felt that "the presently submerged plateaus in the Pacific near Australia, including the Minihiki Plateau and the Ong Java area, may also be remains of this ancient continent." A lone reporter, who had been extremely quiet from the beginning of the press conference, slowly rose to ask a question.

"Dr. Nur," he said, "in your own opinion, do you believe that mountain ranges have been formed slowly over millions of years, or do you believe the Appalachian Mountain Range and mountain ranges on the other side of this planet like the Himalayans were pushed or thrust up suddenly?"

Dr. Nur replied, "The Himalayas are a good example of continental collision. These mountains were formed by the Indian subcontinent pushing up into Asia."

Dr. Nur and Dr. Ben Avraham have decided to rename this ancient submerged continent—called Mu ("the Motherland") by experts on ancient symbolism for thousands of years—"Pacifica."

The entire Pacific Northwest of the United States geologists today have demonstrated was once buried beneath a massive lava flow a mile high around 6,000 years

---

[2]Again, Plato, quoted by Zink.

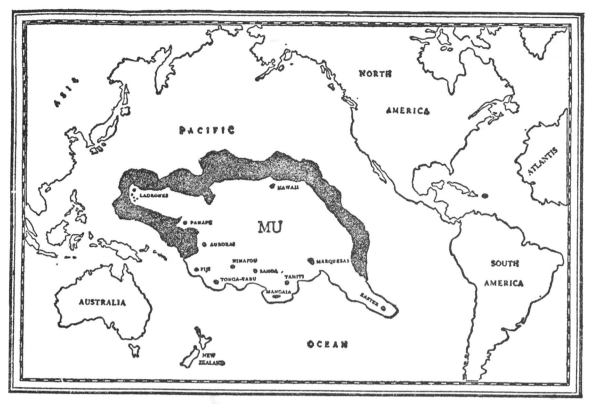

2:3 *The Continent of Mu.* Col. James Churchward, before the theory of continental drift was developed, in his book *The Lost Continent of Mu* described a submerged continent in the Pacific Ocean, foreshadowing by more than half a century the Nur-Avraham discovery of the Pacific plate. "Serious" scientists of Churchward's time ridiculed the idea of a Pacific plate, although such a plate makes the Pacific seafloor consistent with the rest of the world.

---

ago. The thermal energy and pressure pulses produced by a major collision between the earth's plates is awesome: large tracts of earth are swallowed, mountain ranges are thrust up in an instant, global hurricanes sweep the earth destroying forests and all but the most permanent of manmade structures. A cataclysm of this magnitude leaves only small physical examples and fragments of any prior advanced civilization. If New York City were destroyed tomorrow by a natural cataclysm, would anthropologists of the future, from pornography scribbled on the surviving underground steam tunnel walls, deduce that the *whole culture* of New York was degenerate? Would anthropologists of the future, finding broken and fragmentary remains of plastic golden arches in apparently important places, deduce and record something like the following?

Although there are no records, *it is assumed* that the cult of the Golden Arches was a religious cult, apparently heavily involved in the sacrifice of meat, a fanatical and sexually oriented cult whose high priest, Ronald McDonald, sadistically recorded the number of meat sacrifices performed each year.

Could the ancients have accurately predicted earthquakes or foretold cataclysmic shiftings in the earth's crust in advance, thousands of years ago? Does the displacement of the Great Pyramid's interior stones record a massive displacement or shifting in

movement of heavenly bodies occur periodically causing the destructions.[3]

From its beginning in 4000 B.C., the Priesthood of Egypt perpetuated itself year after year, century after century, millennium after millennium; their teachings survive today.

 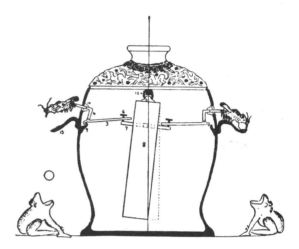

2:4 *The Chinese Earthquake Weathercrock.* As early as A.D. 130, Chinese scientists had enlisted the aid of the population in predicting earthquakes. When a quake struck, the inner pendulum on the weathercrock moved to let a bronze ball fall from the mouth of one of the eight dragons, each positioned towards one of the cardinal points (North, Northeast, East, Southeast, etc.). Which ball dropped indicated, by comparisons taken later, the direction of the quake's movement in relation to the earth's tectonic plates.

the crust of the earth in 1486 B.C.? Early records of past civilizations and their destruction by cataclysmic earth changes were dramatized by the Priesthood of Egypt in their secret religious mysteries.

The ancient Greek Plato, in his *Timaeus,* describes Solon's visit to the Egyptian city of Sais. Solon learned from the Priesthood of Egypt that (emphasis added)

You Hellenes [Greeks] have no heritage...certain perturbations in the

Following Solon's suggestion, Plato journeyed to Egypt to study with the Brotherhood of Egypt. It was Plato, not Solon, who was to discover from the inner core of the Egyptian Priesthood that "our origins stem from our founding by rulers of *foreign countries*" (emphasis added). As to whether Plato was referring to the ancient Hyksos, rulers of foreign countries mentioned in Chapter One, or to the ancient Aryan race, we will investigate further.

Pythagorus, called "The Master" or

---

[3]Velikovsky demonstrates that the Earth experienced a shift in its axis as Venus nearly collided with it. During such a shift the stars would "appear" to move as the Earth rolled over.

2:5 Pythagorus and friends traveling in Egypt — Encamped at night.

"That Man" by other mystical Greek Scholars, upon completing his initiation into the ancient religious mysteries of Egypt changed his name to a name beginning with the Greek letter *P* for symbolic religious reasons—as did Plato, Pliny, Prometheus, and other "illuminated" Greek gods who had studied *in situ* with the ancient Priesthood of Egypt. A Priesthood that from its inception greatly altered the future evolution of Mankind on the planet Earth, a Brotherhood that instructed early Hebrew and Greek scholars. The founders of the ancient Hebrew and Greek alphabets incorporated into the letters of their alphabets sometimes one, sometimes two or three symbolic meanings. The Greek alphabet and numbering system are related to the Hebrew alphabet and numbering system. Both languages sprang forth from the hidden inkwells and pens of brilliant intellects as far removed from the average intelligence of that age as the average man of that age was removed from the great apes—intellects

schooled, disciplined, and instructed for seven years in the ancient wisdom of Egypt by its priesthood. Both languages contained and communicated *symbolically* an earlier concealed science and system of religious belief. A highly developed and articulate system of belief learned by the Priesthood of Egypt concurrent with the establishment of the Egyptian government.

The founders of the Egyptian priesthood understood man as a force of energy contained in a physical vehicle containing seven centers (see Plate 2:6). These centers, running from the base of the spine to the top of the head on man's physical body, were hinted at by early Christian painters when they artistically portrayed a young, martyred, Aramaic-speaking carpenter and his disciples with glowing auras or *halos* surrounding their heads. Jesus spoke Aramaic, but like Moses and other great teachers Jesus spoke several languages. The Priesthood of Egypt in 4000 B.C. taught that the halo-glow or aura surrounding man's physical body had *seven* centers—swirling rings of colored lights (or "chakras" as the Hindu call them) clearly observable to a person with spiritual development. In the ancient Greek language the word *"halos"* meant a luminous ring of white or colored rays surrounding man's physical body. (Hebrew and Aramaic are related to Greek.) In the ancient Greek alphabet, the letter P symbolically represented a man (l) who, having overcome his lowest nature (his sexual center), joined his emotional nature (his heart center) with his intellectual center (ᴾ) in his physical body (P)—thus representing a man in control of his physical, emotional, and mental nature. Thousands of years before early Christian painters depicted Jesus with a halo, knowledge of the aura field, chakras, and *Kundalini* fire (spirit energy which the ancients believed ascended from the base of the spine, the lowest chakra, to the topmost chakra in the head) was taught in the temples of India. The symbol of Kundalini energy is seen today as a physician's staff (cadeucus), a winged rod entwisted by two serpents. Could the early Christians have been taught these concepts by Jesus? If not by him, then by whom?

Through the study of ancient symbolism, one may learn the name Musons, sons of Mu, the Motherland, is where the ancient name of the Order of Freemasons originated. What ancient legends, truths, or inner teachings could the Order of Freemasons have continued to pass on to this day? Is it even possible, by the farthest stretch of one's imagination, that an ancient order or brotherhood might know certain behind-the-scenes stories that have had a most profound effect on the history of Mankind on this planet?

It is recorded in ancient scrolls that "there have always been Tilers or Keepers of the Temple."[4] Before the Hebrew tribes were brought into Egypt by Joseph, before Moses received his final lesson in the law of "Frank Judges"[5] from the mysterious High Priest of Midian[6], before the Greeks studied in Egypt, Phoenician scholars, architects, and sailors had studied in Egypt's oldest temple, the *sanctum sanctorum* or "King's Chamber" of the Great Pyramid. The mathematical, astrological, religious, and astronomical reasons for the architectural connection between the ground floor plan of the temple of King Hiram of Tyre (a Phoenician king and intimate friend of King David, Solomon's father), the ground floor plan of King Solomon's Temple in Jerusalem, and the ground floor plan of the "King's Chamber" in Egypt's Great Pyramid will soon become obvious, as all three are the same. It is written that Tilers, "Keepers of the Temple," were the ones who tiled, repaired, and closed the door of the Great Pyramid shortly after a global destruction during which Moses led the children of Israel out of Egypt.

CATACLYSMS

This massive earlier shifting in the planet Earth's crust, 1486 B.C., buckled, twisted, and shifted the earth's tectonic plates, producing a cataclysm in which vaults supporting the earth gave way. The earth groaned and upheaved; volcanoes exploded, cloud-

---

[4]See, for instance, Masonic documents. Tilers are doorkeepers.

[5]Or "free judges," with some autonomous authority.

[6]Who suddenly appeared to Moses to ask, "What is this thing that thou doest to the people? The thing that thou doest is not good." (Exodus 18:5-23)

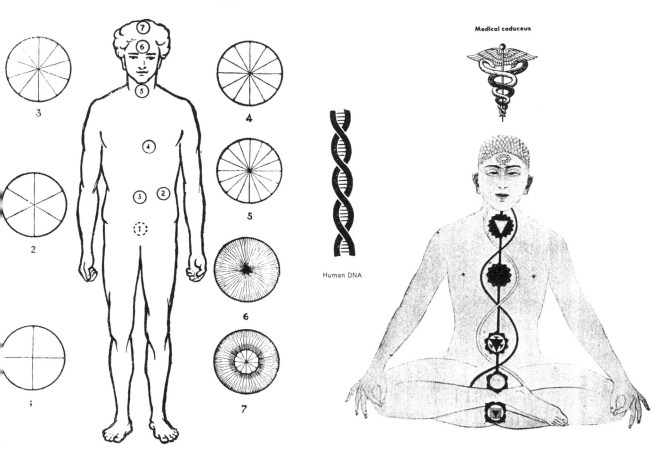

2:6 *The Seven Chakras.* (1) the base of the spine; (2) the spleen; (3) the navel or
solar plexus; (4) the heart; (5) the throat; (6) the "third eye" between the eyebrows;
and (7) the top of the head.

ing the air with volcanic ash; noise, volcanic ash and turmoil filled the air; steaming lava a mile high ran upon the globe's upper strata; oceans were thrown upon the continents; mountain ranges were instantly thrust up; islands were quickly submerged; advanced civilizations disappeared in a day and a night, to become only a vague idea in the collective unconscious of Mankind. Seas became deserts; rivers changed their direction of flow; the already shaking ground was suddenly ripped apart, forming yawning chasms; fires raged unchecked; hillsides collapsed, burying the towns and the screaming populace beneath them; millions of men, women, and children on earth died. The sun was blocked out by volcanic dust, the sky darkened, and men moved into caves to escape the fury of the elements.

This massive displacement of the earth's tectonic plates generated the necessary pressure, hitting the Great Pyramid from the north in the form of a shock-wave, to spring open the sixteen-ton swivel door of the Great Pyramid (see Plate 2:7), a door fitted and hinged millennia earlier by master craftsmen. Someone, between 1486 B.C. and Al Mamun's arrival in 820 A.D. (±4 years), had closed the door on the north

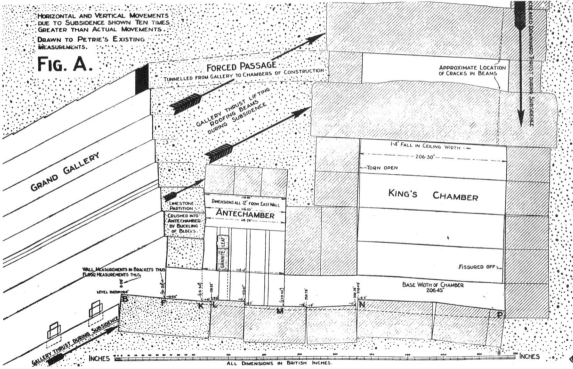

2:7 *Movements Due to Subsidence in the King's Chamber.* The designer of the constructional details of the Great Pyramid foresaw the conditions of subsidence: he foresaw that the central mass of the Pyramid's masonry, in such case, would bring its maximum intensity of pressure to bear upon a square considerably internal to the Pyramid's base square, and that such local concentration of pressure would, by dynamic impulse of momentary subsidence due to earth tremor, punch the central area, along its fissure surfaces, below the level of the natural rock base. That the designer of the Great Pyramid, in his details, devised to meet the expected *vertical movement* is effectively proved by the fact that the passage lengths, in spite of subsidence, have remained unaltered.

face of the Great Pyramid. Could it have been the "keepers of the temple," who, like shadows in the dark, beckon man on continually?

Angelos G. Galanopoulos, Director of the Seismological Institute of the Observatory of Athens, became a professor in 1959 and has since represented Greece in the General Assemblies of the International Union of Geodesy and Geophysics and the Conferences of the European Seismological Commission, and as President of the Subcommission on *Tsunamis* (tremendous sea waves produced by volcanic eruptions, celestial movements, or underwater earthquakes). Professor Galanopoulos co-authored with Edward Bacon (author and editor of a number of books, including *Digging for History*, *Vanished Civilizations*, and the *Life in Ancient Lands* series) a book entitled *Atlantis: The Truth Behind the Legend*, published in 1969. The authors establish that volcanic activity of gigantic proportions (equivalent to a surface blast of 300-450 megatons—in other words, an explosion 22,000 times greater than that of the atomic bomb dropped on Hiroshima) destroyed the island of Santorin in the Aegean Sea, with the explosion generating a sea wave "at least 690 feet high". Based on dramatic geological and archaeological research, the authors suggest a link between the tremendous volcanic explosion of Santorin "around 1500 B.C." and the Exodus of the Israelites.

Dr. Immanuel Velikovsky in 1950 published a book entitled *Worlds in Collision*. The scientific academy of the 50's was outraged, reacting in much the same manner as did the Church of Rome to the theories of Copernicus in 1543 A.D. No major claim made by Velikovsky in *Worlds in Colli-*sion has had to be retracted; in fact, many of his predictions (e.g., Venus is an extremely hot planet; Jupiter is a source of radio waves; remnant magnetism will be found in moon rocks) are today proven true. Schooled in many disciplines including the natural sciences, law, history, biology, medicine, and psychoanalysis, Velikovsky spent years developing his (at the time) unorthodox theories. Velikovsky, on the basis of his analysis of the mythological traditions of ancient peoples, ancient religious theories, texts, astronomical records, and a complex knowledge of the universe, presented evidence that Venus originated as a comet in the second millennium B.C.; that it made a close approach to Earth, causing volcanoes to explode, giant sea waves, and other forms of destruction; that it changed its cometary orbit and was still a comet during the tenth to eighth centuries B.C. Velikovsky dates the Exodus of the Israelites in 1495 B.C., during a great natural devastation of the earth, an occurrence of a shift in the bodies of the heavens which brought Egypt's Middle Kingdom[7] to a close. Knowledge of the movements of heavenly bodies was not restricted to Egypt alone. The High Priest of Rama in India, a prodigiously old man called Manu (a name concealing AUM), is responsible for the "law of eternal recurrence."

David Davidson, a structural engineer (M.C., M.I. Struct. E.), dedicated his life to proving that the Great Pyramid was a representation in scale of the earth's northern hemisphere. During his life Davidson authored an enormous amount of papers and articles over a period of 25 years, including *Early Egypt Babylonia and Central Asia: A Connected History*, *The Hidden Truth in Myth and Ritual*, *and in the Common Culture Pat-*

[7]See Velikovsky's *Peoples of the Sea*, p. 108.

2:8 Joseph making himself known to his brethren.

42

2:9 *Miscellaneous Detail of King Solomon's Temple.* Showing the Ark of the Covenant, the Table of Shewbread, the Golden Candlestick, the Altar of Incense, the Pillar of Brass, the Louver, the Molten Sea, the Altar of Burnt Offering, the Cheribein (Cher-U-Bim), the Tree of Life, and the Key Stone.

tem of Ancient Meterology, *The Structural Aspects of the Great Pyramid*, *The Exodus of Israel: Its Date and Historical Setting*, and his monumental book (the size of a volume of the *Encyclopedia Britannica*), *The Great Pyramid: Its Divine Message*. Davidson, relying on twenty-five years of architectural research on the Great Pyramid (research which only today is being re-analyzed) and upon the ancient architectural and religious history of Egypt, places the date of the Exodus at 1486 B.C., nine years earlier than Velikovsky. Thus:

—Angelos Galanopoulos dates the Exodus "around 1500 B.C."

—Immanuel Velikovsky dates the Exodus "at 1495 B.C."

—David Davidson dates the Exodus in 1486 B.C.

Davidson says, "five years after the death of Ramessu II (the Pharoah of the oppression)," which would agree, as Davidson says, "with the age of Moses at the Exodus, eighty years, according to Deuteronomy 29:5, 31:2, and 34:7 and Exodus 7:7—Moses having been born in the first year (of co-regency) of the Pharoah of the oppression (Exodus 1:8-12, 2:1-10)".[8]

2:10 The mummy of Ramses II.

It was during this world-wide cataclysm that Moses was to lead his people out of Egypt, taking the mummy of Joseph with him and thereby fulfilling the oath of Joseph to the children of Israel: "God will surely visit you, an ye shall carry up my bones from hence." (Genesis 50:25) "So Joseph died, being an hundred and ten years old: and they embalmed him, and he was put in a coffin in Egypt." (Genesis 50:26) Man today assumes that everything to be seen is visible on the surface—a one dimensional view.

Ipuwer, an Egyptian scribe, noticed a curious rippling action in his morning glass of goat's milk while sitting at his breakfast table. Concentrating his visual attention on these curious ripples, Ipuwer suddenly heard a sound over his right shoulder, like distant thunder. The sound grew closer and louder at an alarming rate. Curiously but cautiously, Ipuwer stepped outside his house. The sound-wave (from the volcanic explosion of Santorin triggered by the close approach of the comet Venus), by then resembling the sound of a thousand bulldozers, engulfed him. Moments later all was chaos. Ipuwer survived this epeirogenic shifting in the earth's crust. His writings give us an Egyptian version of this catastrophe.

In 1828 the Museum of Leiden in the Netherlands acquired the papyrus containing the writings of Ipuwer. The text of Ipuwer is now folded into a book of seventeen pages, and is listed in the Museum's catalogue as Leiden #344. The text of Ipuwer is written in the fast-flowing writing style used by Egyptian scribes, a manner of writing quite different from hieroglyphs. The story of Ipuwer is written on the face (recto), and on the back (verso) is written a hymn to God. The front and back of the text are to-

---

[8]The Talmud, preserving Jewish tradition, gives the Exodus as five years after the death of the Pharoah of the oppression.

day differentiated by the direction of the fiber tissues. It is only by a careful examination of the writings of the Egyptian scribe Ipuwer, when compared and examined beside the writings of the Hebrew writer of Exodus, that one can see if indeed both writings describe the same event, the same cataclysmic disaster.

PAPYRUS IPUWER 2:5-10 Plague is throughout the land...blood is everywhere. (2:8) The land turns round [over] as does a potter's wheel...Earth turned upside down...land upside down; happens that which never [yet] had happened. (2:10) The river is blood.

Rusty ferruginous dust filtered down upon Earth from the tail of the comet Venus. This, combined with the iron oxide in the ash from the volcanic eruption of Santorin, imparted a bloody red hue over land, sea, and pyramids. The volcanic ash, sliding down the steep sides of the Great Pyramid, accumulated at the base.

EXODUS 7:21 There was blood throughout all the land of Egypt.

PAPYRUS IPUWER 2:10 Men shrink from tasting; human beings thirst after water.

Volcanic ash covered the surface of the Nile, depleting the river's oxygen level, suffocating fish and other forms of aquatic life, which floated to the surface to decay.

EXODUS 7:21 And the river stank.

PAPYRUS IPUWER 3:10-13 That is our water! That is our happiness! What shall we do in respect thereof? All is ruin.

EXODUS 7:24 And all the Egyptians digged round about the river for [fresh] water to drink; for they could not drink of the water of the river.

PAPYRUS IPUWER 9:2 Cattle are left to stray, and there is none to gather them together.

EXODUS 9:19 Gather thy cattle and all that thou hast in the field; for upon every man and beast which shall be found in the field, and shall not be brought home, the hailstones [meteorite showers from the tail of the comet] shall come down upon them, and they shall die.

PAPYRUS IPUWER 9:3 Each man fetches for himself those [cattle] that are branded with his name.

EXODUS 9:21 And he that regarded not the word of the Lord left his servants and his cattle in the field.

PAPYRUS IPUWER 4:14, 6:1, 5:12 Trees are destroyed...No fruits, no herbs are found...Grain has perished on every side...that has perished which yesterday was seen. The land is left to its weariness like the cutting of flax.

EXODUS 9:25 And the hail smote every herb of the field, and brake every tree of the field.

PAPYRUS IPUWER 2:10, 7:1, 11:11, 12:6 Gates, columns, and wall are consumed by fire. The sky is in confusion.[9]

EXODUS 9:23...and the fire ran along upon the ground.

PAPYRUS IPUWER 10:3-6 Lower Egypt weeps...The entire palace is without its revenues...to it belong [by right]

---

[9]**Velikovsky demonstrates that the Earth experienced a shift in its axis as Venus nearly collided with it. During such a shift the stars would "appear" to move as the Earth rolled over.**

wheat and barley, geese and fish.

EXODUS 10:15...there remained not any green thing in the trees, or in the herbs of the fields, through all the land of Egypt.

PAPYRUS IPUWER 10:3, 2:11, 3:13 *Lower Egypt weeps...The towns are des-* troyed. *Upper Egypt has become waste...all is ruin...The residence is overturned in a minute.*

Dr. Immanuel Velikovsky, author of the books *Worlds in Collision, Ages in Chaos,* and *Earth in Upheaval,* says, "Only an earthquake could have overturned the residence in a minute."

2:11 *The Astronomical Temple of Eduf.* This temple, later known as Appolonopolis Magna, was found and drawn by Dominique Vivant Denon, one of Napoleon's savants, in 1798. Why did Napoleon find a land inhabited by people totally incapable of duplicating these structures? What had become of the ancient builders? Why was the temple found half-buried in sand?

A. H. Gardiner, in his book *Admonitions of an Egyptian Sage from a Hieratic Papyrus in Leiden*, comments on the distress of Egypt—the collapse of the civil service, violence ripping the country, invaders preying on the defenseless population, the wealthy stripped of everything by unruly mobs of the ignorant: "It is no merely local disturbance that is here described, but a great and overwhelming national disaster."[10] Ipuwer speaks of this sudden, violent cataclysm and of how it left his homeland:

N o   f r u i t s   n o r   h e r b s   a r e found...hunger...All animals, their hearts weep...Cattle moan...It is groaning that is throughout the land, mingled with lamentations...The land is not light [sun obscured by volcanic dust]...men flee...Tents are what they make like the dwellers of [the] hills...Years of noise.[11] There is no end to the noise. Oh, that the earth would cease from noise, and tumult be no more...Forsooth, great and small say: I wish I might die...He who places his brother in the ground is everywhere. (6:1, 5:5, 3:14, 9:11, 10:2, 4:2, 4:5, 4:2, 2:13)

"*Forsooth, those who are in the place of embalmment are laid on the high ground*"—that is, coffins protruded from the graves. The coffin containing the mummy of Joseph was found, shaken from its tomb and lying upon the high ground. The Egyptians, like the later Guatemalans, were to bury their dead twice. Rock deep in the earth below Egypt changed in electrical resistance.

2:13 *Nubians Drawn by Denon in 1799.* Dominique Vivant Denon, who later became superintendent of the Louvre and director of the Beaux Arts, accompanied Napoleon on his expedition to Egypt and produced a series of drawings and etchings for the twenty-one volume *Description de l'Egypte.* A Freemason like his emperor, Denon incorporated in his drawings certain Masonic signs, especially evident in his drawing of Napoleon visiting the Great Pyramid's "King's Chamber." His drawings and etchings clearly show only ruins of what at one time was a great and powerful civilization. See *Napoleon in the King's Chamber* (Exhibit 4:2).

---

[10]See A. H. Gardiner, *Admonitions of an Egyptian*, note 1:8. Quoted in Velikovsky, *Worlds in Collision;* see especially pp. 64-91.

[11]Galanopoulos states that the volcanic eruption on Santorin may have lasted for as long as 25 years.

Kuseberg X.J. MEISTER

48

Ipuwer said:

> *Forsooth: the children of princes are dashed* [thrown] *against the wall...children of princes are cast out in the streets...the prison is ruined.* (5:6, 6:12) *Forsooth, public offices are opened and the census-lists are taken away...the laws of the judgement-hall are cast forth...men walk upon* [them] *in the public places...the storehouse of the King is the common property of everyone...Behold, the fire has mounted up on high.* (6:7, 6:9, 10:3, 7:1)

Moses took Joseph's mummy with him when he departed Egypt:

> And Moses took the bones of Joseph with him: for he had straitly sworn the children of Israel, saying, God will surely visit you; and ye shall carry my bones away hence with you. (Exodus 13:19)

Moses, within the framework of Akhnaton's great release of knowledge, was instructed and educated into the secret Egyptian mysteries by the High Priest of Egypt, the High Priest of a mysterious religious system instituted by a band of *rulers of foreign countries* who, working unobtrusively in the foreign country of Egypt, instituted and re-established in 4000 B.C. the ancient Brotherhood of Man. Moses subsequently reburied Joseph with grand honors as his brethren, led by Moses, moved from the right to left around the tomb three times, as was practiced in that age.

Historians, unencumbered by religious superstitions, perverted thought; ignorance, in other words, uncurbed desire; and fear in the form of destructive actions; will remember that the writings of an Egyptian scribe and the writings of a Hebrew scribe, both at the same time in Earth's history, both in the same geographical location, are not necessarily direct proof that such a world-wide destruction occurred. If indeed such a gigantic world-wide disturbance actually occurred, as Immanuel Velikovsky describes and as the editors of *Pensee* suggest happened,[12] then a gigantic, celestially influenced disturbance in the earth's tectonic plates would certainly have been reported by scribes in countries all over the surface of the earth, even in Mexico—a land of pyramids.

The sky "rained not water, but fire and red-hot stones," we read in the Mexican *Annals of Cuauhtitlan*. The Mayan *Manuscript Quiche* states that the earth quaked and water in the rivers "turned to blood." One reading Velikovsky's books, exhaustive in their documentation and detailed in their arguments, remembers the words of one of the ancient priests of Egypt, a prodigiously old man, to Solon in Plato's *Timaeus*, concerning "certain perturbations in the movement of heavenly bodies":

> 'O Solon, Solon, you Greeks are always children: there is no such a thing as an old Greek.' And on hearing this he asked: 'What mean you by this saying?' And the priest replied, 'You are young in soul, every one of you. For therein you possess not a single science that is hoary with age. And this is the cause thereof: There have been and there will be many and divers destructions of mankind, of which the greatest are by fire and water, and lesser ones by countless other means. For in truth the story is told in your country as well as ours,

---

[12]See *Velikovsky Reconsidered*, by the Editors of *Pensee* as listed in the Bibliography.

how once upon a time Phaethon, son of Helios, yoked his father's chariot, and, because he was unable to drive it along the course taken by his father, burnt up all that was upon the earth and himself perished by a thunderbolt—that story, as is told, has the fashion of a legend, but the truth of it lies in the *occurrence of a shifting of the bodies in the heavens* which surround the earth, and a destruction of the things on the earth by fierce fire, which recurs at long intervals...and when, after the usual interval of years, like a plague, the flood from heaven comes sweeping down afresh upon your people, it leaves none of you but the unlettered and uncultured, so that you become young as ever, with no knowledge of all that happened in old times in this land or in your own. Certainly the genealogies which you related just now, Solon, concerning the people of your country, are little better than children's tales; for, in the first place, you remember but one deluge, though many had occurred previously. (Emphasis added.)

Almost all experts in their fields of study are virtually unaware of new discoveries in other fields, yet they take sides in debating, "Is Velikovsky right?" There are mysteries of great import that need to be addressed. Is the Great Pyramid more than a tomb?[13]

Who were the ancient cartographers who drew the original map from which the 1513 A.D. *Piri Re'is Map* was copied? This ancient map, its authenticity beyond question, clearly depicts the South Pole *without* ice, indicating that the topography of the Antarctic continent was either derived by highly developed scientific techniques, or at some point in the earth's past men mapped the South Pole when it was not buried under the oppressive weight of the ice mass presently obscuring it.[14] Who made the Antikythaera Computer, a sophisticated planetary computer capable of advanced astronomical calculations—found at the bottom of the Aegean Sea in 1900 A.D., in the wreckage of a ship containing oil and wine vases accurately dated 65 B.C.?[15] Who were the ancient miners who worked the Ngwenya Iron Mine in Swaziland for iron ores of ochre and specularite in 41250 B.C. (± 1,300 years)—a fantastic date confirmed by both the Yale Radiocarbon Laboratory in America and the Gronigen Laboratory in Holland?[16] This recital of unexplained anomalies indicating prior advanced civilizations could be continued indefinitely. While the experts argue, the planets of this solar system, like a giant cosmic triggering mechanism, once again are rapidly moving into an anciently dreaded position: a position which will, by the planets' combined pull (cf. Newton's Law) on the now over two-mile thick ice mass of Antarctica and the fragile 15,000-foot thick *sedimentary* rock composing the Edsel Ford Mountain Range

[13]See Peter Tompkins, *Secrets of the Great Pyramid,* for a thorough discussion of this point.

[14]See Charles H. Hapgood, *Maps of the Ancient Sea Kings,* as well as his previous book, *Earth's Shifting Crust.* In a forward to that book Albert Einstein said that Hapgood's idea could be of "great importance to everything that is related to the history of the earth's surface."

[15]See *Scientific American* (April 1974); also M. Clagett, *Gears from the Greeks* and *Greek Science in Antiquity.*

[16]See James Bailey, *The God-Kings and the Titans,* listed in the Bibliography.

in Antarctica, contribute to the next cataclysmic shifting in the earth's crust. An "occurrence of a shifting of the bodies in the heavens," as described by the High Priest of Egypt to Solon, is incorporated into the Hebrew religious traditions: "Let them be [the planets and stars] for signs, and for seasons, and for days, and years." (Genesis 1:14) It is earlier found in the "law of eternal recurrence" of Manu, a prodigiously old priest of Rama, India. This planetary alignment and its possible effects on the Antarctic ice mass are discussed with Colin Bull, Dean of the Polar Research Institute, later in this book.

2:14. *Ancient Egyptian Temple with Masonic Symbols.*

...every aspect of Egyptian knowledge seems to have been complete at the very beginning. The sciences, artistic and architectural techniques and the hieroglyphic system show virtually no signs of a period of 'development'; indeed, many of the achievements of the earliest dynasties were never surpassed, or even equalled later on. This astonishing fact is readily admitted by orthodox Egyptologists, but the magnitude of the mystery it poses is skillfully understated, while its many implications go unmentioned.

How does a complex civilization spring full-blown into being? Look at a 1905 automobile and compare it to a modern one. There is no mistaking the process of 'development'. But in Egypt there are no parallels. Everything is there right at the start.

The answer to the mystery is of course obvious, but because it is repellent to the prevailing cast of modern thinking, it is seldom seriously considered. *Egyptian civilization was not a 'development', it was a legacy.*

John Anthony West
Serpent in the Sky: The High Wisdom of Ancient Egypt

VANDALS

How many years after a series of aftershocks Man turned his eyes toward the Great Pyramid as a handy quarry for stone, no one knows. But we do know today (1982) that as recently as 586 years ago, 5,396 years after the Great Pyramid was completed, Man was still busy at work ripping off the remaining surface stones for his own use.

Baron d'Anglure believed that the Great Pyramid was used by Joseph during the seven biblical years of plenty to store Pharaoh's grain. The Baron wrote in 1396 A.D. that

> Certain ouvriers massons qui a force desmuroient les grosses pierres tailles qui font la couverture de desdits greniers, et les laissoient devaller a val. (Certain masons demolished the course of great casing stones which covered these granaries, and tumbled them into the valley.)

But for the vandalism and ignorance of Man in one age, the Great Pyramid and the pyramids of Mexico, the work of men of a far earlier age, would still be intact today.

From the time of Baron d'Anglure in 1396 A.D. to today is 586 years, which together total 1,982 years; adding 1,982 years to 4,000 years gives one a total of 5,982. Just 18 more years gives one a total of 6,000 years and a date—5 May of the year 2000—a date exactly six thousand years after a band of our ancestors stood quietly watching movements in the northern sky above a moonlit Egyptian desert—a date when for the first time in 6,000 years all the planets of our solar system will be arrayed in practically a straight line across space (See Plate 2:15 computed by J.D.W. Staal, Director of Fernbank Science Center's Planetarium,

Emory University, Atlanta, Georgia)—a date when some modern research, discussed later, indicates Antarctica's ice mass will be over three miles thick, possibly four.

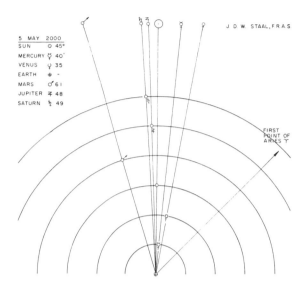

2:15. *The Position of the Planets on 5 May 2000.*

This date heralds an event a band of astronomer-stone masons believed would affect the wobble of this planet producing a catastrophic shifting of the Earth's tectonic plates.

Is it logical to assume that a band of men in 4000 B.C. would go to all the trouble of coordinating and orchestrating the multi-disciplined effort needed to erect the Great Pyramid simply because oral tradition may have given them cause for alarm?

Isn't it more logical to think, from the evidence presented above, and throughout the rest of this book, that these men had actually witnessed and survived a sudden shift in the Earth's terrestrial axis triggered by the growth of one or more of its icecaps?

One might ask, "Why would these men who had survived a terrible event which had destroyed their civilization care enough to communicate an altruistic message of warning and hope across the gulf of space to a generation of men and women 6,000 years in the future?"

This question may be rationally answered by the fact that 6,000 years ago men believed in reincarnation. So, perhaps, this was not an altogether altruistic effort. Perhaps these men built the Great Pyramid to be a huge and surviving symbol which would, in their "future lives," trigger in their minds a remembrance of their past lives. Perhaps they erected the Great Pyramid as a symbol to trigger in their collective unconsciousness a memory of how their civilization was destroyed so that they, in their next reincarnation, could warn others and stop the ice.

Perhaps they have reincarnated. Perhaps they are here now.

Perhaps...

CHAPTER THREE
DARK SHADOWS ACROSS A LAND OF SUN

Peter Tompkins, the son of two extraordinary parents, Laurence and Molly Tompkins, as a child spent many an enjoyable hour on the lap of George Bernard Shaw. The emotional relationship between Shaw, whose plays earned him the Nobel Prize in 1925, and the young American couple, nearly half a century his juniors when they arrived in London in 1921, was to develop and mature until Shaw's death in 1950. The relationship between the grand old man of literature and the beautiful, occasionally maddening girl from Atlanta is best described in the book *Shaw and Molly Tompkins*, written by her son.

Shaw's formal education ended at the age of 14, a fact to which he attributed his being so well-educated. At Shaw's suggestion, Peter returned to America to continue his schooling. Peter attended the University of Georgia and was an undergradute at Harvard until he returned to Europe to continue his education at the Sorbonne in Paris.

During World War II, as a member of the Allied Psychological Warfare Branch, Tompkins covered the war in Europe and Africa until 1943, when he transferred to the Office of Strategic Services to concentrate on military intelligence. Less than a year later Tompkins found himself sitting in the wet bottom of a yellow, squishy rubber dinghy, "like the ones I had used so many times in Sicily to practice secret landings," approaching the coast of Italy in the middle of the night to land behind the German lines. At the tender age of 24 Tompkins, because he had been educated abroad and had spent so much time in Italy that he could speak Italian fluently in various local accents, was picked by the OSS. Under the personal blessing of Major General William J. Donovan, Tompkins was given *carte blanche* to organize an efficient spy ring in the heart of Rome. It was a grim business Tompkins was engaged in: the next knock or ringing doorbell could be the beginning of a German SS raid. Tompkins was always on the run, always expecting that the next meeting would be a trap; many close friends were caught and cruelly tortured before they were killed. Some, hung through the chin on meathooks, died in agony hanging from lamp posts. Others were (comparatively speaking) mercifully paraded before firing squads and machine-gunned to death. Several heroically refused to talk; some did talk. Nevertheless, Tompkins continued to expand his underground intelligence network. Each day his web grew larger. Each day the stacks of intelligence reports grew larger—more information, more stacks of reports, some valid, some false, and some enemy plants. Working faster and faster, working first in one place and then rapidly moving to escape Hauptmann Erich Priebke, the SS captain fanatically determined to catch him, Tompkins continued his work. Dissecting fact from fiction and priority information from unimportant information, encoding the

The Sphinx and Pyramid.

Though the unwary reader would never know it from a casual reading of popular scientific journals or from the popular press (even the self-appointed 'responsible' press) a real revolution in human thought is already under way (compensating with intensity for what it perhaps lacks in numbers).

John Anthony West
Serpent in the Sky:
The High Wisdom of Ancient Egypt

Gurdjieff used to say, "Fairness? Decency? How can you expect fairness and decency on a planet of sleeping people?" And during the first World War, he said, "Of Course, if they were to wake up, they'd throw down their guns and go home to their wives and families."

Robert Anton Wilson
Cosmic Trigger: The Final
Secret of the ILLUMINATI

essence of the information into a coherent report, Tompkins would clandestinely broadcast his anxiously awaited bulletin to the Allied High Command at the end of the day. It was exactly this type of training that twenty-five years later would prove of great value to Tompkins when he began organizing all the literature on the Great Pyramid for his book *Secrets of the Great Pyramid*.

Living by his wits alone, Tompkins impersonated at various times an auxiliary policeman, a black market food dealer, a corporal in the Fascist Republican Army, and a captain in the Command of the Open City of Rome. He endured the incessant pressure, living in a variety of apartment hideouts that only a brave and basically optimistic man could have survived in—a women's tailoring shop run by an old homosexual with his giggling young lover ("a fat-bottomed boy"), where Tompkins became so infuriated that he almost left; a house of assignation; and an aristocratic palazzo subdivided into flats. Tompkins not only endured, but lived at a perpetual peak of nervous energy and found relaxation in brandy, gin, wine, and accommodating young women. After the War Tompkins wrote three books on a war he had intimate knowledge of: *Italy Betrayed, The Murder of Admiral Darlan*, and *A Spy in Rome*.

In 1971 Tompkins's book *Secrets of the Great Pyramid* was published. Egyptologists, brushing the cobwebs aside, clambered into their mummy caskets to hide. Some of the bolder ones, pathetically unable to refute any of Tompkins's discoveries, advanced shaking handfuls of tanna leaves and shouting, "Heretic!" Today, however, many younger Egyptologists are seriously following up on Tompkins's work and the work of Livio C. Stecchini, Professor of Ancient History and Quantitative Science at William Patterson College, who wrote the mathematical appendix for Tompkins's book.

The following spontaneous interview with Peter Tompkins was kindly supplied me by Atlanta radio station WQXI, largely through the efforts of Ike Newkirk, who interviewed Mr. Tompkins.

Newkirk: We're talking with Peter Tompkins, the author of a book entitled *Mysteries of the Mexican Pyramids*. You might say that it's a sequel to his original smash selling work, *Secrets of the Great Pyramid*. Mr. Tompkins, one would seem to think that you're pyramid bound. How did you get on this particular path or is this something you have loved for a while?

Tompkins: Nobody could tell me what it was all about.

Newkirk: The pyramids?

Tompkins: Yes. The only way to find out was to go look and then go poke in the libraries. If some guy tells you that it's just somebody's tomb or that they performed some mysterious rite on it, it's just not enough. I had to go find out. Also, it was a great adventure. In the first book I followed the adventures of those strange characters who dug into the pyramid in Egypt; and just as incredible and fascinating characters went poking around in Meso-America and Central America and Mexico, Chiapas, Yucatan, Guatemala, to find those unbelievable structures, and there may be another ten or fifteen thousand of them still buried in the jungle.

Newkirk: Where did it all begin for you?

Tompkins: It began during the Second World War when I first saw the Great Pyramid. You take a look at that enormous pile of masonry and you've got to wonder why would anyone go to all that effort. You have to see it and climb it to really appreciate what it would take in human endeavor to build it. Now, it seemed to me that nobody would build such an enormity just for a tomb, it had to have some other function. Then I discovered—it took me about twenty years—that in point of fact, it was a library in stone, a sort of university of mathematical, astronomical and geodetic data so carefully put together that coming by thousands of years later you could extrapolate from it the data and see what it was. Then, I wondered if the same thing was applicable in Mexico and Central America; so I went down and poked around and pretty soon I found some very extraordinary people had done some very ex-

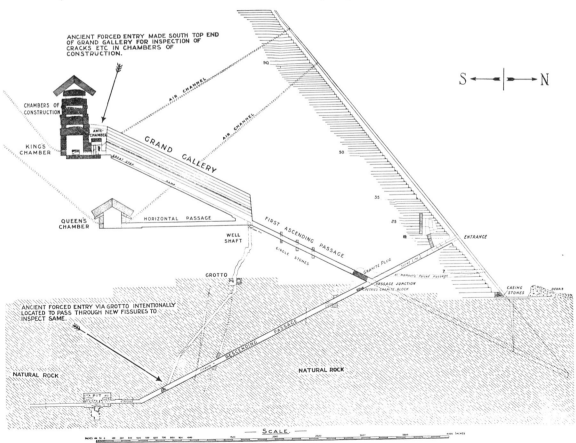

3:1. *Passage System of Great Pyramid, Looking West.*

traordinary work, and the Meso-American pyramids do have the same sort of data built into them. So some advanced civilizations with a sophisticated knowledge of astronomy, geodesy and mathematics built these things. Where they came from and what happened to them, there's one of the great mysteries.

Newkirk: Were the similarities between the Great Pyramid and the Mexican pyramids of such a nature that you could go so far [as] to say the same people were involved in the construction of both?

Tompkins: That's what's so interesting to look for and the data is tenuous, but perfectly obvious. There's a man who worked twenty years with NASA who is an astronomer. His name is Maurice Chatelain [one of the NASA technicians responsible for the Apollo flights]; he's come up with some remarkable figures. The figures have been there all along, but the question was to relate them and understand what they were. There is an amazing number which appears in the Babylonian cuneiform tablets [found in Assurbanipal's Ninevah library] in Mesopotamia. It's one hundred ninety-five trillion nine hundred fifty-five billion two hundred million [195,955,200,000,000].

That is a lot of millions! Who would put down such a number and why? Then you get to Meso-America and find on a stelae numbers going back in the millions of millions, why?[1] What are they trying to tell you? What were they doing it for? It cannot be idle because these people had observed and recorded the synodic returns of the planets to four points of decimal—really quite extraordinary. They knew, of course, that the earth rotated on its axis; that it went around the sun; that the planets went around the sun, and the relationship between them, and that these relationships had a definite effect on people, on vegetation, on all kinds of things on the planet, on growth, on the cycles of disease, on hurricanes, earthquakes; that's what they were studying. Now, when you find the same numbers appearing on both sides of the Atlantic and both are based on what I discovered in Eqypt, on a system based on a second of time, it has to be more than coincidental. You cannot have any science without measurements and a unit of measure of length and a unit of measure of time are the prime elements and they—the ancient astronomers— worked out a second of time. They worked out a second by making the day twenty-four hours, of sixty minutes and sixty seconds, just as

[1]To quote Peter Tompkins from his book *Mysteries of the Mexican Pyramids:* "Chatelain says he got the shock of his life when he realized the number (195,955,200,000,000) was 86,400 times 2,268,000,000 and that 2,268 million was the number of days in 240 precessions of the equinox (of 25,890 years each)" (p.301).

we have today, and they took a circle and made a second of arc, which is the essential way to break up a circle. You can break it up any way you like, but they did it in 360 degrees just as we do today, with sixty minutes and sixty seconds, and from these two seconds [of time and arc] they derived their system of measures which covered the whole Middle East, and all the way out to China. And when you find the same thing in Meso-America, you begin to wonder; it begins to become obvious that the same system is at work. And more extraordinary, the Maya God, the supreme deity, is Hunab Ku— "sole distributor of measure."

3:2. *The North and West Faces of the Great Pyramid, Looking Southeast.* "Few buildings in the world embody the mass of the Great Pyramid, nor do they enjoy such a prominent area of visual command. It's an unusual set of circumstances," said James M. Hagan, Vice President of Heery Associates (a construction program management firm with offices in New York and Atlanta). After viewing a long series of exterior and interior color slides of the Great Pyramid, I asked Mr. Hagan: "If I gave you unlimited manpower, whatever unskilled labor you needed, whether it was 4,000 men or 4,000,000 men given wood mallets and bronze chisels, could you direct them to build this pyramid?" He replied, "No. I see no way unskilled people could have built this. It took highly skilled people in management, design, and execution (quarrying, measuring, cutting, shaping, transporting, and placing, as well as finishing)."

Newkirk: So the obvious inference is there.

Tompkins: Of course, and the other interesting point is that the cosmology is the same there. Their ideas of how the universe got put together, what the formative forces are in it and such notions that the elements have goals, and that hydrogen and oxygen perform in the same way because they are organized and have goals and that there are force fields—a more metaphysical power behind these things—which is what modern science is inevitably coming to, all of this they knew and they knew it on both sides of the Atlantic. And this leads one to the suspicion, more and more, that: (a) we know that there was much more intercourse between the Mediterranean and the Caribbean hundreds, thousands of years ago. All of this nonsense about Columbus discovering America is garbage, of course. But, people, and the Italians, who insist on clinging to it, are silly, because if they looked a little bit further back, they'd find that Marco Polo had discovered the other side of America before Columbus, so they're not going to lose any kudos....

Newkirk: You know, almost everyone who has been through school, high school or college, has been taught that the people,

especially the Egyptians, are always depicted as a people of lesser intelligence without any capabilities at all, and by the same token, the Maya.

Tompkins: It seems to me that the same sort of notion applied to the Blacks in the South up until very recently and it's just as incorrect. The Spaniards when they came here, "the Conquistadors", came with a notion that they were dealing with savages, and for 300 years of history, historians kept putting them down. They said native Americans were savages; they said they hadn't built any palaces, that it was all an invention. It's fascinating when you see in the book, from chapter to chapter, the guys who came here and saw something and then went back to be ridiculed like Gemelli Careri. He was the first one who brought back a report on Mexico to Europe and they just called him a fraud, but far from being a fraud he was a very accurate reporter.[2] And this notion that Americans were savages was, of course, the only defense for a bunch of the most barbaric savages you've ever seen, who came over here looting the gold, massacring the people, raping the women and infecting everybody with the pox—these Spaniards were really not very nice characters—but their only defense

[2]Giovanni Francesco Gemelli Careri, a Neapolitan jurist arrived in Mexico in 1697, his last stop on a five-year trip around the world. Prior to his visit to Mexico, Careri visited the Great Pyramid while in Egypt. Careri mentions in his eight-volume work that Strabo believed that the Great Pyramid was used as an astronomical observatory. His report of history, entitled *Giro del Mondo*, was published in Venice in 1719 by G. Malachin.

was to say that what they found was terrible, when, in point of fact, they destroyed all the records they could of a civilization, which, in many respects, was superior to their own.

3:3. Montezuma welcoming the conquistadors.

Newkirk: Your initial work, *Secrets of the Great Pyramid*, spawned a host of writers who looked into the area and many seem to implicate travellers from other planets, from other systems, as giving the Egyptians, and I would imagine this would carry over into the Mayans, the tools and the knowledge they needed to construct these pyramids. Would you happen to subscribe to that philosophy?

Tompkins: It's a great theory, but where is the evidence? Now, I am not the least bit loath to subscribe to the theory. It makes a great deal of sense, especially when we don't know where the Mayans came from or where they went to. They came out of nowhere that you can trace and they abandoned their cities overnight. Boom! Just like that. It's a very mysterious notion. Chatelain, who worked for NASA for twenty years, who is a space man, is perfectly convinced that these people got their notions and their wisdom from space people, but he hasn't got the evidence anymore than Von Daniken or anybody else has yet to nail it; and so when you ask me...I'm perfectly open to the notion, but please let's get some artifacts or some solid data.

Newkirk: And there's absolutely no evidence to support that theory at all?

Tompkins: Circumstantial evidence yes, but not hard yet. And that's what we're looking for. Very interesting, but I have to stick to facts. I sort of broke ground with the *Great Pyramid*. If in that first book I could have been shot down, it might have put the whole subject back again another hundred years, because for the last hundred years you couldn't mention it in public; to talk about the Great Pyramid as being a scientific, instrument, people gave you the horse laugh. Now they cannot deny it because the facts are cold. In this Mexican book, I've gone a little bit further. I've wet my feet a little bit more; but I try to step on solid ground as best I can so that those who follow won't fall on their faces. You see, the minute you get into pre-history, you've got to go on what there is and I am not the least bit loath to use, as I do in a whole chapter, the readings of Edgar Cayce, who was America's leading sensitive, for I've long since discovered that dowsing is not charlatanry, but is a perfectly obvious science. But, the scientists don't know why and how it works, they don't know how magnetism works, they don't know how electricity works, yet, we light our electric bulbs. Well, with dowsing you find water, and what I've been doing recently down in the Bahamas, which is very exciting, is dowsing for archeological sites because dowsers can lead you in hundreds of square miles of empty sea right to where there is a wreck, right to where there's an object. And so we found columns and pediments, etc., etc. But before you can analyze them and find out whether it is just a recent wreck or a Phoenician wreck or something that may go back thousands of years, you have to *find* the object. And the dowsers are doing it. Psychic archaeology is going to be the fascinating subject of the next year or two.

Newkirk: What kinds of methods did you use for your research work? You had to, of course, have been guided by the historians, the people who recounted—

Tompkins: Misguided by the historians.

3:4. Gold-hungry conquistadors attacking their Indian hosts.

Newkirk: Yes, right without a doubt.

Tompkins: That's the whole game. When I came back from World War Two, I said, 'Uhh-ahh, I've seen enough of this at too close hand and too close to the top,' and I could see that history was being re-written, just simply to suit the victors. So I went to the archives. Now, if you go to the archives, it's fascinating. They will burn and destroy everything they can, but as in the Italian campaign, which was a fascinating thing—there, all the generals of the General Staff got up in court and swore on a stack of Bibles that such-and-such a report never existed. And it was very important to us because it was our landing at Salerno and it could have cost us, and it darn near cost us, the invasion at Salerno. Now all these Italian generals were swear-ing there was no such thing, but twenty years later in the archives came out a piece of paper where a major was told to burn all these messages, and in good protocol manner, the major said 'I hereby burnt message so-and-so and message so-and-so.' So twenty years after the fact, you could see it was obvious that had those generals said, 'Oh yes, there was such a report, but it didn't say what general so-and-so says', they would

3:5. *Spaniards Destroying Mexican Temples Under Papal Supervision.* At the time Cortez sailed from Spain, human rights in Europe were but feebly discerned. Superstition reigned over most hearts and consciences with a fearfully despotic sway. Cortez, commending himself to God and the Virgin, unfurled his sails and steered resolutely toward Mexico. Landing in Mexico, he "converted the inhabitants to the religion of Jesus (sic)" with the energies of fire and sword, misery and blood, fanatic priests, horses rushing to the charge and death-dealing artillery. Let Philosophy explain the enigma as she may—no intelligent man will venture the assertion that Cortez was a hypocrite. He was a frank, fearless, cruel, deluded enthusiast.

have gotten away with it. But they thought because they had burnt it that they could get away with saying it hadn't existed, and that's why they were caught *in flagrante* as plain liars—well, that's what history is made up of, *in flagrante* plain liars, most of the time usually the victors. That's what happened in Meso-America with the Mexicans. When Cortez and his boys got through with them, there wasn't a record; they burnt all the codices they could lay their hands on and it's just by chance that a few survived and we're still having a terrible time deciphering those. But every day a bit more is being cracked and what comes out of it is stupendous data. I mean, those

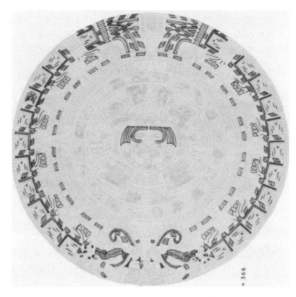

(b) Years before Leon y Gama, Raul Noriega found astronomical computations that demonstrated that this calendar enabled its priests to compute not only the rhythmic cycle of solar and lunar eclipses but also the passage of the sun at zenith, the passage of Venus across the face of the sun (four times in 243 years), the equinox and solstice, the phases of the moon, and the heliacal rising of Venus, the morning and evening star.

3:7. *The "Aztec" Sun Calendar.* (a) Leon y Gama, from the perfection and uniformity of the circles on the great stone and the exact division of it into parts, recognized that its designer had a profound understanding not only of geometry but of astronomy as well.

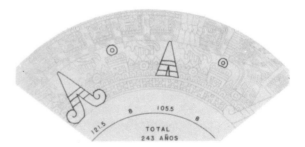

(c) Raul Noriega's research of the "Aztec" sun calendar demonstrates that the calendar incorporated a 243-year passage of Venus before the sun. This phenomenon was first calculated again by Kepler in A.D. 1631. This same information was, of course, available to the ancient priest-astronomers centuries earlier in the "Tizoc" calendar stone.

codices are virtually computerized mechanisms for giving you the cycles of Venus going into thousands of years—a perpetual calendar. They are very, very extraordinary pieces of work.

Newkirk: Could we get any reason why all of this information was destroyed, the Mexican codices, the secrets that lay behind their building? Was it the normal act of a victor or conqueror of these people—

Tompkins: It's one of the first things done almost everywhere.

3:6 Entry of Alexander into Heliopolis.

That's what Alexander the Great did, and it put us back badly. With his destruction of Persepolis and Heliopolis, he destroyed the wisdom of thousands of years. Then he tried to make amends. He, or rather, later Greeks, tried to make amends by building the Library of Alexandria. But then the Christians came along and burnt that— and more horror has been perpetrated on this planet in the last 2,000 years in the name of Christ than in the 2,000 years before, or in history, as far as I can see. What they did had no bearing or relation to the spiritual values of Jesus or any of the prophets or any of the wise Gnostics of the past and, you know, I get tired of it, I get tired of our going into Vietnam and butchering and napalming and defoliating and—we're ready to do it tomorrow. I mean, we came close to doing it in Angola; that's the kind of civilization we have, and I think it's time we changed and went back to the spiritual values that Christians purport to preach.

Newkirk: Man is responsible for his own destruction?

Tompkins: And also for his own creativity. That's the other thing I've found. On the Mexican pyramids, played out on the steps of the pyramid were religious dramas, which a very fascinating philosopher called Szekely[3] has

---

[3] Edmond Bordeaux Szekely, a Sanskrit and Aramaic philologist, whose forefather, Csoma de Koros, compiled the first grammar of the Tibetan language, author of *La Filosofia del Mexico Antiquo, How the Great Pan Died, The Origin of Christianity, The Soul of Ancient Mexico, The Essene Book of Creation,* etc.

tied in with the Persians, and of course, there is this constant tie-in between the Middle East and Middle America. But he describes a ritual on the stairs in which at the top of the pyramid if you go off, it is into spirituality—a return to your natural essence as a spiritual being. If you can climb the steps of the game by your good deeds, by creativity, by love, by conservatism, you can fly off the top, and the opposing elements are vacuity, aggression, destruction and so on. Man, in the middle, is always capable of choosing whether he wishes to go towards spirituality or towards materialism. If he goes off the bottom of the steps of the pyramid, he gets chewed up by Tezcatlipoca, the jaguar, and he'll have to go through the cycle again and that's where we're heading with our gross materialism. If you turn around and go the other way, you return off the top to the plumed serpent, Quetzalcoatl, symbol of wisdom and spirituality. So all of this, and a cosmology which is very close to what modern science is finally coming up to, was played out on the steps of these pyramids, and apparently in a much more ethical manner, as part of a more ethical and social civilization which gradually got obliterated. And what Cortez found when he arrived was a degradation of ancient rites which no longer made any sense, anymore than *our rites* bear relation to what was said by Mohammed the Moslem, Moses the Hebrew, Lao Tzu of China, Mahivira the Jain, Buddha of India, or Jesus of Nazareth.

Newkirk: By virtue of your studies of the Mexican pyramids, did you come to the conclusion that these people had a greater understanding of life than perhaps people of—

Tompkins: Oh—

Newkirk: —a supposed higher civilization?

Tompkins: Very definitely. I mean, I think we've lost the light of day nowadays, simply because we became so overweighted into materialism, and at that point it ceases to be a game; when it starts to be a butchery there is no fun in it anymore. A duel of honor as used to be practiced in the South, in this state, in Georgia, was quite a different game from butchery and *that's what we've lost.* We've lost the ethics and the aesthetics of the game; but we're coming back. It's not so terrible; everywhere you turn now, people are waking up and there's an extraordinary spirit of awareness, and love, tenderness and creativity about. Why?

Newkirk: Another result of your massive research work into the Great Pyramid and other pyramids has been the spawning of the idea of so-called 'Pyramid Power'. There is a great host of people around today who ascribe characteristics, phenomenal powers to the Great Pyramid. Do you believe that the shape of these pyramids means more than what it's suppose[d] to mean, if it's suppose{d} to mean anything at all?

Tompkins: Oh, there's no question that very strange phenomena take place. For instance, N.I.H. in Washington has done these experiments; if you put some eggs into a pyramid, they vitrify instead of going bad. Well, a Frenchman, Antoine Bovis in an 'intuitional flash', discovered this phenomenon in the 'thirties', but, what's so extraordinary is that if you come along and say: 'Hey, if you take a pyramid, this thing happens which regenerates razor blades, it changes the quality of water, etc., etc.' everybody says, 'Ahh' but, if you take a magnet and start fooling around with metal shavings, they will say, 'Well, that's only a magnet.' Then you say, 'How does it work?' and they say, 'I don't know how it works, it just works!' They take that for granted; they take gravity for granted; if you drop an apple they say it falls, but, they don't know why—they haven't a clue as to why. So just because this is a new form of energy, relatively, though I suspect it's the same energy discovered by Paracelsus, Mesmer, Reichenbach, or Dr. Wilhelm Reich with his orgone, I think that's what's going on. But, the fascinating thing is that the shape of things, and this is what the Meso-Americans knew already—the Maya, the Olmec—they knew that the shape of things, old Masonic lore, affects energies and that wave lengths do travel between humans. Everything radiates on wave lengths, and the conjunction and overlapping and forming of them is what really makes reality out of what is, actually, unsubstantial. We are 'such stuff as dreams are made of', pure and simple. It's only because we look at it through materialistic eyes that a table is solid to us, and we can't go through a wall, but analyze it and it's just a lot of wave lengths.

Newkirk: Another one of the conclusions that you come to is the fact that the pyramids may well contain the secrets of the universe. They've been around so long, thousands and thousands of years, and man hasn't latched on to that notion yet and I am wondering why? Is it because our civilization believes that we hold all the answers and are loath to look upon something created by so-called lower civilizations?

Tompkins: I don't buy this lower civilizations—I thought we got rid of that subject—

Newkirk: Okay, maybe that just stuck in my mind.

Tompkins: Well, we're running that one out, fast.

Newkirk: Okay.

Tompkins: And it's just a point of view and usually wrong. That there were more advanced civilizations before this one is obvious; that they go in cycles is obvious; that people get wiped out, whole civilizations get wiped out on this planet, is becoming more and

3:8. *Bas-Relief From Palenque with Masonic Symbols Drawn by Waldeck.* Jean-Frederic Maximilien Waldeck at the age of fifty-six travelled from France to Palenque, Mexico. Waldeck, initially financed by his publisher Berthoud, spent a year *in situ* at Palenque and produced some ninety extraordinary drawings; he smuggled his original drawings back to England with the aid of the British consul. Arriving in England, Waldeck was abandoned by his publisher—because his story was too complicated to be "believable."

3:9. *Waldeck's Drawing of the Tower at Palenque*. Waldeck's book and drawings, although finan-
cially abandoned by his publisher, soon became a collector's item fetching 3,300 francs per book.
Waldeck, in this drawing, shows the tower of Palenque, the eastern galleries on the left and the
western galleries on the right. Waldeck chose sunset deliberately to draw attention to other bas-
relief figures on the front of the eastern galleries.

70

3:10. *The Caracol Tower at Chichen Itza: An Ancient Astronomical Observatory.* That the Caracol Tower was used as an astronomical observatory was discovered as early as 1875 by Dr. Augustus LePlongeon, one of the first explorers of the Meso-American pyramids. Dr. LePlongeon, author of *Sacred Mysteries: Among the Mayas and the Quiches*, lived for twelve years among the descendants of the ancient Maya. LePlongeon was a 33° Freemason, the first white man to learn the ancient Maya language, the first explorer initiated into the Maya secret society of Sh'Tol Brothers, the first outsider to witness their shamanic ritual, carefully hidden from non-Indian eyes for hundreds of years after the Spanish invasion. LePlongeon, much like Carlos Castaneda of today and the ethnobotanist Robert Gordon Wasson before him, discovered many extraordinary remains of a prior advanced civilization.

The day following LePlongeon's initiation into the ancient "sacred mysteries of the Maya" (or "Mysteries of Xibalba," described in the second book of the *Popol Vuh*), LePlongeon wrote that the "elders" or "those who know" were able to surround themselves with a cloud-like white light and to materialize certain strange and mysterious scenes of the past. Later that same day LePlongeon fell into a trance; suddenly, jumping up, he cried, "Dig here!" His Maya helpers began to dig. They dug ten feet into the earth; sweating profusely in the jungle heat and loving this crazy Americano H'Menes (wise man), they dug another ten feet into the damp, stinking earth. LePlongeon confidently urged them on. The air in the hole became harder to breathe. LePlongeon stressed, "Just four more feet." Twenty-four feet into the earth spade bit into stone and LePlongeon was the proud discoverer of the Chac-Mool—an astonishing sculpture, not in relief, but in the round.

71

more obvious. And they come back again and go in cycles. But, of course, that makes for a much more fascinating game because if you really had it all worked out into a glorious welfare world where would be the adventure and the fun and the excitement and novelty of it? You know nobody wants to be pensioned off at age ten. So I think that there are two kinds of guys, those who make it bad by hiding and controlling and the others who try to open it up and clear it, and as long as you have that intercourse between the two *yin-yang* {negative-positive}, you have some fun. But, when it gets all on one side in the game, you've got to re-shuffle and start again. It's not so much that Tezcatlipoca, the jaguar, is necessarily the villain and Quetzalcoatl, the plumed serpent, is the hero; one is playing the hero role and the one is playing the villain role because if you go to the movies and there's no villain, what kind of a movie have you got?

Newkirk: Are we getting to the point where we can really accept history for what it is? Do we still want to color it, do we still want it to support our own beliefs?

Tompkins: Oh, I think history is entirely written...I mean it's the notions of the guy who's writing it. I've written enough history to know that.

Newkirk: Where next for Peter Tompkins? Another pyramid study or...

Tompkins: No, though I must say I would be fascinated if I could get—and I've asked the Chinese if I can go—to have a look at and dig into their huge pyramid out there. Of course, you're going to find I'm probably going to let the mantle fall on the next hard working guy, because I've done my share. But, I think you're going to find pyramid remains all over the United States. You're going to find remnants of ancient civilizations that we have simply bull-dozed over and put concrete over and not looked at. Why archaeology in this country is so neglected, when there are apparent vestiges, of perhaps an Atlantean civilization, all up and down the east coast of America, and up and down the Mississippi there are plenty of pyramids for the next generation to go dig in.

Newkirk: Still a lot to learn for the ambitious researcher then....We've been talking to Peter Tompkins, the author of a sequal to his Great Pyramid study—this one entitled *Mysteries of the Mexican Pyramids.*

Tompkins' books on the pyramids remain the most intelligent, uncensored and comprehensive books ever written on the subject to date. The subject of, and the almost subliminal message embodied within, the Great Pyramid is of such a vast, complex, and difficult nature that any explanation is best presented in a multidimensional or serendiptitious manner.

If you are reading this book, it will have been published exactly as I perceive the facts to be. It is not a book about sex, nor is it a book about flying saucers. This book is about the human race; it's a history of us, of our origins and our destiny as a species.

3:11. *The Caracol Tower, its Main Axis Aligned to the Rising and Setting of Venus, Viewed from the West (Front).* In 1875 LePlongeon's assertion that the Caracol Tower was an astronomical observatory was met with laughter and ridicule. One hundred years were to pass before LePlongeon's work would be vindicated. 6 June 1975, Anthony F. Aveni, professor of astronomy at Colgate University, Sharon L. Gibbs, a research associate in the history of astronomy at Colgate University, and Horst Hartung, professor of architecture and urban studies at the University of Guadalajara (Guadalajara, Mexico), published a confirmation of LePlongeon's work in the prestigious *Science* magazine.

3:13. *Peter Tompkins at the Base of the Great Pyramid.*

3:12. *LePlongeon and his Chac-Mool.* Replying to laughter and ridicule, LePlongeon said, "But who are these pretended authorities? Certainly not the doctors and professors at the heads of the universities and colleges in the United States; for not only do they know absolutely nothing of the ancient American Civilization, but, judging from letters in my possession, the majority of them refuse to learn anything concerning it. Can they interpret one single sentence in the books in which the learning of the Maya sages, their cosmogonic, geographical, religious and scientific attainments are recorded? From what source have they derived their pretended knowledge? Not from the writings of the Spanish chroniclers, surely. These only wrote of the natives as they found them at the time, and long after the conquest of America by their countrymen. The so-called learned men of our days are the first to oppose new ideas and the bearers of these."

WHOM ARE WE TO BELIEVE?

Most Egyptologists tell us that the Great Pyramid was built sometime around 2600 B.C., solely as a tomb for an ambiguous pharoah named Khufu. Tom Valentine, in his book *The Great Pyramid: Man's Monument to Man*, cautions us that "We must always remember that history is precisely that— *his* story and nothing more." Tompkins said, "Oh, I think history is entirely written, I mean it's the notions of the guy who's writing it." That simple statement I have found to be so true.

People always have an opinion on a subject, whether or not they know anything about it. During man's long history on this planet there have been many historians. Some, with a gun to their heads, wrote what they were told. Some write what they believe to be true at any cost. Again the question, "Whom are we to believe?" rings inside our heads. The answer is that we must each decide what is true for himself. A scientific approach requires first reading, then thinking, and finally the expression of an opinion. A clever writer, by presenting only *his* story—evidence that is favorable to his opinion—defeats himself from the beginning. So in the pages ahead, the reader will be exposed to both the pro and con of a debate that contains profound clues to our origins.

Listening to Peter Tompkins, we suddenly realize that we don't know where the builders of the Mexican pyramids came from or where they went. Some of the great minds of our age agree with NASA scientist Maurice Chatelain that the ancients received their wisdom

"Boom! just like that" from outer-space people. Chatelain, scientist turned author, expresses his views in his book *Nos Ancetres Venus de Cosmos (Our Ancestors Came From Outer Space)*. Other people believe that the ancient pyramid builders in Mexico were destroyed as a result of a shifting in the earth's axis. Still others advance the theory that they escaped a cataclysmic shifting in the earth's tectonic plates by constructing airships capable of evacuating three to five hundred people per ship into the earth's upper stratosphere until the major destruction was completed. These same people say that, returning to earth a week later, they were heralded by primitive people who had survived in isolated areas as gods from outer space. A similar event could happen today. A space capsule, blown off course, para-chutes earthward. Landing deep in the Amazon jungle, part of the capsule opens and two white men clad in shiny material emerge. Silent figures watching from the thickness of the jungle turn their eyes skyward as the stillness is broken by the thunder of jets and reconnaissance planes circling overhead. Another "strange bird" arrives. Hovering over-head, it lifts men and capsule upward and departs. Stillness returns. What stories would be told around the campfires that night we can only imagine. Would a shrine be erected? Would the event become a part of the Indian's religious traditions, and if so, how accurately would it be transmitted from one generation to the next? What would an anthropologist or ethnologist make of the story years later? Did gods from outer space land on earth in our past, as Von Daniken suggests so ardently, or did man at some distant point in our uncertain past possess the secrets of flight, as Rene Noorbergen states in his book *Secrets of the Lost Races?* We have put men on the moon, but one can still see real shrunken heads in a curio shop in modern Panama.

Other researchers suggest that the earth's climate slowly changed, prompting the original builders of the Meso-American pyramids to migrate. Others say it was a rapid climate change. Others mention war, famine, cultural disintegration, religious beliefs, etc. One fact remains that is certain; an astronomically and mathematically advanced civilization disappeared from the face of the earth. Why? Will it happen again on May fifth of the year 2000? Will ice play a part in the disappearance of our present civilization or will the people at large, once informed of an ultimate disaster, respond to this ultimate challenge? Will they turn off their televisions and demand that their elected representatives in Washington lobby for the necessary scientific funding to answer this question?

The only scary thing about this becomes evident when one pauses to consider how many people will not pause.

CHAPTER FOUR
PYRAMID POWER

In the previous chapter, Tompkins comments on a phenomenon today called "pyramid power." What exactly is the nature of that elusive energy phenomenon? Why does Tompkins, a trained and disciplined spy, suspect that "it's the same energy discovered by Paracelsus, Mesmer, Reichenbach, or Dr. Wilhelm Reich with his orgone"? Why did Dr. Reich, Vice-Director of Freud's Psychoanalytic Clinic in Vienna from 1922 to 1928, die heartbroken in a United States federal penitentiary? Why did agents of the U.S. Food and Drug Administration hamper and interrupt his work, and, at his death in 1957, destroy all his books they could lay their hands on? Imagine book burning in America! A few of his books, like *Ether, God and Devil*, survived. What had Reich discovered?

Dr. Wilhelm Reich (1897-1957), M.D., psychiatrist, and psychotherapist, claimed to have discovered a new type of energy which he called "orgone energy." Dr. Reich advocated a new and extraordinary kind of healing with his unorthodox (in the fifties) inventions.[1] How is all this connected with a structure known as the first wonder of the ancient seven wonders of the world? Is what Paracelsus and Franz Anton Mesmer called "animal magnetism," what Karl von Reichenbach called "odyle," and what Dr. Wilhelm Reich called "orgone energy" the same thing we today call "pyramid power?"

Today in America there lives a man who stands at the very heart of pyramid power. His name is G. Patrick Flanagan. Like Reich before him, he became interested in the subject while only a little boy. Investigating the secrets of the Great Pyramid without mentioning pyramid power would be like walking around all day in a pair of lace-up shoes without laces. On 7 June 1975, I interviewed G. Patrick Flanagan, a child prodigy who at age 11 had invented a guided missile detector and who three years later invented the Neurophone and was recognized by *Life* magazine[2] as one of the top ten scientists in America. That same year, 1962-63, Flanagan was listed in *Leaders in American Science* (see Plate 4:1) at age eighteen as "an inventor and scientific genius. We are going to follow his career with much interest." At age 22 Flanagan began a scientific study of psychic phenomena and related fields. His inventions now include the Square Wave Speech Generator, a high-speed speech scrambler currently in use by super-intelligence agencies. His most recent invention is a device he calls the Pyramid Energy Generator. His recent books *Pyramid Power* and *Beyond Pyramid Power* explain his theories.

Having read Flanagan's books, which are somewhat technical, I decided to tape an interview with him in order to discover more about pyramid power.

---

[1] Transcripts of Dr. Reich's trial, FDA case #261, are now available under the Freedom of Information Act.
[2] 14 September 1962.

The concept of Pyramid Power is based on the observation that foods and other items placed in a small model of the Great Pyramid are affected in a positive way.

Dr. G. Patrick Flanagan
Pyramid Power II: Scientific Evidence

The quality of the orgone energy that seems to explain and make possible the genesis or creation of matter in the superimposition of orgonotic streams is its negative entrophy, also called the orgonotic potential; that is, when two systems with different orgonotic strength or charge approach each other, the stronger system will attract orgone from the weaker one.

Ola Raknes
Wilhelm Reich and Orgonomy

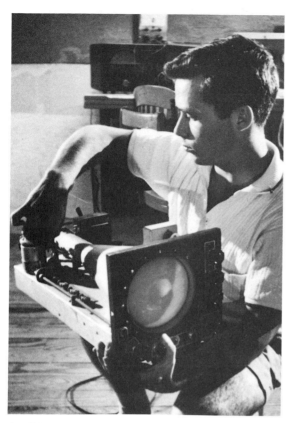

4:1. "FLANAGAN, Gillis Patrick (Mr.), Inventor, 5102 Linden, Bellaire, Tex. BIO-ELECTRONIC RESEARCH. b. Oklahoma City, Okla., Oct. 11, 1944. s. Gillis Chas. and Betty (McKiddy) F. Edn.: Senior, Bellaire H.S., Bellaire, Tex., 1962-63. Exp.: Television Tech., Television tr., Bellaire, Tex., 1959-62. Mem.: Sertoma Internatl.; Aircraft Owner's and Pilot's Assn. Gen. Int.: Amateur Radio License since age of 11; Private Pilot's License since age of 16; Spectacular Gymnast; Grand Award Winner, Greater Houston Sci. Fair, 1959. Areas of Rsch.: Inventor of Neurophone Radio Hearing Aid for Deaf; Research in Human Factors Concerning Effects of Radio Waves on Human Nervous System and Muscle Tissue; Research in Radio Detection of Nuclear Blasts." (*Leaders in American Science*)

Noone: Patrick, you seem to have been instrumental in attracting, stimulating and developing the public's interest in this type of research. How did you become personally involved in such a speculative subject as pyramid power?

Flanagan: Well, I've been interested in unusual energy phenomena since I was a child. In fact, I became world-renowned when I was fourteen years old, when I invented a device called the Neurophone.

Noone: What is a Neurophone?

Flanagan: It was an electrical hearing aid that no one could understand how it worked, because it transmitted sound directly to the brain by an unknown means, bypassing the normal nerve systems normally used for hearing, and as a result of this, plus earlier studies—I became interested in Yoga, for instance, when I was eight years old—as a result of this early interest in unusual things, my Neurophone sparked my interest in attempting to understand what you might call unusual phenomena, unusual energy fields, different teachings that are taught in Asia and in the Orient, such as acupuncture and this sort of thing. So the idea that a pyramid shape and other related shapes had unusual energy fields fascinated me, and these ideas have been around since before the turn of the century, but no one really knew how they worked. When I heard about this pyramid razor-blade sharpener in Czechoslovakia, I started investigating the pyramid phenomena.

81

Noone: What prompted your interest in science at such an early age?

Flanagan: Well, I was fortunate in that when I was eight years old I had a series of dreams that stimulated me to learn everything that I could learn, to read everything that I could read. I became an experimenter, you might say, and a prolific reader, at a time when most children are out playing baseball and things like that. I was indoors learning science, chemistry, electronics, and this sort of thing. I became a ham radio operator when I was nine, and a private pilot when I was sixteen, so throughout my life knowledge has been my major pursuit. I really became interested in research very early. I am just fortunate in that I got started earlier than most people would.

Noone: Did you believe, when you first heard of pyramid power, that it—that there was anything to it?

Flanagan: When I first started, I approached it with the idea that it didn't work. To begin with, I was really quite skeptical about it when I first began because I actually did not believe that the shape of an environment could have any effect on the thing in the environment—it just didn't make any sense to me at all. So I started it sort of as a lark because, as I've said, I had read in various books of Asiatic and Eastern teaching about *Kundalini* energy and other unusual energies, so I pursued it initially as a lark. But as I got into it, I realized there was something to it. I was getting results, although the results were inconsistent. In other words, some-

times it worked and sometimes it didn't work, but it worked enough for me to realize that there was something going on. Ultimately, what I realized was that the pyramid shape is actually a lens or an antenna for energies, and that just like a magnifying glass could be considered to be a lens or a focusing device or an antenna for the sun's energies; the pyramid works sometimes and sometimes it doesn't, in much the same way. For instance, if we were trying to start a fire with a magnifying lens and a cloud goes over the sun, it won't work. This doesn't mean that the lens is no good, this just means that at that moment there's no energy available. So in pursuing this I ultimately have come up with a lot of most unusual theories regarding those energies and some real breakthroughs in the area of communications, fertilizers, and a number of other potential devices for real energy usage which I think would be very valuable for mankind in the future.

Noone: My research tells me that the Great Pyramid will be 6,000 years old in the year 2,000 A.D. I mean, when we stopped using B.C. and changed to A.D, this building was already 4,000 years old, so why, in your own opinion, has it puzzled man for so long?

Flanagan: Well, the Great Pyramid naturally has been an enigma to man because it stands out in the desert like a sore thumb. The Great Pyramid is an unbelievable structure. If you walk up to it and look at it, it's as large as a mountain, and when you realize that this was man-made, and realize that it has certain features that we cannot even accomplish in this day and age, as far as building construction...for instance, the fact that it's level over an area of thirteen and one-half acres. It's level to one-half of one inch, which is better—far better—that we can do on any of our buildings today.

Noone: Is the inside of this structure built as perfectly as the outside?

Flanagan: You will find inside the King's Chamber granite blocks that are extremely hard granite, so hard that it's extremely difficult, even today, to machine—and yet these granite blocks are perfectly smooth over nineteen-foot lengths to within 1/100 of an inch—and it just goes on and on. Whoever built the Great Pyramid had a knowledge of construction techniques, and the earth and alignment techniques that we possibly don't even possess today!

Noone: The most fascinating debate today about the Great Pyramid is that it's said that if one studies the measurements of the Great Pyramid, one will discover all kinds of so-called 'secret knowledge.' I myself wonder if you have looked into the mathematics of the Great Pyramid?

Flanagan: I've gone quite extensively into the mathematics of the Great Pyramid, and it's fascinating to note that the Great Pyramid incorporates within its architecture mathematical formulas that were not supposedly known until four hundred years ago. Like we say, the pyra-

mid is almost, by modern agreement, at least 6,000 years old. I've gone quite extensively into the mathematics of the Great Pyramid, and it incorporates—almost as if it were an encoded structure in which, if we analyze it, we may learn many things that we don't already know—it's got mathematics that are considered today to be quite modern. Today when we build buildings and bridges, we often incorporate in the cornerstone, in a hollow space, what we call a time capsule of information about life as we presently know it, so that some future generation, when they eventually demolish that building, will find these time capsules and be able to obtain an understanding of life as we presently know it.[3] And I believe that the Great Pyramid was placed there as a beacon from the past, to guide modern man in certain directions—and I believe this simply because of the advanced nature of its mathematics. It incorporates many features in its measurements and mathematics that we are only beginning to realize.

Noone: For example?

Flanagan: It incorporates in its measurement system measurements of the earth that we only found recently in the International Geophysical Year. So whoever built the Great Pyramid knew the exact measurements of the earth. This leads us to believe that an advanced race did build it, and that they did leave it there as a message. And I believe that somewhere incorporated within the Great Pyramid is a new discovery which

[3]The reader is referred to Chapter 1, p. 28, paragraph 1.

83

will lead us to an understanding of our true past as a civilization.

Noone: Do you believe that the pyramid may still contain another undiscovered secret chamber?

Flanagan: As you may well know, in any legend there is usually some basis of fact somewhere in the background, and there are enough stories from different sources that the Great Pyramid has a secret chamber and that within that secret chamber is a library of knowledge which will indicate to modern man his true history, why the Great Pyramid was really built, and where we really came from, and why we're really here on this planet. This legend has been going around for literally thousands of years. When I was in Egypt, I had the opportunity of interviewing various Bedouin chieftains and Arab guides. They all told this story, the story that the Great Pyramid is considered to contain within it the knowledge of

4:2. *Napoleon in the King's Chamber.* Drawing of Napoleon visiting the Great Pyramid's third chamber. The fact that the artist incorporated Masonic signs and symbols into his art is noteworthy. An empty granite box, a double square or rectangular box around which the whole building was constructed, a box whose interior dimensions, biblical scholars have shown, would accommodate the mysterious Ark of the Covenant perfectly: the same Ark which Moses carried out of Egypt along with the mummy of Joseph, and which was eventually deposited in the Holy of Holies in King Solomon's Temple (see Miscellaneous Detail of King Solomon's Temple, Plate 2:9).

84

man's past, present, and future, and that someday a person will come from the West, and that that person will ultimately reveal to the world the secrets of the Pyramid.

Noone: America is the only continent immediately west of Egypt today. Could it be that someone from America will ultimately reveal to the world the secrets of the Great Pyramid?

Flanagan: I believe that someday we will discover, truly, a hidden chamber or a library similar to or with knowledge that was possibly contained once in the library at Alexandria.

Noone: I've read in history that Napoleon Bonaparte, while touring the interior of the Great Pyramid, asked to be left alone in the so-called King's Chamber. When he rejoined his men, his generals noticed that he was strangely quiet, and his behavior for some minutes afterwards was "as one in an hypnotic trance." Have you heard anything of this?

Flanagan: My wife and I spent the night in the Great Pyramid in September of 1974, and we had many unusual experiences that were not expected, almost of a psychic nature. We heard various strange sounds and noises, choirs singing, people chanting, sounds coming literally almost from the air in the pyramid, and a lot of very unusual experiences that were out of the ordinary. But when we checked back upon the history of different people who have meditated in the pyramid, various others have experienced similar things. A man by the name of Ouspensky, who was a great writer, spent many hours alone in the Great Pyramid meditating, so

this is not unusual that we have experienced such things.

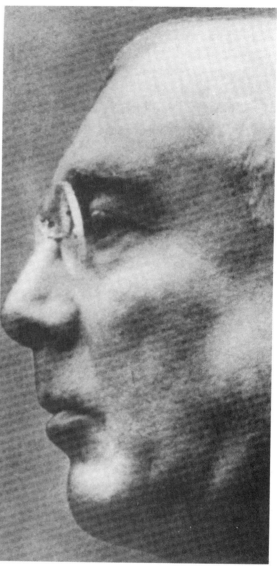

4:3. *P. D. Ouspensky.* A Russian writer who wrote many books around the turn of the century, including *A New Model of the Universe,* which deals with principles of the psychological method in its application to problems of science, religion, and art. His teachings, along with those of a fellow Russian philosopher, Georges Ivanovitch Gurdjieff, are being taught Americans today at training centers in Miami, Atlanta, Pittsburgh, Los Angeles, San Francisco, and Washington, D.C.

Noone: What is the relation, or how does pyramid energy connect, with the Great Pyramid?

Flanagan: Well, when the fathers of modern electronics were first investigating radio energies, they had a very difficult time in determining what kind of antennas would best receive radio signals, what kind of antenna structure would best transmit these signals, and the fact that there were various frequencies involved—and well, what we now have today in the science of radio electronics is that we have literally thousands of different antenna designs, and each one is an efficient design for different frequency ranges and for different applications. And what we find is that the pyramid itself is what we would call a refractive lens or a refractive resonator of what I now call a Tensor Energy Field, and that these energy fields are related to the earth's magnetic fields.

It is well known that as energies approach the earth from different cosmic sources, including the sun and other galaxies, these energies often align themselves with the earth's magnetic field and actually follow the magnetic lines of force of the earth. In order for these pyramid models to have effect, they must be aligned, like the Great Pyramid, to the magnetic field forces of the earth. So, in how they work, it's again like a radio antenna except this particular antenna is for an energy field that we have just discovered—this energy field, as I mentioned, I now call it Tensor Energy, because of certain characteristics, which I have described in my books—and these energy fields are, I believe, the unifying factor between electromagnetic energies and gravitation energy, the unifying factor which Albert Einstein was looking for up until his death.

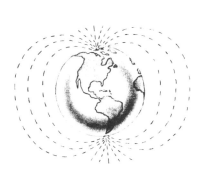 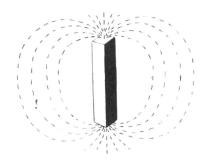 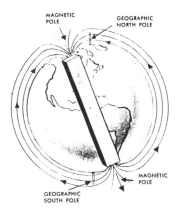

4:4. (a) *The Earth's Magnetic Field.* (b) *The Magnetic Field of a Bar Magnet.* (c) *The Earth's Magnetic Field of Force Similar to that of a Bar Magnet.* The ancient mariners who sailed the seven seas believed that there was a "mountain of lodestone" in one of those seas, which could wreck even the most seaworthy ship if it approached too close, by attracting magnetically every piece of iron on board and thus drawing the ship irresistably closer. They recorded in their legends that as the ship drew closer all the loose pieces of iron would fly straight to the mountain, all iron bolts and nails in the ship's timbers would be pulled out, and the ship would fall apart. One of the heroes in *The Arabian Nights,* Sinbad the Sailor, was shipwrecked by a "mountain of lodestone."

Noone: Doctor, there are many nations that are much further advanced than the United States in the study of parapsychology and related fields, and I am wondering: why?

Flanagan: I believe that what you say is true, as far as nations being advanced. However, I believe that there are individuals in the United States that are easily as advanced or possibly more advanced than work being done in other countries. Russia, for example, and some of the other iron curtain countries are seriously investigating this phenomenon by using government funding, and the result of that is that the scientists in those countries who are investigating this kind of phenomenon are receiving tremendous support from their governments. Unfortunately, the United States government has shown no serious interest in funding this kind of research, and this is why the United States as a whole, you might say, is far behind some of the other countries.

Noone: The individuals that you mention that may be just as far advanced, or even more so than the Europeans—who are they?

Flanagan: Well, I consider that in my own area of research I am probably further advanced than anyone in Russia in this particular field. I had considered—there is a scientist in Japan, whom I recently visited, who is possibly one of the most advanced people around in these energy areas. He's actually investigating heavily the subject of gravity, and I believe that I am possibly one of the most ad-

vanced as far as practical knowledge and practical scientific devices. I have devices right now that—for instance, we have a communication device that will transmit information through the earth, whereas normal radio signals will not travel through the earth. We now have a communication device where we can transmit signals at great distances through the earth without impeding, stealing these energy waves, and I have not heard of anything like this coming from the iron curtain countries.

Noone: What benefits will the public derive from this energy, and if this energy has been known for several years, why hasn't more been done to, say, gather or store it in a battery or something?

Flanagan: In the past, my own experience has been that because these areas are so advanced and so unique the consumer is the person who determines in the end whether or not something is workable. So I believe that as a result of this research, that in the years to come we will see many exciting devices coming out on the market. For instance, I've got to mention the fact I mentioned earlier—we've developed a seed control, seed treatment system that has increased crop yield by as much as three hundred percent in last year's crop testing. This is very exciting, because this is something that you can sink your teeth into. This is something that is solid, indisputable evidence that something unusual is going on. So in the years to come I believe that we will find many exciting inventions and devices coming out on the market that utilize these energies.

Noone: In what other ways could these devices be helpful?

Flanagan: One of the major problems that we have right now, of course, is in the area of pollution and of energy research. Although there is a tremendous amount of energy research in many different areas, I sincerely believe that we will have within the next, possibly, five years a new device that uses gravitational energy, which is a form of Tensor Energy Field, as an energy source. And I believe that it will be non-polluting, and may ultimately become the major energy source on this planet.

Noone: How long will all this take?

Flanagan: Time will tell. In the past it has taken approximately one hundred years for a new discovery to make its way from the laboratory into general public usage and knowledge, in much the same way that pyramid energy has been known since the turn of the century—it's taken this long for it to become popular. However, the rate of change of

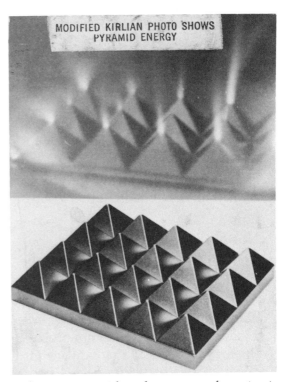

4:5. The antiquity of the Great Pyramid is obvious when one considers that we are closer in time to Caesar and Cleopatra than they were to the construction of the Great Pyramid.

4:6. *Flanagan's Pyramid Energy Generator.* (a) The pyramid energy generator is a 4″ x 5″ series of twenty 1″ scale models of the Great Pyramid arranged in a grid. Within the grid is a magnetic circuit board consisting of steel bars and magnets, which supersede the Earth's magnetic field. The shell or housing itself is composed of dielectric plastic. (b) Kirlian photography and time-lapse photography photograph of Flanagan's generator combined to illustrate and visually show "pyramid energy" issuing from the apexes.

knowledge to actual usage is increasing at a very rapid rate, so it's very possible that these new energy sources will be in use within the next ten years and completely accepted by the orthodox science.

Flanagan's theories—like anyone's ideas that probe and poke behind the veil of mystery we call life, like Copernicus's theories before him—were ridiculed by those who presumed they knew all the answers. There are few who dare to be great, and so far in our history it is these special men and women—the Lindberghs, the Joan of Arcs, the Voltaires, the great thinkers and teachers in any age—who have, perhaps because of an intensely burning inner light, by their efforts contributed and propelled us forward in what we today call evolution. Is Flanagan a singular example, or are there others who share his conviction that the Great Pyramid's shape may contain a clue to the discovery of a source of energy, perhaps a non-physical energy, known at some distant point in man's past? Flanagan's interview, taped on 7 July 1975, lay silently in my safe for the next three years. Then, on 5 September 1978, I interviewed William A. Tiller.

CONFIRMATION

Noone: Where were you born?

Tiller: I am a Canadian, grew up in Toronto.

Noone: When were you born?

Tiller: 1929.

Noone: Gad, you look younger.

Tiller: Yeah.

Noone: Much younger.

Tiller: Well...that's the inner light! [Laughter] I took my degree work at the University of Toronto.

Noone: What was your degree work in?

Tiller: Undergraduate degree was engineering physics, and the graduate degree was physical metallurgy. I then spent nine years in industry at the Westinghouse Research Lab, Pittsburgh.

Noone: What type of research were you pursuing then?

Tiller: Research on the formation of crystals and perfection of crystals, materials of that nature, surfaces, solid-state physics, thermodynamics, that kind of area. I came to Stanford in 1964 as a full professor and have been either a full professor and/or Department Chairman here since '64. I am no longer Department Chairman—I gave that up in '71 when I came back from sabbatical. I had a Guggenheim Fellowship to the University of Oxford in England 1970-71. I have published about 150 papers in the conventional area of science, about 40 papers in the area of psycho-energetics, and have co-authored a couple of technical books. Have been and am general consultant to government and industry.

Noone: What is your present research centered around?

Tiller: It is centered around the science of crystallization, surfaces and interphases between materials, interphases between two media. It's centered around bio-materials and psycho-energetics.

Noone: How might the enormous quantity of tremendously heavy blocks used in the Great Pyramid's construction have been transported?

Tiller: What I am doing deals with physical substance and etheric substance—the etheric, which goes faster than the velocity of light, having negative mass, would give rise to a levitational force. So it would be a *combination*[4] of these two kinds of substances which could ultimately give rise to a net levitation, that is, a force which would balance out the gravitational so that, basically, the mass of what appears to be some physical substance would gradually decrease and eventually begin to slow and would become negative.

Noone: Gad! Dr. Tiller, please slow down, as only some of my readers understood what you just said. Could you simplify that statement for those who don't want to reread what you just said?

Tiller: Well, okay. Here we have gravitational forces where things if you drop them will fall to the floor. There could be the utilization of "levitational forces" where if you have an object you can cause it to be raised in the air without touching it, physically, and maybe the builders of the Great Pyramid, some way, had that technology— so that they could levitate the blocks off the ground and move them more easily and put them in place.

Noone: What do you think makes 'pyramid energy' special?

Tiller: The pyramid shape, it seems to me, is a special one of the large class of shapes, and I'm inclined to think it has some special characteristics in terms of the ratio of the base width to the height. So one could imagine "energy resonances" occurring in space that would be particularly good to *excite* things in a pyramid. One can imagine that the pyramid is a kind of device that converts a new type of energy, even perhaps a non-physical energy, into a physical energy, and that the individual himself cooperatively couples with the device. If the individual is a strong-willed individual and really wants to get the positive results, then he'll probably get it.

Noone: Could you elaborate on this non-physical energy?

Tiller: Well, I just mean an energy that is different than those which we measure in the laboratory or those that we even theorize about, that is— it's not electro-magnetic energy, it's not gravitational energy, it's not the short-range nuclear force, etc., that kind of thing. It's not one of the conventional energies that physics deals with today.

Dr. Tiller's research on the formation and perfection of crystals brings us back to Prince Abdullah Al Mumun and his penetration into and exploration of the Great Pyramid's interior system. Let us take a momentary diversion from our interview and reconstruct this exploration in our imaginations.

After breaking into the Great Pyramid's descending passageway, Mamun and his men crept upward towards what seemed to

[4]What Dr. Wilhelm Reich termed "inter-reaction."

90

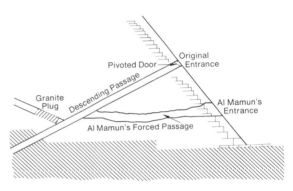

4:7. *The Descending Passage.* (a) The north face of the Great Pyramid, showing the original entrance surmounted by a ridged double-discharging arch formed by four enormous blocks, their ends mitered together, resting on a gigantic lintel. The original entrance is at the seventeenth course; Al Mamun's tunnel is to the right, ten courses below at course number seven. (b) Section showing the relationship of Al Mamun's entrance and forced passage to the original entrance and descending passage.

---

them to be a faint ray of sunlight (See Plate 4:7). Arriving at the uppermost point of the Great Pyramid's descending passageway, they stood before a door—a door they had sought for in vain days earlier. Mamun was to abide his time in patience, until suddenly one of his masons lifted his torch upward and illuminated a strange mechanism. Al Mamun smiled, then reached up and easily pulled down on a bar centered in the center of gravity of a casing stone which served as

the door. The door flew open. As sunlight streamed into and mingled with the darkness of the Great Pyramid's descending passageway, Al Mamun reflected on the lengthy digging, how he had pushed his men. Then he laughed inwardly at himself, his thoughts drifting back to something he had overheard his father say years earlier.

At the time he had not even been crowned Prince, yet now the memory came rushing back. His father, Harun Al-Rashid,

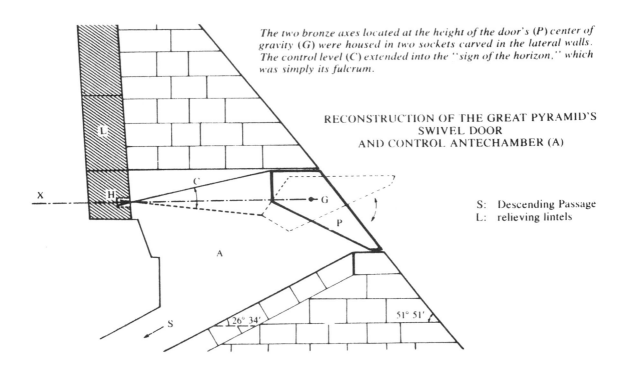

RECONSTRUCTION OF THE GREAT PYRAMID'S
SWIVEL DOOR
AND CONTROL ANTECHAMBER (A)

S: Descending Passage
L: relieving lintels

4:8. *Reconstruction of the Great Pyramid's Swivel Door and Control Antechamber.*

the Caliph of Baghdad, had returned from a late-night meeting. Awakened by conversation, his way lit by the light of the full moon, Al Mamun had approached the balcony overlooking his father's study. Looking down, straining to catch the words spoken below in hushed tones, he saw his father engaged in conversation with the most renowned author in the realm—the author of the *Arabian Nights*. His father was discussing one of the chapters in the *Arabian Nights*, "Ali Baba and the Forty Thieves," with the author. It was winter, and outside the house the wind screamed like a banshee, whipping the desert sand against the house with an irritating, rasping sound. Logs snapped and cracked in the fire below, further obscuring the conversation. Ashamed of himself for eavesdropping, yet knowing that someday he would be Caliph, Al Mamun strained to hear what his father

and the famous author were discussing. Lying down and spreading his weight evenly over the squeaky wooden floor planks, the child inched himself forward until his left ear was pressed between two of the balcony's railings. Broken words drifted up from below. His father was speaking.

"In this chapter, my brother, you—" The fire popped. "—revealing too much. You would have a much more effective and popular book, I believe, if, instead of attempting a complicated description of a relatively simple lever mechanism, you might substitute a magic word like 'open cave!' or 'come forth seed!' or 'open sesame!' "

"Yes, My Caliph," the author responded, "I believe the subjects of your realm at this time would understand that easier, but...perhaps in the future...." The wind wailed.

Al Mamun's father, sensing that his sug-

4:9. Sandstorm in the desert.

gestion was being accepted, continued. "We must remember the lesson we learned from the Grand Master tonight."

A shiver travelled up the boy's spine. He had heard old stories of the "Master," but had always considered them legends.

"But why did Moses..." the author was asking his father. A rasping sound created by almost microscopic grains of sand whipping across the roofing tiles momentarily distracted and heightened the tension felt by Al Mamun. The whole house seemed alive and surrounded by some unseen force.

"You and I must remember..." his father was saying, "that Moses and Trismegistus and all of the great Masters in line before them—" A moth flew against the boy's forehead. "—truth must be purified and that is why they reveiled it. For that, my friend, is the meaning of the word *reveal*."

"But," questioned the author, "why would they cover the eternal law with a new veil?"

The rails bit into the boy's scalp as he pressed a fraction of an inch closer. Suddenly all external sounds around the house stopped; it was as silent as a tomb, with only a cricket chirping rhythmically in the corner. He heard his father's answer as his father rose to his feet, signalling an end to the night's conversation. It seemed to thunder in the sudden stillness.

"My friend, more is concealed than is revealed. Each revealed leads to more concealed. Each concealed leads to undreamed of heights."

The author, rising to his feet, replied, "La ilaha, illa Allah" (there is no god except God), and in turning to exit smashed into the huge indented brass coffee table, staggering back as the coffee urn, cups, and waterpipe fell to the floor with a crash.

"My Prince! My Prince!" The cry echoed up the descending passageway. "Look what I found!"

4:10 Caliph of Baghdad.

Snapped out of his daydream, Al Mamun looked down the descending passageway where one of his men was bending over a large prismatic stone. Seconds later Al Mamun knelt by his workman. Examining the stone's bevelled edges, his eyes flashed upward. There in the passage's ceiling was a hole from which the stone had fallen. Grabbing his workman's torch and thrusting it upward, he remembered the dull thud his workmen had heard, which had prompted

his decision to tunnel east. There in the torchlight above him was what appeared to be another passage sloping upward into the

4:11. *The Granite Plug in the Ceiling of the Descending Passage.* Still tightly wedged in place today, it shows less than 1/16th of an inch clearance around the plug.

heart of the building. Al Mamun wondered if the vibrations from the explosion of the "Chinese snow," (a curious mixture of saltpeter, sulphur, and charcoal) purchased through his underground connections from that strange Chinese alchemist to hasten the tunnelling, had shaken the prismatic stone loose, producing the dull thud. Directing his attention to the rest of the descending passageway, which disappeared at the steep angle of 26 degrees into the inky darkness below, Al Mamun and his men descended into the unknown.

Descending 345 feet into the solid bed-

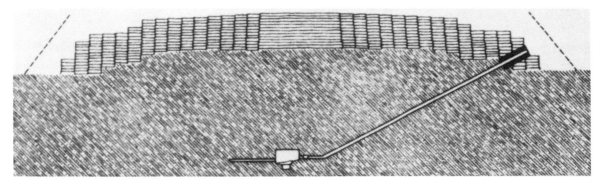

4:12 Underground Passage.

rock of the plateau, Al Mamun and his men reached the Great Pyramid's lowest chamber. Finding only a roughly hewn chamber, its uneven floor littered with dust and debris, its ceiling smooth and cut in layers, a narrow pasageway in the south wall leading nowhere, and a well shaft cut in the floor and also leading nowhere, Al Mamun became confused in this "chamber of chaos." From the black smoke smudges and graffiti on the white limestone ceiling,

Al Mamun deduced that the chamber had been visited in classical times when the location of the door had been known, and that anything of value must be above and behind that granite plug.

Struggling on hands and knees back up the slick descending passage, Al Mamun wondered: how and by what means could this extraordinarily straight and long tunnel have been constructed? The tunnel was 345 feet long, with a mean variation from a cen-

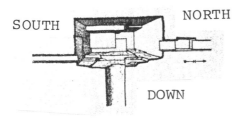

4:13, *The Subterranean Pit.* In the *Egyptian Book of the Dead* (Budge translation, 1895), the earliest codification of moral tenets basic to an outstanding world religion and prior, of course, to Judaism's Ten Commandments, this chamber was called the Chamber of Chaos, symbolically representing the chamber of "Enter Apprentice." See also the Adams' translation, 1897. In this chamber the first degree of the Egyptian Mysteries were conferred.

4:14. *The Pyramid in Fantasy.* In the *Arabian Nights*, the Great Pyramid was reputed to contain great treasures, which most imagined to be gold—overlooking the great wealth of knowledge to be obtained from studying the building itself.

tral axis along the entire length containing a margin of error *less than 1/4"* in azimuth (from side to side) and only *.1* in altitude (up and down.)[5] Al Mamun wondered how men, hacking away at the powdery limestone in the narrow confines of the tunnel, could have breathed with all the limestone dust in the air. Arriving at the granite plug, Mamun slowly realized that if this stone had fallen because of the vibrations of his tunnelling, then this passageway was an original discovery, a discovery unknown to all who had preceded him—perhaps even unknown to his father, whose nocturnal excursions through Baghdad provided the starting point of more than one chapter in the *Thousand and One Nights.*

Determined to go on until the answer was obtained, Al Mamun (realizing the weakness of the Chinese thunder-and-lightning powder against granite, as well as his own ineptitude with this new Chinese invention of gunpowder) directed his men to circumvent the granite plugs by tunnelling around the three granite plugs in the softer limestone core blocks. Excavating a large cavity in the body of the Great Pyramid, west of the ascending passage, Al Mamun was able to circumvent three impenetrable granite plugs and be the first man in history to proceed upward into the mysterious interior of this rock of ages by its ascending passage.

Leading the way with his torch held low, Al Mamun and his men, their backs bent low and seared by the heat of their torches, struggled to retain their footing in the slippery upward-sloping ascending passage as they crept cautiously upward. As Al Mamun continued up the 129 feet of the ascending passage, he noticed three "girdle stones" placed at regular intervals of 17 feet 2 inches. Passing the third of these girdle stones, Al Mamun suddenly realized that the angle of slope of this passage (26° 2 minutes 30″) was almost exactly identical to

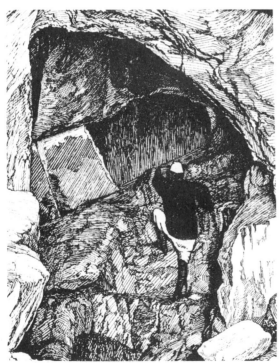

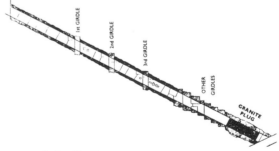

4:15. *The Ascending Passage and Girdle Stones.*

that of the descending passage (26° 31 minutes 23"); he committed this fact to memory. Marvelling at this geometric perfection, Al Mamun arrived at a level floor in his difficult upward struggle. Handing his torch to the next man up and placing his hands on the small of his back, Al Mamun stretched and saw directly before him a horizontal passageway leading south. Taking his torch

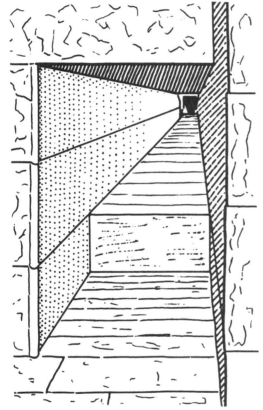

4:16. *Passage Leading to Queen's Chamber* as seen from within the Queen's Chamber.

---

back and bidding his brother to have his men follow as they arrived at this first level, Al Mamun entered the passage alone. Walking as rapidly as possible in a passageway only 3 feet 9 inches high and 3 feet 5

inches wide, Al Mamun plunged ahead. Almost at the end of the 127-foot length of this passage, Al Mamun suddenly jerked to a halt before the Great Pyramid's Middle Chamber (symbolically called in the *Egyptian Book of the Dead* the Chamber of Second Birth.)

There in the darkness immediately before him, illuminated only by his feeble torch light, a sudden drop of 1 foot 11 inches mysteriously appeared in the floor of the passageway. Gingerly stepping down, Al Mamun stood before another doorway a few feet away — a doorway which provided access to the Queen's Chamber, a name incorrectly applied to a non-Arab building and indeed even a non-Egyptian building.[6] If a band of men built this building to survive any disaster, could they have established a fraternity for communicating their message orally?

4:17. *The Queen's Chamber.*

---

[6]**A misnomer, so-called by early Arab explorers because the Arabs buried *their* queens in tombs with pointed roofs and their kings in flat-topped tombs.**

Entering this second chamber, holding his torch high and praying that the elemental forces of the earth were with him, Al Mamun entered and saw a chamber with a pointed room 20 feet five inches high. Pivoting slowly from east to west and back again, he surveyed the entire chamber more closely. The chamber's floor dimensions would prove to be 18 feet 10 inches from east to west, and 17 feet 2″ from north to south (the exact distance that separates the girdle stones).

4:19. *The Niche in the East Wall of the Queen's Chamber.* Today, in the back of this niche, there is a tunnel cut to some depth. Egyptologists explain this tunnel by saying, "it was *probably* cut by treasure-seekers." One cannot help but think, as the tunnel extends for well over 38 feet through solid core blocks ending in a large bulb-shaped cavern, that these treasure-seekers were rather dim-witted to continue digging for such a long time, to such a great depth, without the faintest indication as to why. After 50 years of research, Edward Kunkle, author of the *Pharoah's Pump,* believes that this tunnel (with its flat, level floor, its almost perfect right-angled left side and its particular shape) was an original part of the construction—a part which served a mechanical purpose discussed in the text.

4:18. *The Middle Chamber, Looking East.*

Al Mamun's eyes quickly scanned the chamber, then darted to a corbelled niche 15 feet 4″ tall, indented in the east wall. Cocking his head to one side like a curious and puzzled crow, he examined the niche. As he gazed into the back of this niche, Al Mamun saw what men today can only guess at.

Everything he came across was a mystery to him. Almost absent-mindedly, Mamun shuffled closer to the east wall, wondering what had become of the treasure, wondering what had become of the secret maps and tables of the stars, wondering why this chamber too was empty. Lost in his thoughts, he failed to hear a gentle rustling

4:20. The Niche.

behind him. Almost subconsciously, Al Mamun lifted his torch over his head and as if guided by some unseen presence looked at the wall—only to see a wall covered with "crystals." Whirling about, he saw that the whole chamber was alive with them—they were growing everywhere! Dragging his fingernail through crystals that grow by reproducing themselves, whose individual particles vibrate back and forth, he placed his fingertip to his lips as any modern explorer might do, and tasted salt.

Noone: Dr. Tiller, why would the Middle Chamber of the Great Pyramid be such a magnet, or a repository for these crystals?

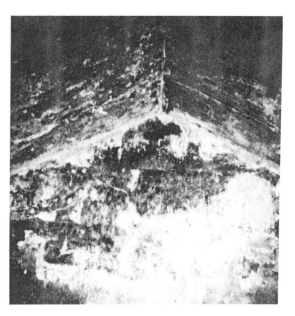

4:21. *West Wall of the Middle Chamber.* This photograph shows heavy incrustation of salt crystals (see Plate 4:21). Edward Kunkle, in *Pharoah's Pump* (pp. 38, 47, 50), shows this chamber was subjected to tremendous compression and *river* water. The Queen's Chamber, situated below and offset by 24 feet from the building's *mass centroid* (see Mathematical Appendix), turns out to be quite an extraordinary crystal-producing factory. These facts may help explain (considering that "interference patterns" from multiple spherical sources fill space with an omni-triangulated pattern of stable standing wave patterns) the surprisingly low salt content of the crystals in question.

Tiller: That's really tough to imagine, because you basically have got to have (a) either some salt water which was in there and evaporated and then deposited this because it got very hot, or (b) it was at some time under the ocean and [the water] seeped in, or (c) somehow the "energies" converted what was in the walls to sodium chloride. None of these, however, makes any sense at all to me. I regret I don't have, at this point in any event, a really good answer for you.

State of Arizona
Bureau of Geology and Mineral Technology

Mineral Technology Branch
University of Arizona
Tucson, Arizona 85721
(602) 626-1943

November 27, 1978
Sample No. 56411

Source of Innergy
P.O. Box 18224
Tucson, Arizona 85731

Dear Sir:

The sample submitted to the Bureau of Geology and Mineral Technology
is predominantly calcite (calcium carbonate) with some halite (sodium
chloride) and gypsum (calcium sulfate).

Since the material was reportedly from Egypt and not Arizona, we are
required to charge $3.00 for the above analysis.

I hope this information is of use to you. If we can be of any further
service, please let me know.

Sincerely,

Robert T. O'Haire
Associate Mineralogist

/bo

cc: W. H. Dresher

This is to certify that the material given to the University of
Arizona was a transparent, crystaline deposit from the walls of
of the Queen's chamber of the Pyramid of Cheops.

G. Patrick Flanagan, Ph.D.

4:22. Certification of Composition of Crystals from Middle Chamber.

100

4:23. *Dr. Flanagan at the Second Pyramid of Giza.*

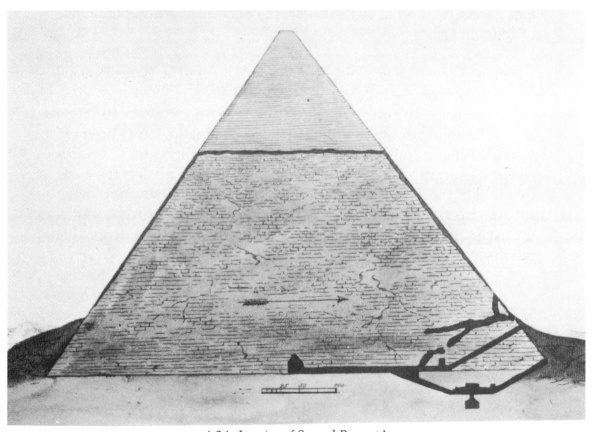

4:24. *Interior of Second Pyramid.*

A street in Teotihuacan, in its easterly direction, was oriented to 106.9°...the street points toward the rising of Sirius or the Egyptian Dog Star, Sothis...The other end of this street points to 286.9°.

Dr. David Zink
The Ancient Stones Speak

A circle of 3,652.42 pyramid inches circumference, equivalent to the number of days in a solar year on a scale of ten inches to a day, falls precisely internal to the outer ring of stones forming the circle of Stonehenge.

Basil Stewart
The Great Pyramid

As archaeologists were mapping and reconstructing Teotihuacan...they realized the city had been meticulously oriented so that its main thoroughfare ran from 15°30 minutes east of north to 15°30 minutes west of south. The dominent structure, the huge Pyramid of the Sun, however, was precisely oriented at right angles to the street. Thus, it faced 15°30 minutes north of west, which meant its azimuth—the angular orientation clockwise from due north—was 285.3°.

Vincent H. Malmstrom
Science Digest

Vol. 89, No. 11, Dec. 1981

CHAPTER FIVE

EXHIBIT A: CONCRETE FACTS AND A VALIANT OLD WARRIOR

Temporarily leaving Al Mamun to ponder the crystals in the Middle Chamber, it's time for some concrete facts. Being of the third generation of an old Southern legal family, I was conditioned and disciplined from a very early age to seek out facts. This childhood training was to become deeply ingrained in my whole being. Suspicion, skepticism, and open-mindedness became second nature to me. These factors were to prove extremely helpful to me years later when I was to present the public with my most difficult case—*The Various Experts vs. The Great Pyramid.*

Most people who have spent their whole life learning a trade or profession, who have a second mortgage on the house, a child in college, and numerous other expenses, are not likely to announce publicly: "Because of the presentation of new evidence, everything I thought I knew is false." Many who live in quiet desperation, having learned from childhood "Don't rock the boat," would be hesitant to change boats in midstream come middle age. Most would imagine that such a public announcement would bring to an end the cherished professorship, the enjoyable mental and physical state of being at the top of one's profession, and the grant money—that all-powerful and desperately needed source

of income. On the other hand, there are many experts today who are not intimidated by new discoveries—discoveries which, like the rapid clicking of the teletype in a newsroom, continually transmit new data about the origin of man.

One of the first "facts" I learned about the Great Pyramid was that hundreds of thousands of slaves, using nothing more advanced than wooden mauls and soft copper chisels, had erected this building *in twenty-three years* (cf. quote from I.E.S. Edwards, p. 167). This statement, published in Dr. Edwards' book in 1947, seemed suspicious to me, simply because of the many recent discoveries I had previously read about. Egyptologists were asking me to believe that the 2,600,000 core blocks of the Great Pyramid and the 115,000 precisely finished casing stones were quarried, cut, transported, elevated into place, and cemented together (with an extraordinary cement 1/50th of an inch thick and rivalling epoxy in tensile strength) by uneducated slaves—all in a space of *twenty-three years!* Something was dreadfully wrong with this supposition.

It seemed to me that the first step in my detective work would be to find someone who would know a great deal about quarrying huge limestone blocks. The world's greatest quarrier of limestone should make an expert witness. I discovered that the Indiana Limestone Institute of America (consisting of 33 quarries) was considered by most architects to be the world's leading authority on limestone. Calling long distance information, I soon found myself speaking to Merle Booker, Technical

Director of the Institute. I was lucky, for this day was one of those special last days that Merle would make it to the office. Dying of cancer before the publication of this book, Merle understood what an important contribution his last research project, sandwiched in between painful chemotherapy treatments, would mean to the world.

Merle explained to me that today limestone is quarried by the fastest and most efficient methods our present technology can supply. Once the huge blocks are fractured and broken loose from the bedrock, electrically powered high-speed diamond-tipped drills cut into the rock with amazing swiftness and precision. Modern forklifts, giant cranes, and other recent inventions stand ready to lift, lower, and load the blocks onto flat-bed trucks or railroad cars for rapid transportation to the building site. Special precautions are then taken by the shipping department to avoid fracturing of the blocks while in transit from strong jolts and various other hazards encountered in shipping.

When quarried, limestone contains groundwater. This is commonly known as "quarry sap." Normally "buff stone" does not require drying beyond the usual sixty to ninety days of quarrying, sawing, and fabrication process. Limestone, however, used on the exterior of a building, such as the "casing stones" that covered the Great Pyramid, should be allowed to dry out for a minimum of six months prior to setting in the wall. This allows the organic matter in solution to stabilize. The organic matter will oxidize upon exposure to the elements, causing the stone to lighten in color with age. The old adage common to all masonry applies: KEEP THE WALLS DRY.

Egyptologists tell us, looking into their crystal balls across the gulf of time, that the builders of the Great Pyramid used wooden mallets, soft copper chisels, and brute force. Old textbooks such as Dr. I.E.S. Edwards's are today used to instruct students specializing in the field of Egyptology. These textbooks perpetuate a much earlier attempt to fit the construction time of the Great Pyramid neatly into the enigmatical twenty-three-year reign of the Pharoah Khufu. These books are directly responsible for the fact that the student of Egyptology receives today only a cursory description of the tallest building erected on this planet until the twentieth century. If anyone seriously challenges their time theory with concrete facts (pardon the pun), they instantly and magically pluck another 400,000 imaginary and unsubstantiated workers out of the air to accomplish the task!

Merle Booker pointed out to me that his time study presupposes that there would be an adequate amount of railroad cars available to transport the blocks. He also told me that the time study did *not* include any delays created by "railroad strikes, train derailments, equipment breakdown, material delays, the engineers and union bosses, the signal whistle and pay lines, the Nile not flooding that year," and of course, "the re-evaluation of cost estimates in the years to come."

Ladies and gentlemen of the jury, I believe that the second paragraph of Merle's letter of 19 December 1978:

> Utilizing the entire Indiana Limestone industry's facilities as they now stand, and figuring on tripling present average production, it would take approximately 27 years [for 33 quarries] to quarry, fabricate and ship the total requirements.

December 19, 1978

Mr. Richard Noone
Allied Imports, Inc.
3541 Clearview Parkway
Atlanta, GA 30340

Re: Great Pyramid
    Egypt

Dear Mr. Noone:

As a follow-up to our letter, dated June 26, 1978, we have had various Indiana Limestone industry members working out realistic quarrying and fabricating time studies for all of the necessary blocks that would be required to duplicate another Great Pyramid, like the one built in Egypt centuries ago.

Utilizing the entire Indiana Limestone industry's facilities as they now stand, and figuring on tripling present average production, it would take approximately 27 years to quarry, fabricate and ship the total requirements.

The quantities of various type of blocks were based on a 755'-9"x 755'-9" base figure for the pyramid and side slopes of 51°-51'-14.3". Also based on providing a king's chamber, queen's chamber, grand gallery, ante-chamber and passage ways on the interior.

All exterior and interior blocks were figured on the basis of 12'-0" X 8'-0" X 5'-0" size. Approximately 264,216 rectangular core blocks would be required, plus 12,723 exterior sloped blocks with very precise joint surfaces. The total quanity of blocks required would equal 131,467,940 cubic feet of quarried, finished stone.

Sincerely,

Merle B. Booker

Merle B. Booker
Technical Director

MBB/lp

5:1. *Letter From Merle B. Booker, Technical Director of the Limestone Institute of America.* The letter specifies the time necessary for duplicating the Great Pyramid with modern techniques.

5:2. *Workers in Limestone.* Egyptologists have taught that the Great Pyramid was built with the primitive techniques illustrated in the first picture.

demonstrates beyond a shadow of a doubt that the theory of the time of construction of the Great Pyramid espoused by the Egyptologists is in dreadful error.

Realizing that the Great Pyramid's time of construction is now seriously questionable, and realizing that the earliest theories of its construction are primarily based upon different religious beliefs, I wondered what priest, rabbi, guru, preacher, or nuclear physicist would actually be intimately familiar with the construction techniques employed in its erection. What I needed now was an architect.

I needed not only an architect, but a very special one—an architect who would be not only a master of architecture, but one intimately familiar with the exterior and interior dimensions of the Great Pyramid—and in addition, a scholar of ancient history and ancient religious beliefs. I had little hope. In this age of over-specialization, could such a multi-disciplined man exist? The odds against finding such a man seemed wildly implausible at the time; however, it struck me that from the moment I had initiated this investigation of the Great Pyramid, an unusual series of events had been occurring. Every time I reached a dead end and thought the problem was insurmountable, my problem would be solved by the arrival of the rare out-of-print book I was seeking, an interview granted with a difficult-to-reach professor, monetary assistance, news of a discovery in some far-distant part of the world reaching me years before it could be printed and available in book form to the general public, or by the arrival of a great teacher.

On 18 November 1976 I read that the Governor of Georgia, George Busbee, had just declared "Architects' Week" in the state of Georgia, in honor of Wilfred J. Gregson.

Later that week I was to read that the Honorable Mayor of Atlanta, Maynard Jackson, had declared "Architects' Day" in the city of Atlanta in this architect's honor. I read on. A short time later our paths crossed.

On 7 April 1977 I interviewed Mr. Wilfred J. Gregson, an architect possessing all three of the needed qualities I was seeking in an architect. Mr. Gregson was graduated in the top of his class in 1921 from England's College of Engineering and Naval Architecture. Completing additional courses in architecture at Liverpool University and London University, Gregson immigrated to the United States in 1921. He furthered his studies in this country by completing additional courses in architecture at the Pratt Institute of Design, the Beaux-Arts Institute, Hirons Atelier, Columbia University, and New York University. Completing his studies, Gregson practiced architecture in the city of New York for the next five years under the name of Wilfred Gregson and Associates. Then in 1929 the stock market collapsed. During this period of little construction Mr. Gregson became such a familiar sight to the librarians of New York City that every morning they would have whatever subject he was studying that week laid out side by side in three, sometimes four, different translations. Following the worst of the great depression, Gregson's services were retained by the United States Government, in whose service he travelled to every state in the Union as an Associate Architect.

In 1939 Gregson moved to Atlanta, Georgia, and registered as an architect. He soon was registered as a practicing architect in the states of Alabama, Tennessee, Florida, Ohio, North Carolina, South Carolina, Virginia, and West Virginia, and had become a member of the National

Council of Architects Registration Board. Mr. Gregson later served for five years on the Architects Examination and Registration Board in Georgia. He was awarded the 33° in Freemasonry for his educational work in the Ancient and Accepted Scottish Rite. Besides English, Gregson speaks French, Spanish, German, Arabic, Hebrew—and reads Sanskrit and Egyptian hieroglyphs. He has also authored a book entitled *Evidences of Masonry in Ancient Civilization.*

It is not surprising, therefore, to discover that Mr. Gregson is the founder and past president of the Society of American Registered Architects.

Noone: Mr. Gregson, as you may well know, there is going to be a CBS television special two weeks from now on the Great Pyramid.

Gregson: I was aware of that.

Noone: It is a one-hour television special probing the mystery and controversy surrounding the Great Pyramid.

Gregson: I was planning on watching it.

Noone: All of my interviews are recorded on tape, so that at some future point in time no one I interview can claim legally that I misquoted him. Is that all right with you?

Gregson: Get on with your questions.

Noone: In the Great Pyramid's King's Chamber, there are two air shafts about—

Gregson: Nine inches in diameter.

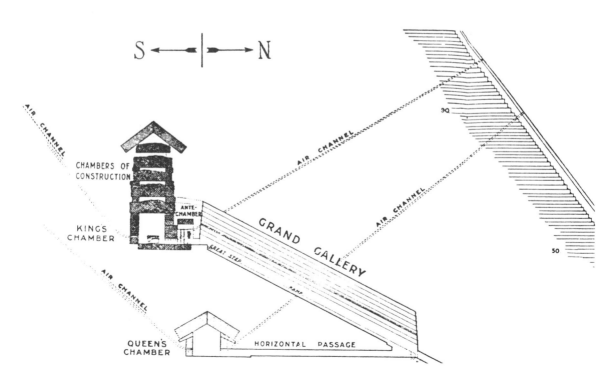

5:3. *Cross Section Showing Air Channels.*

5:4. Peter Tompkins Examining Air Shaft Opening.

Noone: Yes, one running north from the King's Chamber and a similar air shaft running south. Both of these air shafts slope upwards through 180 feet of solid masonry to the building's exterior. Now whoever built the Great Pyramid would certainly have realized that when it rained, as it occasionally does in Egypt, the rainwater running down these shafts would create puddles of water on the floor of the King's Chamber. Now, if this whole building was, as Egyptologists say, constructed for the sole purpose of protecting a mummy, it is certainly suspicious that the builders, by the addition of these two air shafts, created access for what every mummy dreads most—water,

moisture, mold and mildew. So my question to you is why would these two air shafts—

Gregson: Have been constructed?

Noone: Yes.

Gregson: Well, obviously the idea was to get air moving into the pyramid. You can't exist very long breathing stagnant air. So my principle is that this was a temple of initiation, as were certain other pyramids. The Caracol Tower at Chichen-Itza [pronounced Che-Chan-It-Sa] meaning 'Home of the Holy Ones,' very definitely was, because the knowledge has been found there. This being the case, it was built to carry instruc-

5:5. Ruins of an Ancient Temple in Mexico in which Masonic Symbols were found. In his book *Evidences of Masonry in Ancient Civilization*, Wilfred J. Gregson, a Thirty-third Degree Freemason, writes:

Throughout the entire Chichen-Itza complex are thousands of symbols of Masonry two thousand years ago. There are thirty symbols that are recognized today as Masonic including a very hard to find square and compass beautifully set at the center of an enormous panel of delicately carved tracery of signs and symbols.

---

tions through to a later generation—initiation means teaching a new group of people information that an older group of people knew, and this is what the principle would be. You could not have done that—you couldn't have done any teaching inside the Great Pyramid—if the air was foul, if air was not being circulated inside the building. The carbon monoxide would suffocate you in a matter of time. This is why Dr. Harvey, the discoverer of the fact that blood circulates in the human body, was amazed that John Greaves, a 16th century mathematician and astronomer, did not find any air shafts during his exploration of the Great Pyramid. Seeing that we never breathe the same air twice, new air is required to a new inspiration, the *succus alibilis* of it being spent in every expiration. So you would have

5:6. Ruins of an ancient temple in Mexico covered with vegetation. In his book *Evidences of Masonry in Ancient Civilization*, Gregson writes:

One symbol of great prominence throughout all ancient civilizations is the snake or serpent, where it has symbolized "Divine Wisdom". In Yucatan it is featured in practically every structure. At Chichen-Itza the temple at the East of the quadrangle has a great many repeats of a huge sun burst, from the middle of the sun burst is the huge head of a serpent whose mouth is open. This needs little explanation. The sun representing "God" and the serpent "His Divine Wisdom", holds man's head so that he can neither see the serpent "Divine Wisdom", nor the Light of God from which it comes. To do so he must turn around in the opposite direction, like many other poor blind candidates in a state of darkness.

———————

to have air shafts.[1] Another thing about it—I believe that it's possible, that at the time they were built it was possible to make astronomical observations through those shafts. Whether falling stones have changed it any today, I don't know. I know that in the Yucatan, the Maya had observational openings in certain buildings to observe the various planetary movements at the height and the low period of their movement around the heavens and where they rise around the circumference of the earth. They were used, in the clear, generally cloudless skies of Yucatan, where the atmosphere is so pure and transparent that stars are clearly visible to the naked eye that require the aid of a telescope to be seen in other countries, to make observations very, very accurately. I know that these shafts or openings, during the building's construction, were for observing certain planetary and star movements, celestial movements, groups of stars, and keeping track of them, and at least to see what movement was taking place.

Noone: It is quite apparent, from the study of history, there have been men studying the Great Pyramid in every century since its completion. One of Napoleon's scientists, Edme-Francois Jomard, first caught my attention when he espoused the theory that the builders of the Great Pyramid, not the Greeks, were the founders of geometry. I began to explore Jomard's theory, and was

———————

[1] The discussion as to whether or not the Great Pyramid was ventilated, between Dr. Harvey and Professor Greaves in 1638, was not resolved until 198 years later. In 1836 Colonel Howard-Vyse cleared the debris from the air shafts in the north and south walls of the King's Chamber. Once cleared, the shafts allowed air to circulate inside the Great Pyramid. From 1836 to today, the King's Chamber maintains a constant temperature, 68°. Today 68° is the constant temperature that rods, bars, or other standards of measures are kept in, to eliminate shrinkage, expansion, tarnishing, or oxidation.

soon to discover to my horror that more books have been written about the Great Pyramid's measurements than any other subject on earth—excepting, of course, religion. Wading through many quaint and curious volumes of forgotten mathematical lore, I noted a constant, a common denominator, in which all of these men's measurements were in agreement. First, the entrance to the Great Pyramid is offset from the exact center of the Great Pyramid's north face, towards the east, by 286.1022 inches. Second, the base square of the Great Pyramid is short of 36,524.2" by 286.1022".[2] Third, the difference between the height of the ascending passage and the height of the Grand Gallery is 286.1022". Fourth, the King's Chamber is offset from the east-west axis of the Great Pyramid by 286.1022". And fifth, the difference between the present-day truncated top of the Great Pyramid and where the top of the capstone would be, had the truncated building continued to a perfect point, is 286.1022".[3] So my question to you, Mr. Gregson, is: Would this particular mathematical constant have been embodied five times in the Great Pyramid's construction by chance?

Gregson: No. It obviously had some purpose in mind. In other words, if it had been 287, *seven* would have gone into it 41 times, wouldn't it? So that you may have a point there. I feel, as I explained to you before, I thought the number *seven* was a very important measurement in connection with pyramid building, and the number seven would have gone into this 41 times, which has another possible consideration. But I would say offhand that whoever measured the building to four points of decimal was exaggerating somewhat, because even the irregularity of the stone would make much more of a difference than that, so it would be extremely difficult to measure to that degree of accuracy. One point of decimal would be as close as you could get. Anything beyond this is just imaginative.

Noone: What large buildings have you constructed?

Gregson: Well, Millegeville State Hospital in Georgia, as far as horizontal planning is concerned, about 1,500 to 2,000 feet long. That was a very large building, and it houses 1,200 inmates. We have built three others that were somewhat smaller, about 300 feet less in length. They are about the largest I have

---

[2]The base perimeter equals 36,524.2 pyramid inches, which is the number of days in a year multiplied by 100. The inner circle of Stonehenge measures 3,652.42 pyramid inches. (See *Stonehenge Decoded*, by Dr. Gerald S. Hawkins, astronomer at the Smithsonian Astrophysical Observatory and Chairman of the Department of Astronomy at Boston University.) See also the Mathematical Appendix of this book.

[3]Among scientific works consulted: Jomard, John Greaves, C.P. Smyth, Isaac Newton, Giorgiode Santillana, Champollion, John Taylor, John F. Herschel, Robert Menzies, W.F. Petrie, David Davidson, Morton Edgar, Lyle Borst, Alfred Watkins, Schwaller de Lubiez, Adam Rutherford, Livio Stecchini. The most useful works are listed in the Bibliography.

built. Of course, the biggest and most expensive was the San Juan Hospital, which was a ten-story structure—and it, around the base, was about 500 feet in each direction—rectangular in form, so that was a pretty large job. *But the accuracy of it would not be anywhere within the accuracy of the Great Pyramid.* If we were within an inch, we would consider it very good.

5:10. *The Atlanta V.A. Hospital.* Another very large structure built with the aid of a mock-up, this hospital is unique in that it was the first V.A. Hospital embodying a newer concept of hospital design and operation. Through utilization of the Friesen concept of hospital operation, an effort was made to cope with increasing costs of hospital care. This design provides the proper tools to work with, when and where they are needed. Under this concept, professional and allied skills are not diluted with functions and duties that could be performed by less skilled personnel.

Noone: Mr. Gregson, a few weeks ago I interviewed Jim Hagan, a brillant young architect who is a member of the design team that participated in the design of the Atlanta football stadium, the design of the Sports Palace in Cincinnati, Ohio, and recently the design of

5:11. *720-Bed V.A. Hospital.* This medical/surgical hospital built by Gregson & Associates for the Veteran's Administration in San Juan, Puerto Rico, has 548,836 square feet and cost around $18,800,000.00. It was built with the aid of a mock-up, as was the hospital pictured in Plate 5:10.

Atlanta's new subway system, MARTA.

Gregson: I am familiar with him.

Noone: Well, then, as you may well know, Hagan is vice president of Heery Associates, a construction program management firm with offices in New York, Atlanta, and the Middle East country of Jordan.

Gregson: Yes, they are internationally known.

Noone: Recently Hagan and I spent several nights going over the blueprints of the Great Pyramid, its interior and exterior dimensions, and the structures that surround it.

Gregson: Yes?

Noone: We-l-ll, I am not an architect or a structural engineer, but I did observe, night after night, Hagan's continual amazement with the color slides and the in-detail diagrams of this ancient monument. Once the complexities of this building's construction were unfolded to him,

Hagan expressed greater and greater amazement with the building techniques obviously employed in the erection of the first of the seven wonders of the ancient world. Soon Hagan, called to Jordan to assist in the design of the construction of the University of Jordan, was close to the Great Pyramid. Completing his tasks in Jordan, Hagan left Jordan and flew directly to Cairo at his own expense, and next morning examined many of the anomalies we had discussed. He returned to the United States to tell me, 'Listen, Richard, until now structures—football stadiums and sports palaces—have not required nor achieved the constructed accuracy of the Great Pyramid. Placing structures perfectly in relationship to the globe has only recently gained import as an energy response.' I failed to ask him, so I'll ask you, what possibly might have been the motivation for a band of men—what would be the point of making this building so perfect?

Gregson: Well, you know of course my theory of the 51° 51 minutes 14.3 seconds?

Noone: What is that?

Gregson: That is the angle of the Great Pyramid, which is very, very close to another one of my sevens. If you divide that, the number seven, into the 365 days of the year, you come very, very close to your 51° 51 minutes 14.3 seconds. So you are only about nine minutes out, which is very, very close. My theory, again, is that it is a religious edifice, and as such it would embody some certain structure. So looking at it from my standpoint and remembering that all architecture is 'frozen language' expressing the ideas and beliefs of the builders, I would say there are three chambers, and then, above the King's Chamber, there are five layers of stone. So you get three and five. Then on the outside there are four faces of the Great Pyramid, each of three sides. Four and three are seven, so you have 3, 5, and 7, totalling 15, which have tied in very tightly with early ideas or symbols of Man's development and divine development, of planetary movements and the like of that. [Note placement and number of steps behind George Washington in Plate 1:8]. So that let's say this, in the beginning of time those who were observant and noticed that the planets moved in different orbits from the stars would also note that they had different periods for showing up, coming around—and the ancient masons built a great many structures to keep check of them. The ones in Babylon, the ones in Yucatan which were built with holes so you could observe Venus at the different positions and settings, showed a great deal of ingenuity—and the Mayas also integrated the revolutions of Venus with that of the earth. They came up with a very fine idea that the whole world repeated itself every 52 years. So with this, they up and left wherever they were and went somewhere else, just because they figured the world was ready to start again. It was an inadequate observation, but nevertheless they followed very closely along the lines of an ancient Hindu known as Manu. Manu was responsible for what is known as the law of *karma*, eternal recurrence. In other words, he said that everything in the whole universe repeats itself again and

5:7. *One of the Smaller Pyramids Seen with the Great Pyramid.* In the foreground, one of the three smaller pyramids can be seen to be inferior in comparison with the Great Pyramid in the background. Depending on which Egyptologists one reads, the three smaller pyramids were built for King Khufu's Aunt Frances, his mother, members of the royal family, or "other relatives."

again, but on a much longer span of time than the 52-year cycle of the Mayas. So we get back to the fact that wherever you went, even with the American Indians, they were interested in the study of the stars. I think that this was largely built as a monument to the stars, plus an attempt to pass on to civilization some knowledge that the designers of the structure felt was vital. I don't think that we really have gotten it yet. I think that the secret of the Great Pyramid is yet to be discovered. I don't believe what you have now is any more than an indication that the Great Pyramid

does contain a great deal more solid thinking than was originally expected.

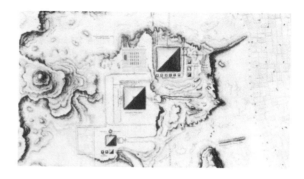

5:8. *The Complex of Pyramids at Giza.* This diagram shows the north-south meridian through the center of the Great Pyramid, and the alignment of other buildings in the complex.

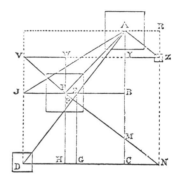

5:9. *Pythagorean Triangles Formed by Perimeters and Centers of the Three Major Pyramids.* This drawing has been supplied courtesy of Alexander Abramov, the Soviet space engineer, and shows some of the relationships among these pyramids.

Noone: If someone asked you to build a copy of the Great Pyramid, could you duplicate the structure with the exactness that it was built with over five thousand years ago, or do our present standards fall short of such perfection?

115

Gregson: Well first off, as an architect I would say an architect would not have the intimate knowledge necessary without getting into an arrangement with astronomers to get their story and their concepts. So you would have to have a combination of skills. The contractor or the builder, the one responsible for the actual building, would have probably some greater experience in construction than the architect would, so you would have at least three in it. And inasmuch as my concept of religious background—you would also have the priesthood. So chances are you had a whole group of people who were responsible for it. *I know of no architect today* who would have the knowledge necessary to build what we know of the Great Pyramid, let alone what we don't know. I think, again, that there is more concealed within the structure than we have discovered, and I think that the purpose of the Great Pyramid was to pass on to later generations what they did discover. It is possible that the Cabbalistic teaching of the Hebrews was more related to this than has yet been known, because they had a whole series of numbers. Each number and each letter in the alphabet had a relative meaning, a lot of which has been completely lost. It's said that Noah preserved the Cabbalah and took it across in the flood, and that Moses received it from the Priest of Midian. A great many people have spent lifetimes trying to interpret and understand it. It has a great deal of deep secrets, and there is a very, very strong possibility that it came from a very early civilization that may have been related to the Great Pyramid's construction.

Noone: According to Egyptologists, the Great Pyramid was constructed by hundreds of thousands of semi-illiterate slaves as a tomb for the Pharoah Khufu. Egyptologists theorize that all this effort was done so grave-robbers would not find Khufu's mummy and loot it. Most Egyptologists also theorize that Khufu was the father of Chephren, and attribute the construction of the second largest pyramid at Giza to Chephren.[4] After a great deal of research, I sensed a problem with this theory. Mr. Gregson, it would appear that if the Great Pyramid was built by Khufu, then one might expect Khufu's son's pyramid to show some improvement, or at least be equal to, his father's pyramid. However, this is not the case. There is no indication of any structural, mathematical, or engineering knowledge being transferred from the builder of the Great Pyramid to the builder of the second pyramid. Would this tell us anything about the sequence of construction?

Gregson: Architecturally, it very definitely points out that they were not related. The improvements

---

[4]For a different opinion, see Chapter 124, p. 199, of Rawlinson's translation of Herodotus, Vol. II. See also a very salutory note (9), on p. 205, by Sir G. Wilkinson. Both state the Chephren was the *brother* of Khufu.

should show in a second development—this is true of our buildings wherever they are. The first building always leaves much to be desired that is incorporated into the second or the third or the fourth building, and perfection is increased up to the point where then they go backwards and become sloppy about it. First to second, and second to third should show a direct improvement, but this is not the case here. I would say that *the theory of the sequence of construction of the pyramids is in error.* [Emphasis added.]

Noone: That is what I thought, because if Khufu and Chephren were father and son, or even brothers, they each may have witnessed some phase of each other's pyramid construction, or used the same builders. Now on the Great Pyramid's east side there are three little pyramids, which Egyptologists theorize were built for members of Khufu's family. These three small pyramids appear to have been just crudely thrown up, without any levelling of courses. Different kinds and sizes of rocks were used, as if piled up by schoolboys, which is quite different from the superb construction techniques evident in the Great Pyramid....Why would the builders just throw up three sloppy little pyramids when they were capable of magnificent work? What would this tell us?

Gregson: Well, it might tell you another interesting thing. As I have already said, the first one would show a great deal of error, the second one would perfect it, and the third one would perfect the second. It is possible the first three pyramids were put up rather crudely to test a theory. If there is some way of dating them ahead of time, then they could have been used as a scale model of what was expected, and the exterior casing may have been removed as much of the exterior casing of the Great Pyramid was. I would suggest that they could have been three samples.

Noone: Well, this is an original thought, which has never been considered. If I am understanding you correctly, these would be like today, before a building is built, a scale model is made of the finished structure.

Gregson: Correct. It always struck me that the one standing off in the corner had a very close relationship to the Great Pyramid, and therefore it could well have been used as a mock-up. I know that frequently when you are building something on a large scale it pays to make a mock-up of it, or a model. For example, the V.A. Hospital in Atlanta and the San Juan Hospital in Puerto Rico—we made a model of both of these before completing them—

Noone: You built the V.A. Hospital in Atlanta?

Gregson: Yes. We built the two, the one in Atlanta, which has just signed us to add a $9 million extension to it, making it a $21 million hospital, and the $20 million hospital in San Juan. We also built a $2.5 million hospital in Augusta, Georgia, right opposite Talmadge Memorial Hospital, a $10 million hospital which I also designed. These were large structures, and in each case it was necessary to make something in the way of a mock-up to work out in more detail just what we were doing. Even more important, when we knew what we were doing it was more important to show other people, because you may have a concept, but it is hard to get it across unless you can show somebody visually. Few people can conceive from a drawing what something is going to look like. So it is possible the first pyramid was built and the owner, or the pharoah, or the chief, or the king, or whoever was there at the time had his own ideas or suggestions, so that the second one was made embodying those corrections, and then he may have passed on and his son or his grandson may have had the third one built. All three of them were built to show improvements, and from the last one the Great Pyramid itself was constructed, in my opinion.

Noone: Mr. Gregson, the measurements of the Great Pyramid have been measured repeatedly, studied, and discussed by great thinkers in every age since its completion. In the sixth century B.C. Thales, the father of Greek geometry, deduced an approximation of the Great Pyramid's height by measuring its shadow, and his own shadow, at the time of day when his shadow was equal to his height. Today, almost two thousand years after Thales, great thinkers are still studying, measuring, and discussing its awesome dimensions. Livio Catullo Stechinni, Professor of the History of Science at William Patterson College (characterized by contemporaries in his field as 'the Copernicus of this century'), believes the Great Pyramid is 'a representation in scale of the earth's northern hemisphere.' Because of the Great Pyramid's awesome dimensions, the intricate complexities of its geometry and construction, the excitement, curiosity, and interest expressed in its measurements by brilliant scholars throughout the ages, I questioned the theory espoused by Egyptologists that the foundations of the Great Pyramid were measured by s-t-r-e-t-c-h-e-d string.

Gregson: You can take a small piece of string and it will expand and contract whether it is moist or wet or dry or hot or cold. When you consider the heat of the desert during the sun time of the day and the coolness of night, that your instruments of measurement would be subjected to a vast amount of change in length, how can you come out with a building and then later people come along and measure it to four points of decimal? That is why I question whether anyone measuring it within a quarter of an inch or one-half an inch, on a structure that big, is within the bounds of reason. The problem of designing it was terrific, because of the necessity of having the three chambers in different locations, and these chambers centered onto the center of the pyramid in the way they are. Because of this—

Noone: Excuse me for interrupting.

Gregson: Yes, certainly. Go ahead.

Noone: Dr. I.E.S. Edwards[5] and other Egyptologists say this:

Pharoah Khufu, who reigned for 23 years, originally planned to have his mummy deposited in the subterranean pit beneath the Pyramid. But he changed his mind and decided to alter the original project by substituting a burial chamber higher up in the body of the building for the chamber already under construction beneath the Pyramid at a time when the building had already been built to some height. It was at this time that the Ascending Passage was hewn upwards through the existing core blocks of masonry already laid. At the top of the Ascending Passage, a level passageway was constructed leading south to what is known today as the Queen's Chamber or Middle Chamber which lies exactly midway between the north and south sides of the Pyramid. Once the Middle Chamber was constructed, with a corbelled niche in the east wall, *it is assumed* [emphasis added] Khufu changed his mind again and wanted to be buried still higher up in the Pyramid. At this point his masons constructed two of the most celebrated architectural works of the ancients—the Grand Gallery and the King's Chamber of the Great Pyramid.

Now Mr. Gregson, I wondered—

Gregson: That doesn't make any sense. Egyptologists often come up with an idea to fit their theory, but from a standpoint of design, in any structure, you design with the whole structure in mind. It is pretty obvious that this building was designed with the idea that it was going to be a pyramid from the very beginning. Even your interior wall shapes and angles and so forth indicate that it was intended to go to a top, and without a question of doubt it was originally designed that way--anything else would be straight foolishness. In ancient philosophy, in many countries and religions, "old stories of the development of mankind" all have relationship to certain centers, or *chakras*, in the human body. This knowledge would necessarily be incorporated into a structure that had its intent as a monument for Mankind.

Noone: Have you spent many hours in the study of ancient history, ancient religions, and ancient philosophy?

Gregson: Only about 45,000 hours since 1928. An interesting point is that if you consider ancient philosophies which have to do with the centers in humans, the *chamber placement* in the Great Pyramid relates very strongly to these centers, this philosophy. If you take the lowest chamber in the Great Pyramid, the subterranean pit, and consider it as the lowest CHAKRA, the sex organ, and if you consider the Middle

---

[5]See Edwards, *The Pyramids of Egypt,* Chapter IV.

Chamber [the Queen's Chamber] as the heart CHAKRA, and the King's Chamber as the head CHAKRA, this would make three centers or Chakras in the human body in pretty much the same relationship as you find them in the Great Pyramid. It is—again my opinion—that you have these three centers, and chances are you also have four more that you have not yet found. It is my belief that there will be *seven* of them found inside the Great Pyramid, in some

way, shape or form. This is to be discovered at a later date, simply by following along the ancient principles of the centers of Mankind.

Noone: A peculiarity shared by the Great Pyramid with no other Egyptian pyramid, Mexican pyramid, or any of the Pacific island pyramids, is each of its four sides is indented about three feet at the center of each face. What structural advantage would this have?

5:12. *The Giza Pyramid Complex from 4,000 Feet.* This unique air photograph of the complex was taken before sunset at an elevation of 4,000 feet. The west slope of each pyramid is shown reflecting the light from the setting sun, and the south slope of each pyramid is in shadow. The south stepped "slope" of the Great Pyramid reveals a V-shaped depression in this photograph. The V-shaped depression, or hollowing-in, occurs in all four slopes of the Great Pyramid—a structural feature that does not appear on any other pyramid in the world.

5:13. *The "Hollowing-In" Feature from Ground Level.* This special feature of the Great Pyramid, extremely difficult to observe from ground level, did not escape the trained eye of Napoleon's artists, as may be seen in the etching above. A century was to pass before the structural engineer David Davidson would relate this "hollowing-in" feature to the three lengths of the year—solar, sideral, and anomalistic.

Gregson: Its apparent advantage would be for draining water, preferably to bring it down one channel instead of all over the surface. Water is nature's destructive mechanism. Water in stone followed by freezing, or water in stone followed by vegetation, will ruin any building. In the Yucatan it has ruined them by the vegetation that grows within the joints. In Ireland it's ruined them by rot and mold. In any building that is not occupied, they go to pieces very, very fast with water acting as the destructive agent. Knowledge of this must have been known beforehand in order to make these gutterways for the water to come down. However, from a structural standpoint, the very business of carving stone with a minute angle in it, in addition to the angle of the slope of the pyramid, and in addition to the necessity of keeping the sides rectangular, square with the base, created an extremely difficult operation for carving at the quarry. It is no amateur job to carve stone in that fashion, much less to get them as smooth as they did.

Noone: The Great Pyramid's King's Chamber is built entirely of granite, and I'm wondering why. Only the

(Hollowing-in of core masonry GREATLY EXAGGERATED to show effect.)

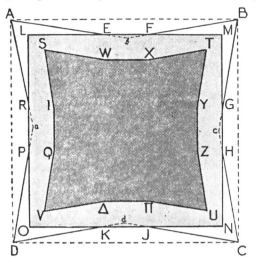

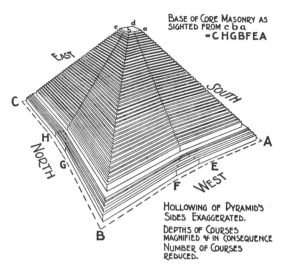

BASE OF CORE MASONRY AS SIGHTED FROM c b a = CHGBFEA

HOLLOWING OF PYRAMID'S SIDES EXAGGERATED. DEPTHS OF COURSES MAGNIFIED & IN CONSEQUENCE NUMBER OF COURSES REDUCED.

5:14. *Diagrammatic Perspective View Illustrating Features of Great Pyramid's Core Masonry.* This study is by David Davidson. An interesting aspect of the construction of the Great Pyramid is the unit of measurement used. Scientists and Egyptologists today agree that whoever built the Great Pyramid used a "unit of measurement," and that this unit was employed throughout the building's construction. What was that unit? From where did we inherit the "inch" in use today? What is the origin of the inch? In 1638 John Greaves attempted to determine the true circumference of the earth by measuring the base perimeter of the Great Pyramid; from Greaves's data Sir Isaac Newton determined that the Pyramid was built on the basis of two different cubits, the "sacred" and the "profane." Sir John Herschel postulated a unit "half a human hair's breadth longer than the inch" as the only sensible earth-commensurate measurement. In 1864 Piazzi Smyth determined the Great Pyramid's true meridian, but William Flinders Petrie "proved" Smyth's discoveries to be false. David Davidson corrected Petrie's "proofs," thus vindicating Smyth. In 1971 Tompkins and Stecchini published their findings, which have been debated by scientists and Egyptologists. In 1979, 341 years after John Greaves attempted to find an "earth-commensurate" measurement, William R. Fix published *Pyramid Odyssey,* resolving the difference between the "pyramid inch" and the inch we use today.

King's Chamber is constructed of granite—all the rest are constructed of limestone. Why would an ancient band of men have constructed—why would only the King's Chamber of the Great Pyramid have been constructed entirely of granite?

Gregson: Well, granite is the hardest common stone known to man today. It is extremely hard to cut or move. If you hit it with a chisel, the hammer will bounce back off the chisel towards your forehead, hardly making a dent in the stone. It is only with our modern equipment that we can grind the stuff and get it smooth and polished. So how in the world these people did it is beyond me. Carving granite is, to say the least of it, a very difficult, slow, and precise operation. Even breaking it out from the quarry is difficult. In present-day granite quarries, they core-drill around the sides and generally dynamite it loose from the base of the bedrock. Then you have to cut away the irregularities of the stone and bang away at it with chisel and hammer or chisel-powered hammers. The best they had here was bronze, no iron, and this would create a very, very difficult operation. It's extremely hard to know how in the world, at a time when steel was not available and the various advantages we have today were not available, how did they get this stone even roughed out, let alone polished? It is an extremely difficult operation.

Noone: I am beginning to see that.

Gregson: I have a pillar of granite in back of the house by the swimming pool, that I attempted to cut a hole in. [At this point Noone and Gregson went outside.] When I attempted to cut a hole in this pillar, I was unable to do it. The steel rock-drill I used just bounced off of it without making any significant indentation. So since steel is a great deal tougher than anything the Egyptians used, I don't know how they were able to get this granite as smooth as they did.

Noone: Is there any conceivable method available to the ancients that would have allowed them to quarry granite with the speed and efficiency that we process it with today?

Gregson: It is possible that they were able to cut these granite blocks with a string or a fiber utilizing some form of abrasive. It is possible, in some cases, to cut stones with an abrasive. A copper cutting wheel will cut a diamond when it is dipped into a solution of water and carborundum. But they didn't have carborundum, unless they possessed a knowledge of electricity. They may have had diamonds and crushed those up in order to make a paste or a cutting edge. A copper cutting wheel would absorb the diamond dust, which would impregnate the cutting edge of the copper wheel, and it would then become a cutting wheel capable of cutting through any rock, including granite. My guess is that the builders of the Great Pyramid had some form of using an abrasive to cut the stone rather than hammering and chiseling it, because of the extraordinary difficulty in quarrying granite in that way.

Noone: How the people communicated on a building project this vast without telephones is a mystery to me, unless the architect or architects, in advance, had planned in extremely careful detail each facet of the project—which still leaves open how an emergency, mistake, or accident was speedily corrected. It appears to me, Mr. Gregson, someone orchestrated an entire nation to complete this construction project—someone possessing the organizing capacity of a genius.

Gregson: The problem to me is not so much the volume of people, the number of people, but the difficulty in getting the stones into the correct angle and plane to put them in place. To position and place the casing stones, with their delicately finished edges, without damage, required an extremely delicate operation.

Noone: That's right! Of course, each of the 115,000 casing stones would have to be put in place "slowly" and "gently" to avoid chipping the very precise joint surfaces.[6]

Gregson: I can conceive of building the Great Pyramid with modern techniques, modern surveying equipment, steel measures, measurements taken when wind, heat, and the light of the sun would not affect measurements, but I cannot conceive of doing it with primitive instruments.

Noone: When you are building a building, and relating the dimensions of the building to a length that is commensurate with the size of the earth, do you prefer to use the metric system or the more ancient system of feet and inches?

Gregson: You use the one you are most familiar with, and that is the inch. A centimeter is the French method of design, numbering, and so forth. It has its usefulness, particularly on a slide rule and calculator, because it is divisible by ten all the way through, whereas the inch is not. But if you will get the *Cipher...*

Noone: How does that help when you are building a very large building?

Gregson: It just makes it easier to knock off a zero and to add a zero to increase the size by ten than any other way. Multiplication is much easier when you are dealing with ten

instead of 1/8 of an inch, 1/16 of an inch, 1/4, 3/8, or 3/4 of an inch. One inch and then twelve inches to one foot and thirty-six inches to a yard, you are messing around all over the place. When you get into rods, $16\frac{1}{2}$ feet, these are measurements that have been dropped. But I understand if you will get the *Cipher of Genesis* you will find a relationship of these measurements which is quite interesting, and also most helpful in the book that you are writing. Do you have a copy of the *Cipher of Genesis?*

Noone: No, but I'll get one.

Gregson: The *Cipher of Genesis* is based on the Cabbalistic teachings which I referred to earlier. You have two Cabbalistic principles: (a) those of the Hebrew, and (b) the other, the Greek. Both the Greek alphabet and the Greek numbering system are related. The Hebrew numbering system and alphabet are also related, and they conceal an occult meaning that is pretty much lost.

The *Cipher of Genesis*, originally published in French in 1967, represents forty years of perseverence in biblical research by Carlo Suares. Mr. Suares was born in Alexandria, Egypt, in 1892, and now lives in Paris with his wife. A personal friend of Henry Miller and Krishnamurti, Carlo Suares has a considerable reputation as an artist and as an architect.

His book expresses the viewpoint that many people, including historians and religious leaders, are unaware that the first five chapters of the Bible were written in

---

[6]See Merle Booker's letter, Plate 5:1.

code, and that their real meaning cannot be understood without the key, the "cipher," to that number/letter code. Whether one believes in a Supreme Being or not, the *Cipher of Genesis* is exciting reading, because it explains many parts of the Pentateuch (the first five books of the *Holy Bible*) that on the surface appear perplexing, through the use of the letter/number code of the Hebrew alphabet (Aleph = 1, Bayt = 2, Ghimel = 3, Dallet = 4, etc.).

Mr. Suares also presents dramatic evidence that certain crucial parts of both the Old and New Testaments are hopelessly mistranslated in Hebrew. For example, Moses comes down from Mount Sinai with two tablets of testimony, tables of stone, written with the finger of God, containing the Ten Commandments, the most humane law being "Thou shalt not kill" (Exodus 30:13). Arriving at the foot of the mountain, however, Moses orders the death of "about 3,000 men" (Exodus 32:27-28), thereby negating the law while giving it. The first five books of the Bible, when read in the original number/letter code, appear to be the testament of a lost civilization—a transmission from the unknown.

Noone: What was that Greek teaching you spoke of earlier—something about one could walk into a lions' den or a den of thieves and come out untouched in one piece.

Gregson: This again is Pythagorus: 'When you go in peace, when you move in peace, exist in peace, the mind is still, the soul serene, and the heart is tranquil; and you move in harmony with the rhythm of the spheres, partake of the sense of oneness of all that is, and realize the connection between yourself and the Divine,' this is the Pythagorean arrangement of the three centers.

I interviewed Dr. Flanagan in 1975, Mr. Gregson in 1977, and both expressed the opinion that the Great Pyramid contains chambers that will someday be discovered. If and when that day arrives, will the secret chamber contain information that the Great Pyramid was constructed by means other than those so far suggested by engineers? Who really knows what a band of men clever enough and sufficiently advanced enough to design and have had the Great Pyramid constructed may have known?

A year and seven months passed. 23 November 1978 I was talking to Lambert T. Dolphin, Senior Physicist in charge of the Radio Physics Laboratory at Stanford Research Institute. Dolphin and the SRI team, working together with Ain Shams University in Cairo and the government of Egypt's Organization of Antiquities, have been using modern electronic sensing equipment—equipment that located King Tut's tomb in thirty minutes (a project that took Howard Carver six years)—to determine whether or not secret chambers exist within the Great Pyramid. Dolphin now believes:

Dolphin: We think there may be a chamber between the King's Chamber and the Queen's Chamber in the Great Pyramid, but the data doesn't tell us whether we have a chamber there, or whether we simply have a large crack. We do seem to have an anomaly in the Great Pyramid—a large void which shows up on our scannings rather regularly.

Noone: Have you been able to define or pinpoint the exact shape of this void?

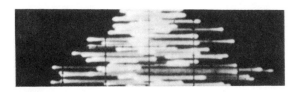

5:15. Location of Possible New Chamber in Great Pyramid. (a) Acoustic echoes, looking through the floor of the King's Chamber. (b) Sketch showing location of possible new chamber in relation to other structures within the Pyramid.

in the Cairo Museum) is thought by Egyptologists to be Khufu, who Egyptologists believe built the Great Pyramid. Although nothing is known with surety about Khufu save a few cartouches (a group of hieroglyphics in a small, oblong area) which may or may not be considered contemporaneous with him, it becomes obvious that this figure could be of anyone, even a "secret master." What *is* known with

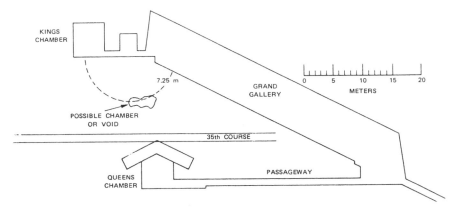

Dolphin: No.

Noone: Am I correct in the assumption that you believe this anomaly may be a hidden chamber?

Dolphin: That's right. We could have used a diamond-tipped drill to look into it this season, but we will eventually—when sufficient grant money is available—return to perform this final test.

Man continues to extract knowledge from the Great Pyramid. And the Great Pyramid, like a Secret Master, continues (like its guardian the Sphinx) to observe the coming of light over the past two million dawns.

SECRET MASTER

The ivory figure shown in Plate 5:16 (now

surety is that this statue was found, not at the site of the Great Pyramid, but 300 miles to the south in the mysterious Temple of Abydos, by Petrie. The shape of the cap on the figure's head, totally unlike regular Egyptian headdress, is also known with surety, and we see its shape and color resembling a High-Degree Mason's hat. The shape and color of the hats worn by High-Degree Freemasons are alleged to be symbolically connected with the different colors of the human corona or aura mentioned in Chapter 2 (See Plate 2:6), a luminous ring or halo surrounding a human's physical body, either of white or of colored rays. Early Christian painters depicted Jesus with a halo; early Hindu painters drew diagrams of the halo divided into seven centers of CHAKRAS (the Hindu word meaning "one of the seven centers of the aura").

What are the hidden secrets of

Freemasonry? What are the new candidates of every 32° Masonic class taught about the Great Pyramid—and why is it a secret? Perhaps an answer to this question might lie in the fact that, were the higher degrees of Freemasonry dramatized before the general public, that same general public might persecute the Masons because of a basic fear of the unknown and unusual.

If the last sentence sounds preposterous, the student of history need only recall the crackle of flames as Joan of Arc burns at the stake at Rouen. Yet she lives on in the hearts and minds of all who remember her refusal to violate her beliefs and solemn obligations.

According to Masonic historians, the hidden secrets of Freemasonry are veiled in allegory and illustrated by symbols. What

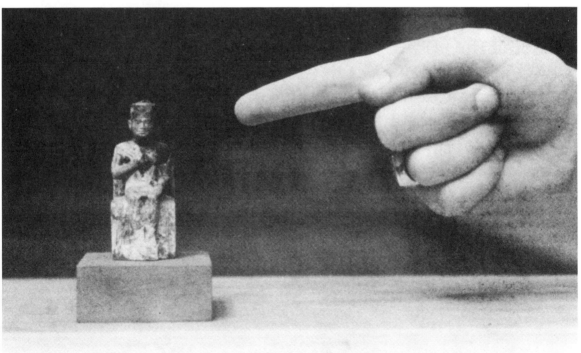

5:16. *Alleged Statue of Khufu.* The name "Khufu" is phonetically similar to the ancient Egyptian word for the Great Pyramid, Khuti, meaning "Glorious Light." The lower photograph dramatically illustrates the actual size of this tiny statue, found in a land of giant "Egyptian" statues.

127

5:17. The Sphinx.

5:18. Joan of Arc. In 1425, on a summer day, at noon, Joan was in her father's little garden. She heard a voice calling her, at her right side, in the direction of the church, and a great brightness shone upon her at the same time in the same spot. At first she was frightened, but she recovered herself on finding that "it was a worthy voice;" and, at the second call she perceived that it was the voice of angels. After this experience, Joan rallied the divided forces of France against the invading English during the Hundred Years War. "I saw them with my bodily eyes," she said six years later to her judges at Roeun, "as plainly as I see you; when they departed from me I wept and would fain have had them take me with them." Asserting her case to the end, she was condemned by the Roman Catholic Church as a witch and heretic and on May 30, 1431, the nineteen-year-old girl was burned at the stake in the marketplace of Rouen. (Quotes from *France*, Vol. II 1869, by M. Guizot and Madame Guizot De Witt).

great secret, revealed in allegory and illustrated by symbols, have sixteen Masonic Presidents of the United States learned? Perhaps they learned that Jacques de Molai, the Secret Master of Masons in France, was imprisoned for five years, repeatedly tortured, and finally burned at the stake by the covetous King Philip IV of France and Pope Clement V for refusing to reveal the hidden mysteries of Freemasonry. As the flames licked higher around Jacques de Molai, he commanded both the King of France and the Pope to appear before their maker—the Pope within forty days and the King within a year. In less than a year King Philip was killed while hunting. Less than forty days after de Molai's pronouncement Pope Clement died screaming that he was "burning up."

How is it possible that today some seven million Masonic members in the United States (to say nothing of its worldwide network of members and lodges in every free country in the world) know and keep the great secret—even from wives and close friends?

In Chapter Two of this book, it was related that J.D.W. Stall, F.R.A.S., Director of Emory University's planetarium, discovered that on 5 May 2000 all the planets in our solar system will array themselves in a grand alignment across space. To discover a knowledge of this planetary alignment (which modern science has only recently discovered) embodied in ancient Masonic lore would be an unsettling experience!

Lord Byron wrote that truth is always stranger than fiction, and it is a fact that Masons use two dating systems. The first is the regular "B.C./A.D." system of dating. The second system used by Masons for dating is *Anno Lucis* (the date memorializing the founding of *Ancient Craft Masonry* in

4000 B.C.), which Masons abbreviate A.L., that is, "in the year of Light." The ancient Egyptian word for the Great Pyramid is Khuti, phonetically similar to Khufu, and both mean "Glorious Light" or "Horizon of Heaven," similar to the aura or corona atop the Masonic pyramid on the back of the U.S. one-dollar bill. (There are twenty-eight secret Masonic symbols on the back of the U.S. dollar bill, including the Star of David, which is formed when one pyramid pointing up is overlapped by another pyramid pointing down to be seen over the eagle.)

5:20. The Great Seal of the United States with a mystical Masonic symbol of the Great Pyramid. The Latin words "Annuit Coeptis" stand for "He has blessed our beginning", while "Novus Ordo Seclorum" translates into "The new order of the Ages".

The rule and guide for the second Masonic system of dating, the A.L. system, is as follows: add 4,000 years to the "Common Era" (the A.D.) date, thus: the numbers 1982, for instance, plus 4000 (the beginning of the A.L. dating expressed in B.C. terms) together equal 5982. Thought of in terms of a six thousand-year cycle of star movements, this Masonic celestial number system gives us the exact date when all the planets in our solar system will once again be aligned across space, a date transmitted from generation to generation by a "band of men," a date only eighteen years from now. (1982).

Freemasonry's highest degree members are initiated, invested, and—all high degree Freemasons wear a golden ring with a pyramid on the front! Inscribed within the pyramid one may observe Yod, the tenth letter of the Hebrew alphabet letter-number code (Aleph = 1, Bayt = 2, etc.) When used to read the first five chapters of Genesis, the letter-number code will cut across many deep-rooted fixations "in the thoughts of man." This mathematical code, explained in *The Cipher of Genesis*, deals with states of consciousness and their relationship to life, which points out that it is not possible to "believe" in a Revelation and at the same time to *be* it. By use of the letter-number code, one discovers the first five chapters of Genesis to be a treatise on thermodynamics which contains the secret of man's transfiguration.

Inscribed on the inside of a High Degree Masonic ring is a Latin description of the "power of the ring." Could Freemasonry be part of a world-wide conspiracy secretly transmitting, from generation to generation, some ancient wisdom necessary for the evolution and preservation of the human species?

As the planet earth precessed or wobbled from the astronomical age of Taurus (the breaking of the Shell, 4000 B.C.) to the present age of Aquarius (the Water-Bearer, begun 20 August 1953), Freemasonry continued to transmit to its own initiates certain inviolate truths and dates, with its

5:19. *The Secret Master.* Wearing a "purple" cap, the Secret Master of Masons in Georgia is seated in the middle high-backed chair in this rare photograph of a secret Masonic class. Seated to his left is "Fishbait" Miller, Doorkeeper and Royal Tiler to the United States Congress ("tiler" referring anciently to the Doorkeeper of the Temple). Between 1486 B.C. (the Exodus) and Al Mamun's arrival in 820 A.D., someone closed and tiled the swivel door on the Great Pyramid's north face after a massive disturbance in the earth's tectonic plates thrust the door open (see Plate 2:7). The connection between the builders of the Great Pyramid and an ancient band of architects, contractors, priest-astronomers, and stonemasons, is, of course, Freemasonry. Modern Freemasonry evolved from the ancient "building guilds" responsible for the seven great architectural wonders of antiquity. In the 32° Masonic class shown above, "Fishbait" Miller is wearing a golden chain around his neck, composed of a series of interconnected pyramids—a symbol rampant in Freemasonry—as well as a "white" cap. Mr. Miller describes his years as Congressional Doorkeeper in his best-selling book, *Fishbait: Memoirs of the Congressional Doorkeeper.* Seated to the Secret Master's right is Wilfred Gregson, architect, Masonic historian, and author of *Evidences of Masonry in Ancient Civilization*, also wearing a symbolic "white" cap. Note the ideogram pattern on the floor.

timeless symbols and in its own special way.

No one has ever satisfactorily explained why Freemasonry has memorialized 4000 B.C. as the Year of Light. The obvious connection is the Great Pyramid—Khuti—"Glorious Light." Originally the Great Pyramid was covered with highly polished white limestone, and when the Egyptian sunlight hit its sides, it glistened with a glorious light. Four times a year the rays of the sun refracted off the Great Pyramid's south side at around noonday became visible for seven days. With the Great Pyramid's perfect alignment to the cardinal points of the compass and its unique slope of angle, the sun's rays refracted off its highly polished surface gave accurately the day upon which the winter solstice, the spring equinox, the summer solstice, and the autumnal equinox occurred. Refracted off the Great Pyramid's south side four times a year, the rays of the sun would become visible because of myriads of minute dust particles[7] suspended in the air. This refracted sunlight, as it slowly became visible, grew in intensity until it formed a brilliant shaft of light resembling the beam of a lighthouse. This radiant shaft of light was visible to all the tribes inhabiting Egypt within a one-hundred-mile radius of the Great Pyramid. Seeing this "glorious light" radiating upward from the Great Pyramid into the noonday sky, the inhabitants knew (depending upon the time of year) when it was time to sow or reap. Not understanding the scientific applications of the Great Pyramid or the seven sciences of antiquity (grammar, logic, rhetoric, arithmetic, geometry, music, and astronomy), the people knew only that they had seen "the Light of the Lord." This belief, preserved by the Hebrew tribes, later surfaced in the Old Testament book of Amos (7:7), "Thus he shewed me: and behold the Lord stood upon a wall made by a plumbline, with a plumbline in his hand."

Noah Webster, another Freemason, best

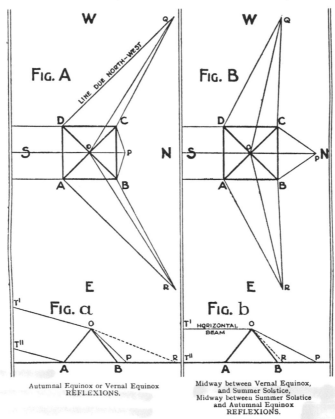

5:21. *Reflections from the Great Pyramid at the Equinoxes.* (See David Davidson's *The Great Pyramid: Its Divine Message,* Plate V).

_____

[7]See David Davidson's *The Great Pyramid: Its Divine Message,* Page 9, paragraph 1.

known for his *An American Dictionary of the English Language* (two volumes, 1828), defines a plumbline thus: "A line having a metal weight attached to one end, used to determine a perpendicular; a line perpendicular to the plane of the horizon." Towering over the surrounding trees in New York City's Central Park stands a huge Egyptian obelisk. Identical in shape to Washington's Monument, this ancient monument contained a plumbline in its Masonic "foundation deposit" (see Plates 1:10 and 1:11).

On 9 October 1880, with 8,000 Freemasons in attendance, the obelisk was raised at right angles with the plane of the horizon. Jesse B. Anthony, Secret Master of Masons of New York State, redeposited the seven ancient Masonic symbols in the foundation deposit under the obelisk, where they will rest until discovered by another generation of some future age. From time immemorial, Masons have laid the cornerstones of public and charitable institutions, monuments, and seats of learning when requested to do so, so that

> when that eternal ocean, whose waves are years, shall have engulfed all who were present at the laying ceremonies, the foundation deposit will remain to tell every passer, by its symbols, that there once existed, upon that perhaps now desolate spot, a monument consecrated to some sacred, moral or benevolent purpose, by the liberality and zeal of those men who perhaps no longer live.[8]

As the deposit was placed, thirty thousand awe-struck spectators wondered what the ancient Masonic rites they were witnessing actually meant. What Masonic rites did the public briefly glimpse?

Did George Washington, Secret Master of a Virginia Lodge of Freemasons, stick a miniature pyramid in the foundation deposit he deposited under the pure white cubical cornerstone of the White House, or did he deposit along with six other ancient Masonic symbols a plumbline?

The seven symbols resting now under the obelisk originally tiled the outer porch of the Temple of Amen, erected by Thothmes III. Why do Christians today, murmuring in their prayers, end their prayers with "Amen?" The word *amen* means the "hidden one," "only one," "secret master," and comes down to us today from the ancient Egyptian Brotherhood of Amen.[9] In the *Egyptian Book of the Dead*, one may read a prayer that begins, "Amen, amen, which art in heaven...." Were the seven symbols deposited under the obelisk at the outer porch of the Temple of Amen by the Brotherhood of Amen brought from a still earlier Empire? Were an identical set of those seven symbols deposited at a much later date in history under one of the two great pillars, Boaz and Jachin, at the outer porch of King Solomon's Temple in Jerusalem? Was it an understanding of all the seven symbols that drew 8,000 Freemasons in 1880 to New York for the redepositing of these symbols? Perhaps only the masons of the ancient building guild who deposited the foundation deposit under the northeast cornerstone of the Great Pyramid would know for sure. However, perhaps some high-degree Freemasons today know how long these symbols have been transmitted from one fraternity to another. With Freemasons all

---

[8]Brock's *Masonic Manual.*
[9]Cf. *Egyptian Book of the Dead*, Budge translation, pp. 46 and 127 of the Introduction.

5:22. KING SOLOMON'S TEMPLE. This is intricate detail showing relation one to another. You can realize from this slide the many, many hours of drawing it required of the architects draftsmen to draw all of this to scale. The plans and drawings are so complete that King Solomon's Temple could be rebuilt today if there was enough money in the world to do it and craftsmen with enough talent to execute the work.

over the world depositing these same seven symbols under the cornerstones of public and charitable institutions, monuments, and seats of learning, one can rest assured that even in the event of a global disaster the seven symbols would eventually be rediscovered by another generation in some future age.

The Revelation of St. John the Divine contains many estoeric references to the Caballistic letter-number code that holds the Bible's secret message. Most historians and religious leaders ignore or are ignorant of the fact that Revelation was the only book in the New Testament that the Councils of Nicea did not change, alter, distort, or intentionally remove (as they removed, for instance, the Gospel according to St. Thomas) to suit their own needs in acquiring new "dues paying" members for their own religion. The Councils of Nicea did not tamper with Revelation, for it contained a great three-fold curse (see Revelation 22:19) to fall upon anyone who dared alter even one word of it. Fortunately, many of these deliberately "lost" writings were discovered early in the 1920's, and are finally available to the public in a book entitled *The Lost Books of the Bible and the Forgotten Books of Eden.*[10]

St. John was very clever, for he knew that the most successful way to hide a secret is to say it openly but casually. Thus one reads in his book of the seven churches, seven Spirits, seven golden candlesticks, seven stars (the Pleiades?), seven lamps of fire, the Book of Seven Seals (or symbols), a lamb with seven horns and seven eyes, a lamb receiving seven blessings, seven trumpets, seven thunders, a seven-headed dragon with seven crowns, a seven-headed beast, seven plagues, seven golden vials, seven angels, seven mountains, and seven kings. So reads a part of the cabalistic writings of St. John the Gnostic. (For support of this interpretation, see the *Cipher of Genesis*, in which may also be found an explanation of the letter-number code, which is beyond the scope of this present work).

Unfortunately the symbols of the wise became as gods to the uninformed, and the personifcation of *maet* (Egyptian: "truth" or "justice") was temporarily lost to all but a few Hermetic fraternal orders. From books written on Masonry by Masons, one begins to wonder if today's high-degree Freemasons have learned the ancient letter-number code, unknown to their wives and close friends. George Washington wore a Masonic apron—is this connected in some way with the "First Great Light" of Genesis, where in 3:7 "they made themselves aprons?"

Is it possible to trace the history of the Cabbalah and the letter-number code? Perhaps simply to catch a glimpse of it here and there as it surfaces is sufficient for the present work.

In the Old Testament, Jacob (whose spiritual name is Israel) gives the Cabbalah to his son Joseph.[11] After Joseph's death, the Egyptian priesthood sought in vain to discover the "magic object" or document. The reason they did not find it is simple—Joseph had entrusted it to the next recipient, who would hold it inviolate and use its force, or simply transmit it to the

---

[10]**Published 1974 by the New American Library.**

[11]**Again the reader is referred to the *Cipher of Genesis* (p. 6) for a complete explanation of Biblical interpretations.**

next recipient.

We next see Moses (Mosheh)[12] receiving the Cabbalah from the *cohen* (priest) of Midian and his seven symbolic daughters. The priest of Midian entrusts the Cabbalah to Moses, changing his name from Reuel to Jethro, and Moses frees the Israelites. The Cabbalah and the mummy of Joseph leave Egypt with Moses during a great and overwhelming national disaster.

For a time the Cabbalah does not surface. But eventually it does.

"And when they brought out the money that was brought into the house of YHWH, Hilkiah the priest found a book of the law of YHWH given by Moses." (II Chronicles 34:14) "And the King and all the men of Judah and the inhabitants, and everybody went up to the House of YHWH [to hear] all the words of the Book of the Covenant found in the House of YHWH." (II Chronicles 34:30).

To answer the question of the origin of the Cabbalah adequately entails considering the possibility of a technologically advanced empire prior to ancient Egypt. It also includes keeping the mind alert to the fact that the *Egyptian Book of the Dead* was discovered in about 4266 B.C.,[13] a date very close to the Masonic Year of Light (4000 B.C.)

According to E.A. Wallis Budge, late Keeper of Assyrian and Egyptian Antiquities in the British Museum, who gave mankind its first translation of the *Egyptian Book of the Dead,*

> The home, origin, and early history of the collection of ancient religious texts which have descended to us are, at present, unknown, and all working theories regarding them, however strongly supported by apparently well-ascertained facts, must be carefully distinguished as theories only.[14]

The oldest edition of the *Book of the Dead*, according to Budge, was discovered "in the reign of Hesep-ti, the fifth king of the first dynasty, about B.C. 4266."[15] Speculating on the origin of these prehistoric writings, Budge writes:

> Whether they were composed by the inhabitants of Egypt, who recorded them in hieroglyphic characters, and who have left the monuments which are the only trustworthy sources of information on the subject, or whether they were brought into Egypt by the early immigrants from the Asiatic continent whence they came, or whether they represent the religious books of the Egyptians incorporated with the funeral texts of some prehistoric dwellers on the banks of the Nile, are all questions which the possible discovery of inscriptions belonging to the first dynasties of the Early Empire can alone decide.[16]

Thanks to E.A. Wallis Budge, we of the present age may read of the discovery of the presently oldest-known chapter in the *Egyptian Book of the Dead* directly from the *Book of the Dead* itself:

> This chapter was found in [the city

---

[12] Whose name in the letter-number code indicates water (as the source of life), cosmic breath, and life.
[13] Budge, p. xiii, Introduction.
[14] Budge, p. xiii, Introduction.
[15] Budge, p. xiii, Introduction.
[16] Budge, p. xiii, Introduction.

of] Hermopolis upon a slab of iron inscribed with lapis-lazuli [an aluminous mineral of a rich blue color used by Tubal-cain and other early artificers] found by the royal son Heru-Tata-F in his inspection of the temples, he brought it to the King when he saw that it was a mystery great unseen and unbeheld.

The text in the *Book of the Dead* goes on to say that the slab of iron, inlaid with lapis-lazuli, was discovered in "the foundation deposit" of an old temple under repair by the foreman of the builders. Writing on the antiquity of the text, Budge says:

> ...the greater part of the texts comprised in the Book of the Dead are far older than the period of Mena [Menes], the first historical King of Egypt. Certain sections indeed appear to belong to an indefinitely remote and primeval time.[17]

Who wrote this earliest-known codification of moral tenets basic to an outstanding world religion and left it to be discovered in a *foundation deposit* by the early inhabitants of Egypt? Surely this document was not compiled by primitives. Was this document brought from Mu? If not from Mu, then where? Who at that time knew how to make iron? Budge documents the fact that the early Egyptian scribes who copied the writing engraved in iron by a master "were perplexed and hardly understood the texts which they had before them."[18] Was the master engraver Tubal-cain mentioned in Genesis 4:22? When this Cabbalah was brought to the Pharoah, the people went to hear the public reading of this mysterious writing, but understood it not. At a little chapel within the Temple of Amen, solemn ceremonies were held and prayers offered in thanks for the return of THE WORD.

A period of stillness hung like a cloud over Egypt for the next several days. Soon the awe-struck Egyptian public caught a rare glimpse of the Secret Master of the Brotherhood of Amen and watched in amazement as he and his brethren performed an ancient rite employed in association with foundation deposits. The seven symbols deposited under the obelisk at the outer porch of the Temple of Amen were to rest undisturbed until moved to Alexandria, Egypt, and later to New York—where they now rest, waiting to be rediscovered in some future era.

Towering over the surrounding buildings in Washington, D.C. stands Washington's Monument, the largest obelisk in the United States. The amount of knowledge we of the present possess about ancient times is only a small portion of the complete story of Mankind. If the mistakes of the past are not uncovered and revealed to the public, we of the present age will soon be doomed to relive the mistakes of the past.

And Moses reburied the mummy of Joseph in Schechem in a parcel of ground which Jacob bought of the sons of Hamor, the father of Shechem, for an hundred pieces of silver, and deposited with it...a small book.

For a time the Cabbalah does not surface. But eventually it does in any age.

---

[17]Budge, p. xiii, Introduction.
[18]Budge, p. xiii, Introduction.

PART II

CHAPTER SIX
THE CASE BEGINS

Two steps become necessary at this point. The first step requires that we return to Al Mamun, whom we left in the Great Pyramid's Middle Chamber "crystal-gazing," and with him make our way up and into the very heart of this awesome citadel of sand kings.

The second step requires that we do not permit ourselves to forget that in all stages and periods of civilization on which we have sufficient data, the highest examples of human development exist alongside more primitive and barbarous individuals who copy the actions of their leaders.

THE MIDDLE CHAMBER

Disappointed at finding the Middle Chamber of the Great Pyramid as empty of treasure as the Subterranean Pit, Al Mamun angrily whirled about and stared directly into the leering, greedy eyes of his men glistening like red-hot coals in the torch-lit chamber. Seeing their sweating faces reflecting his own disappointment, Al Mamun suddenly became as fluid as quicksilver and sprang up the mysterious step he had gingerly stepped down minutes earlier.

In his hasty exit from the Middle Chamber Al Mamun failed to observe a subtle imprint on the left wall of the passage. This column-shaped imprint or depression contains what appears to be the bearded face of a man strikingly similar to the face imprinted on the ancient Shroud of Turin.

The Shroud of Turin is a linen cloth 14½ feet in length and 3½ feet in width, bearing a photographically negative image of a bearded man—scourged, wearing a crown of thorns, crucified, and pierced through the side by a pointed instrument. The shroud is alleged to be the burial garment of Jesus (see Plate 6:1).

The face, alive with expression and its details almost portrait-like, is imprinted on the wall approaching the Middle Chamber of the Great Pyramid. The face imprinted on the Shroud of Turin is similar in appearance (compare Plates 6:2 and 6:3 with Plate 6:1), except that the eyes are open in the face in the Pyramid.

In November 1973, St. John's Cathedral in Turin allowed a team of eminent scientists from different disciplines to examine and subject to various tests (optical, nuclear, radiation) the negative imprint on the shroud. After a series of exhaustive tests with the most advanced scientific equipment available, the only explanation for the imprint's presence—considered by the Nobel Prize-winning organic and nuclear chemist, Dr. Willard Libby—was that at the moment of Jesus's resurrection a microsecond exposure of intense heat imprinted the white linen wrapping with the image of his body.

The Japanese victims of the atomic bomb blast who were "frozen" or negatively imprinted like dark shadows on the downtown walls of Hiroshima are explained today by the intense heat of the atomic blast. Could an extremely intense heat have

Knowledge is power.

Francis Bacon
Meditationes Sacrae

Laws are like cobwebs that entangle the weak, but are broken by the strong.

Solon

Every man has within him his own Pathmos. He is free to venture, or not to venture, upon that terrifying promontory of thought from which one can see into the shadows. If he refrains from doing so, he continues to live an ordinary life, with ordinary thoughts, ordinary virtues, ordinary beliefs and ordinary doubts — and it is well that he should. It is clearly best for his internal peace of mind. For if he ventures on to this summit, he is lost. He will have glimpsed the mighty waves of the Marvelous — and no one can look upon that ocean with impunity... He persists in contemplating this alluring abyss, in exploring the unexplored, in remaining detached from life on the Earth, and in his efforts to penetrate a forbidden world, to touch the untouchable, to gaze on the invisible he returns again and again to the edge of the precipice, leans over, takes one step down and then another — and that is how one penetrates the impenetrable and loses oneself in a limitless extension of infinity.

Victor Hugo
(Quoted in *The Morning of the Magicians*
by Louis Pauwels and Jacques Bergier)

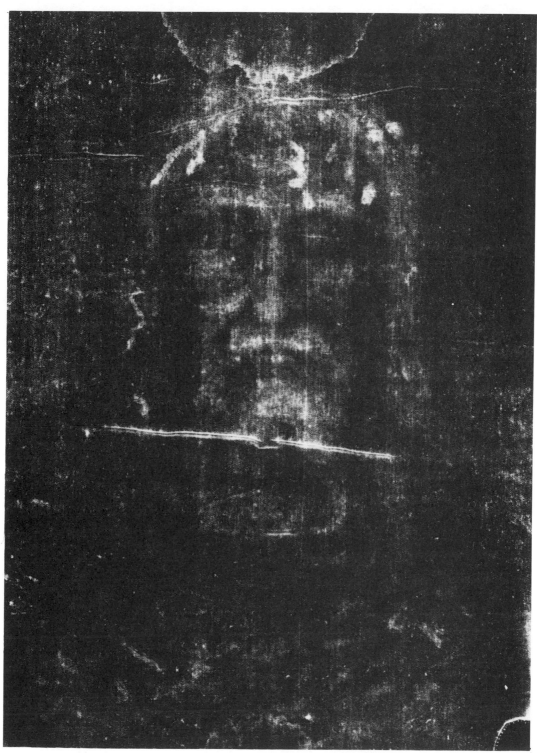

6:1. *The Face on the Shroud of Turin.* Compare this with Plates 6:2 and 6:3.

143

6:2 *The Position of the Face on the Wall in the Passageway.*

6:3. *The Face on the Wall of the Passageway.* This is photographed from within the chamber looking north, as in the diagram in Plate 6:4. The small stone step in the background is a modern adjunct making it easier for tourists to step down the larger step. The bearded face of a man, similar to the face imprinted on the Shroud of Turin, may be seen in the extreme upper left-hand corner of this photograph.

swept through the passageway leading to the Middle Chamber of the Great Pyramid, burning or imprinting someone's image on the wall? The negative and positive terminals of a car's battery will accumulate a buildup of salt incrustation. Could the Great Pyramid's salt-incrusted Middle Chamber have housed some type of battery at some unremembered time in our past? If so, what would its source of power have been? Such speculations may yet lead us to even stranger speculations as we continue upward with Al Mamun.

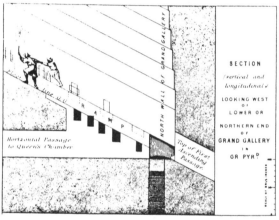

6:4. Section of the Northern End of the Grand Gallery.

Passing this silent sentinel, Al Mamun returned to the level plateau at the top of the Ascending Passage and froze in his tracks. He had sensed the presence of some other life-form. Bidding his men to be quiet, Al Mamun listened. The silence, like that felt beneath the earth in deep mines and caves, was deafening. At first the beating sound he heard he took for his own heart, but the beating sound increased in volume and from somewhere in the ominous void above

drew closer. Raising his torch above his head, Al Mamun saw a huge, strangely constructed corridor sloping upwards into the black and mysterious heart of the building. Suddenly, out of the inky darkness above, a leathery shape emitted an eerie squeak and flew by his head.

6:5. *An Egyptian Bat.* The bats found by Al Mamun in the eighth century A.D. had a wingspread of three feet.

THE GRAND GALLERY

Realizing that it was only a large bat, Al Mamun remembered that he and his men had daily seen large swarms of bats emerging from two small, unexplained openings high on the north and south faces of the Great Pyramid each day at dusk to feed. He cursed himself for being afraid. It had been the bats that had been his first concrete indication that the building *must* have above-ground passages, like those mentioned in his reading of the ancient writings of Ibrahim ben Ebn Wasuff Shah[1] and other Coptic writers.

Standing in this bat-infested cavity, Al Mamun now knew that the ancient writings of Ibrahim ben Ebn Wasuff Shah were

---

[1]The traditions of the later Egyptians were preserved by their descendants, the Copts, whose teachings were held in high respect by the later Arabs.

6:6. *The Grand Gallery of the Great Pyramid, Looking North (Down).* Note first overlap on left exhibits signs of calcination. Compare with Plate 6:21.

true concerning above-ground passages. Suddenly Al Mamun wondered if the other part of the ancient writing could be true—the part that said the Giza complex was built to memorialize a tremendous cataclysm in the earth's planetary system, which "affected the globe with fire and flood."

Pausing a moment to consider the strange construction of this Grand Gallery, Al Mamun wondered what lay at its top. His heartbeat quickened as he considered a room filled with treasure. Using as hand and foot holds a strange series of notches cut into the left and right sides of the Grand Gallery's walls, Al and his men scurried upward into the bat-infested cavity.

When he first saw the Grand Gallery in the early 20's, P. D. Ouspensky, author of *A New Model of the Universe*, described it thus (p. 313):

This corridor is the key to the whole pyramid. What strikes you first is that everything in this corridor is of very exact and fine workmanship.

6:8. *Al Mamun in the Grand Gallery.*

6:7 Grand Gallery.

The lines are straight, the angles are correct. At the same time there is no doubt that this corridor was not made for walking along. Then for what was it made?

Ouspensky first sensed an answer to his own question by the holes, mathematically correct notched divisions, cut into either side of the Grand Gallery. These notches are so precisely divided along the entire length of the Grand Gallery that Ouspensky commented:

And suddenly it becomes clear to you that up and down this 'corridor' some kind of stone or metal plate, or 'carriage', must have moved, which possibly, in its turn, served as a support for some measuring apparatus and could be fixed in any position.

The Renaissance astronomer, Tycho de Brahe, set out to orient his famed observatory at Urambourg to true north; he missed it by about twice what the Great Pyramid misses true north by on its east side. How accurately the Great Pyramid is aligned to the cardinal points of the compass may be found in Dr. I.E.S. Edwards's book, *The Pyramids of Egypt* (p. 255):

...the perimeter of the bed deviates from a truly level plane by only a little more than half an inch. An almost imperceptible amount by which the southeast corner stands higher than the northwest corner.

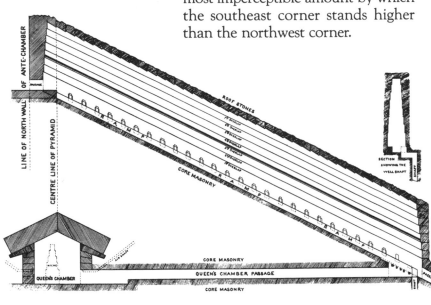

6:9. *The Grand Gallery*. This picture shows three-quarters of the Grand Gallery's length (cut away), showing how even one quarter of its length could be used as a meridian slot for observing the transit of the stars. In Washington, D.C., the U.S. Naval Observatory utilizes a system in which starlight is reflected into a pool of mercury to note a split second in the daily transit of the stars.

The bed or ground the Great Pyramid stands on covers thirteen and one-half acres, or about seven square city blocks. Homes today are not constructed with anywhere near this degree of accuracy. Since the ground was levelled to support the Great Pyramid, no other civilization on this planet has ever completed, *or even undertaken*, such a massive levelling task.

Dr. Edwards goes on to say (p. 256):

> ...it seems remarkable that on sides exceeding 9,000 inches [750 feet] in length so small an error should have occurred, especially when it is remembered that the central mound of rock would have rendered impracticable any measurement of the diagonals to check the accuracy of the square. An exact orientation of the Pyramid on the four cardinal points could only have been achieved with the aid of one or more of the celestial bodies...

The Grand Gallery, aimed like a giant telescope at a particular celestial body in the earth's southern sky—before its view of the heavens was blocked by the completion of the building—points to where radio astronomy has just pinpointed the supernova (or giant stellar explosion) nearest to our solar system of which modern science has any knowledge. The Great Pyramid's Grand Gallery is focused at this particular spot in the earth's southern sky. Is this just chance or coincidence?

In the late 1960's Dr. Antony Hewish, 1974 co-recipient of the Nobel Prize in physics, was working at England's Mullard Radio Astronomy Observatory. Hewish began to track a mysterious rhythmic series of pulses, clearly radio emissions, from a point in the earth's southern sky. Unable to locate even the shrunken remains of a collapsed

6:10. *The Transit Circle, Royal Observatory, Greenwich.* This shows a similar type of orientation to that which may be seen in the Grand Gallery.

---

star visually, Hewish dubbed the phenomenon LGM (an abbreviation that, *half*-jestingly, stood for "Little Green Men").

In another part of the world George Mi-

149

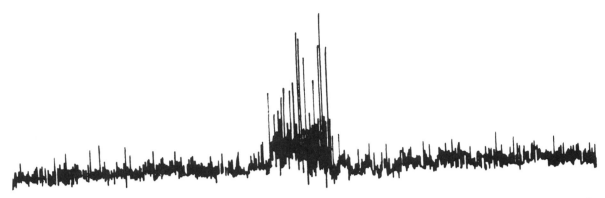

6:11. *The Pulse Record of Vela* X. This radio pulse record of the fast-spinning (eleven spins around its axis every second) remnant of the exploded star Vela X, made at the very moment of its discovery, confirmed the accuracy of the cuneiform star catalogue. Professor M:I. Large, co-discoverer of Vela X, made the original radio pulse record at Australia's Molonglo Radio Observatory, of which the above is a copy. The pulsar this supernova left behind has been registered as PSR 0833-45.

chanowsky, author of *The Once and Future Star*, was deciphering an incredible message cut, carved, and indented in an ancient cuneiform clay tablet (#BM-86378, British Museum). The ancient Sumerian cuneiform table Michanowsky was deciphering described a giant star exploding within a triangle formed by the three stars Zeta Puppis, Gamma Velorum, and Lambda Velorum. These three stars are located in the earth's southern sky, and (unknown to Michanowsky at the time) were being tracked by Antony Hewish at the Mullard Radio Astronomy Observatory in England.

A breakthrough in astrophysics soon allowed Antony Hewis to leap-frog from signal analysis and Little Green Men to pulsars—one of the most monumental scientific achievements of this century. Antony Hewish, employing a method to time the pulse-rate of a neutron star, demonstrated that the strange rhythmic pulses were radio emissions from a star that had collapsed or blown itself up in the earth's southern sky some time around 4000 B.C., a date memorialized in the mysteries of Freemasonry as *Anno Lucis*, the Year of Light.

Michanowsky continued deciphering the Sumerian star catalogue, containing observations going back thousands of years. Working on a "path with heart,"[2] Michanowsky soon read a sentence in the text that troubled and worried him. The remarkably accurate star catalogue now stated that the blazing star that had exploded within the triangle would again be seen by man in 6,000 years. Michanowsky, bothered by this Bible-like bit of prophecy, wondered how in the world a star which blew

[2]In *The Teachings of Don Juan: A Yaqui Way of Knowledge*, Don Juan explained to Carlos Castaneda that "for me there is only the traveling on paths that have heart, on any path that may have heart. There I travel, and the only worthwhile challenge is to traverse its full length. And there I travel, looking, looking, breathlessly."

6:12. *The Cuneiform Star Catalogue.* This clay tablet, containing observations going back thousands of years, is humanity's most remarkable star catalogue. This tablet also informs us of the sources of the names of well-known stars and constellations.

itself up around 6,000 years before could ever be seen again by man.

In 1977 a cooperative effort by scientists at England's Mullard Radio Astronomy Observatory and Australia's Molonglo Radio Observatory provided the answer. Utilizing an ingenious new system, computers were used to collect, analyze, and register the incoming faint light flashes, too dim to photograph, from the collapsed star today named Vela X.

Of course, the very instant this new scientific method was employed to see the remnant light of this "once and future star," the Bible-like prophecy in the ancient cunei-

form tablet was fulfilled. Mankind had indeed seen this ancient star again.

Michanowsky has presented evidence that this gigantic star explosion decisively influenced western religious symbolism and star mythology. In addition, Michanowsky provides a startling explanation for the construction of ziggurats and pyramids, and for their relationship to the origins of the Sumerian civilization.

Michanowsky's research was centered around the ancient Sumerian city of Eridu, located northwest of the present shoreline of the Persian Gulf. Eridu is located at +30° of longitude. Turning a globe, one can see that the Great Pyramid is also located at +30° of longitude. The latitude of the

6:13. *The Grand Gallery Looking South (Up).* The wooden steps and handrails are modern additions.

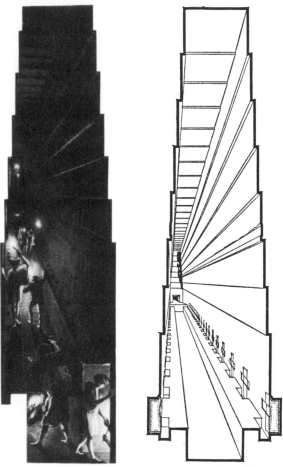

6:14. *Two Views of the Grand Gallery.*

Great Pyramid is 30°00 minutes north. A supernova explosion observable at Eridu would also have been observable at the Giza complex. The question which must now be answered is, would the light of the supernova Vela X have been observable through the Great Pyramid's Grand Gallery in 4000 B.C.?

An answer to this question I knew must come only from a trained and reputable astronomer or astrophysicist. Attempting to

determine exactly how many degrees above the horizon at Cairo, Egypt, Vela X would have been in 4000 B.C. would not be easy. No one as yet has succeeded in constructing a valid formula for calculating the angle of the ecliptic in ancient times, because, as Professor Livio Catullo Stecchini points out:

> The angle of the ecliptic has decreased slowly (today it is 23°27 minutes; it was about at 23°45 minutes in the age of Ptolemy), and accordingly the Tropic of Cancer has moved south. This movement is due to the gravitational pull of the planets, particularly Jupiter and Venus.[3]

When one considers that we are closer in time to Cleopatra and Ptolemy than they were to the construction of the Great Pyramid, the enormous amount of time to be considered becomes apparent. To place the supernova Vela X, after almost 6,000 years, to within ten degrees of the visual angle of the Grand Gallery of the Great Pyramid could only be considered to be due to chance at best. To place Vela X to even within eight degrees of the visual angle of the Grand Gallery might be termed "coincidence" if it were accomplished; to place Vela X within six or fewer degrees of the Grand Gallery's visual field of command would confirm that the Grand Gallery is indeed focused on a position in the earth's southern sky where radio astronomy has just pinpointed the supernova Vela X.

The Great Pyramid's Grand Gallery is focused upward into the earth's southern sky at an angle of 26°. Today the north/south declination[4] of Vela X is -45°. Its present east/west measurement is 8 hours 33 min-

---

[3]*Notes on the Relation of Ancient Measures to the Great Pyramid,* p. 295. **(This is the Appendix to** Tompkins, *Secrets of the Great Pyramid.*)

[4]**The distance of a heavenly body from the celestial equator, measured on a great circle passing through the pole and the body.**

utes, which places it 15° above the horizon at the Giza complex. This position is eleven degrees lower than where the Great Pyramid's Grand Gallery is presently focused. To determine exactly how many degrees above the Giza complex Vela X would have been in 4000 B.C., the earth's "wobble," or precession of equinoxes,[5] would have to be computed.

I called the U.S. Naval Observatory in Washington, D.C. Speaking to Dr. Gart Westerhout, the Scientific Director, I asked his help in determining the precession of the equinoxes in order to determine how many degrees above the horizon at the Giza complex Vela X would have been in 4000 B.C. Being kind enough to help, he called the next day and told me that the right ascension of Vela X in 4000 B.C. was 4 hours 53 minutes and its declination - 40.3°, which would place it 20° above the horizon—only 6° off from where the Grand Gallery presently points.

Dr. Kenneth L. Franklin at New York's Hayden Planetarium, whom I also asked this question, returned my call to tell me that the right ascension of Vela X in 4000 B.C. was 5 hours 10 minutes and its declination - 38.5°, which would place it 21.5° above the horizon—only 4.5° off from where the Grand Gallery presently points. Dr. David S. Evans, an astronomer at McDonald Observatory, University of Texas at Austin, also helped. His figures show Vela X with a right ascension of 5 hours 10 minutes and a declination of - 37.80°, which would place Vela X 22.20° above the horizon—less than four degrees off from where the Grand Gallery now points. Dr. Paul Gorenstien, an astrophysicist at the Smithsonian/ Harvard Institution for Astrophysics, also computed the precession of the equinoxes for me. His computations show Vela X with a right ascension of 5 hours 40 minutes, and a declination of - 37.6°, which would place Vela X 22.5° above the horizon at the Giza complex—also within less than four degrees of where the Grand Gallery now points.

These figures show the possibility of a connection between the most awesome star explosion perhaps ever witnessed by humans and the alignment of the Great Pyramid's Grand Gallery. If the Ascending Passage and Grand Gallery were built to observe this supernova explosion, which appeared as a gigantic light source by night or as a somewhat smaller second sun by day, then perhaps, as Dr. David D. Zink points out in his book *The Ancient Stones Speak* (p. 178):

> ...changes witnessed in the heavens and associated with these catastrophes led ancient man to precise observations of the skies.... The beginning of astronomy was motivated by survival, not superstition.

With the recent discovery of Vela X, the ancient writing of Ibrahim ben Ebn Wasuff Shah:

> The Giza complex was built to memorialize a tremendous cataclysm in the Earth's planetary system which affected the globe with fire and flood.[6]

and later Arabian authors may be looked at in a new light. Thus, Mohammed Ebn Abd Al Hokm:

---

[5]An astronomical phenomenon consisting of a slow movement of the equinoctial points around the ecliptic.

[6]This and the following quotations from C. Staniland Wake, *The Origin and Significance of the Great Pyramid* (appendix).

The Pyramids were constructed by Sheddad Ben Ad before the deluge.

And Abou Mohammed Al Hassan Ben Ahmad Ben Yakub Al Hamadani:

The Pyramids were antediluvian, and they resisted the force of the great flood.

Masoudi, who died in 345 A.D., translated from the Coptic language (an ancient Hamitic tongue used in Egypt until superseded as a living language by Arabic) this tradition:

Surid, one of the Kings of Egypt before the flood, built the two great Pyramids. The reason for building the Pyramids was the following dream, which happened to Surid three hundred years previous to the flood. It appeared to him that the earth was overthrown, and that the inhabitants were laid prostrate upon it; *that the stars wandered confusedly from their courses,*[7] and clashed together with a tremendous noise. The King then directed the astronomers to ascertain by taking the altitude whether the stars foretold any great catastrophe, and the result announced an approaching deluge. The King ordered the Pyramids to be built and also ordered the priest to deposit within them accounts of their wisdom and acquirements in the different arts and sciences.

The legends and myths of all ancient civilizations speak of a great destructive flood affecting mankind.[8] Was a worldwide cataclysmic deluge triggered by a sudden change in the orbital geometry of this planet—or did a stellar explosion in the southern constellation Vela significantly melt, like some giant ultraviolet cosmic sunlamp, the Antarctic ice mass to produce worldwide floods?

It is interesting to note that today the female branch of Freemasonry places great emphasis and importance on a symbol representing a *blazing star within a triangle,* which it identifies, in its esoteric rites, with the "Queen of the South" mentioned in I Kings 10:10. Who was this Queen of the South? Immanuel Velikovsky, in his book *Peoples of the Sea* (p. 107) identifies the Queen of the South with the Egyptian Queen Hatshepsut[9] and demonstrates that the Queen of the South, the Egyptian Queen Hatshepsut, and the Queen of Sheba (who visited Solomon's temple) are one and the same.

Approaching the top of the Grand Gallery, Al Mamun saw before him a giant stone step three feet high. Clambering up this step, he stood on a level platform measuring 6 feet x 8 feet. Turning and looking down the gallery he had just climbed (it now being lit along its entire length by the string of torch-bearing men following him), Al Mamun surveyed this strangely constructed corridor more closely.

The Grand Gallery is a spectacular corbelled vault of unparalleled dimensions. P. D. Ouspensky considered this gallery the key to the Pyramid. The architect Wilfred

[7]Velikovsky demonstrates that the Earth experienced a shift in its axis as Venus nearly collided with it. During such a shift the stars would "appear" to move as the Earth rolled over.

[8]See Velikovsky, *Worlds in Collision, Ages in Chaos,* and *Earth in Upheaval,* as well as Suares, the *Cipher of Genesis.*

[9]An Egyptian queen who built a pyramid temple on the west bank of the Nile at Thebes and visited King Solomon's temple.

Gregson expressed his opinion that the number seven would be found to be a very important measurement in connection with the pyramid building. The construction and measurements of the Grand Gallery justify the positions of both these men. The height of the Grand Gallery is 28 feet, divisible by the number 7 four times. Its polished limestone walls rise vertically to a height of 7 feet 6 inches, above which 7 corbelled courses of fine limestone (each course overlapped inward 3″) rise to the gallery's roof. The roof of the Grand Gallery is comprised of forty stones. To receive the bottom of each roof-stone, the tops of the gallery's side walls are cut like sawteeth so that each roof-stone is individually supported (none presses down on its neighbor), and before the building's completion each roof-stone was individually removable.

Because of the research of men like Sir Norman Lockyer (who in *The Dawn of Astronomy*[10] said that the Great Pyramid was "built by a new invading race representing an advance in astronomical thought"), Peter Tompkins and Livio Catullo Stecchini (whose research was reported in *Secrets of the Great Pyramid*), and Giorgio de Santillana and Hertha von Dechend (authors of *Hamlet's Mill: An Essay on Myth and the Frame of Time*), I discovered that the stellar or supernova explosion of Vela X 6,000 years ago was observable from the Grand Gallery of the Great Pyramid. We also know that the ancient architects of the Pyramid could, by the removal of single roofstones, have observed the movement of the planets in the earth's northern hemisphere, as well as pinpointed the earth's pole star (the "North Star").

The overall length of the Grand Gallery is 157 feet. The length of the Ascending Passage is 129 feet. The total length of both is 286.1 feet. In Chapter Five, the architect Wilfred Gregson remarked, "if it [the number 286.1] had been 287, *seven* would have gone into it 41 times, wouldn't it?" The roof of the Grand Gallery is 41″ wide. The floor of the Grand Gallery is 41″ wide. The two side-ramps of the gallery each extend 20.6″ inward, which together total 41″. The 41″ of the gallery's side-ramps and the 41″ of floor which separates the two side-ramps total 82″—double the width of the gallery's roof.

A mysterious track, six inches wide and 3/4″ deep, located 5¼″ above the third overlap, runs the length of the gallery approximately midway between the floor and roof. This track had a mechanical function discussed later in this chapter.

Modern research has demonstrated that the Great Pyramid's Grand Gallery could function much like a modern telescope. This gallery would allow a band of supremely dedicated ancient astronomers to make extremely accurate maps and tables of stellar hemispheres, and to observe a supernova explosion hundreds of times as bright as common novae—a supernova whose violent bursting may have affected the globe with an enormous amount of radioactivity during the junction of the constellations Leo and Virgo at a summer solstice shortly before 4000 B.C. Sir Norman Lockyer believed that the Sphinx, half lion (Leo) and half virgin (Virgo), was built during this junction.

Could the violent bursting of Vela X have affected the globe with fire and flood? Did the violent bursting of Vela X produce an immense flux of high-energy-charged particles which entered the earth's atmosphere, changed its properties, and damaged

---

[10]See the Bibliography for these and other books reporting important research.

6:15. Sir Norman Lockyer.

the atmospheric ozone to let in large quantities of ultraviolet radiation?

Dr. Carl Sagan, speculating on the evolution of human intelligence in his best-selling book *The Dragons of Eden*, discusses the possible effects of a close supernova explosion (p. 145):

> Nocturnal animals, such as the mammals of the time, and deep-sea animals, such as fish, could have survived this higher ultraviolet intensity; but daytime animals that lived on land or near the surface of the waters would have been preferentially destroyed.

In his book *The Once and Future Star,*

George Michanowsky says (p. 5):

> The psychological impact of this celestial apparition on our culture was overwhelming. In addition, the radiation it generated may have had significant environmental and perhaps even biological consequences on earth.

What biological consequences could the explosion of Vela X have produced on earth?[11]

In *The Dragons of Eden* (pp. 27-28), Sagan discusses the biological effect of a close supernova explosion on human DNA (the genetic material of all life on earth, usually arranged in a double helix as is shown in Plate 2:6):

> Mutations are caused by radioactivity in the environment...mutations are required for evolution. A mutation in a DNA molecule within a chromosome of a skin cell in my index finger has no influence on heredity. Fingers are not involved, at least directly, in the propagation of the species. What counts are mutations in the gametes, the eggs and sperm cells, which are the agents of sexual reproduction... Do we owe our existence to a mighty stellar catastrophe that elsewhere destroyed biospheres and worlds?

Sagan says Dr. I.S. Shklovskii of the Institute for Cosmic Research, Soviet Academy of Sciences, Moscow, has suggested the hypothesis that dinosaurs vanished from the earth almost overnight because of a supernova. Brad Steiger, in his book *Worlds Before Our Own*, presents photographs of

---

[11] Three U.S. government scientists, Drs. Paul Crutzen, John McAfee, and George Reid of the Department of Commerce, believe that a supernova may have led to the extinction of dinosaurs. According to their 1978 report a close supernova explosion would lead to depletion of the earth's ozone layer, *cooler* temperatures, and drought, wiping out most of the plants depended upon by *non-carnivorous* dinosaurs for their sustenance.

tracks made by the most vicious dinosaur ever known (tyrannosaurus rex), found side by side with human footprints beside the Paluxy River near Glen Rose, Texas. Some paleontologists (who have never seen the tracks *in situ*) have declared them to be too large to be human, because they measure 16″ from toe to heel. Others who have never examined the tracks and footprints *in situ* have declared them fraudulent because "man did not live when the dinosaur did." Other paleontologists have stated that the tracks and footprints could not be considered unless the tracks and footprints had pressure ridges formed by the displacement of mud around the feet.

Dr. James A. Jensen, a paleontologist at Brigham Young University, Utah, discovered the biggest dinosaur found so far in 1979, on a slope of the Rocky Mountains in western Colorado. When I interviewed Dr. Jensen, he told me he had named the huge reptile "Ultra-Supersaurus" because "its height was about 65 feet; its length was about 80 feet to 90 feet; and its weight about 85 to 90 tons."[12] Until Dr. Jensen's find, the tallest reptile skeletal remains on display were those of a 40′-high reptile in a Berlin museum.

I asked Dr. Jensen if he had ever examined *in situ* the dinosaur tracks and human footprints found side by side in a riverbank beside the Paluxy River. Dr. Jensen told me he had never seen them, but "they must be fraudulent because man did not live in the age of the dinosaurs." Dr. Jensen also told me that all dinosaurs were, without exception, cold-blooded.

It is interesting to note that, although Dr.

Jensen does not believe man lived in the age of dinosaurs, as a bishop in the Church of Jesus Christ of Latter-Day Saints (Mormon Church) he preaches sermons based on the *Book of Mormon*. The *Book of Mormon* is primarily the religious history of two Hebrew colonies who left Jerusalem nearly 600 years before Christ—just prior to the capture of Jerusalem by the warriors of Babylon—and settled in Mexico. The *Book of Mormon* states that these colonies built pyramids and that Jesus, after the resurrection, visited them. The visit of Jesus, they believe, inspired the legend of Quetzalcoatl (the white and bearded god of ancient Mexico, whose symbol was a winged and feathered serpent representing wisdom, or someone who could achieve the union of opposites).[13] The founders of the Mormon religion, while alone in the woods, state that they received the *Book of Mormon* (originally engraved on plates of gold) when "an angel of God came down from heaven, and he brought and laid before our eyes, that we beheld and saw the plates."[14] For Dr. Jensen, a practicing Mormon bishop, to believe the above and not even consider the possibility that man and dinosaurs might have coexisted on our planet seems a little strange.

If an angel can come down from heaven with gold plates, is it impossible to think that a few types of dinosaur survived in small numbers and coexisted with man? If they did, it might explain why early man built his homes of huge and massive blocks of stone. A modern home would offer little protection from a hungry lion or bear, let alone anything larger. As no one has ever explained how early man could have

[12]In *Omni* magazine (November 1979, p. 36) its was pointed out that "Jensen estimates the leg height at 18′ because "no leg bones have been unearthed."

[13]Jesus said (Matthew 10:16) "Be ye therefore-wise as serpents." According to tradition Quetzalcoatl, after teaching in Mexico for some time, left Mexico sailing east — the direction he had arrived from.

[14]*Book of Mormon*, Introduction.

6:19. The Great Wall of Sacsayhuman.

moved and built with cyclopean masonry (such as the great wall of Sacsayhuaman near Cuzco, Peru, which contains one stone whose weight is 440 tons and hundreds of others from 100 to 300 tons), one may speculate that perhaps early man trained one species of dinosaur to pull the enormous blocks. An "Alley Oop" riding on the back of Dino the Dinosaur might help explain why the oldest stone remains are generally the largest and the most perfectly executed. If any species of dinosaur was still around 6,000 years ago, would the explosion of Vela X have destroyed them? Dr. Jensen's speculation that the human footprints must be fraudulent prompted me to investigate further, because a great deal of Earth's history seems to hinge on the extinction of the di-

nosaurs *before* the appearance of man.

If some species of dinosaur was employed by our ancient ancestors to drag enormous blocks from the quarry to their construction site, perhaps it was a warm-blooded dinosaur. Recently Dr. Robert Bakker, a paleontologist at Harvard University, suggested that some dinosaurs were warm-blooded.

I called the Somervell County Museum in Glen Rose, Texas. Speaking to the custodian, Mrs. Jeanette Mack, I learned that a massive investigation of these tracks and footprints had been conducted by Dr. Wilber Fields at the Ozark College, Joplin, Missouri. Calling Dr. Fields, I learned that he had been to Glen Rose many times, and that his research indicated to his colleagues and himself that the dinosaur tracks and human footprints "because of pressure ridges and various other characteristics are without a doubt genuine."

6:16. Dr. Clifford L. Burdick, Arizona geologist, with an example of a giant man footprint and a dinosaur footprint taken from Dinosaur Valley State Park, Glen Rose, Texas. The Paluxy River is the fastest flowing river in Texas. Most of the year the river is placid, but when the yearly floods come the water's tremendous force washes away stones and boulders (some of which weigh a ton or more). Sunday, July 11, 1971, not one drop of water flowed over the dam in Glen Rose. The Paluxy River below the dam was completely dry and on that day Dr. Cecil N. Dougherty photographed man and dinosaur tracks *side by side* in the river bottom.

One may remember Gen. 6:4, Deut. 3:11, Joshua 13:12, 15:8, 17:15, 18:6 and the well known I Samuel 17:4 (the Hebrew cubit equals about 1.5 feet).

Brad Steiger begins his book *Worlds Before Our Own* by saying:

> Archaeologists, anthropologists, and various academicians who play the 'Origins of Man' game, reluctantly and only occasionally acknowledge instances where unique skeletal and cultural evidence from the prehistoric record suddenly appear long before they should—and in places where they should not.

Steiger then goes on in the next two hundred pages of his book to list hundreds of "erratics" (unique skeletal and cultural evidence) appearing long before it is generally accepted that they should have. Many of the "erratics" indicate that man and dinosaurs did co-exist.[15]

Years before Steiger's book was published, Harper and Row published Peter Tompkins's *Mysteries of the Mexican Pyramids*. In that expensive and lavishly illustrated volume, a particular "erratic" stands out. Page 360 of Tompkins's book shows one of the 20,000 engraved stones collected by Dr. Javier Cabrera of Ica, Peru. The petroglyph on the stone shows men fighting dinosaurs.

The whole question of whether or not man co-existed with dinosaurs was not resolved until 1969. In 1945 an accidental discovery of an ancient burial site in Acambaro, Mexico, yielded 32,000 objects of ceramic, jade, and knives made of obsidian (a volcanic material today used in open heart surgery instead of steel because it has a sharper edge which damages the tissues far less than steel). In addition, statues from a few inches long to three feet high or four or five feet long were discovered of great

---

[15]The magazine *Science Digest*, (June, 1981), p. 21, carried a story describing how scientists, using two satellites, are planning an expedition to hunt for a living dinosaur in the rain forests of the Congo.

reptiles—some of them in active association with people.

The people who produced these objects lived on the beach of a lake in a woodland surrounding. Today Acambero is an arid valley with eroded and dessicated surrounding highlands. Geologists have found that the valley itself was filled by a huge lake until sometime after the end of the Ice Age.

Radio carbon dating performed by Dr. Froelich Rainey in the laboratories of the University of Pennsylvania indicated the age of the samples. Additional tests using the thermoluminescence method of dating pottery were performed to determine the age of the objects. The objects are today dated as having been made around 4000 B.C.—about 6000 years ago.

After two expeditions to the site (1955 and 1968 respectively) Professor Charles H. Hapgood, Professor of History and Anthropology at Keene State College of the University of New Hampshire, author of *Earth's Shifting Crust* (1958), *Maps of the Ancient Sea Kings; Evidence of Advanced Civilization in the Ice Age* (1966), and *The Path of the Pole* (1970), recorded the results of his eighteen-year investigation of Acambaro.

In his paper *Mystery in Acambaro: An Account of the Ceramic Collection of the Late Waldeman Julsrud, in Acambero, G.T.O., Mexico*, Professor Hapgood writes that there were many indications that

> These people had close relationships with animals. We see them petting their dogs, riding wild horses or llamas without saddle or bridle, embracing large monkeys or apes, and having loving relationships with reptiles. It seems possible from some of the figurines that they actually domesticated reptiles, as well as anteaters and other mammals. They are shown in friendly relationships with turkeys. It seems as if they identified with animals in a way that we do not.

Professor Hapgood points out the ceramic collection contains unmistakable "representations of the one-humped American camel of the Ice Age." Teeth found beside the ceramics were identified by Dr. George Gaylord Simson, America's leading paleontologist, at the American Museum of Natural History, as belonging to *equus conversidans owen*—an extinct Ice Age horse.

Commenting on the ceramic collection, Hapgood writes:

> The richness of the imagination displayed by the creators of the objects was incredible, it was uncanny, there was almost a touch of the supernatural to it. All observers have agreed that there is no precedent for it in the annals of archeology.

> The close rapport indicated between people and reptiles strongly suggests an occult component in the culture of the people. They may have been the original people of reptile worship. One obtains from the collection itself a sense of the dark forces within the human psyche, an emphasis on the negative power of fear, and a suggestion of witchcraft in an elementary state of development.

Professor Hapgood also writes that:

> There may also have been a true, positive rapport with nature which our society does not understand.

For those who call the tracks of dinosaurs and man, side-by-side, in Glen Rose, Texas, "Preposterous," for those who shout

160

6:17. Acambero Ceramic Collection. (A) General view of a fraction of the Acambero Ceramic Collection. Note dinosaur figurines in foreground and apron on 4-foot tall statue right. (B) A woman in a loving relationship with a reptile. Note the naturalistic representation of the animal. (From MYSTERY IN ACAMBERO, Copyright © 1973, by Professor Charles H. Hapgood. Reprinted by permission of the author.)

6:18. Extinct Reptiles. (A) Suggestions of the Mesozoic Era: An animal resembling a possible species of Plesiosaurus (long neck, with three-toes feet), a giant reptile of an unknown species, and a relative of the kangaroo family. (B) A representation of the extinct American camel-llama. (C) Note the good natural stance and realistic movement by which the animal is tossing the man, seemingly with the intention of breaking his neck.

"Fraud" at Dr. Javier Cabrera's 20,000-piece stone collection showing man engaged in combat with dinosaurs, for those who attempt to prove to the satisfaction of others that which they themselves do not understand or believe, and shout "Impossible" to the ceramic collection at Acambaro, it is suggested that they check the facts.

While these facts are checked, ice silently accumulates at the South Pole.

In light of the above facts, one must wonder if the explosion and resultant radiation of Vela X produced a sudden surge in the Antarctica ice sheet, substantially affecting climatic conditions on Earth 6000 years ago.

I remembered a worldwide phenomenon discussed by Dr. Carl Sagan in his book *The Dragons of Eden*. Sagan proposes the question

> Is it only an accident that the common human sounds commanding silence or attracting attention seem strangely imitative of the hissing of reptiles?

Sagan also proposes the question:

> Could there have been manlike creatures who actually encountered *Tyrannosaurus rex*? Could there have been dinosaurs that escaped the extinctions in the late Cretaceous Period?

Ancient tradition handed down from the Saints who had to read as a religious duty is *Numismatics*, the words arranged circularly on certain old medals or coins, as distinguished from the inscription across them. According to tradition one inscription told of a meeting between the ten kings of Atlantis to discuss how the world might be rid of huge beasts.

In his book *The Dragons of Eden*, Dr. Carl Sagan very positively presents evidence (pp. 146-150) that during a close supernova explosion (such as Vela X) a thinking creature of thought that normally moved about the surface of the earth during the day (i.e., man) to escape an intensely high amount of ultraviolet radiation would move into caves. It is probable that man made this move after his first or second bad sunburn. During this period of intense ultraviolet radiation, the more ignorant dinosaurs continued lumbering around in the daytime while their huge body mass continued absorbing more and more of the lethal solar radiation.

What the skin colors of dinosaurs were, or what sounds they made, no one knows—just as no one knows how hairy early man was. What we do know today is that the skin of any cold-blooded reptile or warm-blooded mammal excessively exposed to abnormally high amounts of ultraviolet radiation will develop blisters, skin cancer, and will eventually die.

Sagan also presents evidence that man (a creature capable of thought and action), in order to escape an intensely high amount of ultraviolet radiation, slept during the day and moved in search of food during the nocturnal hours across the surface of the earth, gathering the eggs of dinosaurs and birds as food. While the dinosaurs, the dragons of Eden, slept, man stole their offspring.

We often forget that our outlook on life has changed considerably during the past ten years, because so much of what we think we know about the world is changing at an unprecedented rate. It is difficult psychologically to have to change our ideas about this history of man on this planet continually, but hardly a year goes by without some remarkable new discovery showing man to be much older than anyone had previously thought possible.

In 1977 anthropologist Mary Leakey announced the discovery of a 75 foot-long trail of footprints made by two human individuals walking on a fresh layer of volcanic ash 3.6 million years ago. The footprints were discovered at Laetolil in northern Tanzania. Ms. Leakey said one of the individuals was smaller than the other and probably a female. "At one point, and you need not be an expert tracker to discern this, she stops, pauses, turns to the left to glance at some possible threat or irregularity, and then continues to the north," she said. "This motion, so intensely human, transcends time. Three million, six hundred thousand years ago, a remote ancestor—just as you or I—experienced a moment of doubt."[16]

Later that same year a U.S. Navy torpedo recovery vessel was deep under water off the coast of Hawaii. Suddenly the submarine jerked. Rising slowly from the great depths of the Pacific, the submarine surfaced. Pouring onto the deck, the captain and crew were greeted by a hideous, nightmarish sight: there at the end of their anchor line, impaled on their sea anchor, was a colossal sea creature shocking and nauseating to look at. Then the wind changed direction. The stench from the ocher-colored liquid oozing from the creature's orifices was overwhelming. A crewman became sick.

The vessel returned to Hawaii towing the still-heaving creature. Scientists from the University of Hawaii found it to be a 1,650-pound, 14$\frac{1}{2}$ foot fish that was like no other sea creature known. It was classified as a member of the shark family, although the scientists were surprised at the existence of such a large shark in such deep waters. Most modern sharks hang out near a continental shelf or upper slope area. This newly discovered species of prehistoric shark has been nicknamed "Megamouth." The nickname comes from the appearance of the shark's lower jaw: like a large bathtub with four rows of needlelike teeth. What other unclassified creatures from a bygone age lurk in the ocean depths or roam the snow-covered higher elevations of vast mountain ranges only time will tell. Until then, these and many other things will remain an indefinable mystery.

A mystery to *me* was why the internal passageways of the Great Pyramid were aligned the way they are. A succession of investigations of the Great Pyramid over the past hundred and some years has demonstrated that the Descending Passage (the one angled upward at the northern sky) could, at this or that point in time, have been aligned with this or that star in the earth's northern sky. I had always wondered what the more spectacular Ascending Passage (the one angled upward at the southern sky) might have been focused on.

Almost all the investigators of the Great Pyramid have been men who travelled to Egypt from the earth's northern hemisphere and have *assumed* that the Great Pyramid's cardinal point was north. Each of these investigators, depending on when he thought the construction of the Great Pyramid was started, has attempted to align the Descending Passage with a "northern" star. But, as A. Pochan in his book *L'Enigme de la Grande Pyramide* points out,

> ...for the Egyptian *of the Old Kingdom*, the cardinal point was not north, but south....During the Old Kingdom the guiding star was not in the Northern Hemisphere but in the Southern Hemisphere, and the cardinal point was south, not north....

---

[16]Reported in a UPI press release.

The guiding star chosen was of the first magnitude.[17]

I am sure other pyramid investigators may have wondered what the Grand Gallery might have been focused on, and I think Peter Tompkins summarized the existing information with delicate perception in his book *Secrets of the Great Pyramid* (p. 147):

> Through this slot they could observe the apparent movement of the panoply of stars, accurately noting their several transits.

After all, there was nothing else there—nothing visible, that is. But 1,300 light years away a once-great star continued sending radio emissions with minute regularity, radio signals that have preserved for us the memory of its explosion.

To the best of my knowledge no other book published to date on the Great Pyramid has ever mentioned the supernova Vela X. The reason for this is that Michanowsky's book *The Once and Future Star* was not published until 1977.

While I was reading Michanowsky's book for the third or fourth time, a number of scattered researches suddenly became related to each other. It was these scattered researches that set me on the path of making the connection between perhaps the most awesome star explosion ever witnessed by humans and the Grand Gallery of the awesome Great Pyramid. This connection would have been impossible for me to make without the kind help of Dr. Gart Westerhout of the U.S. Naval Observatory, Dr. Kenneth L. Franklin of the Hayden Planetarium, Dr. David S. Evans of McDonald Observatory, and Dr. Paul Gorenstine of the Smithsonian Institution. A special

thanks is extended to George Michanowsky for his time and his consideration, which included sharing with me his new discovery: the deciphering of some hierglyphs in the tomb of Tutankhamen (King Tut) which make reference to the supernova Vela X.

The wide range of speculation inspired by the discovery of Vela X is rapidly growing in importance in the field of history and especially in the discipline of historical climatology—an important subject to which we will return later, when we talk with Dr. Colin Bull, Director of the Institute of Polar Studies.

This chapter has raised many questions. Did the explosion of Vela X decisively influence western religious symbolism and star mythology? Is there a Masonic connection between Vela X, a star which exploded *within a triangle,* and the ancient religious symbolism and star dates of Freemasonry? Is there a connection between Vela X and the laborious calculations of the learned Christian archbishop James Ussher, who fixed the date when God said "Let there be light" as 4004 B.C. (a date only four years different from the Masonic Year of Light)? What secrets would the female branch of Freemasonry know about the visit of the Egyptian Queen Hatshepsut with King Solomon? Why is the Middle Chamber of the Great Pyramid encrusted with salt? Why is a bearded face of a man, strikingly similar to the face imprinted on the Shroud of Turin, imprinted on the wall approaching the Middle Chamber[18] (the chamber which according to the *Egyptian Book of the Dead,* the religious text of the Early Empire, is named the Chamber of Second Birth)? Did Jesus visit and teach in Mexico after the resurrection as the Mormons believe, or did Jesus

---

[17]Pochan, pp. 150-226.

[18]And why has no other book about the Great Pyramid mentioned this mysterious imprint?

visit Mexico before the crucifixion as Edgar Cayce and others believe? Why did Jesus say, "Be ye therefore wise as serpents?" Why did Moses, who was trained in all the wisdom of the Egyptians, set a serpent of brass upon a pole? Why is Freemasonry's twenty-fifth degree named "Knight of the Brazen Serpent?" Why did the writer of the Sumerian star catalogue state that Vela X would be seen again? Did man, at some unremembered time in the collective unconscious of mankind, walk the face of the earth with nightmarish reptiles? Did some "carriage," as Ouspensky suggested almost a hundred years ago, move up and down the Grand Gallery serving as a support for some apparatus that could be fixed in any position—a gallery that Ouspensky believed was the key to the whole pyramid? Why does a mysterious track run the length of the gallery midway between the floor and the roof? Could the interior of the Great Pyramid at some time have been exposed to an extremely intense heat? Perhaps we can find answers for these questions when we rejoin Al Mamun and visit the Great Pyramid's final chamber.

Everyone who has written about the Great Pyramid has sooner or later speculated about it one way or another. Perhaps the reason for this is best described by William R. Fix in his book *Pyramid Odyssey*:

Anyone who becomes really involved with the Great Pyramid must face a unique hazard: the Pyramid takes possession of the mind. The behavior of those who have attempted to explain this monument is as interesting and extraordinary as the Pyramid itself.... Time and again serious investigators have completely lost their sense of perspective in searching for and advancing the explanation which suits them.... Understanding this unusual behavior associated with the Pyramid is part of understanding the Pyramid itself. It has changed the lives and altered the consciousness of many. Men feel *compelled* to explain it and to account for it on their own terms, regardless of the evidence, or lack of it. This compulsion to account for it on our own terms arises from the overpowering presence of the Pyramid: it is enormous; it is ancient; it is legendary; it is sophisticated; it is the result of a great enterprise; it is here for all to see at the crossroads of the earth—and it does not seem to belong to our world.

That is the crux of it: the Great Pyramid does not seem to belong to our world, and because of this it is challenging and vaguely threatening. Much Pyramid literature is filled with strange emotions, with impatience and anger for conflicting ideas. Many hold their theories about it at the level of religious conviction. It is almost as if those who have sought to explain the Pyramid have said to themselves: 'I must make this thing fit into what I *believe* about the history and the nature of the world.'

If we are to rise above yet another partisan interpretation of the Pyramid, we must not exclude any significant body of information simply because it is unfamiliar or because it is not what we expect or want. We must keep asking what solid evidence exists for each explanation. If we are to be truly detached and open-minded, we must accept the unsettling possibility that the Great Pyramid simply may *not* fit into what we believe about history and the nature of the world.[19]

The present writer, being keenly aware of the unique hazard of which Mr. Fix speaks, has endeavored to present the facts as discovered. The present writer has chosen to identify what follows in the next few pages as speculation on his part: I am too much of a skeptic to deny the possibility of anything. Having learned that skepticism becomes itself another form of superstition beyond a certain point, I believe that speculation, if identified as such, may have some value in discussing the Great Pyramid. Many times an imaginative look at old evidence has produced startling results.

Standing atop the 6 foot x 8 foot platform at the top of the Great Pyramid's Grand Gallery, Al Mamun was puzzled by the construction of the Grand Gallery. He wondered if the ancient writings of Ibrahim ben Ebn Wassuff Shah concerning a new invading race from an early empire with an understanding of celestial mechanics, astronomical units, epicyclic trains, and history might describe those responsible for this gallery's construction.

Like a close encounter of the second kind, how many tourists, as they are led by their drone-like guides through the internal organs of the Great Pyramid, realize they are walking around in the guts of a prehistoric machine—or to be more exact, a physico-mathematical facility. By the following data presented here, perhaps even a novice machinist can envision two large cogwheels (with teeth synchronized to match the notches cut into the side-ramps

of the Grand Gallery) connected by an axle, itself in turn supporting and moving some device or instrument up and down the length of the gallery. One can imagine, midway between the floor and the roof, two stabilizing arms extending from the device into the two mysterious tracks running the length of the Grand Gallery. Two such stabilizing arms would support the upper half of the device. An epicyclic train—a train of spur or bevel wheels, belt pulleys, or the like, having one or more of these constrained to move bodily around the circumference of another, which may be fixed or moving—would permit the device to move up and down the Grand Gallery with an unusual velocity ratio but without undue complexity of parts (see Plate 6:20).

6:20. *One Form of Epicyclic Train.*

Even the idea that the Great Pyramid was a machine would, a few years ago, have been ridiculed. Today men of science recognize all possibilities, but not without some proof. If a device or instrument moved up

---

[19]William R. Fix, *Pyramid Odyssey,* pp. 34-39.

and down the Grand Gallery with an unusual velocity—if, indeed, the Great Pyramid was a machine with moving parts—there should be some visible evidence, some stress, attrition, or wearing of parts by friction, abrasion, or heat, to support this thesis.

Standing atop the Great Step and looking down the Grand Gallery, Al Mamun saw nothing that was not a mystery to him. The unexpected dimensions of the gallery, the precisely notched divisons in the side-ramps, the straight lines, the correctness of the angles, the very exact and fine workmanship puzzled him. As his eyes slowly worked their way up the length of the gallery, his attention was drawn to a section of the corbelled limestone wall a few feet away. On his left, at the wall's first corbelling, Al Mamun noticed this section of wall resembled a petrified waterfall and was darker, much darker, than the rest of the smooth white limestone. This section of wall strangely resembled melted wax, as if the stone had been reduced from a solid to a liquid or flowing state by an extremely intense heat.

In the photograph of the Grand Gallery (Plate 6:21), the first corbelling or overlap to be seen directly above the head of the first Arab guide (on the left of the picture), exhibits signs of calcination. Limestone does not melt like wax, but when subjected to intense heat it is reduced to a friable or powdery state. By the action of heat, the surface of limestone is reduced to a powder and falls away, leaving the undersurface appearing as if melted, dissolved, or fused. To initiate calcining on limestone requires a high degree of heat, extremely intense—measuring no less than 1500° F[20] Comparing the 75-year-old photograph in Plate 6:21 to the

modern photograph of Plate 6:6, the reader can see two photographs—taken seventy years apart—of this calcination.

6:21. *The Grand Gallery.* This 1905 photograph, taken from atop the Great Step and looking down the Grand Gallery, shows the gallery without the fluorescent lights, metal handrails, and wooden walkway now installed for tourists. The shallow grooves in the floor were cut in the eighteenth century by early explorers to make ascending the steep, slippery floor easier. Note first overlap on left exhibits signs of calcination. Compare with Plate 6:6.

What extremely intense heat source during some ancient time would have been *no less* than 1500° F? The first commercially successful application of gas welding occurred in 1906, when the French engineer Eugene Bournonville developed a torch

---

[20]**Source: Indiana Limestone Institute of America, Inc.**

that mixed oxygen and acetylene.[21]

An epicyclic train, moving up and down the Grand Gallery with a high velocity, suddenly braking or stopping at the top of the gallery, might over a period of time cause some wearing away by friction, or possibly heat this section of the wall. However, an epicyclic train moving up and down the Grand Gallery would have to have a source of power. Could the Great Pyramid's Middle Chamber, with its salt-encrusted walls, have once housed some type of battery or system of batteries? Perhaps it housed a system of connected Leyden jars which could be discharged together to drive an epicyclic train. Leyden jars and dry cell batteries were in use thousands of years ago.

That the ancients had an understanding of electricity was first discovered by Dr. Wilhelm Konig, a German archaeologist, while employed by the State Museum in Baghdad, Iraq, in 1938. His assertion that a box of 2,000-year-old strange clay jars was a collection of dry cell batteries was called preposterous by experts at the time. Confirmation of Dr. Konig's research did not come until after the Second World War. Willey Ley, a science historian, set to work with Willard Gray, a technician at the General Electric High Voltage Laboratory in Pittsfield, Massachusetts, to construct a duplicate of the ancient clay pots discovered years earlier by Dr. Konig. When Ley and Gray constructed a duplicate of the jars, they found each clay jar housed a cylinder of sheet copper capped at the bottom with copper discs sealed with bitumen or asphalt. An iron rod suspended into the copper cylinder and sealed at the top would, with the addition of copper sulfate, acetic acid, or even citric acid, produce an electrical current of 1.5 to 2.75 volts of electricity.

[21]Cecil G. Bainbridge, *Welder's Handbook.*

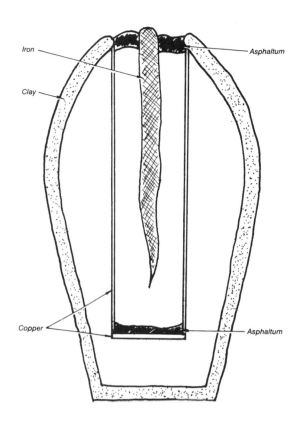

Iron

Clay

Copper

Asphaltum

Asphaltum

6:22. Baghdad Battery. Willard Gray of the General Electric High Voltage Laboratory produced the sketch above based on the specifications of the 2000-year-old Baghdad battery. With the addition of copper sulfate, acetic acid, or even citric acid, this battery will produce an electrical current. In the *Grand Dictionaire Universal du 19th Siecle* the French archaeologist Auguste Mariette writes that while excavating in the area of the Great Pyramid at a depth of 60 feet, he discovered gold jewelry whose thinness and lightness "make one believe they had been produced by electroplating."

Might not a band of men from a technologically advanced early empire have discovered that thin iron or copper rods connecting the clay jars into a series of cells would produce a battery with a much stronger voltage? Today we use batteries to propel an electric car. A series of batteries housed in the Great Pyramid's salt-encrusted Middle Chamber may have propelled an epicyclic train that bore some device or instrument up and down the length of the Great Pyramid's Grand Gallery. Where would the batteries receive a source of energy strong enough to keep them charging while producing enough voltage to move some device or instrument, which could be fixed in any position, up and down the entire length of the gallery? (See Plate 6:22)

Between the huge blocks forming the walls of the Grand Gallery, the joints are precision-cut. The joints are almost invisible. It is impossible to insert a needle anywhere. One tiny pin-hole or air leak would prevent the gallery from being a vacuum. The Grand Gallery, with its walls tilted inward five degrees, is a structure built to withstand atmospheric pressure like a vacuum electron tube. An electron is the elementary, subatomic, negatively charged particle orbiting about an atom's nucleus. The modern science of electronics is a study of the phenomena related to the emission, behavior, and effects of electrons, as in vacuum tubes, and their application in radio and television.

Could the device or instrument moving up and down the gallery have been an apparatus for producing electric currents by induction and for utilizing them? Could the device have been an induction coil?

When the Great Pyramid's internal parts are thought of in terms of "machinery," the pyramid can be seen as a complicated apparatus, or combination of mechanical powers, designed to increase, regulate, or apply motion and great force. The mysterious track running the length of the gallery is no longer mysterious, but can be recognized as an essential part of the whole machine.

Could a series of batteries housed in the salt-encrusted Middle Chamber have received a source of energy strong enough to charge them from something in the chamber at the top of the Grand Gallery?

Overwhelmed and confused by all he was seeing in this hall of mountain kings, Al Mamun whirled about on the Great Step at the top of the Grand Gallery, and immediately before him saw yet another horizontal passageway, leading south—a small passageway measuring *forty-one* inches high. Hesitating, then thrusting his torch ahead and bending low, Al Mamun cautiously entered the passageway. Moving forward a few feet in a crouching position, he was again able to stand upright and observe that he had entered a small antechamber. Except for the north wall behind him, Al Mamun noticed that this antechamber was constructed of granite. For a brief instant he wondered why the builders had changed building material at this stage of construction. Then, peering over the granite bar blocking his progress, Al Mamun noted that the east and west side-walls of this chamber were divided into three sections with half-round tops. Ducking under the granite bar, Al Mamun found his eyes drawn to four half-round grooves cut in the wall above another passageway forty-one inches high, directly ahead. He wondered if some system of rollers and pulleys had been employed here to lift stone valves up and down in the three slots in the side-walls, regulating the admission of something to or escape of something from what lay ahead.

Instinctively, Al Mamun felt he was about to discover something of great value. The hairs on the back of his neck bristled. With growing anticipation he once again

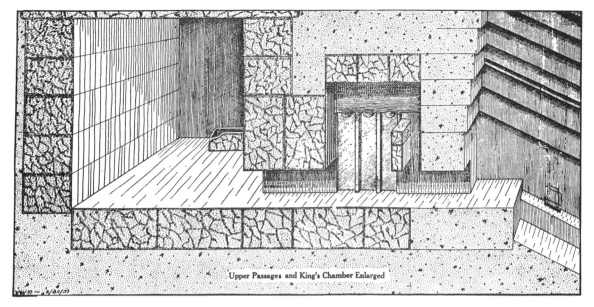

6:23. *Upper Passages and King's Chamber.* This cutaway drawing of the upper passages and King's Chamber is enlarged from scale for clarity.

thrust his torch into the inky darkness, and bowing his head low for the third time he moved into the unknown. His eyes started to smart and water from the smoke of his torch, his torch began to fade, and darkness closed in around him.

Al Mamun suddenly noted that his torch was not fading, but that its light was only appearing to dim because he had entered a large, well-proportioned chamber built entirely of meticulously wrought and polished red granite blocks. These hard granite walls, because of a surprising matte-like finish, absorbed light and sound—producing a soft, ethereal feeling such as one may experience in the vast hall of a cathedral. If the Great Pyramid was a machine, then the surface of the walls could have been given a certain function; e.g., the matte finish retains moisture that a slick finish could not.

Al Mamun saw that the four walls of this chamber were created of exactly one hundred large granite blocks, stacked five courses high. These blocks are composed of mica, feldspar, and a high percentage of quartz crystals. Al Mamun noticed the entire top course of the chamber to be constructed of only *seven* granite blocks—a number symbolizing perfection in the ancient world. He did not notice, however, that the distance between the north and south walls was 17 feet 2″, the same distance as was found between the north and south walls in the Middle Chamber and between the girdle stones in the Ascending Passage.

Moving into the King's Chamber with three swiftly executed steps, Al Mamun noticed out of the corner of his right eye a dark shadow at the western end of the chamber. Startled, he turned to face the shadow, hesitated, then advanced towards it holding his torch in front of him. Moving a little closer, he saw the shadow was a large chocolate-colored box cut from a single block of granite (later found to contain an

171

extremely high percentage of quartz crystals). Unlike the walls, which absorbed the light, this box sparkled with an almost incandescent light as if it held something ancient and sacred. Stepping back from this large rectangular box in the *sanctum sanctorum*, Al Mamun remembered the Middle Chamber with its crystals alive and growing everywhere.

His heartbeat quickened as visions of gold and precious jewels danced in his head. A scarab, the sacred beetle of ancient Egypt, slowly moved across the floor between Al Mamun and the box. Al Mamun's heart pounded as greed overcame his better judgment and he rushed forward to tear and strip from the mummy of Khufu the gold and precious jewels he knew the greatest Pharoah of Egypt would certainly have been adorned with prior to burial. The scarab lay crushed on the floor behind him.

An almost inhuman scream escaped the lips of Prince Abdullah Al Mamun, echoing and reverberating up and down the Grand Gallery, as he gazed into the box and saw....

Outside the Great Pyramid that same day, life was proceeding normally. Mary (a name concealed within the word "pyramid") was taking a urine sample to the high priest of the Temple of Amen to determine if her unborn child would be a boy or a girl. Receiving Mary, the priest passed her sample on to the temple technicians, who would soak a bag of barley and wheat with equal amounts of the specimen. If the child was to be a boy, the growth of the wheat would be accelerated. If the unborn child was to be a girl, the growth of the barley would be stimulated. In 1926 modern science rediscovered the urine pregnancy test.

In 1933 laboratory tests confirmed the acceleration of wheat and barley growth in connection with pregnancy. Mary soon received word that the growth of the barley was stimulated. She smiled at her good fortune.

Deep inside the Great Pyramid, Al Mamun wondered what had become of his good fortune. Nothing! Absolutely *nothing* was in the box. Al Mamun could not believe it was empty. *He* would not be cheated. His mind reeled, searching for an explanation. Where was the treasure? Where was the gold, the precious jewels, the magic *Scripture of Magick?*[22] Where were the secret maps and tables of the celestial and terrestrial spheres, the glass which would bend but not break (strangely reminiscent of plastic) described in ancient legends thousands of years before? Where, in fact, was the mummy of Khufu?

An electric jolt raced through the mind of Mamun: *Could someone have plundered this sanctum sanctorum before me, removing things of value?* Considering the enormous amount of difficulty he had experienced in gaining admission to the Great Pyramid's center chamber, he doubted it.

Could someone have entered the upper chambers of the Great Pyramid before Al Mamun? Perhaps when we talk with Dr. Edward Wente, an eminent Egyptologist, we will discover the answer to this important question.

---

[22]*A document which Aleister Crowley burned out most of the molecules in his ladder-like helical chain searching for in vain.*

172

6:24. King's Chamber.

We're destroying our species' most precious resource — our intelligence.

Professor Ernest J. Sterglass
Speaking on the deleterious effects of nuclear
radiation on the brains of young children.

Our attitude toward Earth was healthier when we were pagans who believed that spirits resided in everything, that man and beast were on equal footing, and trees had to be placated before cutting.

Kenneth Brower

Recently, some archaeologists and historians have been revising old theories about the fall of numerous elaborate and powerful civilizations of the past, such as the Indus, the Hittites, the Mycenaen, and the Mali empire of Africa. There is considerable evidence that these empires may have been undone not by barbarian invaders but by climate change.

—1977 CIA Report

CHAPTER SEVEN
AN EGYPTOLOGIST AND A HIEROPHANT

On 19 April 1977, twelve days after I interviewed the architect Wilfred Gregson, I interviewed Dr. Edward Wente, an eminent Egyptologist at the Oriental Institute of the University of Chicago. The Oriental Institute was founded by Dr. James Henry Breasted as a "laboratory for the study of the human career," and is considered one of the most excellent schools of Egyptology in the world.

Dr. Wente received his doctorate in Egyptology in 1959 and later became Professor of Egyptology at the Oriental Institute. He worked for ten years with the Epigraphic Survey at Luxor, Egypt, recording monuments and temples, and he was Field Director of that project from 1972 to 1973.

Dr. Wente's book *Late Ramesside Letters* was published by the University of Chicago Press. He has also co-authored with Dr. William Kelly Simpson, Curator of the Egyptian Section of the Boston Museum of Fine Arts, a book entitled *The Literature of Ancient Egypt*. Dr. Wente is Chairman of the Department of Eastern Languages and Civilization. His current book is entitled *An X-Ray Analysis of the Royal Mummies*, which he co-authored with Dr. James E. Harris.

Noone: Dr. Wente, as you may know, there is going to be a CBS television special on the Great Pyramid tomorrow night.

Wente: Is it tomorrow night? I didn't know when it was going to be.

Noone: It is a one-hour special probing the mystery and controversy that surround the Great Pyramid.

Wente: Yes.

Noone: I would like to record this conversation, so the information that goes in my book is exactly as you give it to me—that way there can't be any misquotes. All right?

Wente: Well, I guess that is all right.

Noone: The first question I would like to ask you is this: There seems to be a great deal of controversy surrounding the origin and purpose of the Great Pyramid. Different researchers have written that the pyramid is a scale model of the earth's northern hemisphere, incorporating the mathematics and science of an antediluvian civilization. Others have written that it was, or is, a granary, a Bible in stone, a temple of initiation, a treasure vault, a huge water pump, a cosmic reservoir, a time capsule, and many other things. What exactly is the Great Pyramid, in your opinion?

Wente: It was built as a tomb for the Pharaoh Khufu, and it was part of the total funerary complex. The Great Pyramid contains the chamber and sarcophagus in which the king's mummy was placed. It also had, at the east side—east of the pyramid—a mortuary temple.

Noone: Was the mortuary temple physically connected to the Great Pyramid, or is this temple just built near the Great Pyramid?

Wente: It bordered it, and there the cult of these two kings would have been celebrated. Extending, that is, the daily cult. After he had died and been buried in the pyramid, the daily ritual would have taken place in that temple. Then you proceed from there eastwards, where there was a long causeway which Herodotus informs us had painted reliefs, and actually bits of these reliefs have been found from Khufu's complex.[1] A number were incorporated in later pyramids of the Middle Kingdom. At the bottom of this long causeway, there was what we call a 'valley temple,' which stood at the edge of the cultivation so that a ship could come up to the quay of the mortuary of the valley temple. There was the lower temple, so that when you have a king's funeral eventually this complex was put into action. Certain rituals were performed in the valley temple with the king's mummy there, and then the mummy was transported up the long causeway to the funerary temple. Further rituals were carried on from that point to his final interment. Through the—of course it would have to be through the north entrance of the pyramid. So basically we look at the Great Pyramid exactly as we look at the other pyramids, as the burial place for the king, and that was what it was designed for.

Noone: What became of the body of Khufu?

Wente: Well...Khufu's body seems to have been...uh, removed and destroyed. It could have been stolen, as no trace of the body of Khufu has ever been found.

Noone: Dr. Wente, there seems to be a great deal of controversy concerning the validity of these statements. The book *Secrets of the Great Pyramid* by Peter Tompkins and the book *The Great Pyramid: Man's Monument to Man* by Tom Valentine, to name two, point out discrepancies in the theory you have espoused. Number one is that the tomb theory is based on the hearsay evidence of Herodotus, who travelled to Egypt around 440 B.C., thousands of years after the Great Pyramid was completed, and little more. I would like your opinion on these books.

Wente: Well, I must admit that I've never read the books.

Noone: You've had your Ph.D. in Egyptology since 1959?

Wente: That's right.

Noone: What specifically is your degree in?

Wente: My Ph.D. was in Egyptian Philology, certain aspects of the Egyptian language as revealed in the written documents of ancient Egypt.

Noone: Architects are puzzled as to how the ancients could have constructed the Great Pyramid with

---

[1] An initiate in the ancient mysteries, Herodotus never told all. Speaking of the Egyptian mysteries, he says: "I know the whole course of the proceedings in these ceremonies, but they shall not pass my lips." (Book II, p. 142)

primitive means of measuring a geographical length on earth, then relating that length to a second of movement in the vault of the heavens, linking together both the measurements of time and distance, incorporated both these measurements in their building.

Wente: Yes, well, we know engineers express great admiration for the building achievements of the builders of the Great Pyramid, but I think astronomically—it was oriented on an astronomical basis.[2] One of the major things was to level off the plateau and to secure a square of such large dimensions. I think there have been various hypotheses as to how this might have been done. The Egyptians did use cords to measure with in their foundation ceremonies.[3] Oh, some people say there would be too much stretching, too much leeway. Others have suggested using water to secure a level.

Noone: Would I be correct in assuming that in your opinion we don't know how the thirteen-and-a-half-acre base of the Great Pyramid was measured or levelled?

Wente: I would say that.

Noone: Architects tell me they cannot conceive how a people supposedly only one step removed from the Stone Age could have been in possession of the mathematical and astronomical data necessary to

erect this edifice. Dr. Wente, how do you believe the Great Pyramid was constructed?

Wente: I would probably go along with the theory proposed by Dr. Dunham at the Boston Museum as to how it could have been done. You had a number of ramps—now there is some question about the placement of these ramps. Some say the ramps sort of went around the Pyramid. Sort of like those pictures you may have seen on the Tower of Babel construction. You could have had ramps in various positions, or there might have been only one rather long large ramp constructed of brick and fill. As the Pyramid was built higher and higher, they could also elevate the ramp.[4]

Noone: Then in your opinion we don't know for sure how the Great Pyramid was constructed?

Wente: Yes.

Noone: Is there any truth to the ancient legends that the Great Pyramid was built first and the rest of the pyramids in Egypt are just poor copies of the original?

Wente: Certainly not. It certainly was not the first pyramid.

Noone: How is this determined?

Wente: From a chronology. The oldest one is not a true pyramid—that is the step pyramid of Zoser, a king of the third dynasty, at Saggara. Then we have several

---

[2]The Great Pyramid is oriented astronomically correct to the four cardinal points of the compass.
[3]See page 132 of the interview with Wilfred Gregson.
[4]Today the single-ramp theory is doubted because by the time upper levels were reached the single ramp would consume four times more material and labor than the pyramid itself.

7:1. Romantic nineteenth-century depiction of the Tower of Babel. Gregson, in his book *Evidences of Masonry in Ancient Civilization*, writes:

To Babylon were brought the priests and teachers of Egypt, Palestine, Zoraster, Mithra, Greece and masters from all parts of the known world. Kings sought to be initiated into the rites of the mysteries. Pythagorus, initiated into the mysteries of Egypt, spent four years in Babylon where he and the Magi exchanged their knowledge of the hidden mysteries with the brethren who had received masters wages from foreign parts. To the profane, this gathering of foreigners became a "Babel of Tongues". Could one of these tongues come from Yucatan? It is more than likely since the Observatory Building at Chichen-Itza follows closely the design of many of the Ziggurats (pyramid structures) of the Asiatic Babylonian (Chaldean) period B.C. 4000 - B.C. 1275. The *Hall of 100 Columns*, at Persepolis, built by Darius, B.C. 521 - B.C. 485 in the northeast corner of the palace temple complex was duplicated in the northeast corner of Chichen-Itza. There are a great many other resemblances that like these noted above are more than could be expected accidentally.

178

pyramids connected with King Seneferu.[5] He built the Bent Pyramid at Meidum and the northern pyramid at Dahshur, the first true pyramid. The angle of this pyramid is not as steep as the angle of the Great Pyramid.

Noone: There seems to be a great deal of debate about the angle of the Great Pyramid, because its angle, 51° 51 minutes 14.3″, is the angle which shows the Pyramid incorporates a value for pi.

Wente: I think that it was probably that pyramid builders arrived at a more satisfactory angle that was structurally sound. One might say that perhaps the angle of the Bent Pyramid was a bit too steep, so then the builders tapered it structurally.

Noone: Then perfection was missing in the Bent Pyramid.

Wente: Yes. So the angle of the Great Pyramid seems to have been arrived at after a great deal of experimentation in the building of pyramids.

Noone: Is there any reason for the entrance to the Great Pyramid to be offset the center of the north face, measuring from side to side, 286.1″?

Wente: I can't figure any reason for that.

Noone: Out of the other eighty-nine major pyramids in Egypt, how many of these have northern entrances offset toward the east 286″?

Wente: I can't say for sure just how far off center other ones might be. Well, they are all on the north face, put it that way.

Noone: Are you sure they are all on the north face?

Wente: The Egyptians...not all of their ... uh-h-h ... structures, even in history and art, totally balance their measurements. There are deviations ... uh ... Deviations occur sometimes—we are unable to explain why deviations from what one would normally expect to be in a balanced position occur.[6]

Noone: Is there any proof that the Great Pyramid incorporates any mathematical formulas or astronomical knowledge?

Wente: I wouldn't say so. I think Egyptian mathematics were rather pragmatic, more arithmetic than involved mathematics, I would say.

Noone: Professor Livio Catullo Stecchini, a Professor of Ancient History at William Patterson College, has advanced the theory that the box in the King's Chamber was a standard of volume and measurement, a measurement deeply ingrained in Egyptian religion, and—

Wente: I don't believe anything of that sort. I think all other Egyptologists would agree with me that the rectangular box in the King's

---

[5]According to the late E.A. Wallis Budge in the *Egyptian Book of the Dead* (page 18, footnote 2), "The building of the pyramid of Meidum has usually been attributed to Seneferu, but the excavations made there in 1882 did nothing to clear up the uncertainty which exists on this point."

[6]The Bent Pyramid has an entrance 15 yards south of the middle of its *west* face, also an entrance on its north face, but no other pyramid in Egypt has an entrance offset from center 286.1″ or an angle of 51°51 minutes 14.3 seconds. It's incredible that a professor of Egyptology would be so unfamiliar with the most amazing and ancient structure in Egypt.

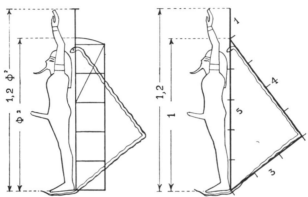

7:2. In his book *Serpent in the Sky: The High Wisdom of Ancient Egypt*, John Anthony West correctly points out that this relief from the tomb of Rameses VI shows the direct evidence of Egyptian knowledge and use of the 3, 4, 5 Pythagorean triangle. West writes that Egypt waned and ultimately fell through the misuse of knowledge. He states:

> This is but one valid reason for keeping certain types of mathematical knowledge secret. There are many others pertaining to the course of development and initiation of the individual: the man found incapable of keeping a simple secret cannot be entrusted with a more complex, more dangerous secret.
>
> In every field of Egyptian knowledge, the underlying principles were kept secret, but made manifest in works. If this knowledge were ever written in books — and there is mention of sacred libraries whose contents have never been found — then these books were intended only for those who had earned the right to consult them.

Chamber was designed solely to put the king's mummy in. Its being used for any other purpose than putting a mummy in is ridiculous.

Noone: Have you read Professor Stecchini's work?

Wente: No.[7]

[7]According to Stecchini, "Egyptologists do not understand that there are theological reasons why a coffer should be empty. For example, the symbol of the god Ammon, at Thebes, was a bag full of air." This quote from Stecchini comes from a letter taken from a series of letters and telephone calls between Professor Stecchini and the author.

Noone: If the Great Pyramid was used as a tomb, how was it sealed after the burial?

Wente: Well, the Great Pyramid and others—one thing they had was sliding stones.

Noone: Structural engineers tell me that to slide the granite plugs [which block the Ascending Passage] down the Ascending Passage from somewhere above would require three-fourths of an inch clearance around the plugs and darned good ball bearings.[8] Measured today, these plugs show less than one-sixteenth of an inch clearance, which makes it physically impossible for them to have been slid down the Ascending Passage.

Wente: Well, I am not sure about that. The important columns—

Noone: Excuse me for interrupting, Doctor, but I am not talking about columns as there are no columns in the Great Pyramid. I am talking about the three granite plugs which Al Mamun tunnelled around to ascend the Ascending Passage. You see, Dr. Wente, if the granite plugs could *not* have been slid down the 129 feet of the Ascending Passage, they must have been built in place—blocking the passage before the building was completed. This would go a long way towards discounting your theory that the Great Pyramid was a tomb, wouldn't it?

Wente: Yes, but I think that must be an inaccurate observation. What one presumes is that wooden supports, or some kind of supports—

Noone: Did you say that this is what one *presumes?*

Wente: Yes, I don't think we have any evidence of wood. I presume that wood was what was used to hold up these stones—or something of that sort—until after burial, and I would say that they may have used some compartmentalizing of sand so as to ease the terrific bang that may have occurred. We are just not certain, but I don't think there is any particular problem with this.[9]

Noone: I think my final question would be: Peter Tompkins makes the point that most Egyptologists have no more qualifications to give an authoritarian opinion on the Great Pyramid's structural design than an architect on Egyptian philology. What would your opinion be on this statement?

---

[8] Professor J. Brachet, a French architect, went to Egypt to measure and verify this point. Returning to France, he published an illustrated book on this point, in which he agrees with David Davidson, author of *The Great Pyramid*, that the granite plugs *could not* have been slid down the Ascending Passage unless the walls were as smooth as glass. In 1965, he found the walls of the corridor to be roughly finished. See Brachet, *Nouvelles Recherches sur la Grande Pyramide* (Aix-en-Provence: La Pensee Universitaire, 1965), for further discussion of this point, which bears directly on the improbability of the Great Pyramid's having been built as a tomb for Khufu.

[9] This debate is dealt with fully in 19 pages complete with illustrations of Tompkins' book *Secrets of the Great Pyramid* (pp. 236-256). In these pages the idea of putting sand at the bottom of the Ascending Passage to cushion the big bang as the granite plugs supposedly came rocketing down the Ascending Passage is shown to be spurious.

Wente: I think there might be some truth in that; as I said, I am an Egyptologist—philologist and historian.

Dr. Wente shows that not only do orthodox Egyptologists believe a Pyramid is a tomb is a tomb is a tomb, but why.

Anyone who examines in detail the Egyptologists' opinion that this monolithic building was only a tomb will discover many gaps in the logic, gaps which raise many questions. The mummy of King Tut, a relatively insignificant ruler (compared to Khufu, supposedly the greatest Pharoah of Egypt) was found inside three large coffins. Isn't it odd that the granite box in the King's Chamber is only large enough to hold a body within a very small and thin-walled coffin?

Although Dr. Wente quoted the historian Herodutus on one point, he did not mention that Herodotus states that Khufu was buried *under* the Pyramid:

> ...the underground chambers, which Cheops [Greek for Khufu] intended as vaults for his own use: these last were built on a sort of island, surrounded by water introduced from the Nile by a canal.[10]

When Herodotus describes the second pyramid, he states:

> It has no subterraneous apartments, nor any canal from the Nile to supply it with water, as the other pyramid has. In that, the Nile water, introduced through an artificial duct, surrounds an island, where the body of Cheops is said to lie.[11]

No such chambers have been found, and on this type of hearsay evidence Egyptologists build their case.

In his book *The Mysteries of the Great Pyramid*, A. Pochan reflects Herodotus's account, writing that Khufu

> ...has lain in his crypt carved out in the bedrock at the level of the Nile's low water—that is, 58 meters beneath the Pyramid's base and 27 meters beneath the subterranean chamber known to us at present.[12]

A few small holes drilled into the bedrock might answer this question. To find the mummy of Khufu is something that Egyptologists dare not dream of, but nevertheless do.

Edward J. Kunkel, author of *Pharaoh's Pump*, believes there are chambers below the subterranean chamber, and that the chambers connect with the Nile by means of an artificial duct. Mr. Kunkel believes the Great Pyramid to be a machine: he believes that the Great Pyramid is a huge hydraulic ram pump, and apparently so does the United States Patent Office, which granted him a patent for a hydraulic ram pump constructed like the internal organs of the Great Pyramid. For years no one would listen to him because one part of his pump was missing. For the past twenty years, Kunkel has insisted that a cavity exists between the Middle Chamber and the King's Chamber in the Great Pyramid. During the 1977 field work at Giza, a joint Egyptian/American research project applying ground-penetrating radar techniques discovered a cavity exactly where Kunkel had said it would be (see Plate 5:15).

[10]*History,* Book II, p. 125.
[11]Ibid., p. 126.
[12]Pochan, *Mysteries of the Great Pyramid,* p. 287.

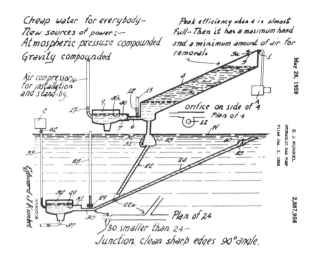

May 26, 1959

E. J. KUNKEL
HYDRAULIC RAM PUMP
Filed Jan. 3, 1955

2,887,956

7:3. *Kunkel's Hydraulic Ram Pump.* This drawing shows the ram pump based upon the design of the Great Pyramid, exactly as filed with the United States Patent Office in 1955.

Ed Kunkel began to wonder how the ancients could have moved and built with such great mass. He made a list of the basic methods by which a mass could be moved:

(1) manually; (2) the use of the wedge, or the screw, or the inclined plane; (3) the lever, the use of gear wheels, the pulley, and the crane; (4) the expansion of a gas, or the changing of the pressure of a gas, such as the internal combustion engine, the steam engine, the use of dynamite, a windmill, or an airplane; (5) the buoyancy of a gas, as it is used in a dirigible; (6) the use of a magnet, or magnetic fields, which includes the whole field of electricity; (7) by the use of pumps, hydraulics, or water power.[13]

After many years of research, Kunkel built a working model.

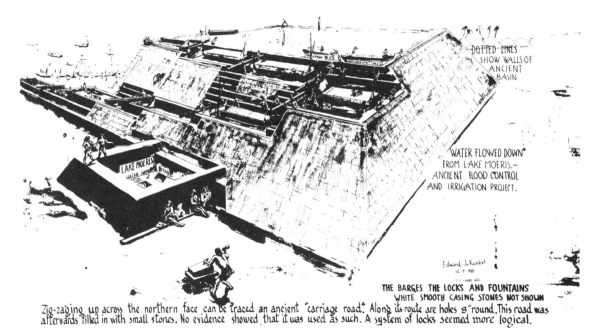

7:4. *Edward Kunkel's Depiction of how the Great Pyramid could have been constructed utilizing a system of water locks to float the blocks to the next highest course of construction.*

[13]Kunkel, *Pharoah's Pump*, p. 5.

Kunkel points out in his book *Pharaoh's Pump* that nearly all authors writing on the Great Pyramid have omitted difficult and hard facts of history when discussing the Pyramid. He makes the point that the omission of these facts

> ...perpetuates the modern conception of the ancient Egyptian. Indirectly, it has a tendency to belittle the achievements of the ancients, in medicine, literature, social consciousness, astronomy, geographical exploration, metallurgy, the mechanical arts, mathematics, and engineering.[14]

Applying the principles he used to build a working pump modelled after the Great Pyramid, Kunkel developed a new type of dam which can supply cheap electrical power.

One man believed Kunkel, way back in 1932. Robert Lee Spencer, Dean of the School of Engineering of the University of Delaware, after studying Kunkel's blueprints for the new type of dam, said

> Engineers feed on new ideas. Give them a new idea, and they will equip it with so many gadgets, that even *you* will not know what they are for. They will develop an automatic ignition system, special fuels, use inert gases, and all sorts of pressure and vaccuum gauges—tubes could be made big enough to run a boxcar through, with everything else in proportion—a bushel of wood should operate it for a day.[15]

In this energy-conscious age, as we build more and more nuclear power plants on earthquake-prone zones, one could hope that engineers will soon begin building dams such as Kunkel designed, supplying inexpensive electrical power. The accident at Three Mile Island (built on an earthquake-prone zone) compounded by an earth tremor would have had tragic consequences for anyone living within a fifty-mile radius. In his best-selling book *We Are the Earthquake Generation* Dr. Jeffrey Goodman points out that as the earth once again enters into a period of greater surface instability, architects of the future will find it necessary to learn more about plate tectonics if they are to retain the responsibility and respect afforded them by the people they build for. During an earthquake, a bushel of wood would damage far less property and hurt far fewer people than the eruption of a nuclear power plant.

The Great Pyramid — is it an astronomical instrument set to signify the changes of the seasons, the physical expression of all-prevailing principles of geography and astronomy, a tomb, or a huge hydraulic ram pump? Perhaps it is all these, and more.

In his book *Cosmic Trigger: The Final Secret of the Illuminati* Robert Anton Wilson writes of the double star Sirius and the intrigue that surrounds it. Most of that intrigue is a result of a ten-year labor by Robert K. C. Temple, a Fellow of the Royal Astronomical Society of England and author of *The Sirius Mystery.* Temple's ten years of research has led him to believe that an advanced race from a planet in the system of the double star Sirius visited Earth around 4500 B.C. The heliacal rising of the star Sirius in 4240 B.C. established

---

[14]Ibid, p. 22.

[15]Quoted in *Pharoah's Pump*, p. 79. A copy of this book is available from Mr. Kunkel by writing to him at 295 West Market Street, Warren, Ohio 44481.

the ancient Egyptian New Year—and the founding of Egypt as a unified kingdom.[16] The oldest chapter in the *Egyptian Book of the Dead* was discovered in the foundation deposit of an ancient temple by Heru-tata-f, the royal son of Men-Kau-Ra, while he was making an inspection of the old temples around 4266 B.C.[17]

Duncan MacNaughton, in his book *A Scheme of Egyptian Chronology*, points out the 41"-high passage at the top of the Grand Gallery as being aligned with the trajectory of Sirius, which moved between 26°18 minutes and 28°18 minutes around 4000 B.C. in the earth's southern sky (other astrophysicists believe that the heliacal rising of Sirius around 4000 B.C. had a trajectory of 23°). The founders of the Egyptian religion named their supreme being *Osiris*. Sirius is the only fixed star with an unvaried cycle of 365.25 days, and it played an important part in the Egyptian calendar. The German Egyptologist Ludwig Borchardt believes that the establishment of the Egyptian calendar took place in 4240 B.C.—almost the exact date when the oldest chapter of the *Egyptian Book of the Dead* was found in the foundation deposit. Schwaller de Lubicz in his *Le Temple de l'Homme* is also convinced that the year was 4240 B.C. Sir Norman Lockyer, who wrote *The Dawn of Astronomy*, believed that the Sphinx was built during the junction of the constellations Leo and Virgo at a summer solstice shortly before 4000 B.C. The entire Christian world, until the last century, believed that the world was created in 4004

B.C., based on the calculations of Archbishop Ussher.[18] Freemasonry records 4000 B.C. as the Year of Light. Professor Charles H. Hapgood in his book *Maps of the Ancient Sea Kings: Evidence of Advanced Civilization in the Ice Age* presents evidence that Antarctica was mapped around 4000 B.C. when its coasts were free of ice. Could the explosion of Vela X around 4000 B.C. have significantly melted the ice that covered the coast of Antarctica? If so, it would clear of obscurity how someone could have mapped Antarctica almost 6,000 years ago, a time when "experts" tell us our ancestors were walking around in a constant state of stupor trying to figure out how to count their toes. Hugh Auchincloss Brown presents evidence in his book *Cataclysms of the Earth* that the ice mass in Antarctica has been steadily growing for the past six thousand years.

It seems from the body of material that I have examined that some horribly destructive cataclysmic event took place on earth between 4500 and 4000 B.C. Was this event a pole-shift?

In *Cosmic Trigger* Robert Anton Wilson points out:

> ...whether we approach the Sirius mystery from the modern end and work backward from Aleister Crowley, or start from the ancient end and work forward from the Egyptians, we continually collide with the mysterious and enigmatic history of Freemasonry.[19]

---

[16]See John Anthony West, *Serpent in the Sky: The High Wisdom of Ancient Egypt*, p. 107.

[17]See Budge, p. 13 of the Introduction.

[18]In the seventeenth century, Irish Archbishop Ussher established that the world was created in the year 4004 B.C. at nine o'clock in the morning of October 26. He arrived at this date by his understanding of biblical chronology. Fossils until the last century were considered by many good Christians to be the work of the devil. It was imprudent to doubt such Bible wisdom.

[19]Robert Anton Wilson, *Cosmic Trigger: The Final Secret of the Illuminati*, p. 234.

I felt that it would be unwise to dismiss Freemasonry—an international sociological phenomenon—especially if the Masons knew some esoteric behind-the-scenes part of history concerning this event preserved in their ancient rituals. If we forfeit the right to seek answers to questions which sometimes appear unanswerable, then we forfeit our right to claim any difference from the animals.

What connection exists between Freemasonry, the Great Pyramid, and the ancient world was a question I felt would best be answered by a high-degree initiate of the Masonic Order. In the preface to the Golden Anniversary Edition of his book *An Encyclopedic Outline of Masonic, Hermetic, Qabbalistic and Rosicrucian Symbolical Philosophy*, Manly P. Hall writes:

> To live in the world without becoming aware of the meaning of the world is like wandering about in a great library without touching the books. It has always seemed to me that symbolism should be restored to the structure of world education. The young are no longer invited to seek the hidden truths, dynamic and eternal, locked within the shapes and behavior of living beings.

The prepublication sale of Mr. Hall's book has been without known precedent. The subscription list for the first edition was closed a year before the manuscript was given to the printer. The second, third, and fourth editions were sold before the finished volume was received from the printer. The book is massive in size, measuring 13" x 20". It contains 54 full-page color plates, 200 illustrations, an elaborate topical cross index, and numerous ancient written documents which still exist from ancient times—the German translations required nearly three years, to say nothing of the Latin, Italian, French, Spanish, Hebrew and Egyptian translations. It weighs ten pounds, retails for $125.00, and is one of the most beautiful books ever published. Originally published in 1925, this book and hundreds of others written by him have made Manly P. Hall the widest-read author of prehistory in the world.

Here was a man to answer questions—if he was still alive. A short time passed.

Noone: Mr. Hall, in your opinion what is the Great Pyramid?

Hall: I do not personally regard it as having been built as a tomb for the Pharoah Khufu. I feel that it was an antediluvian building, and it was built long before that time. I realize that is a highly controversial point, and I can only support it in a sense by a study of the whole antediluvian situation. I would suspect that perhaps the original meaning was clarified much later during the early Christian period, around the second or third century in Alexandria, when it was advanced that the Great Pyramid was the actual tomb of Hermes. Hermes is a semi-mythological personality, and is a personification of wisdom as the synthesis between the Greek Hermes and the Egyptian Thoth or Tehuti. Both represent the divine intelligence, and I have a feeling that it was originally a repository, monument, or diagram in miniature of an ancient wisdom belief, or perhaps one of the earliest scientific monuments in the world.

Noone: Would you care to advance an opinion as to who may have built it?

Hall: That's always a little difficult, because there are so many conflicting opinions on the subject. I doubt very much if it was built at or near the time in which it is historically assumed to have been built. I think it is a much older building, and I'd be inclined to suspect that it might have been built when the star Vega was in direct line with the Descending Passage, so that the ray of the star determined its location. I think it has strong astronomical importance.

Noone: When do you believe that was?

Hall: I think that was much earlier, perhaps fifty to sixty thousand years earlier. Incidentally, most of my opinions on the subject are in my published writings already. We have an article in the publication called *The Phoenix*, and in our large symbolical book, and some direct and indirect references to the Great Pyramid in my books *Freemasonry of the Ancient Egyptians* and *The Lost Keys of Freemasonry.*

Noone: Would there be any direct connection between the teachings of Freemasonry and the Great Pyramid?

Hall: I think there is definitely a connection. Now, [as to] whether the connection is direct, or whether Freemasonry in combining its rituals and so forth from ancient sources perhaps included both direct and indirect sources...There is a publication from the Library of Congress on the Great Seal of the United States. It is out of print, but we have a photostatic copy of it in our library. In that publication there is a considerable discussion of the reverse of the Great Seal. The author of the subject declares that the reverse of the Great Seal of the United States is a rather meaningless symbol derived from a secret society, and he goes into no further details.

Noone: The reverse of the Great Seal, showing the Great Pyramid, and the obverse both appear on the back of a one-dollar bill then?

Hall: Yes. I don't know if you ran across my little article on continental currency, but in that article I reproduced the drawings which appeared on the first continental currency, the first paper dollars. One of the drawings is the Great Pyramid, so it was used considerably before the designing of the Great Seal—which very few people know. Also, on another one of the seals the all-seeing eye in the triangle appears surrounded by three candlesticks on the old American banknotes produced around 1775-1780. So there was evidently a tradition back in there somewhere relating to that subject. And of course in the hieroglyphics of *Horopolo Nilus* the use of the Great Pyramid as a symbol is emphasized. That was one of the first efforts made during the early post-Christian period to interpret the hieroglyphics of Egypt. It is now considered one of the most important symbol or emblem books. My feeling is that from the general consideration of the presence of pyramids on various tombs and so forth, small ones particularly, in written hieroglyphics, I think it represented at that time a temple of

7:5. Egyptian Room, Masonic Temple, Philadelphia, Penn.

initiation of some kind into the Egyptian mysteries. Apparently the Great Pyramid was connected underground with some outside point, and the rituals carried on there would parallel very closely, I think, some of the basic rituals of Masonry, including the death and resurrection in the King's Chamber. The chamber coffin is certainly not adequate for the elaborate mummification and various coverings and so forth that were put over the bodies of these kings by nobles. They couldn't fit in. Also there seems to be no reason why a legitimate tomb should have air vents going from the King's Chamber out to the surface.

Noone: With all your studies, what did you find for yourself to be the easiest way to reach nirvana [a state transcending the limitations of earthly existence]?

Hall: Well, that's off the discussion of the Great Pyramid, but perhaps it *is* in there. In other words, perhaps the symbolism of that is there. If you want to ask such a question as Nirvana, I think the best authority would be to go directly to Buddhism. I don't feel I would want to do it, but I have a sneaky suspicion that it's a situation very much like certain degrees in Freemasonry: they have to be earned, and the symbols have to

7:6. The Symbolic Crucifixion in the King's Chamber of the Great Pyramid.

189

be correctly interpreted and applied directly to the personal conduct of the individual. In other words, if you want to be enlightened, you must live towards enlightenment.

Noone: Many writers have written that the Great Pyramid enshrines truth, and I wondered—what is truth?

Hall: Well, that question Jesus refused to answer. The term is just too big. We play with it too much. The truth of the thing is the reality of it, and the realities are all more or less concealed in a world of causation. And all we get are their shadows in this world. I think the only way the individual can really come to know truth in its fullness is to become one with it.

Noone: Numerous writers on the Great Pyramid have stated that the builders of the Great Pyramid came from the ancient continent of Mu. What do you think?

Hall: That I don't know. It doesn't seem to me that that is as likely as it would be that it is related more directly to Western culture. Perhaps the Atlantean Empire. There is a description somewhere—it might be in one of the unofficial degrees of Freemasonry, but there is a description—of the magnificent pyramid temple in the City of the Golden Gate, which was apparently the great capital city of the Atlantean Empire. Now I know pyramids of various kinds have recently been discovered in China, and just recently the enormous pyramid complex in northern Guatemala, and

to a degree the pyramid structure goes throughout the world, but the principal examples of it—particularly with very exact mathematical and astronomical relations—these are principally in Egypt and in the Western Hemisphere, through Central America, and with certain modification in South America. I would suspect that the Great Pyramid was a monument or marker of great importance, perhaps an effort to create a structure that would survive practically any disaster that could occur to the world. I feel that the pyramidal structures in Central America and Mexico and down even into the Andes represent a definite allegorical presentation of something more than the current belief. The codices support this point of view. Years ago I talked to Dr. Breasted, Sr., at the University of Chicago Oriental Institute, concerning the ritual of the *Egyptian Book of the Dead.* I asked him if he considered it possible that this was not intended merely as a talisman to carry the soul into another life, but might actually be a ritual performed among the living by a masked hierophant, and he replied, 'That certainly inevitably is true. I have actually seen a papyrus in which the prompter's marks are marked in the margins.' I did not see the papyrus, I only have it on the authority of Dr. Breasted, who is a pretty reliable authority and [was] the greatest living Egyptologist of his time. Also, the same is true in your ancient carvings, monuments, paintings and so forth—highly stylized symbolically. Now there is a possibility that there is a kinship

7:7. Top: The step Temple of the Inscriptions at Palenque resembles the Egyptian pyramids.

7:8. *Top*: Egyptian Pyramid. *Bottom*: Mexican Pyramid.

7:9: Step temples on both sides of the Atlantic. *Top:* Reconstruction of the Marduk temple in Babylon (about 600 B.C.) with the Temple of the Convocation (Esagila) on the left and the stage tower (Etemenanki) in the walled temple courtyard. *Bottom:* Reconstruction of the temple complex of Copan (Honduras), about A.D. 200-500. The "relationship" between this Maya temple and the Marduk temple in Babylon is striking. The stage tower could have been brought to Mesopotamia and Mesoamerica by the intermediary of the more ancient Atlantean civilization.

193

between these monuments and monuments in Asia, Tibet, Java, and Angkor Vat. The pyramidal form in all cases has been used to explain cosmic mysteries, and they belong to a realm of ideology that at the present time is very different from the ideology among most investigators.

Noone: Why would that be?

Hall: Because many are staunch materialists. I know in Mexico I discussed the pyramids of San Juan with several Mexican archaeologists, and they're all of one opinion—that these pyramids, like the Pyramid of the Sun, are very, very much older than the appraisals that have been put on them by non-Mexicans. They

7:10. Pyramid of the Sun, Teotihuacan, Mexico, west face.

are convinced that those pyramids were there long before the rise of the Aztec Empire or the Maya Empire, and that they represent a diffusion of a certain high cultural level, which extended almost entirely around the world.

Noone: What happened to such an advanced race and their culture?

Hall: I think Plato's account is correct, based on Solon, who in turn was supposed to have been able to examine the columns in the subterranean chambers of Sais, Egypt, in that they were memorials to a lost people. These people as a central hub of culture disappeared. These places that survived were originally colonies of the central source. When the central source vanished, the colonists were isolated. In every case, practically, that we trace, the original colonizer or the original leaders came from another land and promised to return. They never returned, and as a result of that each of these cultures gradually developed an indigenous form and developed its own specialized concepts. The common origin faded away for lack of support, but was preserved in legend and myth as the people who had gone long before. Mythology in my mind is really a history of prehistoric times. Please always bear in mind that my suggestions and comments are personal, in the sense that I claim no great authority for them. I claim only thoughtfulness and many years of contemplation of the philosophical aspects of these things.

Several months after I interviewed Mr. Hall, scientists measuring the growth of the ominous Palmdale Bulge (which covers 32,000 acres and straddles the 600-mile San Andreas fault at the intersection of the Gralock Fault) recorded the swelling was becoming more rapid. And, according to the latest research on earthquake activity, it's just a matter of time before California is struck by an earthquake much larger than the one that struck Guatemala on the morning of February 4, 1976, leaving one million human beings homeless and 23,000 dead in the twinkling of an eye. Californians are living in what scientists call "the ring of fire" and nature has a tendency to shake things off its back every once in a while.

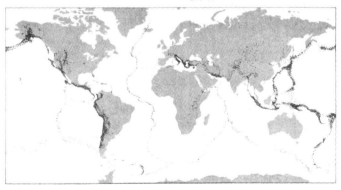

7:11. *The Ring of Fire.* This map shows the distribution of earthquake and volcanic activity which encircles the world where friction between the earth's tectonic plates is greatest.

If the collective unconscious of man contains memory of catastrophic experiences, which his collective consciousness normally represses, then this may explain why some people, more acutely sensitive to the subtlest earth tremors than their neighbors, have already moved out of seismically active California. William Mullen, one of the editors of *Pensee*, writes in the book *Velikovsky Reconsidered:*

> ...increased experimental sophistication has only revealed greater complexity in genetic structures, leaving the possibility of the subtlest kinds of transmission wide open. Inheritance of behavior patterns laid down in catastrophic circumstances might explain a number of biological enigmas: bird migration; swarming; acute sensitivity of many species to the subtlest earth tremors, solar eclipses, etc. The inheritance of memory has already been suggested by experiments on rats and worms.[20]

In 1972, David E. Smith, a geophysicist with Goddard Space Flight Center, developed a new technique—laser beams bounced off an orbiting satellite—to measure the movement of the San Andreas Fault. The Goddard team conducted experiments in 1972, 1974, and 1976. The experiments indicated far more subterranean activity than previously suspected. This in turn suggests that energy is rapidly accumulating and that its release will produce an earthquake of enormous magnitude. Many Californians have developed a unique defense against the coming earthquake: they ignore it.

The Richter Scale is a measure of ground motion as recorded on seismographs. Every increase of just one number means a *tenfold* increase in magnitude. For example, a reading of 7.5 reflects an earthquake ten times stronger than one of 6.5. A reading of 8.0 or above is a superquake. Jerry Eaton of the U.S. Geological Survey's Earthquake Research Center in Menlo Park said, "The 1857 and 1906 (California) earthquakes will be repeated—there's simply no way around it." Estimations as to when the superquake will occur vary; some place it as early as 1982, others as late as 1989. When it will happen remains the big question.

In 1974 Dr. John Gribbin, an astrophysicist, and Dr. Stephen Plagemann, who holds a doctorate in physics, published a book entitled *The Jupiter Effect*. They believe that the alignment of the planets around Christmastime late in 1982 will cause great sunspot activity and unprecedented earthquakes in California. Drs. Gribbin and Plagemann believe that the extra pull of the planets will act like the straw that broke the camel's back, triggering a release of the enormous amount of pent-up energy in the San Andreas Fault.

To what extent do the planets affect Earth? Does the moon affect the earth's high and low tides? Humans are about 95% water—could the gravitational pull of the moon affect the specific gravity of humans? Police report an increase in crimes during a full moon; perhaps this is why ancient Latin criminals were called "lunatics." Could the gravitational pull of the planets affect earthquake activity on Earth? Earlier in this book four of the best astrophysicists in the United States were kind enough to compute the position of Vela X in 4000 B.C. for me. Their carefully calculated measurements were all slightly different.

---

[20]The editors of Pensee, *Velikovsky Reconsidered*, pp. 284-85.

Why? The answer is that the angle of the ecliptic has decreased slowly, and accordingly the Tropic of Cancer has moved south. Why has the angle of the ecliptic decreased slowly? Why has the Tropic of Cancer moved south? Professor Livio Stecchini, in the mathematical appendix of Peter Tompkins's book *Secrets of the Great Pyramid*, points out that "this movement is due to the gravitational pull of the planets, particularly Jupiter and Venus."[21] If Drs. Gribbin and Plagemann are correct in their calculations, then as Dr. Jeffery Goodman points out in his book *We are the Earthquake Generation*, "one can only shudder at what the greater alignment and more significant positioning of the planets to occur in 2000 might bring."[22]

If Manly P. Hall, a high-degree initiate of Freemasonry (apparently including the same truths Herodotus learned from a masked hierophant in an ancient Egyptian mystery school), is after sixty-five years of research correct in his assertion that a certain high cultural level extended almost entirely around the world, where is the proof? "Where are their cities?" the unconscious mind of the uninitiated skeptic might ask. "Who wants to know?" the rational soul of the world might answer.

Earlier in this book Peter Tompkins prophetically said, "There may be another ten or fifteen thousand of them still buried in the jungle."

A serpent, its tail rattling slightly, caressed the base of the Pyramid Dr. Ian Graham stood upon. Ian Graham, of the Peabody Museum, Harvard University, was deep in the northern Guatemala jungle, two days' walk from the nearest village.

Standing atop the pyramid, Ian Graham felt a shiver run through his body as he measured and recorded the unexpected immensity of the site and the monumentality of its principal pyramids—far, far larger than the ancient pyramid ruins of Temple IV at Tikal, Guatemala. Standing like an alien atop a huge pyramid in the steamy jungle of northern Guatemala, Ian Graham suddenly realized he was measuring architecture that would revolutionize thinking on pre-Colombian history. From atop the principal pyramid of the ancient site called *El Mirador* by the Indians, he surveyed more than 200 buildings and a dozen pyramids six times larger than those at Tikal. The ruins cover so many hundreds of square miles that Ian knew the mapping would have to be done by laser and computer. He thought back to 1978, when archaeologists actually began to cut through the mounds of soil and vegetation that covered the remains of the once-huge metropolis. He remembered the words of Dr. Raymond Matheny of Brigham Young University: "We might have run across the first true city of the New World...It is one of the greatest concentrations of public architecture in the ancient world."[23]

The base of the pyramid Ian was standing on had been roughly measured at 750 feet per side or about 3000 feet around its base, and he remembered that Egypt's Great Pyramid measures 755 feet per side. From the archaeological field work already done and the thousands of ancient artifacts classified, Ian knew El Mirador was founded long before Tikal, long before Christ. He wondered why the oldest megalithic sites

---

[21]Tompkins, p. 295.

[22]Goodman, p. 178.

[23]*Foundation for Latin American Anthropological Research Newsletter.*

exhibited a higher level of workmanship. The pyramid he was standing on contained stones far larger than those at Tikal, and Mirador's houses have none of the characteristic cobblestone vaults so characteristic of all other discovered cities in Mexico and Central America. Field work already done showed that the ancient architects of Mirador apparently stopped building generations before Tikal collapsed, a newly discovered chronological fact that totally confuses the traditional historical sequence for the collapse and abandonment of Maya cities in Peten, Guatemala.

Everywhere Ian Graham looked, he could sense valid mathematical and astronomical relations, including the basic constants of our three-dimensional math. As with many ancient pyramid sites, it seemed that the builders were concerned, as if their very lives depended on it, with the movement and alignment of the planets and perhaps with the accumulation of ice at the earth's South Pole.

Turning his eyes from the twin altars at the end of the vast plaza, Ian looked over a sea of greenery. He could see the remains of a vast and ancient highway system radiating outward across the jungle in every direction to other cities in the realm. In the distance he saw the citadels of Tintal and Nache. He remembered that in 1880 Claude Joseph Desire Charnay had discovered in a very ancient Mexican cemetery 13,000 feet up Monte del Fraile ancient *wheeled* toy chariots.[24] If these people had wheeled toys, is it not logical to assume that they also had wheeled vehicles? The highway system radiating outward like a spider web from the pyramid complex reminded Ian Graham of the highway system on the Pacific island of Malden.

On the barren Pacific island of Malden, remnants of a vast and ancient highway system radiate outward like a spider web from a temple complex of forty stone temples. The highway system, composed of large blocks of basalt fitted together so precisely that grass will not grow between them, runs across the island, crosses the beach, and disappears under the waves of the Pacific. Isn't it illogical to assume that these huge, precisely engineered roads were constructed simply for people to *walk* on? Fifteen hundred miles south of Malden Island, another section of the same type of road emerges from under the waves, crosses the beach, and disappears into the jungle of Rarotonga Island. This suggests that many Pacific Islands are the remains of a presently submerged Pacific continent. Three thousand four hundred miles west of Malden Island lies the Pacific island of Ponape. A vast ruined city called Metalanim (renamed Nan Madol around the turn of the century) sits on its southeastern shore. Ninety walled artificial islands covering eleven square miles comprise the site. The city is constructed of huge natural crystalline log-like blocks of basalt. Manmade canals capable of passing a modern ocean liner divide the city. A colossal breakwater to protect the city was laid in the ocean, with a large sea gate for passing ships in and out. Stone walls 40 feet high and 18 feet thick (Were these walls built eighteen feet thick to keep the people in or to keep something huge, powerful, and terrifying out?), artificial waterways, colossal breakwaters and sea gates, unlike the primitive buildings one associates with the natives of the Pacific, give evidence of a former powerful and well-organized culture which vanished within the "Ring of Fire."

[24]Cf. Tompkins, *Mysteries of the Mexican Pyramids,* p. 152; also Charles Berlitz, *Mysteries from Forgotten Worlds,* p. 54.

J. Macmillan Brown in his book *The Riddle of the Pacific* says:

> ...the hauling up of these immense blocks, many of them from five to twenty-five tons in weight, to such height as sixty feet must have meant tens of thousands of organized labor; and it had to be housed and clothed and fed. Yet within a radius of fifteen hundred miles from this as a center there are not more than fifty thousand people today. It is one of the miracles of the Pacific..."[25]

Colonel James Churchward in *The Lost Continent of Mu* describes the ruins of a great temple on Ponape, a temple 300 feet long by 60 feet wide, which he believed at one time was part of the presently submerged Pacific continent he called Mu—the Motherland of Man.

> On the walls are the remains of carvings of many of the sacred symbols of the Motherland. This temple is connected with canals and earthworks, and has vaults, passages and platforms. The whole is built of basaltic stone. Below the pavements of the great quadrangle, on opposite sides, are two passages or gateways, each about 10 feet square. These are pierced through the outer wall with passageways leading down to the canal. Within the great quadrangle is a central pyramidal chamber, unquestionably the holy of holies.[26]

Churchward believed the city on Ponape was one of Mu's capital cities, one of the Seven Sacred Cities of the early Empire of Mu. Churchward presents evidence that the writings today named the *Egyptian Book of the Dead* were brought to Egypt from Mu by holy men who were acutely sensitive to the subtlest earth tremors and left the Early Empire before it was obliterated by earthquakes.

In *The Lost Continent of Mu* (1930), *The Children of Mu* (1931), *The Sacred Symbols of Mu* (1933), *The Cosmic Forces of Mu* (1934), *Cosmic Forces as They Were Taught in Mu Relating to the Earth*, Volume Two (1935), Churchward describes a once great civilization with a population of 64,000,000, which was obliterated by earthquakes and vanished beneath the waters of the Pacific. Back in the thirties, before the theory of continental drift was developed, the defenders of the conventional wisdom ridiculed the idea of a submerged continent in the Pacific Ocean. In 1977, however, Dr. Amos Nur, a Stanford University geophysicist, and Dr. Zvi Ben Avraham of the Israel Oceanographic Institute renamed this submerged Pacific continent "Pacifica."

Churchward's research suggests that many Pacific islands are part of what at one time was a vast continent crossed with many beautifully paved roads cunningly constructed to represent the web of the gray-and-black pointed spider. Churchward draws parallels between the *Seven* Sacred Cities of Mu and the *Seven* Rishi (sacred) Cities of India and the *seven* superlative intellects of the *seven*-headed serpent which gave *seven* commands. Churchward states that while in India he read in the Naacal clay tablets that the earth was created in *seven* periods of time.

In *The Ultimate Frontier* we read:

> The Pacific Basin is ringed by mountain ranges, often volcanic, which were raised when Lemuria

[25]J. Macmillan Brown, *The Riddle of the Pacific*, quoted in Berlitz, pp. 124-25.
[26]James Churchward, *The Lost Continent of Mu*, p. 76.

7:12. Nan Dowas Temple, Nan Madol, Ponape, 1968.

7:13. Nan Dowas Temple, Nan Madol, Ponape "Commoners' Gate" at left, 1968.

7:14. *The Submersion of Mu.* "Temples and palaces came crashing to the ground."

[Mu] sank. Near the prehistoric city of Tiahuanaco, which is on the shore of Lake Titicaca in the Andes Mountains of Peru, are the remains of stone-lined canals which served as a connection between the Pacific Ocean and the geologic Amazonian Sea which was formerly part of the Atlantic Ocean. The canal is now about two-and-a-half miles above sea level. Tiahuanaco is built along the same lines as Metalanim on Ponape and is also intersected by canals.

Excavations south of Mexico City revealed a former ocean port which is now far inland at an elevation of 7,000 feet. When this ancient buried city was unearthed by William Niven, it had a total of thirty-one feet of debris above it consisting almost entirely of boulders, gravel and sand. The only way so much material of this type could have been deposited is by a tidal wave of colossal magnitude. If nothing else, these archaeological findings indicate that man was well civilized during the last era of mountain raising and that he experienced floods of appalling destructiveness.[27]

In the ancient records of all peoples, in temples and monuments to the planets, in precise charts of the heavens, astrological canons, religious texts, secret societies, sacrificial rites, legends and myths, are recorded the fact that the earth more than once in historical times has been

[27]Richard Kieninger, *The Ultimate Frontier,* p. 69.

Atlantic Ocean.

7,000 feet above sea level

Pacific Ocean,

⊙ Mexico City.
⊕ Niven's Buried Cities.

7:15. Conventional sketch, present conditions surrounding Niven's Mexican buried cities.

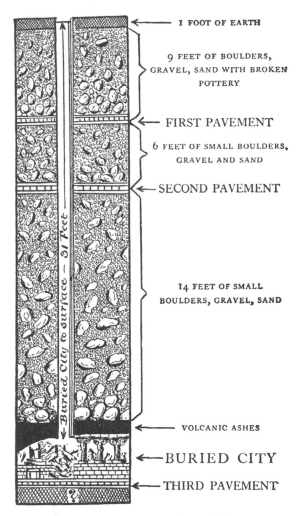

<- I FOOT OF EARTH

9 FEET OF BOULDERS, GRAVEL, SAND WITH BROKEN POTTERY

<- FIRST PAVEMENT

6 FEET OF SMALL BOULDERS, GRAVEL AND SAND

<- SECOND PAVEMENT

14 FEET OF SMALL BOULDERS, GRAVEL, SAND

<- VOLCANIC ASHES

<- BURIED CITY

<- THIRD PAVEMENT

Buried City to surface – 31 Feet

7:16. Niven's Mexican Buried Cities.

fundamentally altered by global cataclysms. Almost every year, as if to bear witness of global cataclysms, ancient cities like Mirador, buried for centuries, are uncovered and speak to us of their sudden demise. Ancient texts speak of a shift in the terrestrial axis of the planet, and of the magnetic poles of the earth having been suddenly flipped over.

How, the skeptic might ask, could the earth's magnetic field have flipped over? Will the earth's magnetic field flip again on the 5th of May 2000?

As the planet Earth rotated on its axis, the sun *appeared* to rise above the horizon like a grave and giant ball of fire. Above the Galapagos Islands the sky began to grow light. The hull of a ship, slapped by the waves of the Pacific, became visible in the gray light of dawn. In the bowels of the ship life stirred—intelligence stirred, drank coffee, and began a new series of experiments on board the research ship *Glomar Challenger* at a site almost midway between the Galapagos Islands and the west coast of Ecuador.

On the morning of 23 July 1979, British, Soviet, and American scientists aboard the research ship *Glomar Challenger* were heading home. The vessel has, over the past eleven years, drilled 800 core holes at 501 sites deep into the sea floors around the earth. The *Glomar Challenger* is the only ship in the world capable of such deep-sea drilling. The international team of specialists on board had concluded the most extensive experiments ever conducted on core samples of the earth's sea floors, using magnetic, chemical, acoustical, and electrical devices as well as radioactivity.

Just before the mission ended, as it sometimes happens, in one of the last experiments conducted, a Soviet device, a rotating ultrasonic beam pulsing 2,000 times a second, lowered into one of the core holes, documented that the earth in its mosaic past had reversed its polarity—meaning that compasses would have pointed south, instead of north!

Immediately above the stratum showing the reversed magnetic field was another stratum "normally" polarized. This showed the scientists that the Earth's magnetic field had later flipped back to the present magnetic field (see Plate 4:4). In the section of the report dealing with what the immense force might have been which caused the magnetic field of the planet to flip over and reverse its polarity, and then suddenly flip back over to its present polarity, was one word: "unknown."

What immense force of kinetic energy could have brought about a total reversal in the magnetic force fields of the planet? The query marked "unknown" is unanswerable. However, some specialists privy to the report who had families in California moved their families out of California. It may be pointed out that alterations between strata are abrupt—so are cataclysmic disasters, tornadoes, typhoons, earthquakes, and a sudden surge of a major part of the Antarctic Ice Sheet. Outer space influences, like the explosion of Vela X, are also sudden. One would think that man would be satisfied with all these natural disasters—natural disasters that are difficult to predict and, with all our present technology, impossible to control or prevent.

If one thinks of the earth as an egg with cracks in its shell, then one can visualize the crust of the earth as composed of several tectonic plates. Between these tectonic plates are the cracks in the eggshell—huge cracks like the San Andreas Fault in California, the Brevard Fault in Georgia, the Motagua Fault in Guatemala, etc.—pieces of shell (tectonic plates) separated by cracks (faults). The faults that separate the earth's tectonic plates form an interconnecting web which encircles the planet.

Before the 1976 Guatemalan earthquake, pressure built up in the Motagua Fault until it found a point of release. Before that earthquake, rock deep in the earth below Guatemala changed in electrical resistance, and a percentage of the pressure was transferred from the Motagua Fault into the next intersecting fault, the San Andreas Fault. Pressure in the earth, like water or ice, seeks the path of least resistance and moves from one fault to another.

On the morning of 29 November 1978, the U.S.S.R. detonated *two* nuclear devices underground. The first blast registered 5.6 on the Richter Scale; the second blast registered a huge 7.1—almost a 20% increase of ground motion. Rock deep in the earth below Russia changed in electrical resistance. Pressure moved rapidly underground from one fault to another until it found a point of release. A few hours later that day, a slight tremor moved under Mexico City and was followed almost immediately by a second and stronger tremor, which collapsed office buildings and sent office workers streaming into the streets.

Later that day a percentage of the pressure moved north into the San Andreas Fault. One remembers the words of Professor Aranja as he explained the Guatemalan earthquake to his trusted field foreman Emmanuel: "When we speak of a major earthquake, we are working with a global event. It shakes the entire planet."

To my knowledge no seismological laboratory has conducted a major study of the relationship of underground nuclear explosions and earthquake activity. Since November of 1976 scientists have been disturbed by a flurry of minor tremors, measuring up to 3 on the Richter Scale, that have occurred along the San Andreas Fault southeast of Palmdale, California. Don L. Anderson, Director of Cal Tech's seismological laboratory, speaking of the flurry of minor tremors, says: "Until these recent swarms there has been very little action along this section of the San

7:17. The stone masonry technique employed in a corner of the Valley Temple adjacent to the second largest pyramid at Giza, Egypt (allegedly the Egyptian Kephren's), is obviously similar to the stone masonry technique employed in the corner of the temple of the three windows on the other side of the Atlantic Ocean at Machu Picchu, Peru. One major difference in construction techniques between the two is the use of polygonal blocks and the absence of cement between the stones in Peru. Another difference between the two is that the stone masonry at Machu Picchu, Tiahuanaco, and other South American sites employed a keyway or slot cut into one stone in the wall opposite a keyway cut in the stone next to it. Metal clamps fitted into the slots joined the stones together. Thus, each stone employed in the building of the temple was joined together into a stone masonry system admirably suited for stability during a period of earthquakes.

Andreas Fault. It could be significant."[28] The Guatemalan earthquake was one of fifty earthquakes recorded around the world by the U.S. Geological Survey during 1976.

The U.S. Geological Survey reported that 35,000 human beings—and possibly two or three times that number—died in earthquakes around the world in 1976. The U.S.G.S. said the count was far from complete because official fatality reports from the significant earthquakes in China in July and August and the significant quakes in the Soviet Union in April and

[28]U.P.I.

May were unobtainable. The U.S.G.S. believes the Chinese quakes may have killed over 100,000 people. In addition, the death count did not include the earthquake of 25 June in Western New Guinea, which agency officials believe killed 6,000 people. The total death toll, somewhere around 200,000 "makes 1976 the worst year for earthquakes during the last fifty years," a 1976 UCLA report said.[29]

During 1976 the United States exploded thirty-six nuclear devices in the Pacific Ocean alone. Official figures on how many nuclear devices the Soviet Union, China, and other Iron Curtain countries detonated during 1976 are unobtainable. This withholding of facts by Iron Curtain countries makes it difficult for scientists to evaluate how extensively the detonators of nuclear devices are damaging the planet's state of equilibrium, depleting the ozone layer, or increasing the incidence of cancer in humans. How extensively the explosion of nuclear devices in the air, under the seas, and in the ground are affecting natural disasters—earthquakes, volcanic activity, floods, freakish weather patterns[30]—on the planet is also a question at present unanswered.

Two weeks before the devastating earthquake that hit Iran in September 1979, Soviet seismologists predicted the quake. How could they predict the quake? Perhaps they knew of an upcoming test. Thirty-six hours before the quake, the Soviet Union detonated a nuclear device underground, 4,000 kilometers away. The bomb (about ten megatons) was considerably larger than most. The earthquake which struck Iran registered 7.4 on the Richter Scale, and in seconds *twenty-five thousand* innocent men, women, and children lay dead.

Naturally earthquakes are almost always followed by less powerful aftershocks within a day or so. None were detected.

The question, "What have the detonators of nuclear devices wrought?" thunders forth in silence. The implications are awesome. As Charles F. Keetering has said, "I am vitally interested in the future, because I am going to spend the rest of my life there." As the precession of the equinoxes inexorably moves us closer to 5 May 2000 A.D., this question will grow in importance until finally even the very least cognizant people on this planet will urgently begin to ask this question .

A question asked too late is seldom answered in time.

---

[29]See Goodman, op. cit.

[30]See The Impact Team, *The Weather Conspiracy,* which includes two CIA reports: "A Study of Climatological Research as it Pertains to Intelligence Problems," and "Potential Implications of Trends in World Population, Food Production, and Climate."

The molecular structure of quartz is spiral, and may be left-handed or right-handed just as on the carved decorations at Newgrange [Ireland]. It is also piezoelectric: that is, it expands slightly if given a slight charge of electricity. If placed under pressure — as it would be if charged while inside another stone — alternate edges of its prism give off positive and negative voltages on what can reach a dramatic scale: a force of 1,000 lbs. applied on each face of a half-inch crystal of quartz creates 25,000 volts.

Francis Hitching
Earth Magic

According to Maurice Denis-Papin, descendant of the famous inventor, the Arc of the Covenant was a sort of electric capacitor capable of producing an electrical charge of 500 to 700 volts. The Arc is said to have been made of acacin wood, lined inside and out with gold: that is to say, two conductors separated by an insulator. On either side were garlands which may have served as condensors. Denis-Papin says the Arc was placed in a dry spot where the magnetic field reached a normal 500 to 600 volts per vertical meter. Insulated from the ground, the Arc is said to have given off fiery rays, acting like a Leyden jar.

Peter Tompkins
Secrets of The Great Pyramid

And when they came to Nachon's threshing-floor, Uzzah put forth his hand to the ark of God, and took hold of it: for the oxen shook it.
And the anger of the Lord was kindled against Uzzah, and God smote him there for his error; and there he died by the ark of God.

2 Samuel 6:6-7

(The ark of the Covenant was an adaption of the Egyptian Ark, even to the kneeling figures upon its lid. Bas-reliefs on the Temple of Philae show Egyptian priests carrying their ark — which closely resembled the Ark of the Hebrews — upon their shoulders by means of wood staves like those described in Exodus.)

CHAPTER EIGHT
HISTORY REPEATS ITSELF

Pyramids, cyclopean stone walls, titanic stone remains of archaeoastronomy containing a knowledge of orbital geometry,[1] magnetic forces,[2] and thermodynamics,[3] prove beyond a shadow of a doubt that our grand and august ancestors were far, far more intelligent than most historians are willing to admit, especially from the time they began to think of our ancestors as hairy, tailed quadrupeds, probably arboreal in their habits. In reality our ancient ancestors were far more interesting than monkeys.

Today scientists like Dr. Ronald D. Nadler at Yerkes Regional Primate Research Center (Emory University, Atlanta) are conducting fascinating research work with monkeys and the great apes. Scientists like Dr. Roger Fouts at the University of Oklahoma and Stanford University's Penny Patterson, to name a couple, are teaching monkeys and the great apes how to communicate with humans. Monkeys and apes have been taught to "talk" with humans by being taught Ameslan, the American Sign Language used by the deaf. Monkeys and apes at Yerkes Primate Center have been taught Yerkish, a computer language developed there.

This research work has raised many questions. Dr. Carl Sagan, in *The Dragons of Eden*, points out that if monkeys and the great apes are capable of abstractions, how smart do they have to become before killing them constitutes murder? He asks how smart they must become before religious missionaries consider them worthy of conversion. Could a band of men in some ancient age have "talked with the animals?" Could our ancestors have taught monkeys and great apes to perform simple tasks? Is it within the bounds of reason to imagine our ancestors may have taught teams of great apes to move huge blocks of stone—or did the ancient ones (as some believe) command a knowledge of magnetic forces, thermodynamics and other natural forces of nature that we are only now rediscovering?

The old adage, "Intelligence commands respect," becomes applicable when one considers that man during times of hunger would imprison, breed, and deliberately kill monkeys and apes for food, before he would deliberately kill one of his own kind.

In his book *The Conquest of Civilization* Dr. James Henry Breasted shows an ancient Egyptian relief of gazelles, addaxes, oryxes, ibexes, and hyenas, now found only in a wild state, eating at their mangers in stables along with cattle and goats. Records so far discovered do not tell us to what extent the Egyptians domesticated monkeys and apes. Breasted writes:

It is interesting to see how the ad-

---

[1] See Tompkins, *Secrets of the Great Pyramid* and *Mysteries of the Mexican Pyramids*.

[2] See the report of the Foundation for Latin American Anthropological Research on the curious magnetic properties of giant stone statues at Monte Alto, Guatemala. Also *Newsweek* (16 July 1979), p. 85.

[3] See Suares, *Cipher of Genesis*.

vancing desiccation of the Sahara thus brought man and the wild animals together, so that finally the ox, the sheep, the goat, and the donkey, all once wild, gave up their free life and became what we call domestic animals, the servants of man.[4]

As scientists continue to educate monkeys and apes, will we, as in some scene from the movie *Planet of the Apes*, have primates picking cotton, collecting garbage, and performing other menial tasks? Would they be subject to the draft?

Were man and monkey at some ancient time one? It is significant that Charles Darwin did not use much fossil evidence that worked against his theory. Journalists have misled people into thinking that there is one particular "missing link," which if found would prove the common origin of man and monkey. Point in fact: there are millions of "missing links." It has been hoped that in the hundred or so years since Darwin popularized his theory of evolution many of these intermediate species would be found. They have not. Rather than a gradation between forms in the fossil record, we find clear-cut gaps—the same gaps that exist between present-day forms. Anyone who examines the fossil record will be struck by the remarkable persistence of many types down through the alleged geological ages. Fossils of plant leaves claimed to be 70 million years old—sycamore, birch, willow, poplar, grape, oak, hickory, walnut, palm, fern, and many others—are all identical with their present-day counterparts.[5] Where is the supposed "evolutionary development" between the fossil form and the present? Starfish fossils dated at 750 million years ago are indistinguishable from "modern" starfish.[6] Shouldn't they have changed into something else during all that time? In comparative anatomy class we were taught to pay our respects to the venerable *coelecanth*, "one of our fish ancestors that lived four hundred million years ago." Evolutionists claim that they were able to detect from the fossils of these fish that their front fins were turning into legs! How great was their embarrassment when in recent years a living coelecanth was found off the coast of Madagascar with its front fins no further evolved than those of its 400-million-year-old fossil counterpart.[7]

"There is probably no area of science more filled with nonsense and unscientific guesswork than that branch which deals with fossil man," writes George Mulfinger, a persistent and dedicated researcher of many deceptions embodied in the theory of evolution. In his book *The Flood and the Fossils*, Mulfinger states, "From a few fragments of bone, a generous supply of plaster of paris and a vivid imagination, whole races of men are fabricated and colorful myths are constructed concerning their [supposed] primitive beastlike mode of life."[8]

George Mulfinger is a science faculty member at Bob Jones University, Greenville, South Carolina. He received his B.A. in chemistry, summa cum laude, and his M.S. in physics, both from Syracuse Uni-

---

[4]James Breasted, *The Conquest of Civilization*, pp. 26-27.

[5]See Byron C. Nelson, *After its Kind*, quoted in George Mulfinger, *The Flood and the Fossils*.

[6]Ibid., p. 59.

[7]Ibid., pp. 55-56. Cf. p. 293 of this present work.

[8]George Mulfinger, *The Flood and the Fossils*, p. 8.

versity. He has pursued additional graduate studies in several of the physical sciences at Syracuse, Harvard, and the University of Georgia. He holds memberships in the American Association for the Advancement of Science, the American Physical Society, the South Carolina Academy of Science, Sigma Pi Sigma, Pi Mu Epsilon, Phi Beta Kappa—and like Dr. G. Patrick Flanagan is listed in *Leaders in American Science*. He was the recipient of a National Science Foundation Research Participation Grant in 1964.

In his book Mulfinger discusses the Piltdown Man:

> The Piltdown Man hoax marked one of the low points in the history of science. A practical joker filed down the teeth of a chimpanzee jawbone to pass for human, treated it chemically to give it the appearance of great age, and planted it in a gravel bed where it was subsequently 'discovered' by a team of anthropologists. Many of the greatest experts in the field accepted it as a legitimate fossil. In fact they were fooled for 41 years! If the most eminent physical anthropologists in the world are so easily deceived, how far can we trust their pronounce-ments?[9]

Another good example of this type of misinformation being accepted by the lay person as truth is the Nebraska Man. The Nebraska find was used in the Scopes Trial in an effort to confound William Jennings Bryan. Bryan stated wisely that the evidence was too scanty. What was the evidence? The evidence, as Mulfinger points out, "was a single tooth!"

On the basis of *one* tooth a whole new race of man was created and even dated—at one million years. The name chosen for this new great find, "proving" the missing link between man and monkey, was *Hesperopithecus Haroldcookii*, in honor of its discoverer, Harold Cook. Further study revealed, however, that the single tooth found was the tooth of an *extinct pig*. Mulfinger says:

> In the meanwhile, though, the 13th Edition of the Encyclopedia Britannica had carried it as a legitimate human fossil with 'all the honors.' In the *14th* Edition it became necessary to explain it away. Rather than admit that it had been a wild pig's tooth, the author simply stated that it had belonged to a 'being of a different order.'[10]

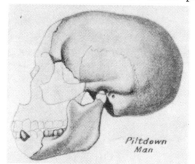 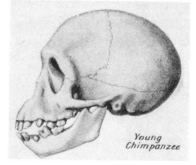 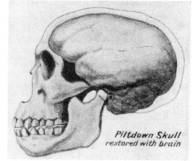

Piltdown Man

Young Chimpanzee

Piltdown Skull restored with brain

8:1. Mythical Piltdown Man.

[9]Ibid., p. 9.

[10]Law students may wish to ponder the part of extinct pigs in the Scopes trial. Ibid., p. 10.

The well-known Java Man find consisted of only a small piece from the top of the skull, a fragment of a left thigh bone, and two teeth.[11] Mulfinger points out, "These were found in sand in a riverbed in central Java, over a span of about a year, scattered over a range of 50 to 70 feet. There is therefore no guarantee that the bones all belonged to the same creature. Dr. Dubois, the discoverer, took them to Europe where they were examined by twenty-four of the most eminent scientists of the day. These leaders of the scientific world were unable to reach any agreement as to the identity of the bones. Ten of them felt they had come from an ape, seven thought they were human, and the other seven were convinced that they were from some kind of 'missing link.' "[12]

Dr. Dubois, who had originally sided with the latter group, eventually reversed his position and concluded that the creature was a gibbon (an ape of the Indian Archipelago, slender in form and with very long arms). A second Java Man later turned up in the literature, based only on what was thought to be a part of a skull. However, modern science knows this piece of skull, as Mulfinger points out, to be the kneecap of an extinct elephant.[13]

In 1959 the famous *Zinjanthropus* was found at Olduvai Gorge in Tanzania, East Africa. Since that time Mulfinger states "three different artists' conceptions have made the rounds of various periodicals—one drawn like a man, one like a gorilla, and one like a chimpanzee."[14] Originally hailed as one of our remote ancestors, the *Zinjanthropus* is now considered by its discoverer to be most like a gorilla. He states that it was at least "95% ape."[15] Mulfinger says:

> We would be willing to go the other 5% and say that it was 100% ape. Other impressive names such as *Australopithecus* and *Paranthropus* have appeared in the news. These are nothing but extinct apes, having a brain capacity comparable to that of the modern gorilla.[16]

  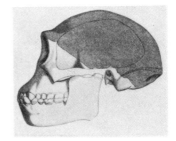

8:2. Mythical Java Man. Ape, Mythical Java Man. Shaded area shows the kneecap of an extinct elephant.

[11]Nelson, pp. 126-130.

[12]Mulfinger, p. 10.

[13]Ibid., p. 11.

[14]See Arthur C. Custance, *Fossil Man in the Light of the Record in Genesis*, p. 7. and Mulfinger, p. 11.

[15]Dr. Leakey is quoted by Mulfinger, p. 11.

[16]Mulfinger, p. 11.

Until just recently there were only two theories to explain man's presence on this planet—Darwin's theory of evolution and the biblical theory of creation. New research on organic evolution, genetic drift, and random evolution has raised questions as to whether or not Darwin's theory is the whole story.

Dr. David M. Raup, Curator and Chairman of Geology at the Field Museum of Natural History in Chicago, questions whether Darwin's theory tells the complete tale of how life developed on earth. In an article entitled "The Revolution in Evolution," written for the 1980 *World Book Science Annual*, Dr. Raup points out that Darwin's theory does not explain the whole process of evolution, and that this has caused many evolutionary biologists and paleontologists to believe that there is more to the story. For example, Dr. Raup says:

> ...suppose there is a very small population of pigs—say only five of reproductive age. One of the five pigs carries a mutation that makes it resistant to swine flu, a common disease among pigs. This mutation makes it better adapted than the other four. Theoretically, the better adapted animal will live longer and have more offspring than the other four, so the next generation will have a higher percentage of pigs carrying the flu-resistant trait. Such a change would be evolution because the species would change, and it would be Darwinian evolution because the change would be in the direction of a better adapted organism.
>
> However, suppose that a tree falls on the superior pig before it has produced offspring. The tree could have fallen on any of the others. It was just bad luck for the species that it fell on the better adapted animal. As a result of this non-Darwinian event, the superior animal—and its genes—would be removed from the population. This is one form of a process that biologists call genetic drift.[17]

Going back to the bones and the dates and the statistics, geneticists and molecular biologists are pulling genes apart and recombining them in hopes of finding out why life turned out the way it did. While Dr. David M. Raup and Drs. Stephen Jay Gould of Harvard University, Thomas J. Schopf of the University of Chicago, and Daniel S. Simberloff of Florida State University search for a connection between natural selection and random evolution, other scientists (who have forgotten that the extinction of a species can prevent the evolutionary system from ever reaching an equilibrium or steady state) continue building nuclear power plants and detonating nuclear devices, creating greater surface instability in the crust of this planet as we inexorably move closer to 5 May 2000—an anciently dreaded date embodied in the Great Pyramid's mathematical symbolism.

That symbolism contains a message from an early empire to a civilization of the future sufficiently advanced to decipher it. No language was used in the message, because a language might be lost or altered with the passage of time. For example, 2,000 years ago the word *meek* was a word used to describe a chariot horse so well disciplined that with the lightest touch of the rein on the right side of its neck the horse would instantly respond and turn to the right. At that time the word *meek* meant well disciplined. So when the Master Adept Jesus

---

[17]David M. Raup, "The Revolution in Evolution," in *World Book Science Annual* (Chicago: 1980)

said, "Blessed are the meek: for they shall inherit the earth," we can understand that he was saying, "Blessed are the well disciplined, for they shall inherit the earth."

After twenty-five years of intense research, David Davidson, a structural engineer, architect, astronomer, mathematician, and historian, published his analysis of the Great Pyramid's message. His monumental book (568 pages—the size of an encyclopedia volume) is titled *The Great Pyramid: Its Divine Message.* Using geometry, astronomy, stone construction, and allegory from the *Egyptian Book of the Dead*, Davidson says that the designer of the Great Pyramid was

> ...projecting his knowledge into a future stage of civilization that could interpret his intention. He [the designer] foresaw that the contemporary language in which the facts could be conveyed would lose its meaning and idiomatic significance. It might be lost entirely, or at least be capable of mistranslation or misinterpretation. This foresight has certainly been justified.[18]

Davidson, an agnostic and a sober structural engineer from Leeds, England, originally became interested in the Great Pyramid when he read of the theories of Robert Menzies. According to Menzies, a Scottish religious enthusiast, the Great Pyramid contained a 6,000-year prophetic history of the world commencing in 4000 B.C.

A quiet genius, Davidson set out to disprove the "idiotic" theories of Menzies. The more Davidson attacked the data used by Menzies, the more he dug into them, the more he was forced to accept them. He blueprinted every stone of the Great Pyramid's interior system, and after twenty-five years of intense research Davidson the agnostic became a deeply religious man. His book is the most extensive, thorough, and analytical book ever written on the Great Pyramid.

Davidson used time-honored scientific laws to explain the Great Pyramid's mathematical symbolism. In the seventh edition (1937) of his book, Davidson talked of the number of days in a solar year, the hollowing-in feature of the Great Pyramid's faces in relation to the anomalistic and sidereal year (see Plate 5:14), the common culture pattern in ancient measures, the Great Pyramid's external definition of the planet Earth and its orbit in relation to the zodiac and its apparent movement, the precessional movement of the north celestial pole, a perspective view of the southern heavens up the south end of the Great Pyramid's Grand Gallery. As with Einstein with his "special" theory of relativity, few people of the thirties understood Davidson's explanation of the Great Pyramid's mathematical symbolism. His explanation was simply too thorough, too scientific, too analytical. The overwhelming bulk of Davidson's detailed mathematical computations swamped the average reader, and only a few understood why a band of men almost 6,000 years ago stood on the sands of northern Africa quietly waiting in the dark, their eyes scanning the heavens.

The people of Stelle, Illinois (see the photograph at the end of the Preface), are certain they understand the message of the Great Pyramid. They are making preparations to airlift at least 250,000 persons above "the physical danger inherent in the seismic reapportionment of the world's land masses and the various accompanying conditions"[19]

---

[18]**David Davidson,** *The Great Pyramid: Its Divine Message*, p. 139.

[19]*See below.*

214

they believe will take place on 5 May 2000. A skeletal structure of their program is outlined below:

I. Overall Objective
   Develop and Assemble the technological means for surviving the turn of this century.
II. Interim Goals
   A. Community of Stelle to become totally self-sufficient so as to buffer the effects of the coming economic collapse and the conditions to exist between that time and the turn of the century.
   B. Develop a plan by 1980 to accommodate 10,000 people in the community.
   C. Assist in the building of a second community outside Dallas, Texas, so a community stands at the beginning and end of the country's beef food-chain, i.e., the stockyards of Texas and the slaughterhouses of Chicago.
   D. After developing the city of Adelphi outside Dallas, assist in the building of Philadelphia, a third city to be constructed on an island in the Pacific Ocean.
III. Parameters, Criteria, and Conditions to be Considered
   A. Prepare for an increase in the frequency of destructive winds, droughts, floods and generally disruptive atmospheric conditions nearing the end of the century.
   B. Seismic and volcanic activity will increase in frequency and destructiveness as the century draws to a close.
   C. After 1998 we may have to deal with effects from the final war and battle of Armageddon in terms of nuclear fallout and atmospheric

disturbances.
   D. By May 5, 2000, we must be ready to airlift at least 250,000 persons above the physical danger inherent in the seismic reapportionment of the world's land masses and the various accompanying conditions.
   E. After May 5th, we must be prepared to cope with hurricane-strength winds generated in an atmosphere filled with dust, fumes, and noxious gases.
   F. Must plan that the sun will be blocked out by dense volcanic ash and other atmospheric contaminants, preventing the use of solar energy.
   G. Great walls of water will roar across the land, whisking away almost everything in their path.
   H. Immediately following the cataclysm, soil conditions will make conventional food propagation unfeasible.
Basic Needs to be Fulfilled
   A. Pre-cataclysm site preparation for Stelle, Adelphi, and Philadelphia.
      1. Need to develop earthquake-resistant structures in order to minimize later rebuilding.
      2. Need to determine how to store building materials and useful goods that are not practical for airlifting.
   B. The airlifting of at least 250,000 persons to an altitude of approximately 14 miles for a period of approximately 14 days in special vertical take-off-and-landing craft. These vehicles are to be about the size and shape of a Boeing 747 fuselage, maintain a stable and horizontal position, and carry approximately 200 passengers

215

each.
1. Need a practical power system.
2. Need a practical propulsion system.
3. Need to develop a life-support system package for the craft that will meet all of the basic needs for 200 people (per craft) over an extended period of time. Some of those needs include: Pressure Control, Temperature Control, Air Purification, Potable Water, Food, Waste Handling, Lighting.

C. Post-cataclysmic rebuilding and new construction
1. Need large temporary shelters with the necessary utility systems for heat, water, wastes, etc.
2. Need to establish food propagation operations.
3. Need to fabricate building materials from whatever indigenous resources exist, and salvage whatever materials and goods survive the upheaval.

The city of Stelle is sixty miles south of Chicago, Illinois, a few miles from Cabery, Illinois. To learn more about this unique city, I talked with Robert B. Machiz at the Stelle Administration Building.

Noone: Do the people of this city believe there will be a cataclysm of massive earthquakes and *tsunamis* [giant sea waves] on Friday, May 5th, 2000?

Machiz: As far as the Stelle Group is concerned, the answer is: yes, there will be tremendous changes as the tectonic plates shift in search of equilibrium. These expected changes are the outworkings of geophysical and astro-mechanic forces. This unusual combination of factors may be referred to as the "Doomsday Effect."

Noone: What are the components of the Doomsday Effect?

Machiz: Many factors within our earth are conjoining to produce great surface instability, but in brief they are: (a) structural weakness in the continental arches, which has occurred as a result of thousands of years of earthquake and volcanic activity—volcanoes and earthquakes are the earth's way of relieving the stresses and pressures created by a slight shrinkage of its overall size; (b) the polar icecaps have been building up in a lopsided manner, especially at the South Pole, adding further to surface instability; (c) on May 5th, 2000, the planets will be aligned in practically a straight line, which will exert sufficient gravitational pull to trigger a major reapportionment of the earth's land masses.

Noone: Would this have anything to do with religion or an act of God?

Machiz: The Stelle Group does *not* believe that these geological changes are being brought about by God or higher beings. Rather, they are the natural outworkings of physical factors.

Noone: Many Christian fundamentalists are saying that these are the 'later years' spoken of in Chapter Sixteen of Revelation.

Machiz: Under their scenario a

vengeful God has become disgusted with the growing multitudes of sinners and non-believers and these shall be destroyed when Doomsday or Judgement Day is 'visited upon them.' Of course, the true believers will be saved from this terrible ordeal as God intervenes on their behalf. Typically, the source of their information is through revelatory experience or interpretations of the Bible. The scenarios do not appeal to a person's logical and analytical faculties—rather, the appeal is an emotional one. Underlying such a world view we usually find the concept that 'by grace are ye saved.' Pure belief in God is enough to please him and gain his favor and blessings.

Noone: How did the Stelle Group gain advance knowledge of the coming world events?

Machiz: The information concerning the Doomsday Effect was provided by the Brotherhoods, which are comprised of men and women from our planet. The information is neither a vision nor an interpretation of the Bible, although parts of the Bible deal with these events. The Stelle Group does *not* believe that it will be saved by an act of God. Each person is responsible for his or her life, and predestination of any kind is *never* imposed upon us by higher beings. Stelle seeks to develop the technology which will allow civilization to continue after the predictable events at the turn of the century. Sitting on our laurels and feeling saved will not produce the much-needed technology, nor will it aid us in our attainment of egoic advancement. The components of the Doomsday Effect can be substantiated with scientific evidence. While many scientists will either ignore or blatantly reject this information, there will still be some who will give it the serious attention it warrants. Of the latter, a portion will be sufficiently sympathetic to the Brotherhoods' philosophy to enable them to join the Stelle Group.

Noone: What are the benefits for those who join?

Machiz: If the applicant is sincere, well disciplined, and accepted, he or she shall find at Stelle an environment conducive to both the development of character and the development of the technology which will be needed to withstand the events at the turn of this century.

I interviewed Stelle's Robert Machiz on 24 March 1977, and I realized that all the people living there had read *The Ultimate Frontier* and had then for one reason or another decided to move to Stelle. *The Ultimate Frontier* is a book that most people are bound to feel strongly about, because it strikes uncomfortably deep at the core of almost every human delusion of our times. The book covers a wide range of fascinating subjects: the relations among members of the Brotherhoods such as Pharaoh Akhnaton, Moses, King David, Elijah, Isaiah, Buddah, and Jesus; the adventures and travels of Jesus between his twelfth and thirtieth years as reported from contemporaneous records preserved by the Brotherhoods; the geology of the ancient, sunken continent in the Pacific Ocean called Mu or Lemuria, and the evidence of its once-majestic civilization; the coming trials of mankind during the remainder of this century; and the part the Brotherhoods will play in preserving the finest in our culture.

The book was finished and ready for publication way back in 1959, but publisher after publisher turned it down as "too hot to handle" because it made public certain secrets of almost all the major religions. Other publishers turned it down back in the 50's because of the book's economic predictions for the United States. *The Ultimate Frontier* said that the United States in late 1979 or the first few months of 1980 would encounter severe economic conditions, and of course the publishers back in the 50's knew that no economic adviser worth his salt would dare to predict an economic condition twenty years in the future. March 1980: President Carter addresses the United States with his anti-inflation plan.

Some of the early readers of the book invested wisely, made millions, and built a new city in a cornfield sixty miles south of Chicago. A month before President Carter addressed the nation, a story about the Stelle Group appeared on the front page of the prestigious *Wall Street Journal* (19 February 1980). Was somebody listening?

Rejected by every major publisher during 1959 and 1960, the author was not intimidated. Perhaps he knew that Zane Grey, who gave us so many marvelous westerns, tried to sell his book manuscripts when he was still unknown and was told by a publisher that he had no ability for writing westerns. Or that Louisa May Alcott, who wrote the classic *Little Women*, was once told by a publisher to give up the idea of writing. The author of *The Ultimate Frontier* decided to publish and promote the book himself—something that normally has about as good a chance as a snowball in the place of eternal damnation. *The Ultimate Frontier* soon became the largest-selling underground book in the United States. How the book comes into a person's environment varies. More than one person has said he was casually strolling down the aisle of a bookstore when *The Ultimate Frontier* fell off the shelf in front of him. Most of the time, however, the book is recommended as an interesting and rewarding reading experience by a friend.

In any age a precursor of knowledge speaks to the people. Some listen, some don't. For the years remaining between now and the year 2000, *The Ultimate Frontier* offers a moving and practical message of hope.

Attempting to judge whether or not the earth will undergo a great distortion of its crust in 2000 without adequate information would only lead us to wander around in a desert of indecision. Wandering in indecision is dangerous; one may sometimes stumble into an *auto-da-fe*, which is sometimes fatal. Let us not despair or become fatalistic in our thinking on this subject. At the end of even the darkest tunnel shines a ray of hope. Let us therefore seek answers, and in so doing find the truth—lest the fear of a cataclysm paralyze our mental energy, or (even worse) lest we complacently allow the threat of a possible cataclysm to be woven into the fabric of our modern anxiety and, like the threat of nuclear war, be seldom thought of. However, continuing reports of increasing earthquake and volcanic activity, both near and far, in the newspapers and on radio and television, will prevent us from washing our hands of the subject like some modern Pontius Pilate. In this age of instant news, our hearts will not be waxed gross nor our ears dull of hearing nor our eyes closed to the ever-increasing and ever-present possibility of events we cannot control, ending our lives and the lives of our children. Thankfully, some of us instinctively know the difference between right and wrong.[20]

There are a few in our history who dared to be great, and until their accomplishments are recognized, history will remain distorted. For example, thousands of years ago Zoroaster said:

Be good, be kind, be humane and charitable; love your fellows; console the afflicted, pardon those who have done you wrong.

And Buddha said:

In dealing with others, one should do as he would have done him.

And Mohammed said:

Let none of you treat his brother in a way he himself would dislike being treated.

And Confucius said:

Do not do to others that which you would not they do to you.

And Jesus said:

All things whatsoever ye would that men do unto you, do you even unto them.

And Krishna said:

The true rule is to do by the things of others, as you do by your own.

And in the Torah, the law of Moses, we read:

Do only to another man what you would that he do unto you.

These seven great Adepts have all said essentially the same thing. How many believers in any of these religions practice what the founder of their religion taught? How many modern teachers of these religions today practice sophistry? Few believe in any religion because they have examined the evidences of its authenticity and made a formal judgement upon having weighed the testimony. Had we opened our eyes to the light under the shadows of St. Peter's in Rome we should have been devout Catholics; born in the Jewish quarter of Aleppo we should have condemned Christ as an imposter; in Constantinople we should have cried, "God is Great and Mohammed is his prophet." One of the best ways to learn more about one's own religion is to study someone else's. If Zoroaster, Buddha, Mohammed, Confucius, Jesus, Krishna, and Moses were alive today and meeting together, would they quibble and bicker and slay one another over dogma?

Of course not, we would answer. Yet today in Ireland, Catholics kill Protestants and Protestants kill Catholics in the name of religion, in the name of God. Hebrews quibble with Moslems and Moslems bicker with Christians, and all over the world religion wars against religion while innocent girlhood shrieks in vain to lust for mercy, and gray hairs are dabbled in blood. Until teachers of religion teach tolerance and respect for the religions of others, this planet will continue to orbit the sun a stinking charnel-house, steaming and reeking with human gore, the blood of brother slain by brother for opinion's sake, all to prove whether this or that doctrine be heresy or truth, a horror to her sisters in the universe.

A wise teacher was asked, "On your

---

[20]Researching our history is like wading through a snake-infested swamp barefoot. If you make it to the other side of the swamp, human snakes appear to say venomously that you could not have walked barefoot through a snake-infested swamp. You must have used a boat, they cry. Or there were no snakes at all. What you report must be a lie because, if there were snakes you would not have made it. It is always those who have never walked barefoot through a swamp who cry most vehemently and boastfully.

death-bed, would you call for a priest, rabbi, minister, or some other?" He said, "Until you thoroughly understand your religion and compare it to others, how will you know your last choice in life was the correct one?"[21]

John the Baptist taught some creed older than Christianity, and the body of evidence points out that he was a member of the Essenes. The sect of Essenes, which parallels Christianity, believed that truth was scattered among different religions throughout the world. The Essenes were studious and hard workers, who refused to use or make weapons. They were skilled in the healing arts, practiced benevolence, organized their order into four degrees (each with secret rituals), and hid a part of the Great Pyramid's message in the Dead Sea Scrolls, which they deposited for future generations.

Baptism was a distinctive ritual of the Essenes, who taught the doctrines of reincarnation and the immanence of God. It is an interesting question as to how much Christianity owes to the Essenes. Baptism is a link between modern Christianity, the Essenes, the mysteries of the Cabiri, and the ancient Egyptian mysteries of Osiris. Speaking on the Egyptian mysteries, Herodotus said:

> Upon this lake are represented by night the accidents which happened to him whom I dare not name. The Egyptians call them their mysteries. Concerning these, at the same time that I confess myself sufficiently informed, I feel myself compelled to be silent.[22]

Men have formed secret societies, made use of ceremonies of initiation, employed symbols and emblems and means of recognition in all ages.

Occult teachings and the traditions of the mystic religions state the following: John and Jesus were cousins, and when Jesus arrived to be baptized John did not recognize him, as they had not seen each other since childhood. Jesus made himself known to John by giving John a secret sign or token. Then John returned the appropriate sign or token, to which Jesus gave another secret sign or token, until they had worked their way through a whole system of challenges and counter-challenges. This continued until Jesus, the Secret Master of the Essenes, passed on to higher orders or degrees which John the Baptist had not attained. John (or Johana, which means in Hebrew "Yahweh is gracious") the prophet later became known as John the Baptist because he practiced the rite of baptism—a distinctive mystical Essene ritual.

In A.D. 212, Minacius Felix, a Roman lawyer, wrote a defense of Christians and Christianity in which he said:

> Many of them know each other by tokens and signs (*notis et insignibus*), and they form a friendship for each other, almost before they become acquainted.[23]

Besides secret handshakes, the early Christians would flash the sign for the Pisceian Age, which was usually a small fish carved out of bone. The symbology is obvious: Jesus, the fisher of men. In fact, Christianity in the beginning was a secret religious order. Contemporary writers of the period attest to the secrets of the church.

St. Gregory Nazianzen, Bishop of Con-

---

[21]This anecdote is from the author's personal experience.

[22]Herodotus, p. 142.

[23]Quoted in Pike.

stantinople, wrote in A.D. 379:

> You have heard as much of the Mystery as we are allowed to speak openly in the ears of all; the rest will be communicated to you in private; and that you must retain within yourself... Our Mysteries are not to be known to strangers.[24]

In his book *De Mysteriis* St. Ambrose wrote:

> All the Mystery should be kept concealed, guarded by faithful silence, lest it should be inconsiderately divulged to the ears of the Profane.... It is not given to all to contemplate the depths of our Mysteries...that they may not be seen by those who ought not to behold them; nor received by those who cannot preserve them.[25]

In his second book St. Ambrose wrote:

> He sins against God, who divulges to the unworthy the Mysteries confided to him. The danger is not merely in violating truth, but in telling truth, if he allow himself to give hints of them to those from whom they ought to be concealed.... Beware of casting pearls before swine!.... Every Mystery ought to be kept secret; and, as it were, to be covered over by silence, lest it should rashly be divulged to the ears of the Profane. Take heed that you do not incautiously reveal the Mysteries![26]

St. Cyril of Alexandria (made bishop in 412 and died in 444) wrote in his seventh book against Julian:

> These Mysteries are so profound and so exalted, that they can be comprehended by those only who are enlightened. I should say much more, if I were not afraid of being heard by those who are uninitiated: because men are apt to deride what they do not understand. The ignorant, still today, not being aware of the weakness of their minds condemn what they ought most to venerate.[27]

That the ancient mysteries of Egypt were incorporated into Christianity may be glimpsed in the writings of Theodoret, Bishop of Cyropolis in Syria (born 393 and made bishop in 420). In one of his three Dialogues, called the "Immutable," he introduces *Orthodoxus* by saying:

> Answer me, if you please, in mystical or obscure terms: for perhaps there are some persons present who are not initiated into the Mysteries.[28]

He further writes, in his preface to Ezekiel, tracing the secret discipline leading up to the commencement of the Christian era, that "these Mysteries are so august, that we ought to keep them with the greatest caution.[29]"

---

[24]Ibid.

[25]Ibid.

[26]Ibid.

[27]Ibid.

[28]Ibid.

[29]Ibid.

Origen (born A.D. 135), answering a charge made by Celsus that the Christians had and taught a secret and mysterious doctrine which was taught only a select few initiates, replied:

> Inasmuch as the essential and important doctrines and principles of Christianity are openly taught, it is foolish to object that there are other things that are recondite; for this is common to Christian discipline with that of those philosophers in whose teaching some things were exoteric and some esoteric: and it is enough to say that it was so with some of the disciples of Pythagoras.[30]

To be eligible to receive the teachings of the hidden sciences, Pythagoras consented to be circumcised, a practice brought out of Egypt by the Hebrews. The great secrecy observed by the initiated Egyptian priests for many years, and the lofty sciences which they professed, caused them to be honored and respected throughout all the world. Egypt was regarded by other nations as the college, the sanctuary, of the arts and sciences. The inner circle of the Egyptian Priesthood knew all the secrets of the Hindustani, Persian, Syrian, Arabian, Chaldean, and Phoenician mysteries. These mysteries were taken to America thousands of years before Columbus by Egyptian astronomer-priests. That the Egyptians visited and colonized America is today known with certainty, thanks to the genius of Harvard Professor Barry Fell. In his landmark book, *America B.C.*, Professor Fell presents myth-shattering evidence that Libyans, Celts, Basques, and even Egyptians had in some ancient time established colonies in North America. Professor Fell's book was finished in 1976 and published in 1978.

The early Christians were initiated into the Christian mysteries in three degrees. Members of the first degree were called *auditors*. Members of the second degree were called *catechumens*. Members of the third degree were called the *faithful*. Archelaus, Bishop of Cascara in Mesopotamia, when questioned about the secret mysteries of the early Christian Church, replied:

> These Mysteries the church now communicates to him who has passed through the introductory degree (auditors). They are not explained to the Gentiles at all; nor are they taught openly in the hearing of catechumens; but much that is spoken is in disguised terms, that the faithful, who possess the knowledge, may be still more informed and those who are not acquainted with it, may suffer no disadvantage.[31]

St. Augustine, Bishop of Hippo (who lived to a ripe old age of 83, having been born in 347 and dying in 430), wrote:

> Having dismissed the catechumens, we have retained you only to be our hearers; because, besides those things which belong to all Christians in common, we are now to discourse to you of sublime mysteries, which none are qualified to hear, but those who, by the Master's favor, are made partakers of them…. To have taught them openly, would have been to betray them.[32]

---

[30]Ibid.

[31]Ibid.

[32]Ibid.

He goes on to say that the Ark of the Covenant signified some sort of mystery.

The Wall Street Journal's story on the city of Stelle, Illinois, contained the information that the founder of Stelle, author of *The Ultimate Frontier*, was chosen to establish the city by "a secret, ancient organization."[33] *The Ultimate Frontier* states that the granite box in the Great Pyramid's third chamber was:

> ...the repository of the Golden Ark of the Covenant—the Holy of Holies of the Tabernacle in the Wilderness. This revered relic was placed in the sealed pyramid for safe-keeping.... The Ark had previously been secreted in the long-since destroyed Temple of Isis where it had been brought by Osirians from Poseid.
>
> The Ark was intended to be delivered into the custodianship of the 'Israelites' who would hold it safe. It rested in Solomon's Temple until the Kingdom of Judah was established under Rehoboam, Solomon's son. The Ark served as the symbol of the scepter—meaning Salvation through Christ—which was prophesied to come through the tribe of Judah (Genesis 49:10). Precariously, but continuously, the Ark remained in Judah's possession until Christ was crucified. At that time the Ark was overturned, and it disappeared. It is now in safekeeping by one of the Brotherhoods.[34] (See Plate 2:9).

Moses also took the mummy of Joseph with him when he departed Egypt during a great and overwhelming national disaster.

That the early guardians of the Christian mysteries felt they could not speak freely to the people is evident in the writings of Chrysostom, Bishop of Constantinople (born 354, died 414), when he wrote:

> I wish to speak openly: but I dare not, on account of those who are not initiated. I shall therefore avail myself of disguised terms, discoursing in a shadowy manner....[35]

Why the early guardians of the Christian mysteries felt they could not speak freely to the people is best explained in the writings of Cyril, Bishop of Jerusalem, who wrote in his *Catechesis* before he died in 386:

> The Lord spake in parables to his hearers in general; but to his disciples he explained in private the parables and allegories which he spoke in public. The splendor of glory is for those who are early enlightened: obscurity and darkness are the portion of the unbelievers and ignorant. Just so the church discovers its Mysteries to those who have advanced beyond the class of Catechumens: we employ obscure terms with others.[36]

That the early Christian writers held the Egyptian philosophers in high regard is evident from the writings of Origen:

> The Egyptian philosophers have sublime notions with regard to the Divine nature, which they keep secret, and never discover to the people but

---

[33]For this story see *Wall Street Journal,* 19 February 1980.

[34]Kieninger, p60.

[35]Quoted in Pike.

[36]Ibid.

8:3. Here is the most holy place in the House of God. It is a perfect cube, 20 cubits by 20 cubits (40′ × 40′) 1-Kings, 6th. Chapter) the only piece of furniture in the most holy place was the sacred Ark of the Covenant of the Lord, containing the testimony. This was placed within the oracles, shadowed by the wings of two gigantic angels on olive wood, overlaid with pure gold. Each angel was ten cubits, (20′ high) 1-Kings 6: 25. With an outspread of wings of twenty cubits (40′).

under a veil of fables and allegories.[37]

Clement of Alexandria wrote:

> The Egyptians neither entrusted their mysteries to everyone nor degraded their secrets of divine matters by disclosing them to the profane; reserving them for the heir apparent to the throne, and to such of the priest who excelled in virtue.[38]

In his book *Fragments of a Faith Forgotten, the Gnostics: A Contribution to the Study of the Origins of Christianity*, G.R.S. Mead writes:

> The institution of the Mysteries (Egyptian, Hebrew, Christian, Hindostan, etc.) is the most interesting phenomenon in the study of religion. The idea of antiquity was that there was something to be *known* in religion, secrets or mysteries into which it was possible to be initiated; that there was a gradual process of unfolding in things religious; in fine, that there was a science of the soul, a knowledge of things unseen.
>
> A persistent tradition in connection with all the great Mystery institutions was that their several founders were the introducers of all the arts of civilization.... Analyse any of the great religions, and you find the same factors at work, the same problems of human imperfection to be studied, the many who are 'called' and the few who are 'chosen.' All Hindus, for instance, are not unintelligent worshipers of idols and all

Christians fervent imitators of the Christ.[39]

Who were the founders of the great mystery institutions of ancient Egypt? Who they were and where they came from is itself a mystery; we may know the gift but not the giver. Looking around us today we can still see their influence—the two columns, Jachin and Boaz, which stood at the outer porch of Solomon's Temple, were *facsimiles* of the two obelisks that stood at the outer porch of the Egyptian Temple of Amen, and from them arose the fashion in the Middle Ages of surmounting cathedrals with two towers (See Plates 1:7, 1:11, 2:9).

In Finlayson's *Symbols and Legends of Freemasonry*[40] it is stated: "AMEN—This untranslatable word, the same in all languages, is a name of the great God of Egypt." In Revelation 3:14, God is called "the Amen." The early Christians had three degrees, auditors, catechumens, and the faithful. For centuries before the Christian era the Essene communities performed their secret rituals (of four degrees) beside the shore of the Dead Sea. Earlier, in ancient Egypt, the Egyptian priests performed their mysteries, which Manly P. Hall believes "would parallel very closely the basic rituals of the three degrees of Blue Lodge Masonry including the death and resurrection in the King's Chamber." The earliest written record of the ancient mysteries is in the *Egyptian Book of the Dead*, rituals performed among the living by masked hierophants. The *Book of the Dead* has been translated by two scholars, the first being E.A. Wallis Budge and the second W. Marsham Adams of Ox-

---

[37]Ibid.

[38]Ibid.

[39]G.R.S. Mead, *Fragments of a Faith Forgotten, the Gnostics.*

[40]Symbols and Legends of Freemasonry, p. 20, Finlayson.

ford (in 1897). Sir Gastron Maspero, as a result of Mr. Adams's researches, concluded that the Great Pyramid and the *Book of the Dead* reproduce "the same original, one in words, the other in stone."[41]

Adams translated the ancient rituals written on papyri and considered the title to be *Book of the Master of the House of Hidden Places*. It is from this very literature that the Coptic descendants of the ancient Egyptians derived the mystical and allegorical element that was introduced into early Christian gnosticism. The literature of early Christian gnosticism abounds in mystical pyramid figures and associated astronomical conceptions and constellations. According to David Davidson:

> To the Copts is due the survival, to the present day, of the ancient Egyptian Calendar and month names. To them we owe the retention of a dialect of the ancient Egyptian language, and with it, much that has tended to facilitate and elucidate the translation of ancient hieroglyphic texts. Hence the importance and value attaching to any traditions concerning the Great Pyramid that can be reliably identified as of Coptic origin.[42]

The Institute of Antiquity and Christianity (Claremont, California) has published *The Gospel of the Egyptians* (1975) and *The Coptic Gnostic Library* (1978), and recently furnished a new library for the Monastery of St. John the Theologian on the island of Patmos, Greece. (Women are not allowed on that island.)

Adams's *Book of the Master of the House of*

Hidden Places identifies the Great Pyramid's passages and chambers from the ancient text, which E.A. Wallis Budge had titled *Book of the Dead*. Adams identifies the Great Pyramid's underground chamber as the "Chamber of Chaos." The granite plugs that block the first part of the ascending passage he identifies as the "Gate of Ascent." The ascending passage he identifies as the "Hall of Truth in Darkness." The middle chamber he identifies as the "Chamber of Second Birth" or "New Birth." The horizontal passage from the middle chamber he identifies as the "Path of the Coming Forth of the Regenerate Soul." The threshold of the Grand Gallery, at the top of the ascending passage, he identifies as "the Crossing of the Pure Waters of Life." From the ancient texts Adams identifies the name of the Grand Gallery as the "Chamber of the Orbit" or the "Hall of Truth in Light." Adams made these translations back in 1897, almost a hundred years before modern science discovered Vela X (which I have shown in Chapter Six is the focus for the Grand Gallery). The word "Pharaoh" descended to us through the Hebrew. In ancient Egypt the term meant "Lord of the Orbit." The antechamber at the top of the Grand Gallery Adams identifies as the "Chamber of the Triple Veil," and the King's Chamber as the "Chamber of the Open Tomb" (see drawing by David Davidson, 8:4).[43] David Davidson used time-honored scientific laws to explain the Great Pyramid's mathematical symbolism, but his explanation is too thorough, scientific, and analytical to use in this present work. Thus, working from bottom to top, we have the

---

[41]Quoted in Tom Valentine, *The Great Pyramid: Man's Monument to Man,* and Davidson, p. 88.

[42]Davidson, p. 89.

[43]For confirmation of these names, see Davidson, *The Great Pyramid: Its Divine Message,* pp. 88, 218, 370-2, 382-3.

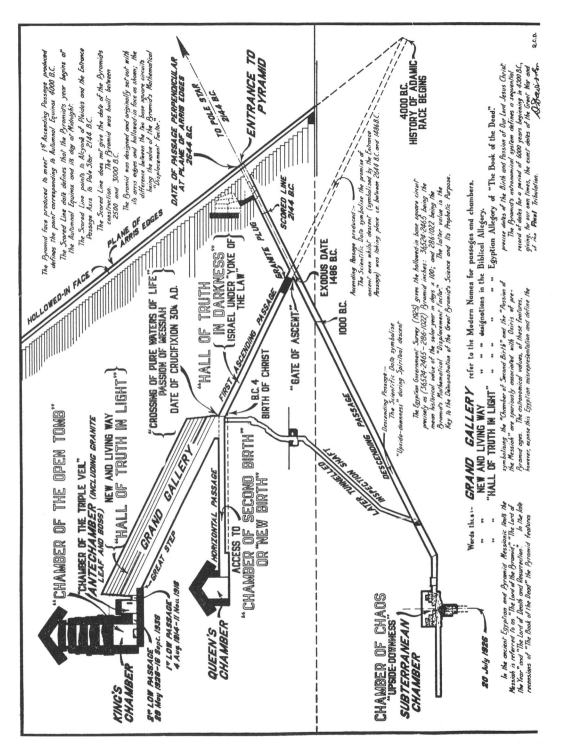

8:4. *Davidson's Drawing.* This cross-section shows Davidson's enlightening translations of the names of the chambers of the Great Pyramid.

227

names of the Great Pyramid's three chambers: Chamber of Chaos, Chamber of Second Birth (or New Birth), and Chamber of the Open Tomb. Symbology is the key, the infallible exegisis, to the inexorable message incorporated in the Great Pyramid by our ancient progenitors. Using symbology, can we decipher a message almost 6,000 years old? Can we keep it simple, yet accurate? Thanks to Tom Valentine, author of *The Great Pyramid: Man's Monument to Man,* we can. His simplification of Adams' and Davidson's long and complicated translations follows:

The *Book of the Master* and the Great Pyramid describe the same path for every individual who lives and dies, then reincarnates again and again to learn the lessons of life. The one tells the story in words, the other in stone.

Every Ego, or Ka as the Egyptians called the discrete bundle of mental energy that makes up a person, descends into incarnation from another plane, and as the incarnation begins—as the child takes its first breath—the Ego loses all conscious memory of its previous lifetime. As one enters the Great Pyramid, it is on a descending angle. There is one hieroglyph inscribed in the limestone above the entrance—it is best translated as 'horizon of heaven.' This corresponds to the allegory in stone. As each of us descends into life, the horizon of heaven narrows and we emerge in darkness.

We invariably reach a point in our descent into life and its unknowns where we may choose to elevate ourselves and begin the ascending path that ultimately returns to the Crea-

tor. However, the 'Gate of Ascent' is blocked; the elevation of one's character is difficult. The way is blocked, and it is much easier to cease the attempt and drift along a descending slant, remaining in the dark regarding life's purposes. About sixty feet from the entrance, we find the ascending passage leading upward into the heart of the Great Pyramid, and the Gate of Ascent is plugged with those three cubes of granite, built deliberately into place.

Those souls or Egos that do not make the struggle to grow upward through the gate of ascent will continue to descend in darkness. They cannot know, for they descend further and further from the light until finally they reach the 'chamber of upside downness,' the chamber of 'chaos.' There are false indications that lead one to believe there is another way out, but these routes lead nowhere. The Ego in this chamber of chaos has no choice but to die in darkness, or climb all the way back up to the Gate of Ascent and make the struggle. All is not lost when one dies in 'unknowingness' because he will be incarnated again, and again, and again so that he may choose to elevate—but the choice must be his own.

In the Great Pyramid, after you reach the granite plugs or the Gate of Ascent, you can continue descending for more than 350 feet in total darkness and close quarters until you finally reach the subterranean chamber carved out of the rocky plateau directly below the Pyramid's apex...this dark chamber is unique. The ceiling is dressed and relatively smooth, the floor is rough and unfinished—it's upside down, the chamber of chaos or upsidedownness. There is what appears to be another corridor, but it leads to a dead end; there is what appears to be a well shaft or corridor leading straight down, but it too is a dead end. Is this chaos? A chamber built upside down with passages to nowhere!

Turning back to the Gate of Ascent, the Ego now incarnate makes the choice to strive for human perfection. He does not know at this point that perfection, rejoining the Creator, is what he is seeking, but he follows an inner urging that demands that he elevate himself. This inner urging is a 'divine discontentment,' very much like nature's urging to a caterpillar, which causes metamorphosis and beautiful butterflies. The aspiring individual makes his way through the Gate of Ascent and finds himself in the 'Hall of Truth in Darkness.' Once you make the effort, you can feel the ascent, but though you are on the right path, it is not immediately made easy—you must continue to make great effort.

In the Great Pyramid, once beyond the granite plugs you still must practically crawl along because the passage or corridor is still narrow and confining. It's also dark, but it does not become progressively darker as does the descending passage. You are moving upward through the Hall of Truth in Darkness.

Your physical life may expire at any point along the way, but you retain in your Egoic memory the lessons that brought you to the particular plateau of advancement

along the path you have made—making it easier for you to choose the proper circumstances of life to incarnate into the next time around. The various plateaus of advancement are indicated by the 'girdle stones' found every 17 feet 2 inches.

As you work your way upward along the Hall of Truth in Darkness, you will reach a corridor leading you toward a major plateau of Egoic development. You enter the 'Chamber of New Birth,' or 'Second Birth.' In this chamber you may take stock of all you have learned during your ascent in darkness, and there will be a realization of what you are struggling toward—a new awareness of consciousness of the purpose of all the effort. You will be filled with joy and new resolve to continue the ascent toward the Creator.

Armed with your new consciousness—cosmic consciousness some like to call it—you return to the ascending passage and suddenly emerge into the 'Hall of Truth in Light.' The grand gallery stands before you, magnificent, spacious, filled with the promise of glory.

Every phrase or name for the chambers or passages is translated directly from the *Book of the Master,* and it is obvious that each fits the interior system of the Great Pyramid perfectly.

Let's look at the cleverness of the symbolism in the actual construction. [See Plate 8:4.] You are climbing upward in the narrow ascending passage, or Hall of Truth in Darkness. You are crouching and practically crawling along so you cannot see what is above; therefore when you reach the juncture of the corridor leading to the Queen's Chamber, or the Chamber of New Birth, it grasps your attention before you notice the Grand Gallery looming just above. Returning from your visit to the Queen's Chamber, your motion is going to take you naturally upward into the Grand Gallery as you emerge from the slanted corridor entrance. You now can stand up and stretch your limbs and move upward more easily in the huge, two-story gallery. It is indeed the Hall of Truth in Light.

As the joyous, growing Ego reaches the upper end of the Hall of Truth in Light, he must climb a great step before he can stand on a level floor. All your effort has brought you, finally, to the floor of the temple. You are on the verge of what the Buddhists and Hindus have called 'liberation.' You have almost reached the pinnacle of this round of existence; once you pass through the 'Chamber of the Triple Veil' before you, you need never incarnate to the physical level again—your Egoic growth will be accomplished on higher levels of existence from this point on.

The Chamber of the Triple Veil obviously has three parts to it. According to the *Book of the Master*, the first part is 'inner conflict,' the second part is 'truce in chaos,' and the third part is 'final tribulation and humility.'

Let's look at the actual construction in the Great Pyramid. [See Plate 8:4.] At the upper end of the Grand Gallery is a great step of limestone and once you climb up onto it, you are standing on the floor level of the main chamber, or King's Chamber.

However, to enter, you must stoop down again and enter another cramped corridor. After the magnificent ascent in the Grand Gallery, it's no wonder one wants to balk a little before stooping to enter the narrow, confining corridor. It's certainly symbolic of inner conflict. You only crawl for a few feet in this first 'veil,' and you can stand up inside a small antechamber. You get a break in the confinement, and you can reflect on your reaction to the confining entrance. You are also standing directly above the Chamber of Chaos hundreds of feet below, and perhaps as you are getting this second 'veil' of 'truce,' you can reflect on the millions of Egos, exactly like you, who have yet to make the ascent. Ahead lies the third veil, and once again you are forced to crouch to enter, but beyond this final low passage lies the main chamber—the 'Hall of Judgment,' the chamber of the 'open tomb.' It is with respect and true humility that you make this final passage through the veil of tribulation and humility.

Once inside the Hall of Judgment, you are initiated into what must be a grand club of joyous, evolved Egos. You have earned, by your own efforts, this lofty position. At the far end of the chamber sits a huge, empty sarcophagus that signifies that the mystery we call death is no longer. The tomb is open, you are immortal.

Every key portion of the philosophy in the *Book of the Master* is embodied in stone within the Great Pyramid.

The allegories in stone and ancient literature match up and define a beautiful, individual philosophy. Yet even more remarkable is how these same allegories match the progress of civilization over the past 6,000 years.

As in all proper allegory, what one sees lies with the beholder and needs no exegesis here. However, what does Valentine mean when he says these same allegories match the progress of civilization over the past 6,000 years?

Valentine, in his book *The Great Pyramid: Man's Monument to Man*, presents evidence that the Great Pyramid contains a secret message (in three parts) from an early empire. Valentine's book deals with the second part of the Great Pyramid's message—a narrative in stone in which abstract ideas are personified, a continued metaphor—hidden in allegory within the construction of the interior system of passages and chambers.

The better part of Valentine's book is given over to explaining how the Great Pyramid's system of passages and chambers is a chronological graph that begins in 4000 B.C. and continues for six thousand years. To cover this in proper detail would require hundreds of pages, and as this has been done by Davidson and Valentine, I will simply cover the high points. Those who desire further information on this part of the Great Pyramid will find sufficient material in either Davidson's or Valentine's book.

Projecting the arris edge of the Great Pyramid beneath the surface rock [see Plate 8:4] to a point where it is joined by a projection of the floor line of the ascending passage gives one a straight line. Beginning at the geometrical point beneath the pyramid where the projected arris edge meets the projected floor line of the ascending passage, we have a straight line that runs up the ascending passage and Grand Gallery ending at the only monument in the pyramid: the granite slab in the antechamber that coincides with the floor line of the ascending passage system. This line measures 6,000 inches. To use this line as a chronological graph, we must have a constant; our constant is a year of 365.242 days. So we have a straight line of 6,000″, and each inch equals one year of time. We now have an inch/year scale covering 6,000 years of 365.242 days each. Starting at the bottom of this line precisely at midnight of the autumnal equinox 3999 B.C., we can move inch by inch, year by year, up this time/distance scale until something catches our attention.

Another constant we will use is the names of the passages and chambers from the *Book of the Master of the House of Hidden Places*.[44] Moving up this inch/year scale, nothing catches our attention (as the reader can see in Plate 8:4, Davidson's drawing) until we reach the juncture of the descending passage and the Gate of Ascent. The date is 1486 B.C., the Exodus of the Israelites from Egypt as the rusty ferruginous dust from the tail of the comet Venus filtered down upon the earth and mingled with volcanic ash from the gigantic volcanic explosion on the Greek island of Santorin. As the volcano emptied itself of tremendous amounts of rock and molten lava, the central part of Santorin collapsed. The sea rushed in to fill the huge caldera, pulling water away from the coast of Egypt. The Israelites "went into the sea upon dry ground" and crossed the Sea of Reeds. As the sea filled the cauldron-like cavity—the present Bay of Thera—it generated a

---

[44]Adams' name for the *Egyptian Book of the Dead*.

231

tsunami at least 690 feet high.[45] This gigantic sea wave returned to Egypt as the Egyptians were crossing the Sea of Reeds, sweeping away "all Pharaoh's horses, his chariots and his horsemen" (Exodus 14:24). The volcanic caldera of Santorin resembles, in its most important respects, that of Crater Lake in Oregon, which was formed by a cataclysmic eruption of Mount Mazama around 4000 B.C.[46] Sliding down the steep sides of the Great Pyramid, volcanic ash accumulated around its base. Prof. Galanopoulos points out that:

> ...the fall of hail and red rain are not unusual in volcanic eruptions. It will be remembered that the first layer of pumice on Santorin is rose-coloured. Volcanic ash carried by high-level winds towards Egypt would fall on surface water and the iron oxide in the ash would dissolve in the waters and colour them [and the Great Pyramid] red.[47]

In his book *L'Enigme de la Grande Pyramide* A. Pochan presents evidence that the Great Pyramid was at one time painted red. In a paper read before the Institut de'Egypte on 7 May 1934 and 2 March 1953, Pochan stated:

> As I proceeded to measure the casing stones of the Great Pyramid, a peculiar fact attracted my attention. Some

detached blocks lined up a few meters from the pyramid, which apparently had once been part of the facing, showed a curious red-brown tint on their flat, sloping side.[48]

In his paper Pochan—unaware of the cataclysmic volcanic eruption on the Aegean island of Santorin—asked the question:

> To what phenomenon could this tint—which the blocks' other surfaces did not have—be attributed? To time? Light? To the sand—as unferruginous as it was.... There could no longer be any doubt: *The Pyramid's facing had been painted.*[49]

To prove his point that the Great Pyramid had been painted red, a theory already doubted by Jean Philippe Lauer,[50] Pochan submitted the four fragments he had in his possession to Professor Boulanger, head of general chemical research at the Sorbonne in Paris. Unfortunately Prof. Boulanger died before he finished his analysis. The chemical analysis was completed by his daughter Francoise Boulanger, assistant professor at the Faculte des Sciences, using the Sorbonne's great spectrograph. Completing the chemical analysis, she reported:

> M. Pochan entrusted us with limestone fragments taken from the Great Pyramid's external facing, which showed, on their flat surface, a

---

[45]Angelos G. Galanopoulos and Edward Bacon, *Atlantis: The Truth Behind the Legend*, p. 112 passim; pp. 192-99.

[46]Ibid., p. 192.

[47]Ibid., p. 199.

[48]A. Pochan, p. 219.

[49]Ibid.

[50]Jean Phillippe Lauer, *Fouilles a Saggarah* (Cairo: Institute Francais, 1935), and other works by him mentioned in the Bibliography.

reddish coloration.... The elements found in the superficial reddish coating *and not in the stone are: iron, manganese, phosphorus, and sodium.*

In addition, as phosphorus is among the rare metaloids that reveal themselves spectrographically, we tried an alkaline treatment with a view toward investigating the other possible anions, and we found—again, by comparision—that the colored coating contained *chlorine* and traces of sulphate; we can assume that the sulphate is in the form of calcium sulphate.

The fact that we found phosphorus and sodium leads us to posit the existence of an organic element accompanied by these two elements.

The presence of iron and manganese fully explains the reddish coloration observed.

We consider these facts to verify M. Pochan's hypothesis, to wit, that the Great Pyramid was indeed painted.

Paris, May 5, 1950 [51]

Painted red the Great Pyramid was—but by the hand of man or by the hand of nature? Considering the extraordinary lengths the builders of the Great Pyramid employed to acquire a smooth white finish for refractive reasons (see 5:21), it is extremely doubtful they would paint it red. In fairness to M. Pochan it should be pointed out that when the chemical analysis was performed little was known concerning the volcanic eruption on Santorin. Volcanic ash contains the necessary elements to produce a superficial reddish coloration on the external pure-white facing stones. A "red rain," as Prof. Galanopoulos mentioned, would also produce a red-brown tint on the external surface. The "organic element" mentioned in the chemical analysis Pochan interpreted as the oil used as a base for his imaginary paint.

A far more credible explanation for the "organic element" is as follows: With the close approach of the comet Venus, petroleum hydrocarbons descended to earth, some in a liquid form, from the gaseous tail of the comet and sank into the pores of the limestone, covering the surface of the Great Pyramid with a fine film of oil. Later the iron-oxide-rich volcanic ash, carried to Egypt by high-level winds, descended earthward and mingled with the petroleum on the pyramid's surface.[52] With the passage of time, the abrasive action of wind-carried sand and the bleaching action of the sun restored the Great Pyramid to its pristine whiteness. Some ancient reports after 1486 B.C. describe the pyramid as colored, but by the time of Herodotus (440 B.C.) the Great Pyramid was again white. This explanation adds more evidence to the accumulating pile of data proving Velikovsky's theory of global cataclysms correct.

Prof. Galanopoulos says:

> The sea-wave which helped the Exodus of the Israelites was produced by the collapse of Santorin; and the collapse occurred after the eruption phenomena which brought about the [ten] plagues.... For those who believe that the plagues and the crossing of the waters were miracles of Divine Providence alone, the miracle...lies in the timing of the occurrences, the

---

[51]Pochan, pp. 221-22.

[52]Editors of Pensee, *Velikovsky Reconsidered*, pp. 135, 235-38, 256. (See also Velikovsky's *Worlds in Collision*, p. 69.)

synchronizing of events. Moses [a highly initiated Cabbalist] is divinely guided to take advantage of the mechanism of occurrences whose manifestation obeys natural laws which are themselves the work of God.[53]

Velikovsky, the editors of Pensee, Hugh Auchincloss Brown, and many others have presented evidence that global cataclysms have fundamentally altered the face of our planet, by a shift in the terrestrial axis of the earth, more than once in historical times. William Mullen, one of the editors of Pensee, said, "Only someone who has grasped the unity of mythical thought in a number of cultures will be in a position to formulate general laws for its mechanisms."[54]

Harvard University professor Barry Fell in his book *America B.C.* has demonstrated that we must include Egyptian, Libyan, Iberian, Basque, and Celtic colonizers in our American heritage. Moses, within the framework of Pharoah Akhnaton's great release of knowledge, was instructed and educated into the secret Egyptian mysteries by men of high intelligence who wisely defended their work against jealous officialdom and the greed of man; uplifted by their deeper insights, they endeavored to promote the betterment of the human condition through selective release of their discoveries. Page 159 of Prof. Fell's book shows a photograph of the Pontotoc stele. On the stele is an extract from the *Hymn to the Aton* by Pharaoh Akhnaton. This stele was found in Oklahoma! Fell points out that the Wabanaki Indians of Maine were reading and writing with Egyptian hieroglyphs before 1738. Champollion, who spent years deciphering the Rosetta stone (a black diorite stele with an inscription of hieroglyphics, demotic script, and Greek, found in Egypt in 1799 by Boussard), cracked the mystery of Egypt's millennia-old hieroglyphs and published the results of his work in 1828. This enabled scholars to read the literature of ancient Egypt. Champollion also had a thorough knowledge of Coptic. Had Jean-Francois Champollion known of the Wabanaki Indians, he could have carried a plaster of paris cast of it to them for deciphering. With the deciphering of Egypt's mysterious writing system (a system of ciphers), at a little chapel a *shofar* (ram's horn) sounded before a black-draped altar with the symbol of the Lion of Judah, as solemn ceremonies were held and prayers offered in thanks for the return of the Word. It is an interesting question as to how much Judaism owes to the Egyptian mysteries.

Moses, like Akhnaton before him, learned the final secret of the Illuminati in the *sanctum sanctorum* of the Great Pyramid. When Moses, already old, became tired in the wilderness his teacher, the priest of Midian, suddenly appeared to his younger student and asked, "What is this thing that thou doest to the people? The thing that thou doest is not good," (Exodus 18:5, 23). The priest of Midian explained the law of "frank judges" and then Moses appointed able men of truth to be frank judges and to bear the burden with him. In private counsel the priest of Midian explained to Moses the meaning of *EYEH ASHER EYEH* (I am that I am). With a quick movement the priest shook a fine layer of volcanic ash from his coat and went his way into his own land to rejoin the tilers of the temple of the mysteries, as there was a great deal of re-

[53]Galanopoulos, pp. 192-99.

[54]Editors of Pensee, p. 287.

pair work to be done.

Passing the first girdle-stone, like Al Mamun as he inched his way across the squeaky wooden floor planks of his father's balcony, we may understand that more is concealed than is revealed. Each concealed thing leads to undreamed heights.

Like the author of *The Ultimate Frontier*, when Henriette Mertz found "no commercial publisher willing to publish my book, I published it myself in 1953." In that year her book, with no promotion, enjoyed modest sales. However, it sparked and sent an electric ripple through the scientific community who understood the value of her research. The reason commercial publishers in the dark ages of the fifties did not publish her book was that they had been advised by "experts" that "what she suggests would cast doubt on generally accepted theories of academia committed to certain firmly established dogmas, one of which held that ancient people crossed neither the Atlantic nor the Pacific before the voyage of Columbus."[55] Her book, *Pale Ink*, with great precision recounts the Chinese exploration of North and Central America by Buddhist missionaries 4,000 years ago. Twenty-three years passed before a courageous commercial publisher (Ballantine Books), published her book under the new title *Gods from the Far East: How the Chinese Discovered America*. In the Buddhist mysteries the symbol of the sun is a circle with a dot in the center. This symbol is universally the same, from the underground caves of Peru to the catacombs of Rome. It is found in the underground labyrinths of Egypt and in every lodge where Freemasons perform their secret "mysteries."

Passing the second girdle stone, we are moving upward in the Hall of Truth in Darkness on our chronological graph, and perhaps as we continue upward some of the gloom cast by two dark ages will be dispelled. In 1973 James Bailey published his book *The God-Kings and the Titans*. In this book we learn that Christopher Columbus, before sailing to America, worked as a cartographer for the Portuguese for seven years, and Bailey tells us further:

> ...the half-Inca historian, Carcilaso de la Vega, records that Columbus had given hospitality to a Spanish crew which had been blown off its course on the way to the Canary Islands and after twenty-eight or twenty-nine days had been blown into the Caribbean. Only five survived the trip to America and back and they stayed with the famous Genoese cartographer Christopher Columbus. He received them kindly but, enfeebled by their sufferings, they perished in his house. So that he became heir, de la Vega says, to their sufferings and adventures. This experience, de la Vega says, was what really prompted Columbus and led to his first voyage.* From this it is a fair surmise, therefore, that he crossed the Atlantic with reasonable knowledge that he would make land ahead. He virtually said so himself.[56]

---

*El Inco, *Royal Commentaries of the Incas*, page 19.

Bailey, in his copiously illustrated book, discusses the mining of South, Central, and

---

[55]Twenty-three years seems ample time to destroy the "generally accepted theories of academia," in this case as in others.

[56]James Bailey, *The God-Kings and the Titans*, p. 33.

North America by people from India, China, Greece, Phoenicia, Palestine, and Egypt, over a period in excess of five thousand years prior to the voyage of Columbus. In his book we learn the myth of Jason and the Golden Fleece is no more a myth than the famed city of Troy. In Appendix I of his book, the voyage of the ship *Argo* is traced geographically; the Golden Fleece turns out to be a lambskin with a map of the South American gold mines on it. Jason crosses the Atlantic, enters the Caribbean, sails south to the Amazon River, from which he makes his way to Lake Titicaca in the Andes Mountains of Peru (where the remains of stone-lined canals that once served as a connection between the Pacific Ocean and the geologic Amazonian Sea may still be seen. These canals are built along the same lines as the canals on the Pacific island of Ponape.) Buildings around Lake Titicaca, the most ancient, stand obliquely—thick at the base and tapering at the top like ancient Egyptian buildings. Today one does not see the ancient canals that at one time surrounded the Great Pyramid. Dr. J.C. McCoan, in his book *Egypt* (published in 1882), writes:

> The excursion to the Pyramids, which was once almost formidable from the inconvenience of crossing the Nile by a ferry and then riding on donkey-back for seven or eight miles along a tortuous track, broken at frequent intervals by *ruinous canals* [emphasis added] or patches of submerged ground, is now a pleasant carriage drive of an hour and a half over the fine iron bridge from Kasr-en-Nil to Ghizeh.[57]

In 1882 it took an hour and a half to travel from the Nile to the Great Pyramid by carriage. To move 2,600,000 core blocks and 115,000 casing stones from the Nile River to the site of the Great Pyramid by dragging or rolling them across the sand would be a time-consuming project. Moving the blocks from the river to the building site by the use of pumps, hydraulics, and water-filled canals, as Edward Kunkel has shown in his book *Pharaoh's Pump* (see Plates 7:3 and 7:4, makes much more sense. Control of water by ancient people for many purposes other than building was crucial: drinking, food processing, cooking, bathing, lime cement production, mining, etc., all depended on the use of water. In Mexico the reservoirs, canals, drains, and other water controls of the Maya civilization have been recently unearthed.[58] At both the La Venta and the San Lorenzo sites, huge basalt stones, some weighing 30 tons, were imported from the Las Tuxtlas Mountains over 100 miles away. The canals also provided food, since fish, edible water snails, and other forms of aquatic life could be harvested throughout the year. In addition to aquatic life, the canals attracted geese, ducks, doves, and quail, as well as deer and other forest animals. The canals could be used to transport crops from the fields to the market (as well as trade goods and building materials). Vegetable mulch, along with canal muck, was used to revitalize gardens. The similarity between the canal systems of Ponape, Lake Titicaca, Egypt, and Mexico is striking. Bailey, in *God Kings and the Titans*, presents evidence of the Egyptian presence at the ruins at Tiwanaka near Lake Titicaca.

From the research of Fell, Mertz, Bailey, and Tompkins (to name a few), we can see

---

[57]J.C. McCoan, *Egypt*, p. 58.

[58]*Science* 193 (20 August 1976).

that there was a great deal of intercourse between the Mediterranean and the Caribbean thousands of years ago. And as Tompkins says above in Chapter Three, "All of this nonsense about Columbus discovering America is garbage." With so many people coming to the Americas, one may wonder why, at the time of Columbus, the location of the Americas was not common knowledge to everyone. At that time trade routes were secret, and one does not walk around talking freely about the location of one's tin, copper, silver, and gold mines. The way to the Americas was known to several peoples in several different countries, which lends credence to the Mormon belief that Jesus visited Mexico and inspired the legend of Quetzalcoatl, the white and bearded god of ancient Mexico who, after teaching in Mexico for some time, left Mexico sailing east—towards Jerusalem—the direction he had arrived from.

Dr. Augustus Le Plongeon (see Plates 3:10, 3:11, 3:12), in his book *Maya/Atlantis Queen Moo and the Egyptian Sphinx*, writes:

Let us take, for instance, the last words, according to Matthew and Mark,[1] spoken by Jesus on the cross, when a sponge saturated with *posca*[2] was put to his lips: '*Eli, Eli, lamah Sabachthani.*'

No wonder those who stood near him could not understand what he said. To this day the translators of the Gospels do not know the meaning of these words, and make him...play before mankind a sorry and pitiful role.... He spoke pure Maya. He did not complain that *God had forsaken him* when he said to the charitable individual who tried to allay the pangs of the intolerable thirst he suffered in

consequence of the hardships he had endured, and the torture of the chastisement inflicted on him: 'Hele, Hele, lama zabac ta ni;' that is, 'Now, now, I am fainting; darkness covers my face;' or, in John's words, 'It is finished.'[3]

---

[1]Matthew, chap. 27, verse 46.
[2]Posca was the ordinary beverage of Roman soldiers, which they were obliged to carry with them in all their expeditions, among which were the executions of criminals. Our authorities on this matter are Spartianus *Life of Hadrian,* §10) and Vulcatius Gallicanus *Life of Avidius Cassius, 5).* This posca was a very cooling drink, very agreeable in hot climates, as the writer can certify, having frequently used it in his expeditions among the ruined cities of the Mayas. It is made of vinegar and water, sweetened with sugar or honey, a kind of oximel.
[3]John, chap. 19, verse 30.

A hundred years ago Dr. Le Plongeon's orthodox contemporaries did not believe him when he wrote that Egyptians and Phoenicians had visited Mexico. They did not believe him when he wrote that the Caracol Tower at Chichen-Itza (Home of the Holy Ones) was an astronomical observatory (See Plate 3:11). And, as none of them spoke Mayan, which Le Plongeon wrote and spoke fluently, they were not about to believe the last words spoken on the cross by Jesus belonged to an elegant and mystical tribe of Central American Indians (the memory of George Custer's disaster being fresh in their minds). A major general at age 23, he retained the brevet

[59]Le Plongeon, *Maya/Atlantis Queen Moo and the Egyptian Sphinx*, p. 38.

rank of major general until he led the 7th Cavalry to the Little Big Horn.

Passing the third girdle stone, we have dispelled some of the gloom of our history, and as we move upward in the Hall of Truth in Darkness perhaps we will feel an inner urging to continue the ascent. Moving upward in the dark, we may stop, pause, and experience a moment of doubt as we forever leave our simplistic view of history behind. As we passed the third girdle stone we may have heard, somewhere in the back of our heads, a gentle click of a door closing behind us.

We are now close to the top of the Hall of "Truth in Darkness," where it intersects the horizontal passage leading to the Queen's Chamber. Approaching the Queen's Chamber or "Chamber of Second Birth" (or New Birth), the floor level suddenly drops mysteriously, 1 foot 11 inches. We, like Al Mamun so long ago, wonder why. We enter the chamber and observe the curious niche with its Pythagorean division, the tunnel (see Plates 4:19, 4:20), the salt crystals reproducing themselves on the walls, and in a brilliant flash we begin to think symbolically as we leave the Middle Chamber and return to the mysterious drop in the passage. Drawing a line from the bottom of the "mystery step" across to where it intersects our 6,000-year chronological graph, our inch/year scale, we have a date (see Davidson's drawing, Plate 8:4). Each inch of our straight line is equal to a year of 365.242 days, and the date we have is 4 B.C.—the Birth of Jesus. We remember the face, like the face on the Shroud of Turin, imprinted on the wall at the entrance of the "Chamber of Second Birth" (Plate 6:3).

The first thing one thinks is, wasn't Jesus born on December twenty-fifth, Christmas, zero A.D.? Of course there was no zero A.D., and as Valentine points out:

> ...when Dionysius Exiguus was calculating the Gregorian calendar we use today, he figured that the birth of Christ took place in the twenty-eighth year of the reign of Augustus Caesar. However, he overlooked the fact that Augustus had ruled Rome for four years under his true name, Octavian. Therefore Dionysius made a four-year mistake.[60]

The twenty-fifth of December is the winter solstice—the time of year at which, owing to the annual revolution of the earth around the sun, the sun is at its greatest distance north or south from the equator and begins to turn back, which happens at midsummer and midwinter (21 June and 25 December), either of the two points in the ecliptic at which the sun appears to be at these dates. In *The Ultimate Frontier* we find:

> ...one Dionysius Exiguus who, in 533 A.D. proposed that the calendar years be counted from the birth of Christ instead of from the founding of Rome. His researches indicated that Christ had been born during the twenty-eighth year of the reign of Augustus Caesar. But here is where the Brotherhoods interfered with Dionysius' reckoning. He failed to uncover the fact that Augustus reigned for four years under his own name of Octavian before he was proclaimed Augustus by the Roman Senate. The Brotherhoods know that Jesus was born on October 4, 4 B.C., but it would have been awkward for Doom's Day to fall on the

[60]Valentine, p. 107.

year 2004 A.D. since certain prophesies make [5 May] 2000 A.D. the preferred year. The time of the great earthquakes is not being brought about by Higher Intelligence but is merely the natural consequence of geophysical forces. However, it suits the purposes of the Brotherhoods to make their plans for mankind coincide with this scientifically predictable cataclysm.[61]

The festival of Christmas is a survivor of a pre-Christian festival, *Natalis Invicti Solis*, which originally coincided with the winter solstice, 25 December. In the early empire this festival was the birthday of the unconquerable sun, which to the ancients was a symbol of God just as the cross is a symbol to the Christian of Christ. Christmas was not a part of the Christian Church until the third century, when the Roman Church, attempting to attract new dues paying members, incorporated this ancient Egyptian (or pre-Egyptian) festival into Christianity.

Moving upward on our inch/year scale from the date 4 B.C. exactly $33^{1}/_{2}''$ (the number of years Jesus lived), we reach the juncture of the Hall of Truth in Light and the precise date on our timeline is 7 April (Julian) A.D. 30—the cruicifixion.[62] As we step into the Hall of Truth in Light we may remember the combined length of the two halls is 286.1 *feet* and the difference between the height of the Hall of Truth in Darkness and the Hall of Truth in Light is 286.1 *inches*.

Continuing up the 157 feet of the Grand Gallery, our inch/year scale reaches the bottom of the Great Step and our date is A.D. 1844 as the angular ascending line moves up

to strike the granite slab in the antechamber. In the center of the granite slab there is an embossed marker. Measuring from this marker to the granite box in the King's Chamber marks the date of 5 May of the year 2000, a date when the people of Stelle, Illinois, will be orbiting the earth to escape a cataclysm of massive earthquakes and *tsunamis* that they believe will destroy much of our present civilization. Returning to earth after a cataclysm of the magnitude they believe will take place, will they be heralded by primitive people who survived in isolated areas as gods from outer space? One fact remains that is certain: astronomically and mathematically advanced civilizations *have* disappeared from the face of the earth before. Why? Will it happen again on the fifth of May? How far advanced beyond our modern technology the builders of the Great Pyramid were is a subject we are only now beginning to investigate and understand.

The first intelligent question that assaults our reason is: How could anyone know the future? David Davidson spent twenty-five years measuring the Great Pyramid's passage system and checking the dates with historical events. During Davidson's life the popular opinion held that Egypt was the first civilization and that prior to Egypt man was merely a hunter and seed-gatherer. Because of this prevailing opinion Davidson, in the end, could attribute the mathematical and astronomical data embodied in the Great Pyramid only to the fact that God must have helped the Great Pyramid's architect by a divine revelation. Egyptologists responded with laughter and ridicule and, having already come to a standstill with the tomb theory, never read the analysis of a

[61]Kieninger, p. 107.

[62]Davidson, pp. 473-89.

239

building by so lowly a person as an *architect*.

I reread Davidson's research once again, but the question as to how anyone could know the future remained unanswered. I talked with the architect Wilfred Gregson and explained to him that none of the books written on the Great Pyramid's inch/year timeline explained how anyone could know the future outside of divine revelation. He told me, "Quit looking so hard. When you go to sleep, put a pencil and paper by your bed and, should you dream, remember to wake up and write down immediately what you dreamed before you forget it." I did not dream that night. The next night, however, I must have dreamed, for when I awakened I became aware that something was written on the paper on my bedside table.

Chuckling, I reached for the paper (which I imagined would magically reveal the complex details of King Tut's laundry list, or how many asps Cleopatra allowed to munch upon her reputedly luscious breast before she died, or other salient secrets most Egyptologists seem to devote a great deal of time to discussing). Imagine my surprise when I read: "The truth of the thing is the reality of it and the realities are all more or less concealed in a world of causation and all we get are their shadows in this world." I remembered that this was a quote from Manly P. Hall from Chapter Seven, which I had just finished.

8:5. Cleopatra.

240

This did not answer how anyone could know the future, but it reminded me of something else. I had just read *Serpent in the Sky: The high wisdom of Ancient Egypt*, by John Anthony West, who proves that the ancient Egyptians were far more familiar with the interplay of the physical forces of nature than had heretofore been known. Comparing the knowledge of the ancients to the new discoveries in the field of subatomic physics, West writes:

> In the world of subatomic physics, time and space in the ordinary sense lose their meaning, and language will not allow physicists to express what they find in terms comprehensible to the rational intellect. Particles that are simultaneously waves can be in two 'places' at the same time, and subatomic events of the 'past' are preceded by events in the 'present'. Matter is not a thing but a pattern of probabilities, the likelihood of which can be statistically determined within a certain degree of accuracy by mathematics.[63]

This in turn reminded me of the research of Fritjof Capra reported in his book *The Tao of Physics*. I remembered that in the new physics, time does not flow smoothly as we perceive it, nor does time move evenly from past to present, so there is no absolute before or after. Space is not flat, but part of a curved space/time, so if you started off in one direction in the universe you would end up right back here eventually.

According to the new physics, space is not an empty container in which there are objects and events, but part of a web that enmeshes everything—so that if you move a leaf you disturb the stars. At that point I remembered the words spoken by Dr. Flana-

gan after spending the night in the Great Pyramid's King's Chamber: "We had many unusual experiences ... almost of a psychic nature."

The King's Chamber is located in the exact center of the Great Pyramid's mass centroid. The history of the Great Pyramid is filled with reports of people experiencing unusual things while in the King's Chamber. I wondered why. Suddenly I remembered Einstein's law: if enough mass is collected in one place the collected mass will distort the time and space we normally experience. Could the mass centroid of the Great Pyramid distort time and space in such a way that anyone in the center of this mass centroid would experience unusual events? For this to be possible, the Great Pyramid's mass centroid would also have to effect a change on gravitational forces. Could the mass centroid of the Great Pyramid affect gravitational forces? The answer to this question is: Yes.

Pages 84 and 85 of Peter Tompkins's book *Secrets of the Great Pyramid* state that Piazzi Smyth, the Astronomer Royal for Scotland, was attempting to obtain the correct latitude of the Great Pyramid *without* having his plumbline "diverted from the perpendicular" by the mass centroid of the Great Pyramid. Should the mass centroid of the Great Pyramid prove sufficiently great to divert a plumbline from the perpendicular, then the King's Chamber (isolated from atmospheric pressure, 14.69 psi) may prove to be a chamber in which subatomic events of the past are preceded by events in the present. If the mass centroid carries an electrical charge, the process of distorting time becomes easier. The mass of the Great Pyramid *is* sufficient to divert a plumbline from the perpendicular (see Appendix A).

---

[63]John Anthony West, *Serpent in the Sky,* p. 122.

Should a device moving up and down the vacuum of the Grand Gallery have been an apparatus for producing electric currents by induction, we would have an electric charge within the Great Pyramid's mass. *Was* there an electric charge within that mass? One Egyptologist believes so. However, he is not your average Egyptologist.

Professor of Egyptology at Rocky Mountain College (Billings, Montana) D.J. Nelson, when not teaching, is a travelling lecturer with twenty-nine seasons and more than 6,000 paid appearances in forty-six states and seven countries behind him. Born in 1925 at Vernal, Utah, he attended the Polytechnic Institute of Technology and the University of California at Berkeley, and his earliest studies in ancient history and archaic languages were under Father Vespo Eliad, Monastery of St. George, Jericho (in Palestine) and M. Zakaria Ghoneim, Keeper of Antiquities at Saqqara, Egypt. Prof. Nelson has a working knowledge of Egyptian hieroglyphics, hieratic and demotic writing, three dialects of Coptic, Persian Cuneiform, and both Meroitic Hieroglyphic and Metroitic Demotic (Old Nubian). His reading skills in the Han language (Chinese) are extensive.

When not teaching or lecturing, Prof. Nelson produces archaelogical, natural history, and travel films. During 1959 and 1960 Nelson walked every foot of ground that Jesus is known to have travelled, filming scenes *in situ* for his television special *The Light from Galilee*, acclaimed as one of the year's best on European television. To reach Moslem holy places, forbidden to Christians, he disguised himself as a Bedouin sheik and shot most of the scenes from a camera hidden inside a gourd water bottle. He has photographed or produced 42 syndicated and network television films for such series productions as *I Search for Adventure*, *Bold Journey*, *Seven League Boots*, *Kingdom of the Sea*, *Wild Kingdom*, *Across the Seven Seas*, *Expedition*, *Great Adventure*, and *Golden Voyage*. He directed and filmed a two-episode presentation on the Dead Sea Scrolls hidden by the Essenes. It was the first film on the scrolls ever telecast in the United States.

Nelson has published more than 130 scientific papers and articles for technical journals. His photographs have appeared in hardback books put out by Reader's Digest, Houghton Mifflin, Griffin, and Time-Life Publications. He did the first translations of the Metropolitan Museum Egyptian funerary papyri of Hor, Amen-Hotep, and Ta-Shert-Min. The translations were published in four works by Modern Microfilm in Salt Lake City.

Nelson's private collection of Egyptian antiquities, including several rare resurrection figures, papyri, and parchments, is one of the most comprehensive in the country. He has directed or been assistant director of four professional digs in the Nile Valley. He is credited with the discovery of the royal tomb of Princess Nefer-Ka-Ra and a late period gallery tomb at Dashur. He has been a member of the Adventurers' Club of Los Angeles for the past twenty years, and is also a definitive authority on the spectroscopic analysis of ancient inks.

Equipped with a working knowledge of nine of the ancient written languages of the Nile Valley and the Holy Land, Nelson has spent over thirty years searching for esoteric knowledge in surviving papyri and parchments of the Near East. In the Foreword of his book *Life Force in the Great Pyramid* (co-authored with David H. Coville, an expert in electronics), Nelson states that by a careful analysis of ancient word roots by means of a character-by-character breakdown of hieroglyphic spellings, he knows that "the

Egyptians of the Pyramid Age had knowledge of aural energy fields, their effects and the methods of manipulating them." He writes that the ink used by the ancient Egyptians was composed mostly of carbon so that the carbon-ink lines, once dry on papyrus, form a primitive condenser "storing, amplifying and releasing pulsating electric discharges."[64]

Nelson's research led him to suspect that the earliest people of Egypt had a degree of intellectual advancement far beyond our present-day physics. On the average, granite contains only 25% silicon quartz. The 100 blocks isolating the Great Pyramid's mass centroid (King's Chamber) contain a silicon dioxide (quartz) content more than double that. Did an ancient band of men isolate only the King's Chamber by hundreds of tons of quartz particles to effect a high electrical resistance and opaqueness to fast neutrons? Edgar Cayce believed pyramids were erected to propagate the original faith and to preserve the "knowledge that would make for a unifying of the understandings as to the relationships of man to the creative forces." Nelson states:

> The great mass of stone above the Pyramid chambers presses downward by gravitational force upon the granite walls thereby converting them into perpetual electric generators.
>
> The inner chambers of the Great Pyramid have been generating electrical energy since their construction.... A man within the King's chamber would thus come within a weak but definite induction field which under certain conditions might disrupt his

brain waves. This field might produce the mental aberrations and hallucinations of the sort described by those who have had the occasion to spend more than a few hours in the Great Pyramid; viz., Napoleon Bonaparte, Captain G.B. Caviglia, Dr. G. Patrick Flanagan and others.[65]

After spending some time alone in the King's Chamber, as Alexander the Great is reported to have done before him, Napoleon came out of the chamber pale and impressed. He refused to tell what strange effect he had experienced and forbade his generals ever to make mention of the event—merely hinting, according to Tompkins, "that he had received some presage of his destiny."[66] Could Napoleon have experienced a distortion of space and time as we normally experience it? Could Napoleon's brain, in this induction field, have experienced a distortion of space and time in which subatomic events of the past are preceded by events in the present? We are all about 95% water, and all our brains are electric-storing, recording, amplifying, and releasing pulsating electric discharges. Could the electric brainwaves of Napoleon in the induction field of the Great Pyramid's King's Chamber have, via internal electric biochemical interruption, experienced a presage of his future?

Given the human race's proclivity for fooling with nature, we may be dealing with an ancient (now greatly damaged) *time machine!*

I recalled the words of Stanford University's Prof. William A. Tiller:

> The Pyramid shape, it seems to me, is

---

[64]*D.J. Nelson and David H. Coville, Life Force in the Great Pyramid, p. 2.*

[65]Ibid., p. 73. (See also pp. 141-2 of this book.)

[66]Tompkins, p. 50.

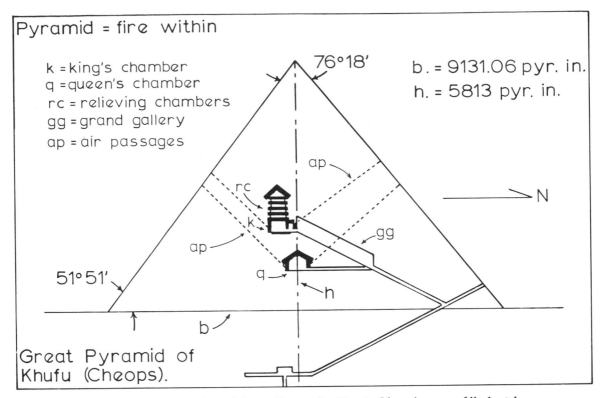

Pyramid = fire within

k = king's chamber
q = queen's chamber
rc = relieving chambers
gg = grand gallery
ap = air passages

76°18'

b. = 9131.06 pyr. in.
h. = 5813 pyr. in.

51°51'

Great Pyramid of
Khufu (Cheops).

8:6. Professor Nelson suggests that if the coffer in the King's Chamber was filled with an aqueous solution of natron (N_AHCO_3, N_ACI, and $N_{A2}SO_4$), the salt-water itself would act as an effective conductor of electricity for the piezoelectric induction from the matt-finished walls of the King's Chamber. This, Professor Nelson points out, would make it unnecessary to line the coffer with metal — the salt itself is an effective conductor of electricity. Professor Nelson correctly points out that such a process would naturally produce poisonous chlorine gas which, somehow, would have been vented from the chamber.

The "stable" organic compounds in human blood are essentially the same as sea-water. A human candidate placed in this coffer during this process would experience a low voltage shock to his brain from the electrolyzed natron solution which Nelson says would have very good "health-restoring properties."

a special one of the large class of shapes and I'm inclined to think it has some special characteristics in terms of the ratio of the base width to the height. So one could imagine energy resonances occurring in space that would be particularly *good* to excite things in a pyramid.

Manly P. Hall, A. Pochan, and a host of other writers have expressed the opinion,

and evidence, that the Great Pyramid was used as a temple of initiation into the Egyptian mysteries. In the Egyptian mysteries the candidate was placed in the King's Chamber (or as it is called in the *Book of the Master*, Chamber of the Open Tomb) for his final degree of initiation. It is certainly possible that, after years of wondering what was inside the temple of initiation and wondering what the final secret degree would reveal, one of the things *excited* in the Great

8:7. After winning the decisive Battle of the Pyramids, Napoleon asked to be left alone in the Great Pyramid's King's Chamber.

Pyramid would be the candidate's central nervous system, which controls his cerebrospinal and autonomic systems. Should a lion-masked hierophant whisper certain instructions in the candidate's ear while in this heightened state of consciousness, then, as Prof. Tiller states, "One can imagine that the pyramid is a kind of device that converts a new type of energy, even perhaps a non-physical energy, into a physical energy, and that the individual himself cooperatively couples with the device."

Isolated from atmospheric pressure in the deep and solemn interior where there was no sun to shine and heat it up by day, no sky to radiate cold at night, but only darkness and a uniform temperature of 68° from year to year, a band of Masters almost 6,000 years ago prepared a candidate for this cooperative coupling with the energies they had set to work. Soon, through internal electrical biochemical interruption, the Elders of the Brotherhood would free forever the candidate's central nervous system from its conditioned perception, thereby elevating another primate brain from the mental bands that bound it. Soon the candidate

would awaken to the fact that there was something of great importance to be known.

All metal or metallic objects were removed from the candidate. Conduits of copper electrodes, running up the "ventilating" shafts to the Great Pyramid's outside electrostatic field, were connected to terminals in the Queen's Chamber. A low hum began to resonate in the King's Chamber from the bottom of the Grand Gallery.

One of the Elders moved toward the granite box composed of 55% quartz crystals. Checking its gold-covered inner and outer surfaces, he satisfied himself that their electric cell was in perfect condition to hold a high-voltage electric charge. Another Elder used quartz crystals to measure and control the frequency of electric impulses.

The moment was at hand. Six flat crystal plates were brought into the King's Chamber. In sets of two the flat crystal plates were arranged in triangular form[67] about the granite box at the west end of the chamber. As pressure was applied to each of the three sets of flat crystal plates, one plate in each of the three sets developed a negative electric charge as the other three flat plates in each set simultaneously developed a positive electric charge. As the pressure was increased between each of the three flat sets of crystal plates, an electrical voltage was created. Once created, this electric voltage (copulating with the piezoelectric induction from the King's Chamber matte-finished walls, which retain moisture) accumulated a slight charge in the granite box. As more pressure was applied to the three sets of triangularly arranged flat crystal plates, an epicyclic train began moving an induction coil up and down the length of the Grand Gallery with an unusual velocity.

[67]See miniature drawing bottom left-hand corner of Plate 1:8. See also Plate 4:2.

It became hot in the Queen's Chamber. The cells emitted sparks, which hit the walls of the chamber. This electric discharge caused the electrolytic ionization of sodium chloride (table salt), releasing poisonous chlorine gas that was vented out of the chamber by the two ventilating shafts. The candidate was placed in the correct position for the elevation. More pressure was applied to each of the sets of crystal plates. The electrical voltage increased until an arc could be observed jumping between each of the three sets of crystal plates, thus forming an electric triangle of three burning tapers arranged in triangular form about the Holy box, which held the Ark of the Covenant.

Co-operatively coupling with the energies for an interval of time, the candidate perceived the events of the past mingling with the events of the present and the events of the present mingling with the events of the future. Then, as if a huge wheel were turning, past moved into present, present into future, and future into past. As one cycle ended and a new cycle began, the candidate moved in harmony with the rhythm of the spheres, partook of the sense of oneness of all that is, and realized the connection between himself and the Divine. The candidate actually experienced history repeating itself over and over and understood the true purpose of his existence, where he really came from, and why he was here on this planet. Elevated, he was placed in front of the granite box that held the golden Holy of Holies around which Moses was to construct the Ark of the Covenant. He saw the *Shekinah* over the mercy seat and heard a voice speak to him from within the cloud of light, and at that moment he became one of a long line of Masters.

"Speculation!" the skeptic would say. Leaving the skeptic to founder in incalculable sums and endless contradictions, let us ask which Brotherhood might have possession of the Ark of the Covenant today. In one book on Freemasonry, I noted that the candidate "walked upon the electric carpet." As to whether this is an indication or reference to the presence of the Ark, I cannot say. Ancient written information about these "Masters" is scarce, but this information is discussed by Nelson in *Life Force in the Great Pyramid*.

8:8. THE VIGIL IN THE KING'S CHAMBER. *The soul in the form of a man-headed hawk departing for Amenti.*

8:9. THE RETURN OF THE ARK. This striking illustration exhibits a party of reapers interrupted in their work and thoroughly surprised by the **Ark** of the Covenant in the distance, coming toward them in a cart drawn by lowing kine, without a driver. The explanation is this: Several months before, the Israelites, having been defeated in battle by the Philistines, sent for the **Ark** to go with them to the conflict, in the superstitious belief that the mere presence of an object so sacred would secure them success. None of them, however, knew how to use the **Ark's** power. The Philistines defeated the Israelites, carried the **Ark** off as a distinguished trophy, and soon found that their gain was a loss. Wherever they took the **Ark** — to Ashdod, to Gath, to Ekron — a strange disease smote the people with emerods. In their terror they determined to send the cause of their trouble back to its original place. To satisfy themselves that this was the right course, they put it upon a new cart, together with certain golden offerings, and then attached the cart to a yoke of milch kine, whose calves were shut up at home; reasoning that if the dumb beasts, contrary to what would be their natural course, took the road toward Israel, it might be assumed that the **Ark** was the cause of their troubles. The experiment succeeded perfectly. The kine followed a straight course to Bethshemesh, turning neither to the "right hand or to the left."

There is a legend to the effect that any who chanced to enter the Holy of Holies in King Solomon's Temple unclean were destroyed by a bolt of Divine fire from the Mercy Seat. If the High Priest had but one selfish thought, he would be struck dead while in the presence of the **Ark**. The other priests could not enter the sanctuary; therefore, when their leader was about to go in and receive the commandments of the Lord, they tied a rope around one of his feet so that if he were struck down behind the veil, they could drag the body out. Perhaps this is in some minor way connected with the Masonic cable-tow.

Many early books on magical philosophy hint that the Ark of the Covenant was oracular in character because of specially prepared chambers in its interior. These by their shape and arrangement were so attuned to the vibrations of the invisible world that they caught and amplified the voices of the ages imprinted upon and existent in the substance of the astral light.

But let us return to Joseph, "sold by his brothers". That episode is a distorted description of an initiatic ceremony. Some of its elements are significant: Joseph was in a state of halfdream, he was stripped *of his coat, his coat of many colours that was on him* (Gen. XXXVII, 23-28). This is a wrong translation. His robe was the robe of spoliation (or dispossession); *he was cast into a pit: and the pit was empty, there was no water in it.* And Yehoudah (Judah) suggested, *let us* sell him, and he was sold for *20 pieces of silver.*

All these symbols are clear to those who know the Qabala.

The essential theme in the myth of Jesus is death and resurrection. This allegory has been introduced with such pageantry that its protagonist has been deified; the brilliance of the drama has obscured its meaning.

But certain clues, especially in Matthew and John, lead us to understand that the Rabbi who gave rise to his own legend knew quite well the original meaning and the cosmic significance of the *Aleph-Bayt.* In other words, we have every reason to believe that he was a highly initiated Cabalist.

Carlo Suares
The Cipher of Genesis

Jesus, a highly initiated Cabalist in the Order of Melchizedek, knew quite well the cosmic significance of the Hebrew letter-number code which he tried to explain to his disciples who, by their own admission, "perceived it not."

See Hebrews 7

CHAPTER NINE
THE EARLY EMPIRE OF NINE SISTERS

It seems that to begin to understand any of the ancient mysteries, one must belong to one of them. For example, writers on Freemasonry state that to understand their mysteries one must belong to the order, "if only because the actual experience is more important and significant than merely 'academic' knowledge."[1] This would be in keeping with ancient wisdom beliefs—that there was something to be *known* in the mysteries, secrets or mysteries into which it was possible to be initiated, and that when certain areas of the brain are stimulated by the secret processes of the mysteries the consciousness of man is extended and he is permitted to behold what he does not normally see.

This may be the reason Freemasonry is banned in all Communist countries. It is also banned in Roman Catholic Portugal and Spain, yet in Rome the mysteries of Freemasonry are conducted within blocks of the Vatican. I remembered reading Abigail Van Buren's column on "Can Catholics Join Masons?"[2] in which this excellent reporter provided the answer to her reader's question by contacting the Most Rev. Fulton J. Sheen and having him answer the question. His answer, as it appeared in her column, follows in its entirety:

Dear Abby: It was a joy to hear from you, and I shall try to answer the question: 'Can a Catholic become a Mason and maintain his standing in the Catholic Church?'

Can a Catholic be a Mason? That depends. According to a letter sent to the presidents of the various National Conferences of Catholic Bishops by Cardinal Seper, prefect of the Vatican's Sacred Congregation for the Doctrine of the Faith, dated July 18, 1974, membership by lay people in Masonic groups is acceptable, provided the groups are not actively hostile to the Church.

Clerics, religious, and members of secular institutes are still forbidden in every case to join any Masonic associations.

Although Canon 2335 of the current Code of Canon Law of the Church continues to remain on the books, it is to be interpreted in the light of the above-mentioned letter.

I wondered why "membership by lay people in Masonic groups is acceptable," yet "clerics, religious, and members of secular institutes are still forbidden in every case to join." This presents an intensely interesting question: If a lay person of the Catholic Church may join Freemasonry, be initiated into its mysteries, and have his consciousness extended far beyond what he normally perceives, then this would mean that lay people of the Catholic Church may know what their priests, bishops, and cardinals are "still forbidden in every case" to learn! I

---

[1] Cf. Pike.

[2] "Dear Abby," *Atlanta Constitution*, 31 October 1978.

wondered why Canon Law 2335 said what it did, and I decided to find out.

History tells us that the Order of Knights Templar, founded in 1118 A.D. for the purpose of guarding pilgrims travelling to the Holy Land, became so vastly wealthy and powerful that King Phillip IV ("the Fair," 1268-1314) entered into a devious plot with Pope Clement V (1264-1314) to destroy the Order and seize their wealth. King Phillip sent a crafty letter to the Grand Master of the Templars, Jacques de Molai (1243-1314) expressing in flattering terms his desire to consult with the Templars as to the necessary measures to be taken for recovery of the Holy Land. Assuring de Molai that the Knights Templars were the persons best qualified to give advice upon that subject, and to manage such a military enterprise, the King advised de Molai to bring his treasure and concluded his letter:

> We order you to come hither without delay, with as much secrecy as possible, and with very little retinue, since you will find on this side of the sea a sufficient number of your knights to attend upon you.[3]

The good knight sailed for France. On his arrival, de Molai placed his treasure in the temple at Paris and reported to the King—who then ordered de Molai to report to the Pope to discuss the best means of regaining the Holy Land.

De Molai mysteriously disappeared—into a dungeon—and did not reappear for nearly five years, and then only to suffer a terrible death. A noted criminal of Beziers, Squin de Florian (who was serving a life sentence in the penal castle), was offered a pardon and reward to swear certain charges against the Templars. With his hand on the *Holy Bible*, de Florian charged de Molai and the Knights Templars with heresy and the commission of a list of weird crimes far beyond *his* mental ability to devise. With a heresy charge in hand, Phillip put the rest of his *coup d'etat* into action by dispatching secret communications to the *bailies* of all the different provinces of France. Accusing the Templars of unnatural crimes, Phillip set about preparing the public for what was to follow by ordering Pope Clement to have his monks and priests (most of them totally ignorant of what was really going on) speak out against the Templars in churches and other public places. As they moved to speak against the Templars, eager to please His Holiness, the monks and priests were horrified at the long list of unnatural crimes imputed to a band of men held in such high esteem by the public. Taking advantage of the ignorance, bigotry, and superstition of that age, Phillip must have smirked as he watched the reaction of the crowd to the diatribes against the Templars, who were alleged to have:

> ...cut up and burnt the bodies of their deceased members, and from their ashes prepared a powder which they administered to the initiates, to cause them to keep their obligations and worship idols; that they worshipped an idol covered with an old skin, which had been embalmed, and that the eyes of this idol were two carbuncles having the brightness of heaven; they then roasted the bodies of infants and anointed their idols with the fat; that the Templar's whole hope of a future was centered in this idol, instead of Christ and His viceregent, the Pope; that in celebrating

---

[3]M.W. Redding, *Scarlet Book of Freemasonry, p. 196.*

252

their secret rites and ceremonies, young and tender virgins were introduced, but for what purpose it was not known; that they had dark caves, deep in the earth, in which they had an image in the form of a man, with two bright glittering eyes; and all who took the obligation of the Order were compelled to deny Christ and foul the cross with their feet, and then sacrifice to their horrible idols; that when profaning the cross the cave was darkened; that when a Templar and a girl had a child, a circle was formed in this cave, and the child was thrown from one to another till life was extinct, then it was roasted, and its fat preserved to anoint the idols with; that to conceal their wicked lives they constantly attended church, and made much almsgiving; that they comforted themselves with edification, and frequently partook of the holy sacrament, always manifesting much modesty and gentleness of deportment, both in public and private.[4]

Phillip and the Pope, having fully matured their plans, set the night of 13 October to surprise and make prisoners of the Knights of the Order. Accordingly, on that memorable night the Knights of the Order throughout France were surprised, arrested, and cast into dungeons. On 19 October the Inquisitor General with his myrmidons opened the Inquisition in Paris. The Knights were turned over to the Order of Preachers (Dominicans), noted for being the most cruel and expert torturers of the age. Among the means of torture were the following: The legs of the Knights were fastened in an iron frame, after which the soles of their feet were smeared with fat and they were placed before a fire, with a screen drawn back and forth between their feet and the fire to regulate the heat and render the torture more exquisite and unendurable; others were fastened to an iron frame so near the flames of a fierce fire that the flesh was burnt from their heels and pieces of the bone came out. The great agony produced by this burning process frequently drove the victims to madness.

9:1. *Top*: Surprised and Arrested, and Tortured. *Bottom*: A Knight Templar's arms being dislocated by jerks on a pulley, as the flesh is burned from the feet of another Knight.

[4]*Ibid., p. 200.*

253

Thirty-six Knights perished while many others lost the use of their limbs and were maimed and crippled for life. Other tortures, too indecent and revolting to describe here, were used to extort confessions from some of the Templars—which they subsequently revoked. From 19 October until 28 March, 546 Templars who had persisted in holding their obligations inviolate and maintaining the innocence of their Order were taken from the dungeons and marched under heavy guard into the bishop's palace, where Pope Clement's hand-picked commission was waiting to give them trial. To make a show of fairness, the commission permitted the Knights to authorize a committee of their number to draw up a written defense.

The Templars asked for an interview with the Grand Master, de Molai. This was denied. Returning to their cells, the Templars consulted and embodied their results in a letter, which they voted Knight Sir Peter de Bolgna to present to the holy commission. The letter gave the origin, objects, and mode of initiation into the Order. It then stated that some of their Order had confessed under terrible sufferings, but that the confessions had been retracted. As many of the Templars were of distinguished birth and noble blood, members of the most illustrious families in Europe, public opinion began to grow in their favor.

King Phillip hastened to take measures to arrest the tide of public sympathy.

As Grand Master de Molai had rendered the church and state such important services as to make him popular with the people, it was deemed expedient to proceed with caution in his case. Therefore, instead of being brought to the stake with the others, he was kept confined in prison and

9:2. *The Torture of the Knights Templar.*

9:3. "Will you now confess?" screams the "holy" father.

frequently subjected to cruel tortures to force a confession from him—and also with a view toward terminating his life in that way. His strong constitution survived all the barbarities inflicted on him, however, and he lay in prison over five years.

For prudential reasons, the fact of his imprisonment had been carefully concealed by King Phillip and Pope Clement from the public. To account for his disappearance, hints were thrown out that he had confessed to the charges brought against the Order in private to the Pope, with a view toward absolution, and then had returned to the Holy Land. On the morning of 18 March, nearly five and a half years after his incarceration, the mystery of his disappearance was solved. The citizens of Paris were startled by the sight of a scaffold being erected before the Cathedral of Notre Dame. They were also startled because everywhere they looked, nailed to every tree, wooden pole, or wooden sign, were white pieces of paper that had mysteriously appeared overnight; there were so many of them it seemed as if a light snow had fallen. Moving closer, the people read a summons by the Pope and the King of France commanding them to be present at, and assist in, hearing the confessions of the Grand Master of the Templars and his companions, by playing the part of the crowd.

"De Molai! De Molai has returned!" An excitement moved through the crowd as if an electrical charge were leaping from person to person. He had returned—now there was hope. Men wept openly with joy, feelings and passions ran high. A little girl with

9:4. De Molai in the Torture Room.

bare feet sweeping the street crossing smiled, though she did not know why. It was only after the inital shock of de Molai's return that the public began to think about why the summons said he would be presented to them on the tall platform erected before the Cathedral of Notre Dame. A north wind began to blow across the platform and into the cathedral.

At the appointed hour, King Phillip smiled as he saw before him the forming of what promised to be a crowd that would exceed in size even the crowd that had once formed before Pilate. He noted Clement—his sweating. This was the first time Phillip had ever seen the Pope sweat, and it worried him.

A few minutes later, four men loaded with chains, surrounded by guards, and haggard from years of long suffering were moved into the public view. A murmur of astonishment ran through the crowd. Clothed in filthy and tattered rags, looking more like chained wild animals than men, de Molai and the three knights shuffled toward the platform.

Pope Clement had planned their first public appearance in over five years just this way. He knew the public was mentally conditioned to seeing anyone of greatness clothed in finery. He knew that de Molai and his knights, presented to the public in this way, would look disgusting—while he, in his flowing white robes, would present to the multitude a fine example of the best in Christianity. During the past five years his hatred of de Molai had increased. He detested the fact that some of the people considered de Molai a hero. He had noticed the murmur of astonishment when the crowd first saw de Molai. His excitement increased: soon the public would hear de Molai's confession.

Phillip noted that Clement was sweating more now, and he reminded himself that it would be better to arrange for a less religious and stronger Pope in the future.

The crowd was struggling to believe that these shabby-looking men were de Molai and Knights of the illustrious Order of Templars. They looked more like the ragpickers who collected rags and bones from the streets and ashpits than illustrious knights. A moron in the foremost rank of the crowd began to snicker.

As de Molai and the knights began to ascend the long flight of steep steps leading to the platform top where the King, the Pope, and the Bishop of Alba awaited them, a man in the crowd moved toward the dungeon. Halfway up the steps one of the Knights, Sir Guy, stumbled and fell. A white handkerchief fluttered downward from a rooftop as all eyes were glued on the fallen Knight. A little-used side door to the dungeon quickly opened and closed as a man slipped inside.

Sir Guy appeared to be experiencing some difficulty in getting to his feet, and as all four of the prisoners were chained together with leg irons the whole procession was stopped, frozen between heaven and earth, halfway up the steps. De Molai's eyes were focused on a certain rooftop, from which two white handkerchiefs soon fluttered earthward, signalling that their man was inside. He touched Sir Guy on the right shoulder and the struggling Knight managed to stand. Some in the crowd, believing that he was afraid to confess his crimes and sensing that this might somehow rob them of their sport, began to jeer and taunt the

9:5. Ragpickers collecting rags and bones from the ashpits in the streets of 13th Century France.

257

prisoners.

Unaware of the events that had transpired out of his line of sight on the steps, Pope Clement (now drenched in sweat) heard only the jeers and taunts of the crowd, which he mistakenly thought were being prompted by his idea of dressing the prisoners in rags. Phillip noticed that Clement's breathing was becoming heavy, his eyes were half-closed, and he seemed to be shivering. As Phillip wondered whether or not Clement would faint, he saw Clement's face become beet-red, his body tense, and his entire self from tiara to white slippers quiver in intensity. Phillip thought that perhaps Clement was praying.

But Clement felt so much better now—he realized as he observed the crowd that the wayward sheep who had believed de Molai to be a hero were now jeering him, and that they would now return to the arms of the church. Arriving at the top of the stairs, de Molai and his companions shuffled to the center of the stage, and the crowd became quiet.

Phillip le Bel gave the signal to the Bishop of Alba to read aloud the eighty-eight articles of accusation and the confessions of the prisoners, whose estates and wealth had years earlier been confiscated. At the conclusion of the reading, the papal legate turned to the Grand Master and requested that he avow the guilt of his Order. To this de Molai replied by stepping to the front of the platform and raising his manacled hands toward heaven, repeating the Lord's Prayer. With an exhilaration born of great fatigue, he exclaimed in a loud voice, "To say that which is untrue is a crime against God and man. Not one of us has ever betrayed his God or his country. I do confess to many sins, but I disdain to add the sin and crime of perjury against the innocent and noble Order of the Temple to my other sins."

King Phillip cursed. Pope Clement fainted. The crowd was struck with stupor and eagerly awaited the denouement of this event that was to echo around the world. Guy, the Grand Preceptor, arose to echo the statement of the Grand Master, but before he had proceeded very far, the King and the Bishop of Alba, astounded at such an exhibition of firmness and defiance from men who they had supposed to be so broken down as to render them incapable of further resistance, hurriedly ordered the Knights back to prison.

Phillip's rage knew no bounds. He decreed that the Knights would be burned at the stake at nine o'clock that evening. But in the gloom of his dungeon the Grand Master was hard at work. He created four Metropolitan Lodges, one at Naples for the east, one at Edinburg for the west, one at Stockholm for the north, and one at Paris for the south. He organized and instituted what afterward came to be called the Occult, Hermetic, or Scottish Rite Freemasonry (see Plate 5:19).

A small island in the river Seine, opposite the King's gardens, was selected as the place of execution, and there, over the spot where later stood the equestrian statue of Henry IV, a pyre was erected into which two posts were set with a quantity of charcoal around them. These preparations were hastily completed on the afternoon of the same day that the prisoners were remanded to their dungeons. De Molai had finished drafting the four documents by eight o'clock that evening, and a few minutes later the little-used side door to the dungeon quickly opened and closed as a man carrying four documents slipped outside and disappeared into the night.

Opposite the King's gardens a large crowd had already collected to behold the tragic scene. They were not kept waiting long. At nine o'clock the Grand Master and the Preceptor were brought under guard to the island and immediately chained to the posts and the charcoal was lit. As the charcoal was arranged to burn slowly, de Molai improved the opportunity by addressing the assemblage in the following memorable and prophetic terms:

"France will remember our last moments. We die innocent. The decree that condemns us is an unjust decree, but in heaven there is an august tribunal, to which the weak never appeal in vain. To that tribunal, within forty days, I summon the Roman Pontiff. O Phillip, my King, I pardon thee in vain, for thy life is condemned at the tribunal of God. Within a year I await thee!"

A shudder ran through the awe-struck crowd. The fires were now closing around the victims, first roasting the feet, calves, and knees, and then gradually rising higher. At that moment thousands of white handkerchiefs throughout France rose to tear-filled eyes as thousands of voices prayed, "Dieu vous garde, de Molai."

Retribution soon overtook Pope Clement in the form of a violent dysentery. *Less* than forty days after the execution, Clement died screaming that he was burning up. His dead body was carried to Carpentras (then the residence of the popes) and placed at night in a church, which soon after, struck by lightning, caught fire and nearly consumed his remains. While Clement's relations quarrelled over his part of the treasure "confiscated from the Knights Templar," a band of men broke into the church at Luca and abstracted his ill-gotten gains from its

vaults. Jewelry, symbols, and ornaments that had belonged to the Templars were also taken. One of the relics of the Templars was missing, a relic to be discussed shortly.

The King of France was also called to his last account *before* the end of the year, fulfilling de Molai's prophesy. King Phillip was but slightly slashed across the calf by a rabid boar while hunting. A few days later Phillip died frothing at the mouth of a strange disease that baffled the art of his physicians—the "Pasteur treatment" for rabies was still in the future.[5] Squin de Florian, who had sworn on the Bible the false charges against

9:6. The death of de Molai.

---

[5]*This account is closely based on Morals and Dogma of the Ancient and Accepted Scottish Rite of Freemasonry by Albert Pike, Clausen's Commentaries on Morals and Dogma by Henry C. Clausen, 33° Sovereign Grand Commander of the Supreme Council of the 33°, the World Book Encyclopedia, Scarlet Book of Free Masonry by M.W. Redding (1889), and France by M. Guizot and Madame Guizot De Witt, Vol. I, 1869.*

the Knights Templar, was soon hanged for an atrocious crime.

That the Order of the Temple lived, under other names and governed by unknown Masters, revealing itself only to those who in passing through a series of degrees had proven themselves worthy to be entrusted with the dangerous secret, is evident from a papal bull written hundreds of years later by another Pope Clement, this time Clement XII. In the archives of the library I found a copy of this bitter bull, written in 1738. A copy follows in its entirety, to which I have added italics for emphasis.

Clement, Bishop, servant of God, to all the faithful, health and apostolic blessing.

Placed, unworthily as we are, by the disposal of the divine clemency in the eminent watch-tower of the apostlehip, we are ever solicitously intent, agreeable to trust reposed in us, by obstructing error and vice, to preserve more especially the integrity of the true faith, and to repel in these times all danger from heretical societies.

It has come to our knowledge, even from public report, that certain meetings or assemblies, commonly called Free Masons, are spread far and wide, and are every day increasing; in which persons, of whatever sect or religion, contend with an affected show of natural honesty, confederate together in a close and inscrutable bond, according to secret laws and orders agreed upon between them, and bind themselves as well by strict oath taken on the Bible as by the imprecations of heavy punishments to preserve their mysteries with inviolable secrecy. We, therefore,

revolving in our mind the great mischiefs which generally accrue from secret bodies, not only to the temporal tranquillity of the state but the spiritual health of souls, and that, therefore, they are antagonistic to civil and canonical laws. Being taught to watch night and day lest this sort of men break as thieves into the house, and, like foxes, root up the vineyard; lest they should pervert the hearts of the simple, and privily shoot at the innocent; that we might stop up the broad way which from thence would be laid open for the perpetration of their wickedness, and for other just and reasonable causes to us known, have, by the advice of the cardinals and of our mere motion, and from the plenitude of the apostolic power, decreed to be condemned and prohibited, and by this our present ever valid constitution, we do condemn and prohibit the meetings of the above-named society of Free Masons.

Wherefore, all and singular the faithful in Christ, of whatever state, degree, or condition, whether laity or clergy, worthy of express mention, we strictly, and in virtue of holy obedience, command that no one, under any pretext or color, dare to presume to promote, favor, admit, or conceal in their houses members or assemblies of this abominable order, nor in any way aid or assist in their meeting in any place, or to administer medicine to them in their sickness, or in any manner, directly or indirectly, by themselves or others, afford them council or help in their hour of trial and affliction, or persuade others to join said Order.

We, moreover, command that

bishops, prelates, and inquisitors shall proceed to inquire into, coerce, and restrain the same as vehemently suspected of heresy, with condign punishment; for to them, and each of them, we hereby give and impart free power of proceeding against the same transgressors, and of calling in, if it shall be necessary, the help of the secular arm.

Let no one, therefore, infringe, or by rash attempt contradict this our declaration, damnation, command, and interdict.

Dated from Rome in the year of the Incarnation of our Lord, 1738, and the 8th of our pontificate.

A. Cara, Vice-Datary
C. Amatus, Vice-Secretary
Visa De Curia N. Antonellus
I. B. Eugenius.

In the above-mentioned day, month, and year the said condemnation was posted up and published at the gates of the palace of the Sacred Office of the Prince of the Aposteles by me, Peter Romolatus, cursitor of the Holy Inquisition.

CARDINAL'S EDICT, FOLLOWING THE ABOVE BULL.

Whereas, the holiness of our sovereign lord, Pope Clement XII., happily reigning, in his bull of the 28th of April, condemned, under severe penalties, a society known as Free Masons, which, under the pretext of being a civil and charitable association, admit men of any sect or religion, with a strict tie of secrecy, confirmed by an oath on the Holy Bible, as to all that is transacted or done in said secret meetings; and whereas such meetings are not only suspected of occult heresy but even of being dangerous to public peace and the safety of the ecclesiastical state, since if they did not contain matters contrary to the Catholic faith and to the peace and well-being of the commonwealth, so many and such strict ties of secrecy would not be required as are mentioned in the aforesaid bull of his Holiness; and it being the will of our Lord the Pope that such secret society be dissolved and broken up, and they who are not constrained by fear of ecclesiastical censure be curbed by rigorous punishment; therefore it is the express order of his Holiness, by this edict, to prohibit all persons of any state or condition, whether secular or regular, or whatever degree or dignity, from joining the Order of Free Masons, or meeting with them, or in any way associating with them under any other title or cloak whatsoever, under pain of *death* and the *confiscation* of their effects.

It is likewise prohibited as above to any person to seek or tempt any one to associate with any such societies, meetings, or lodges, and they who shall furnish or provide a house, hall, or room for said Masons to hold their lodges in are hereby condemned, over and above the aforementioned penalties, to have the house where such lodges are held utterly destroyed and erased from the ground. And it is the will of his Holiness that to incur the above-named penalties any conjectures, hints, or presumptions of the faithful shall suffice for a presumption of guilt, without admission of any excuse whatever.

And it is also the will of his Holiness that any person having notice or knowledge of such meetings hereafter, and do not immediately report the same to the nearest ecclesiastical authority, shall be considered accomplices of said Masons, and likewise be subject to all the pains and penalties they are subject to. But the names of denouncers or informers shall be kept secret.

Joseph, Cardinal Fiaro
Jerome de Bardi, Secretary[6]

Thus according to Joseph Cardinal Fiaro this condemned every Freemason to death and confiscation of his property (or anyone who helped him, or who even failed to inform on him), and damned him to die without salvation.

From the gloom of a Paris dungeon, a document found its way to Edinburgh, Scotland. Later that year the Scots, led by Robert Bruce (the new Grand Master) began their fight for independence from England (confirmed in 1327 by the Treaty of York). The Scot poet (and Scottish Rite Mason) Robert Burns wrote a poem, "Bannockburn," which tells about the Battle of Bannockburn, the most important battle in the history of Scotland.

The effects of papal condemnation, which from the bull cited would seem to be terrifying, might be better judged when one remembers that ninety-nine years before the death of de Molai the Magna Carta, the English charter of human liberty and justice, was presented by Knights of the mystic brotherhood to the people. Pope Innocent III (who reigned 1198-1216) condemned the Magna Carta as follows:

> We...do utterly reprobate and condemn this agreement; and under ban of anathema [a curse] we command that neither the King shall presume

9:7. Tombs of Templars.

[6]Redding, pp. 181-4.

to observe it nor the Knights and their accomplices to require its observation.[7]

History, unaffected by papal curse, records the Magna Carta's overwhelming acceptance by the free men of England, as well as the fact that Pope Innocent died within a year after he condemned the charter.

This type of "Vatican thinking," which demands dominance over the public's freedom of conscience and speech, is evident in some seventeen major encyclicals and allocutions hurled out by the Vatican since 1738. A few examples:

Pope Pius IX (1846-78) condemned popular government.
Pope Leo XIII (1878-1903) condemned public schools.
Pope Pius XI (1922-39) condemned separation of church and state.

In 1933 the very first political action taken by Adolf Hitler and the Nazi party was an order stating that all Masons throughout Germany were to be simultaneously surprised, arrested, and cast into prison. Sound familiar? The Nazis ruthlessly suppressed Freemasonry, imprisoning and murdering its members. Similar actions were carried out in Italy, Japan, and elsewhere. In Italy, within blocks of the Vatican, Mussolini persecuted, imprisoned, murdered, and confiscated the property of Masons, many of whom were Roman Catholic. But the mystic Brotherhood, the world's oldest champion of liberty, justice, and constitutional freedoms, emerged triumphant in the end.

Many American Roman Catholics bravely fought and served with honor and distinction during World War II. Many died. Many were maimed and crippled for life or experienced the monstrous horrors of concentration camps. Yet neither Mussolini nor Hitler, both of whom pretended to embrace the Catholic faith, was ever excommunicated.

During World War II the Vatican's clergy blessed Mussolini's military forces as they went out to fight American soldiers, many of whom were Roman Catholic. The Vatican never condemned the Nazi invasions of neutral nations, nor did the Vatican speak out against the extermination of six million Jewish men, women, and infants—not to mention even more millions of Europeans, *almost all* of whom were Roman Catholic. To condemn the forces of fascism and national socialism would hardly have been a violation of the ecumenical spirit. These acts of craven servility by the Vatican during World War II prompted deep feelings in our American Roman Catholics, and, as history has shown, they only added to the terrible psychic and physical suffering of Europe. Nothing can be sacrificed forever.

One of the four documents sent by the Grand Master de Molai into the darkness was read by the Grand Master of Masons in the state of Missouri, U.S.A., Belton Lodge #450: the thirty-third president of the United States, the fifteenth Masonic president of that country. During World War II the Grand Master, Harry S Truman, consulted with his Grand Preceptor of modern warfare Gen. Douglas MacArthur, who after the war proved his ability as a statesman in his brilliant administration of the occupation and reorganization of Japan. Truman consulted with MacArthur concerning a new weapon a fugitive scientist from Hitler's realm of horror had put together. Truman had already consulted with Vannever Bush, former head of the Carnegie Institute, and had been told by Bush, "Mr. President, the

[7]Clausen, p. 169.

bomb will never go off, and I speak as an expert on explosives."

From the archives of the Library of Congress, the following composite dialogue can be put together. Discussing the bomb, Truman said, "Bush says the damn thing will never explode, but Oppenheimer and the others have assured me Einstein's theory will work out. Einstein has expressed his concern to me that the bomb might be too heavy for air transport to Japan. He suggests it might be floated into Tokyo Bay and then detonated. How the hell he expects us to float it into the harbor is beyond me."

Responding to Truman, MacArthur replied, "I'll work out the logistics."

He left immediately to call a general staff meeting to "work out the logistics." Over the next few weeks a direct series of communications was rapidly exchanged among Truman, MacArthur, and Einstein. At last, a coded message as to whether or not Einstein believed the bomb could be made light enough with the correct air transport was received: "God does not play dice with the universe."

The well-known end of World War II came about a short time later. Liberty, the essence of what that war was about for many of the peoples of the earth, prevailed.

As the winds of freedom, carrying justice and constitutional rights, swept around the world a more tolerant atmosphere was created, in which some people began to ask themselves what use there was to a morality that destroys human beings. In this climate Freemasonry flourished. Medieval fulminations against Freemasonry by the Church of Rome declined, and on 12 September 1960, Houston, Texas, a Roman Catholic said: "I believe in an America where the separation of church and state is absolute—where no Catholic prelate would tell the President, should he be a Catholic, how to act...where

no church or church school is granted any public funds or political preference."

That speech was made by John F. Kennedy just prior to his election as President of the United States. It was Kennedy who declared a national space goal of landing an American on the moon. On 16 July 1969 Apollo 11 was launched to undertake the first lunar landing mission. On board were Neil A. Armstrong, Michael Collins, and a Mason—Knight Templar Edwin A. ("Buzz") Aldrin, Jr.—who would eventually be one of the first earthmen to leave their footprints on the moon. Footprints—a long way from a dungeon in Paris where four documents, one of which travelled west to reach America by way of Edinburgh, were written by another Knight Templar shortly before nine o'clock one memorable night. (The story and results of the other three documents are beyond the scope of the present work.) Other Masonic astronauts have included Leroy Gordon Cooper, Donn F. Eisele, Virgil I. Grissom, Edgar D. Mitchell, Walter M. Schirra, Jr., Thomas P. Stafford, Paul J. Weitz, James B. Irwin, and John H. Glenn, Jr.

As the earth wobbled along in the age of Aquarius, tension between Freemasonry and the Church of Rome declined. Yet the ancient papal pronouncements against Freemasonry, which the Most Rev. Fulton J. Sheen points out continue to remain on the books, have never been rejected or revised despite the ecumenical attempts of Pope John XXIII. However, since the codification of the canon laws in the *Codex Juris Canonici*, almost all Catholic clergy consider the old papal bulls and edicts little more than the expressions of personal opinions. For example, in 1973 at the Chicago Lawyers Masonic Club luncheon the guest speaker was the Rev. John A. O'Brien, Ph.D., who said:

As a Roman Catholic, a research professor of theology at the University of Notre Dame, and a priest for more than half a century, I want to pay a long overdue tribute to the Freemasons for the distinguished contribution which they have made to the civic, commercial, scientific, cultural and spiritual life of our nation. They have given us some of our greatest presidents, generals, legislators, statesmen, citizens and patriots. If that rich and many-faceted contribution were withdrawn, our nation would be impoverished indeed.

During a priestly ministry of more than fifty years, many of my closest and dearest friends have been Masons, and I count their friendship as a pearl beyond all price.[8]

During the anniversary of the Order of de Molai, John Cardinal Willdebrands, Secretariat for Christian Unity, addressed de Molai representatives by saying, "May I, as the President of the Secretariat for Promoting Christian Unity, express my gratitude and joy that the membership of the Order includes Catholics...I pray that the Lord of Hosts may bless you in all your noble work."[9] Bob Dylan has sung, "The times, they are a-changin'," and perhaps someday in the future a Roman Catholic Pope will be a member of Freemasonry. Perhaps it will be someone like Pope John Paul II.

Taking a momentary pause from the present and returning to the medieval time of de Molai, we may remember a specific charge brought against the Knights Templar, a specific charge brought against the Templars saying that de Molai and the Templars had "deep caves" or catacombs in the earth, in which they had an image "whose eyes had the brightness of heaven."

Recent research would seem to indicate that there may be more truth to this ancient charge than has heretofore been suspected. The new evidence would certainly tempt one to believe that the Templars *did* have an image that they kept hidden from the eyes of all but their initiated members. The new evidence would also support the charge made against the Templars that they held this image in high esteem. In point of fact, if this new evidence continues to be shown valid, the whole religious world may be in line for a disturbing shock, and Freemasons may be shocked more than anyone as a result of this new research.

Taking a giant stride further back in history to the time of Al Mamum, we remember Al Mamun leaving the Chamber of New Birth inside the deep and solemm interior of the Great Pyramid. We remember that in his hasty exit from the chamber he failed to observe a subtle image on the wall outside that chamber—an image similar in appearance to the face on the Shroud of Turin, which allegedly bears the image of Jesus.

Could the image the Knights Templar held in such high esteem have been that linen cloth, $14^{1}/_{2}$ feet in length and $3^{1}/_{2}$ feet in width, bearing a photographically negative image of a bearded man, scourged, wearing a crown of thorns, crucified, and pierced through the side by a pointed instrument? Were the Knights Templar the custodians of the burial garment of Jesus?

In his book *Shroud* Robert K. Wilcox presents evidence that the Knights Templar had this shroud in their possession until most of them were killed on the orders of

[8]Reprinted in Clausen, pp. 173-74.
[9]Ibid.

King Phillip le Bel and Pope Clement V. Wilcox points out that after the leaders of the Templars were burned at the stake the church acquired the shroud from the widow of Geoffrey de Charnay, a Knight Templar, burnt to death at the stake by inquisitors at Poitiers, France.

International laws on ownership of ancient relics may be invoked, a world court engagement lasting for years may be involved, with the Vatican and the Supreme Council of Masons in Washington, D.C., fighting over rightful ownership of the Shroud of Turin. In the court battle between the City of Atlanta and the City of Chattanooga over who had rightful ownership of the Civil War locomotive *General,* Atlanta regained possession of the stolen locomotive even though it had been displayed as a tourist attraction in Chattanooga since the end of the Civil War.

With the death of de Molai, another chapter in the story of earthmen was recorded, showing that of all the animal kingdom, none are so cruel and vindictive to their own kind as man when impelled by religious fanaticism and the lust for gain. In the world are three classes of despotism: civil, ecclesiastic, and military, each of which is sufficient to effect the misery of a people.

Looking back on history, the insane events of the past seem today like a storm in a valley seen from a mountain top high above the clouds. Time separates us from the events. Because of this separation, the events are robbed of their reality to us. We did not personally experience the drama. We did not see the events, nor did we discuss them over coffee with friends. Because we did not actually live through or experience the events in our own central nervous systems, they seem remote and foreign to us. They become little more than academic knowledge—and besides, they happened so long ago they are simply not relevant to us because they could never happen today. Or could they?

On the night of 11 June 1977, all Freemasons in the Arab League countries were simultaneously surprised, arrested, cast into prisons, and tortured or killed in an attempt to extract from those captured the names of their fellow members who had escaped the dragnet. Most of the Masons held their obligations inviolate and refused to name fellow members. One did talk, several hours after he was stripped naked and blindfolded and tied to a stake with a large brass bowl strapped over his stomach. Inside the brass bowl was a hungry rat. At first the rat only nibbled at his skin, tasting...then, ravenous with hunger, it ate, squirmed, pushed its head deeper into the body of the young man. He held out long enough for most of the Masons to flee or go underground into hiding before he talked.

The following morning a UPI report dated 12 June 1977 from Cairo, Egypt, read: ARAB LEAGUE CLOSES MASONIC LODGES. Fifty-eight days later, on the morning of 8 August, in a squalid parking lot in downtown Jidda, Saudi Arabia, the 22-year-old Princess Misha'al and her boyfriend were executed for being young and in love. After she was made to kneel, six bullets smashed into the head of the dewy-eyed young princess. Her boyfriend, forced to watch her death, was made to kneel beside her shattered body. A small and apparently dull sword rose and fell, hacking into his neck five times before the bungling executioner felt the head was severed. It was not. The crowd, satisfied that the "will of God" had been done, applauded and returned to work before their next call to prayers, while those who had condemned the children busied themselves buying more American real estate.

That section of the planet Earth was on the same level of mental and cultural development as medieval Europe. Movies, theater, coin-operated games and other forms of entertainment have been banned (beheading people in public remains the most widely attended form of public entertainment), women are forbidden to drive cars, a husband by saying "I divorce you" three times may rid himself of a wife no matter how faithful, woman adulterers are tied in a sack and stoned to death, men and women must wash immediately after sex because sex even between husband and wife is nasty, women are forced to wear veils in public (a law found most helpful by spies moving among the people unnoticed), boys and girls have twenty hours of compulsory religious instruction (brain-washing) every week, possession of alcohol is punishable by public flogging (so there are no bars except those for the rich), thieves have their hands chopped off (making future honest employment difficult), those guilty of religious or political crimes are beheaded in public. Each year thousands more just disappear. Defense attorneys are not allowed in Islamic courts. I was therefore naturally curious to see what excuse the self-appointed rulers of Islamic nations had invented to justify their actions against Freemasonry. The excuse, I soon found, exhibited none of the imagination or clairvoyance found in classical Moslem manuscripts (viz., the Koran, written by Mohammed, who said, "Let none of you treat his brother in a way he himself would dislike being treated"). I was to discover that the Boycott Office of the Arab League (*in charge of non-military sanctions against Israel*) had adopted a resolution saying that the "founders" of Freemasonry had taken part in the first Zionist conference in Switzerland in 1897, and because of this Masonic lodges were banned!

A sudden thought crossed my mind—I wondered if Freemasonry allowed Moslems to join Masonic groups. Through Samuel Weiser, a rare book dealer in New York, I acquired a copy of *Morals and Dogma of the Ancient and Accepted Scottish Rite of Freemasonry* by Albert Pike, who in standard Masonic references is considered to be the highest initiate in nineteenth century American Freemasonry.

In *Morals and Dogma* I found an answer to this question. Pike, now deceased, lives on in his writings to answer the question: Can a Moslem be a Mason?

> Masonry does not *inculcate* her truths. She *states* them, once and briefly; or hints them, perhaps, darkly; or interposes a cloud between them and eyes that would be dazzled by them....all men are of the same origin, have common interests, and should co-operate together to the same end. He that saith he is in the Light, and hateth his brother, remaineth still in the darkness.
>
> Masonry, around whose altars the Christian, the Hebrew, the Moslem, the Brahmin, the followers of Confucius and Zoroaster, can assemble as brethren..."[10]

So it appears that anyone of any religion is eligible to join Freemasonry; however, priests, bishops, cardinals and other members of secular institutes and religious orders of the Catholic Church often do not join because of their church laws, rather than because of any restriction in Masonry itself.

Obviously, the Arab League employs

---

[10]**Albert Pike, *Morals and Dogma*, pp. 218, 226.**

miserable historians, or this charge saying that the "founders" of Freemasonry had taken part in the first Zionist conference in Switzerland in 1897 is simply propaganda used as an excuse to close all Masonic Lodges in a land where freedom of the press is unknown. For as long as demons of ignorance, brutality, baseness, falsehood, slavishness of soul, intolerance, superstition, tyranny, the insolence of wealth, and bigotry are used by civil and religious despots of the Arab League, they will remain a little and barbarous people. Recall the two constitutional principles of religion, that make all religion—love of God, and love of neighbor.

I knew Freemasonry and its founders were far, far older than 1897, as alleged by the Arab League. I remembered a sunny afternoon in London, standing before a door in the British Museum which opened into a room where the Regius Manuscript and other ancient and rare art treasures are kept. The Regius Manuscript was written in Middle English about 1390. It was purchased by King Charles II from an antiquary; George II presented it to the British Museum in 1775. It is a Masonic poem written 141 years before the "founders" of Freemasonry took part in the first Zionist conference. I was also fortunate to see volumes one and two of a rare book entitled *The Sign Language of the Mysteries* by J. S. M. Ward, M.A., late scholar and prizeman of Trinity Hall, Cambridge, England. His book traces Masonic symbols concealed in celebrated works of art—stained glass windows of churches, chapels, and cathedrals; famous paintings; and statuary—back to ancient Egypt. Ward points out that statues of Egyptian Pharaohs show the hands and/or arms in certain deliberately posed positions, and he stresses the fact that these positions indicate the degree of advancement the Pharoah had obtained in the Egyptian mysteries—positions which he says conceal a meaning well known to Freemasons.[11] This is echoed in the writings of Albert Pike:

Masonry also has her mission to perform. With her traditions reaching back to the earliest times, and her symbols dating further back than even the monumental history of Egypt extends, she invites all men of all religions to enlist under her banners and to war against evil, ignorance, and wrong.[12]

On the back of one of two mysterious stone figures brought to the British Museum from Easter Island, I noted an Egyptian ankh (or crux ansata) carved in bas-relief. The fact that it is in bas-relief is important, because if it had been incised, it might have been added at any time subsequent to the original carving. However, the ankh exhibits the same weather-worn disintegration shown by the rest of the statue, which precludes the possibility of its having been an addition. How this symbol, widely used in ancient Egypt, came to adorn the back of this anthropomorphic statue is unknown. As we now know, the ancient Egyptians visited and established colonies in the Americas; the body of evidence still available to the diligent researcher—ancient writings, buildings, and other artifacts— leaves no doubt that the ancient Egyptians moved upon the face of the waters and circled the world.

---

[11]There is a statue of Pharoah with his right foot in the hollow of the left — striking because it is so unnatural.

[12]Pike, p. 311.

"The outcome of any serious research can only be to make two questions grow where only one grew before," Thorstein Veblen has said. Ra was the name of the sun (son) god in Egypt, Easter Island, and Polynesian.[13] Blond-haired mummies have been unearthed in Egypt, South America, and Lexington, Kentucky, and in the islands of the New Hebrides straw copies of mummies were photographed by *National Geographic* in the early 1900s.[14] North and south of the equator, mummies and pyramids have been discovered all the way around the earth. At sometime in the remote past a world-wide early empire of pyramid-builders encircled the earth, a social world far more advanced than many Middle East countries of the present.

In the Arab mind an Islamic nuclear bomb is necessary "because Israel has one." Pakistan does not have oil, but with a nuclear bomb Pakistan, sharing its bomb with its oil-rich Islamic sister countries, is in a very powerful position to command and receive oil, fighter planes, nuclear fuel, etc.—a point of view discussed by two Indian defense specialists in their book *Pakistan's Islamic Bomb*. Events developing now are setting the stage for what will prove to be the beginning of the end of the present power structure in the Middle East. By inductive reasoning and seeing both the outside shell of reality and the scientific principles underlying the developments in the countries controlled by the Arab League—one can predict with a certain degree of accuracy a tremendous destruction taking place in the Middle East in the early 1990's.

With the closing of Masonic lodges in the Moslem world, I realized that history was once again repeating itself. With every day that goes by the simplistic view that sees history as a gradual but inexorable advance loses ground to cyclical theories. That there were more advanced civilizations before this one is obvious, that they go in cycles is obvious, that whole civilizations of people get wiped out on this planet—forcing the survivors to start over—is becoming more and more obvious. Man has discovered that he is a slave to his own scientific inventions. Rather than being a master of his own marvels of science, he trembles in fear of nuclear war—a reflection upon the level of civilization collectively attained. When one pauses to consider nuclear devices being manufactured by countries on the same level of mental and cultural development as medieval Europe, perhaps even lower—one trembles in fear, for there is not the slightest doubt of our present state: the deluge is once again upon us.

As I was rereading the second sura of the Koran and speculating about the present social, patriotic, and cultural values in the Arab League countries, I received another report from Cairo. This report stated that after the midnight Arab League dragnet, a light that had burned without interruption for thousands of years above a large gilt crescent springing from a series of globes was extinguished in a deep cavern on Mount Hira (Jebel Nur). A man draped a black standard over a statue of an *Alborak* (a strange white creature the shape and size of a mule with the head of a woman and the tail of a peacock), which according to Moslem tradition[15] Mohammed rode to Jerusalem. (It was said that upon dismount-

---

[13]*Heyerdahl Observer Magazine* reports on related matters.
[14]*National Geographic* 19 (January 1908): 10.
[15]See 17th sura, Koran; also Manly P. Hall, *An Encyclopedic Outline of Masonic Hermetic, Qabbalistic and Rosicrucian Symbolical Philosophy*, p. clxxxix.

ing at Mount Moriah, he caught hold of the lower rung of a golden ladder lowered from heaven and, accompanied by the Angel Gabriel, ascended through the seven spheres separating the earth from the inner surface of the empyrean.)

Leaving the cavern, this man descended the mountain. The following night a mysterious person, unknown and unsuspected by the oil sheiks of the Arab League, moved among the crowd in the Arab city of Medina and, making his way past the small shops and stalls of the bazaar, turned down a narrow street. There was a stir in the air, such as arose among the Jews before the birth of Jesus, as if a change of large dimensions was approaching. Leaving the city of Medina at midnight, the person moved toward an ancient burial ground on the outskirts of the city. As if guided by the Light of the Prophet, he moved through the darkness over the rocky ground toward his rendezvous.

The Axis (Quth) was waiting for him, attended by two of the Faithful Ones, four of the Intermediate Ones (Evtad), five of the Lights (Envar), seven of the Very Good (Akhyar), and forty of the Absent Ones (Rijal-i-ghaib). These men, renouncing worldliness, had each withstood the test of a thousand and one days of temptation and were all members of the secret Order of Mevlevi: the Keepers of the mysteries of the Islamic faith, founded by the great Persian Sufic poet and philosopher Jelal-i-din. Members of the Order of Mevlevi are also referred to as "dancing dervishes,"[16] whose movements, as Manly P. Hall says, "exoterically signify the movements of the celestial bodies and esoterically result in the establishment of a rhythm which stimulates the centers of spiritual consciousness within the dancer's body" (see Plate 2:6).

As the person approached the ancient burial ground, he wondered how long Islamic people would allow civil and religious despots to control their minds. He felt it would not be long. He knew the future of his country depended on *his* generation—a subject he had often discussed with Princess Misha'al and her friends. The thought of her, and of their clandestine meetings, brought a smile to his face. She had encouraged him to seek the Axis before, but after her return from England, where late one night she had attended a ceremony within "a circle of ancient stones," she had become more persistent on this point. It was the arrest and imprisonment of his brother the night before and the visionary words of Misha'al after the midnight raid on Freemasons that some intuitive frame of mind told him that now was the time to seek the Axis.

He knew Islamic history, and as he stepped over the raised tail of a scorpion without breaking his youthful stride he recalled a time in history when the streets of Baghdad were lit by street lights while Europe struggled through the Dark Ages. Now wholesale slaughters in wars, decapitations, mutilations, and death by fire and torture

9:8. Stonehenge.

---

[16]See J.P. Brown, *The Dervishes* (Philadelphia, 1868); L.J. Garnett, *Mysticism and Magic in Turkey* (London, 1912); and Hall, p. clxxvi.

had replaced the words of the Prophet Mohammed. He thought of his younger brother, whom he must help when he returned. He knew his brother was a good and kind person and strong as a bull, not afraid of anything except rats. His thoughts returned to the greater part of the people, who suffered from poverty, ignorance, ill health, and hunger, while the oil sheiks, who pretended to embrace Islam, continued importing expensive Scotch in boxes marked "glassware" and dressing their concubines in the most expensive gowns from Dior and Yves St. Laurant while they used computers to develop nuclear devices for the destruction of humanity. He knew it was time for a change, a new cycle using the insights and wisdom of the ancient mysteries.

Arriving at the ancient burial ground, he saw a large circle of fifty-six men surrounding the Axis and the two Faithful Ones. A man of weaker character and stamina, whose resistance was inadequate to what lay ahead, would have fled. The person knew, however, that he had chosen this meeting the moment he had entered the deep cavern on Mount Hira, and he felt no need to save himself from whatever drama or test lay ahead in the shadows. He knew that for the return of THE WORD to the people of Islam the Order of Mevlevi, the Keepers of the Islamic Mysteries, must be invoked.

9:10. *Stelle, Illinois.* These people have joined together in this avant-guard community to survive the next shift in the Earth's axis by orbiting the planet in an L-5 orbit. After the destructive shifting they plan to return to Earth. An L-5 orbit was first proven practical by Dr. Gerard K. O'Neill, Princeton University (characterized by contemporaries as the Christopher Columbus of the Space Age), and author of *The High Frontier.*

271

9:9. *Stonehenge*. A 'Druid's Day' celebration at Stonehenge on August 24th. Julius Caesar wrote in *De Bello Gallico*, "It is especially the object of the Druid's to inculcate this—that souls do not perish, but after death pass into other bodies, and they consider that by this belief more than anything else men may be led to cast away the fear of death, and to become courageous. They discuss many points concerning the heavenly bodies and

their motion, the extent of the universe and the world, the nature of things, the influence and ability of the immortal gods; and they instruct the youth in these things." In this photograph one may see the pyramid and the Egyptian cross on the altar. In Old Irish Druid meant "he who knows."

On the other side of the world, seven hours earlier, people in America were dancing in the disco clubs while lean and hungry people were planning events that would forever alter the future for them and their children's children. In Stelle, Illinois, and Adelphi, Texas, however, people were working to prepare for what Alvin Toffler in his new book *The Third Wave* has described as a "regional economy"—an economic situation made known to readers of *The Ultimate Frontier* eighteen years ago, an economic situation which Andrew Duncan, an expert on the Arab world, points out in his new book *Money Rush*:

> Saudi Arabia will be largely responsible for the quality of life in the West during the 1980s. American financial commitment to Saudi Arabia is now greater than it was to Vietnam at the height of the war.[17]

The young man thought, "A night is a dawning, an end is a new beginning, and death is but a waking," as two of the Very Good stepped aside, opening the circle. He stepped inside and the ranks closed behind him. He realized that he must now prove himself deserving of the help of this band of men who had renounced all worldliness. He knew that whatever happened from this point on he must demonstrate that he had advanced far enough in the evolutionary scale to merit their help.

As the circle closed behind him, the Axis smiled. The two Faithful Ones moved east and west to join the circle, which was now moving slowly counterclockwise. The person moved into a position directly in front of the Axis and words were exchanged in disguised terms. The person said, "The one who knows the secret does not speak," to which the Axis replied, "The one who speaks does not know the secret."

Discoursing in hushed tones on the fate of those who in the past had vainly attempted to vanquish Truth, certain ancient rites were performed. The person was surprised when the Axis suddenly thrust an ancient fine gold ring with a string tied to it and a wooden toothpick—the two most important symbols of the Islamic mysteries—into his hand and instructed him to turn around. Turning, he noticed the circle. A moment ago it had been moving slowly counter-clockwise. Now the circle of men was chanting a melodious succession of sounds and skipping—as if attempting to establish a certain rhythm.

As he watched the circle of dancing dervishes move from a skipping movement into a faster dancing movement, a rhythm was established and the night moved before his eyes, burning away the past and its false revelations. He felt strange. He felt the unknowable unknown as an actual presence. There in the darkness of the desert the circle, as it moved faster, seemed to be swarming with all that could be. He felt the movement of its living power transcending all human thought. The circle of dancing dervishes had become to him a pulsation of life, a whirlpool of life, a vertiginous movement of life in which he was tempted to laugh. However, before he could do so the rhythm of the circle increased and his sensorial apparatus was stimulated. *Kundalini* energy ascended his spine, passing through all seven of his chakras, awakening in an uncontrollable outburst of energy something deep within him as he recognized the presence of life as an ally in the impenetrable mystery of being.

The effect of the dance on his mind had

---

[17]Andrew Duncan, *Money Rush*.

been swift and overwhelming, never giving him the chance to fossilize his thinking. He realized that the dance represented the very powerful movement of the universe—an intense movement, a dynamic and immeasurable movement that transcends all conception. He knew that in seeing the movement of this drama, in the hidden depths of its whirlwind motion, he had understood the secret of existence, which had liberated in him a hidden faculty he would use to help the people fight against evil, ignorance, and wrong when he returned from his journey into this kingdom of sand and stone.

Beginning his long journey home, he recalled the last words spoken by the Axis: "The awakening of the Third Eye is worth a thousand corporeal eyes." The string tied to a fine gold ring on his hand fluttered in the night air.

A few hours later a coded overseas telephone call was placed. In America the stillness of the night was shattered by a phone ringing at 1733 Sixteenth Street, NW, Washington, D.C. The phone was inside a white marble building on one of the Capital's finest thoroughfares, a building modelled after one of the seven wonders of the ancient world, whose entrance (guarded by two Egyptian sphinxes) opens into the House of the Temple of the Thirty-Third and Last Degree of the Ancient and Accepted Scottish Rite of Freemasonry of the Southern Jurisdiction of America.

The next day the four original Metropolitan lodges instituted by de Molai—one at Naples for the east, one at Edinburgh for the west, one at Stockholm for the north, and one in Paris for the south—were notified that the ugly head of anti-Freemasonry had again risen. Also notified were the Supreme Councils of the Ancient and Accepted Scottish Rite in 35 other countries, each with hundreds of thousands or millions of members, which have come into existence from the time that the Grand Master Jacques de Molai, an hour before his death, passed a living flame of truth into another hand to be carried forth into the darkness of the world.

With some seven million Freemasons in America, assuming an average membership of only 500,000 for each of the other 39 countries in the Southern Jurisdiction (to say nothing of the Northern Jurisdiction of Freemasonry or the York Rite or the Order of de Molai or the Daughters of the Eastern Star—one of the female branches of Masonry—or its other auxiliary organizations), simple mathematics shows that within hours some 26,000,000 members of Masonry in 40 different countries knew of the putrid deeds performed by the Arab League's Boycott Office.

In his book *The Sirius Mystery* Robert K. G. Temple, a Fellow of the Royal Astronomical Society with a degree in oriental studies and Sanskrit, states his belief that

> ...we may be under observation or surveillance at this very moment, with an extraterrestrial civilization based at the Sirius system monitoring our development to see when we will *ready ourselves* for their contacting us. In other words, we may very possibly be allowed to control the forthcoming contact ourselves.[18]

In a brief but more esoteric annotation, readers of Robert Anton Wilson's book *Cosmic Trigger: The Final Secret of the Illuminati* may have already noticed that the street address of the Supreme Council of

---

[18]Robert K.G. Temple, *The Sirius Mystery,* p. 220.

the Thirty-Third Degree equals the number 23 (17 + 3 + 3 = 23). Readers of Wilson's book, and other genies who enjoy mathematical games, have probably guessed that if one called long distance information and asked for the telephone number of the Supreme Council of the temple they might be told: "Someone, Sirius, detached from the hive economy via internal biochemical auto-experiments should know the first two numbers are 2 and 3, which form the number 23."

Those who understand Maya mathematics or those who understand the *I Ching's* trigrams have already solved, by trans-time signalry between members of a divine effort, that the third and fourth numbers of the Supreme Council's telephone number would also be 2 and 3, which again form the number 23. Chance? The name Scottish Rite Freemasonry has 23 letters. Coincidence?

The "lucky coincidences" or syncronicities—as they are called in Jungian psychology—of the number 23 Wilson believes guided him to "a network of adepts that extends far beyond our Earth," which he connects with the enigma star Sirius. Wilson writes: "I definitely experienced impressions which I thought were communications from Sirius"—a somewhat ambiguous statement, since those who know, know. According to Georg von Rauch, in his book *A History of Soviet Russia*, 23 million human beings were arrested (and shot) by Stalin's orders for unfaithfulness to the Communist Party in a country where the inhabitants are subjected to separate transportation buses, limited school facilities, restricted living quarters; are denied voice in government; are under harsh police control; and are regimented and living in filth, poverty, and hunger—most of which has been brought about by the intolerance of those in power.

The American conception of liberty is unknown in most foreign countries, and that is why no other nation since the early empire predating ancient Egypt has ever possessed the spiritual strength and material wealth we now enjoy. Our civilization is no accident, because it was founded squarely upon the concept of human liberty and continues to exist because we have learned to defend the rights of the individual. If we are to hold these rights of liberty inviolate, we must not follow in the footsteps of Europe, Asia, and Africa, by surrendering bit by bit our heritage, because it can only lead us into economic and political ruin.

Can we turn around and go back to where the mistakes began? To do so would be revolutionary, and besides, it would be too difficult to retrace the footsteps of our forebears. What most of us want is security, and I do not mean economic security alone (although the present and several preceding administrations have seemingly thought so), but peace of mind, unfailing faith in the benevolence of God, the right of free men to control their own government and to enlarge or diminish its power at will. Physical security can be attained only when we banish war.

Mental processes thousands of years ago were similar to those used today. Men computed in billions. The laws of mathematics have remained inexorable throughout the years. God's Ten Commandments are the same. Our government should not plunder the haves to give to the have-nots, it should not punish success and glamorize failure. It should not discourage thrift and invite inflation to the extent that we now accept dishonesty as a necessary ingredient of politics.

"A public office is a public trust" is unfortunately regarded by many as a quaint and ancient commentary by some senile and ancient band of men—we know better now, of course. At the moment the process has taken the form of taxing and spending by the government, which constitutes a serious threat against our constitutional limitations. True security cannot be fashioned out of slavery, injustice, and corruption, but must be founded on the laws of God and dedicated to the dignity of man.

The United States of America is the last refuge on this earth for human liberty. The responsibility of preserving that liberty is yours. You cannot afford to gamble tomorrow entirely upon armament, because there may be no tomorrows.

It was almost daylight in a small hamlet through which the caravans passed on their way to the bazaar. The village was peopled with peasants, carpenters, and shepherds who kept the even tenor of their ways. The soft padding noise of fifty-nine camels as they plodded through the narrow streets awakened a child. As the appearance of caravans so early in the streets was a sight the child had never before witnessed, this caused him to wonder. Running downstairs from his bedroom window, the child opened the front door and stepped into the street. The caravan had vanished. An exotic odor that child had never before smelled superimposed itself over the regular moist, sweaty smell of the street. The child saw a man moving towards him down the narrow street.

Timidly moving into the street as the man drew closer, the child reached out his hand to touch the hand of the man and clutch his ring finger. Looking down at the young boy's face, a transparent drop began to form in the corner of the man's right eye as he thought of millions of such children in hundreds of countries who would grow up prisoners of their parents' religious and political-nationalistic propaganda. The hand of the child was warm. It pulsated with the throbbing of a young and eager heart seeking truth. Looking towards the heavens, the man remembered the words of the Axis concerning a date in May *twenty-three years in the future.* As his eyes locked on the star Sirius, he wondered why so many men try so desperately to prove to the satisfaction of others that which they do not themselves understand or believe. Kneeling, the man made a low sibilant sound as he whispered into the child's ear the seven words: "Love God, and your neighbor as yourself."

The identity of this young man must remain secret, because my Cairo source of information is most insistent:

> Every day he moves among the people of the Arab League countries spreading, in every direction, TRUTH, he becomes like a great tree which shoots forth its branches and roots and attracts more followers. Therefore, he poses a great menace to the corrupt religious infidels who have forgotten the most important words of Muhammad: 'Let none of you treat his brother in a way he himself would dislike being treated.'
>
> Perhaps, a man from the west like yourself will understand that the corrupt religious ideas of a few fanatical religious leaders coupled with the insatiable greed of the oil sheiks and political leaders presently control the free will of millions of Moslems, people who NEVER had the opportunity to learn, as people in your country do, that the devil can often quote Scripture to achieve his own end.

In 1977 these events were unknown to the general public, as many events are now.

9:11. The Axis surrounded by members of the Order of Mevlevi — the keepers of the "Islamic Mysteries" — with the Egyptian Dog Star Sirius in the distance.

A year before the above events in the Middle East took place, I interviewed Tom Valentine, author of *The Great Pyramid: Man's Monument to Man*. Valentine presents evidence of a pre-Egyptian civilization highly skilled in the science of gravitational astronomy—and therefore the mathematical basis of the mechanical arts and sciences—that built the Great Pyramid to communicate a message to a generation of men and women alive on earth 23 years before 5 May 2000.

My interview with Valentine took place on 7 October 1976 (a year whose numbers total 1 + 9 = 10, + 7 = 17, + 6 = 23) at which time I learned...

Noone: Mr. Valentine, how did you become interested in the Great Pyramid?

Valentine: Well, like everyone else, for most of my life I accepted the idea that the Great Pyramid was just a great big pile of stone made by thousands and thousands of slaves. But I read a book in 1967 called *The Ultimate Frontier*. That book profoundly affected my life. In it they made statements about the Great Pyramid being much more than a tomb. Point in fact, it never was a tomb for a pharoah. It is a monument to mankind and human perfection. It is the oldest

9:12. *Tom Valentine at the Base of the Great Pyramid.* In this photo Valentine's foot rests on one of the remaining precisely engineered, angled, and placed casing stones which originally covered the entire building. Note the shadow-box like arrangement of pavement stones surrounding an ancient band of men's Pyramid.

artifact of an ancient system of religious belief. Then I thought, that's something I can check out. I can see if the information in *The Ultimate Frontier* is true or not. I started investigating. I then learned a great number of things about the Great Pyramid. First of all, the ancient Greeks were quite right in calling it the 'first wonder of the world.' When one considers the thought, preparation, and choice of site, one will see that the solid bedrock of the Giza Plateau—the only tableland within miles capable of supporting the weight of the structure—was the most intelligent choice. There is a fantastic amount of literature about the Great Pyramid. Therefore, it is not unusual that we also find a great deal of controversy surrounding it. The British in the 1860's were the first to study the ancient building in a serious manner. By re-examining the theories of the British, which were discarded by the 'experts' of that time, the crux of my book began to take shape.

Noone: Does the crux of your book include the fact that the Great Pyramid may *not* have been built by the ancient Egyptians?

Valentine: Yes. The British did not discuss that possibility. That possibility is my own bit of research. However, most people who study the Great Pyramid realize [that] the civilization we know as 'ancient Egyptian' could not have built the Great Pyramid the way we know today it would have had to have been built. You see, the building is built geometrically perfect, and according to our present conception of ancient history the Egyptians didn't understand highly theoretical mathematics—obviously from the way the other 89 major pyramids in Egypt were constructed. The manner in which the other pyramids were constructed was a very haphazard way of building. They are copies of the Great Pyramid. The Great Pyramid itself is, however, absolute perfection in stone both to the '*pi*' relationship, the relationship of a diameter to the circumference of a circle, and the Golden Mean or '*phi*' relationship, with which we can divide a straight line so that $A^2 + B^2 = C^2$. The reason why it was structured is embodied in the word itself, 'pyramid,'—'lights and measures'—that there are revelation types of lights. The word for pyramid used by the ancient Egyptians was 'glorious light,' and the word has meaning that there are revelations in the measurements. If you pursue this hint, so to speak, you find out that the builders of the Great Pyramid are the same people that wrote the original text of the Old Testament, and they laid out their plan in the Great Pyramid as well as in the Scriptures.

Noone: Who are these people?

Valentine: My opinion is, they were what we call Hyksos (heck-sos or hike-sos), and we find traces of them throughout Meso-America, India, and the Middle East in the earliest of times. The Egyptians had two or three different waves of Hyksos rulers come in. The word 'hyksos' for many years was translated 'shepherd kings,' which is a paradox, you see—looking at life the way we look at it today.

How could a group who were non-warlike come into a land and take over and run things without any fighting? Yet they obviously did, and these ancient builders had a profound influence wherever they went. The years of research I've done tell me that the Hyksos were a group of people who had in their culture information stemming from a previous civilization. I think that our view of history, saying that it started in the 'cradle of civilization,' in Egypt and Mesopotamia, is *wrong*. The surviving evidence indicates both Egypt and Mesopotamia are actually later civilizations—remnants of a far, far greater early empire.

Noone: Do you think the Hyksos race was a race chosen by some greater intelligence to impart a superior ideology to the rest of the human race?

Valentine: Not so much chose, but actually chose themselves. All genius is self-appointed. I would say these people were a remnant from a previous culture, and they had something they wanted to do, and they embodied their thinking in their work, and they influenced people by their works. They came into the land, and there were already humans in the Nile Valley, but they came into the land in an unobtrusive and dextrous maneuver so as not to alarm the existing culture. They came in without fighting. They took the worst land. They didn't try to impress their knowledge on the others. They just did things in a better way. Soon the people in that area were paying attention to them. Once they gained the attention of the people it didn't take very long before they were running everything, because they did everything with better methodology, which is the way life ought to be—you ought to show by example.

Noone: What happened then?

Valentine: Fairly soon after arriving, they suggested to the people that as life was *now* so peaceful and harmonious, it would be a happy challenge to build a monument to the future, to the future of mankind. In my opinion the Hyksos philosophy and the philosophy of many modern people is identical, in that human beings can be perfect if they work toward that end.

Noone: What happened to the ancient tribe, the Hyksos?

Valentine: I think they are still in existence today and have not died out but have gone underground many thousands of years ago. What we call Masonry, Freemasonry, is an offshoot of the group that started out. The Hyksos group became what *The Ultimate Frontier* calls 'the Brotherhoods.' These are a group of people who have knowledge about what it really means to be human, to be a human becoming, to grow toward human perfection—it's a philosophical thing. These people still exist. They still band together in groups here and there, and they show by doing. Again, their lifestyle shows that they really have a handle on what life is all about. They don't try to impress others with numbers or with what they know, they just live doing some-

WASHINGTON AS A MASON.

9:13. In his book *The Sign Language of the Mysteries*, J.S.M. Ward, M.A., late scholar and prizeman of Trinity Hall, Cambridge, points out that Dr. E.A. Wallis Budge's translation of the *Egyptian Book of the Dead* failed to consider the "sacred" symbology of certain Egyptian hieroglyphs ("They have two quite different kinds of writing, one of which is called sacred, the other common." Herodotus, p. 93, Book II) well known today to many 32° Freemasons. Ward's two-volume book was published by the Baskerville Press Ltd., London, in a limited edition of one thousand numbered sets which were sold in 1928 for the extravagant price of 125 pounds.

Ward's book shows Masonic symbols incorporated into the art, paintings, and stained-glass windows of churches, chapels and cathedrals of the Renaissance, and the ancient temples and tombs and statues of Egyptian pharaohs. Most Americans understand Indian sign language — one raised hand means "how" or my hand is empty of weapons — "Peace." Ward suggests that statues of Egyptian pharaohs have two flat hands on their knees, or their arms crossed across their heart chakras, or that other Egyptian pharaohs may have their hands raised palms out as if they were trying to push someone away, which might explain the picture of Washington above.

282

Seti I adoring Osiris-Seker in his shrine.
Mariette, *Abydos*, Vol. I, p. 75.

Seti I offering incense to Osiris.
Mariette, *Abydos*, Vol. I, p. 60.

Nekhebit and Hu presenting life and
sovereignty to the son of Isis.

Uatchit and Sa presenting life and sovereignty to the son of Isis.

Seti I praying to Osiris.   Before the god are the symbol of the bull's skin, and the
ram containing his soul.
Mariette, *Abydos*, Vol. I, p. 61.

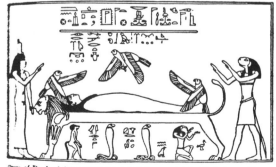

Osiris of Denderah lying on his bier which is supported by Thoth, two goddesses,
and an Ape-god.   The three hawks are Isis, Nephthys, and Hathor.   At the head
stands Isis, and at the foot Ḥeqet.
Mariette, *Dendêrah*, IV, 70.

Osiris Ḥemka begetting a son by Isis, who hovers over him in the form of a hawk.
Anubis, Horus, Nephthys and Shentit are present.
Mariette, *Dendêrah*, IV, 90.

9:14. Egyptian symbols.

thing they want to accomplish while they are here. We know in Egypt these people formed secret societies and that Pharaoh Akhnaton came up 'under the rose' out of one of these secret societies and took over the land of Egypt in a manner that forbids disclosure, at a time in which the superficial popular theology left a want unsatisfied, which religion in a wider sense alone could supply. We know Alexander the Great wanted to get the knowledge of one of these ancient secret societies, because he writes about it a great deal. Pythagorus consented to be circumcised in order to become one of the initiates of these secret societies—which are the Hyksos population carrying their knowledge of science and the universe and cosmology with them and keeping the truth secret so they wouldn't be persecuted and wiped out. You can imagine what society today would do to a group of people like this, were they to perform certain 'ancient rituals' in public. Look what they did to Akhnaton—as soon as he was dead they destroyed the city he built.

Noone: That's right, they tried to—

Valentine: Wipe his name out.

Noone: Yes, because he taught there was only one God.

Valentine: The human tendency in the mass populace...

Noone: When you use the term 'mass populace,' are you referring to a group of people who have become undeveloped on account of a too pleasant or a too severe climate, or

even from physiological or psychological causes?

Valentine: The phrase 'mass populace' was a term used by the ancient ones which usually refers to those in a populace, any populace, in any country, who sit back waiting for some savior to raise them up out of their misery.

Noone: Then you *are* referring to people who are merely living a 'conditioned response' to their environment.

Valentine: Yes. The human tendency in the mass populace is to tear things down rather than to reach up to the excellent, which brings everything down to mediocrity. We're doing that in this country today with our so-called standards from the federal government—everything's got to be brought down. This is just another social indication of this tendency in human beings to bring things down to a lower level so it's easier—instead of striving for excellence. The Hyksos people went after pleasing results and worked hard in this manner. They strove for excellence, and therefore they had to go underground to keep from being persecuted. In almost every case that we can trace, anyone that tried to bring the truth to man has been crucified, or killed in some cruel or barbarous human ritual.

Noone: Do you know how the Great Pyramid was constructed?

Valentine: I leave that puzzle to the engineers, architects, and professors of physics who have researched and

9:15. Alexander the Great. During his campaign in Egypt, Alexander, finding that the various objects of human ambition which he had been so rapidly attaining by his victories and conquests for the past ten years were insufficient to satisfy him, began now to aspire for some supernatural honors, and he accordingly conceived the design of having himself declared to be the son of a god. The heroes of Homer were sons of the gods. Alexander envied them the fame and honor which this distinction gave them in the opinion of mankind. He determined to visit the temple of Jupiter Ammon in the Oasis of Siwah, and to have the declaration of his divine origin made by the priests there.

Marching west along the shores of the Mediterranean he reached a place called Paraetonium. He then left the seashore and marched south, striking at once into the desert. For eleven days he and his escort marched three hundred miles across the boundless expanse, whose solemn silence is far more imposing and sublime than the loudest thunders of the sea. Arriving at the temple of Jupiter Ammon, Alexander attempted to bribe the priests by presents and pay to initiate him into the mysteries. The priests, after conferring in secret with the thought of saving the village from Alexander's wrath, came out with the annunciation that Alexander was indeed the son of the god Jupiter Ammon. Magnificent ceremonies were performed, with offerings, oblations, and sacrifices, after which Alexander returned to Memphis no more the wiser.

studied the building. No one at the present really knows. There are several suppositions, but since no one really knows, that mystery remains to be answered in the next 24 years. And since no one really knows, in my opinion there's no such thing as an 'expert.'

Noone: In that case, how do you believe the Great Pyramid may have been constructed?

Valentine: My information, from people who seem very knowledgeable, says that they built in with water locks and floated the blocks into place. That's pretty hard to conceive of, because they would have had to have been tremendous locks, because the Great Pyramid is up on a plateau at least six miles from the banks of the Nile river. Water with a series of basins and pipes that match the corridor and chamber system of the Great Pyramid's interior system embodies all the laws of hydraulic engineering. For example, the Great Pyramid's Grand Gallery is a perfect 'vacuum bottle' in this pumping system, which I explain in my book as I explore the research work of Edward J. Kunkel, author of the book *Pharoah's Pump*.[19]

Noone: If this tribe of people, the Hyksos, caused the Great Pyramid to be constructed, did they know their message wouldn't be understood for thousands of years, or did they think that humans would grasp its meaning a little bit before that?

Valentine: I think it's quite appar-

ent that they knew it would be grasped in the 20th century. I think that they laid it out so the core of their meaning would be picked up by those who really had the mathematical knowhow. It wasn't until 1905 that we had the real understanding of gravitational astronomy, the astronomy involving the solar system and the movement of the earth around the sun, down so pat that we had all the answers the builders of the Great Pyramid had. They knew as much or more about today's system of gravitational astronomy as we know.

Noone: Do you think this falls in line with a number of other theories that humans were at one time visited by supremely intelligent beings from other worlds?

Valentine: I don't accept that thesis. However, I believe that there is life probably on every little planetoid in the entire universe, life that is similar to ours in [having] a spiritual nature, but somewhat different in physical nature. No other beings from outer space ever came down here and cohabited with the apes, as Mr. von Daniken would say. I would reject that thesis, but on the other hand I *would* say we are indeed created by another intelligence far greater than this planet or even this solar system. You know, it's a funny thing. I was once an atheist. I went through most of my college days as an atheist. I went through most of my college days as an anthropologist, and didn't believe in a creative theory at all, but

[19]See pp. 199 & 200, *supra,* and Plates 7:4 and 7:15 for further details on Pharaoh's pump.

after studying for many years I was forced to accept the fact that I obviously had been created—because it just didn't happen by chance. There's no way. I would say that this theory that something in outer space came down and interfered is quite accurate, in that respect. We are in the image of a creator of some kind that we can't even conceive. Therefore we have the ability to do all kinds of fantastic things. I think there was a civilization 50,000 years ago in the Pacific, now underwater, that had in it achievements that we only think of today.

Noone: Okay, just a minute—let me backtrack here. At the beginning of the interview you mentioned that you began your investigation of the Great Pyramid after you read *The Ultimate Frontier.* What's it all about?

Valentine: Oh, that's a big topic! *The Ultimate Frontier* ties together a history of this planet, the idea and purpose for mankind being a part of it, and a philosophy of growth towards human perfection—and how this philosophy is what life is really all about. The truth of this was lost when the great civilization on the Pacific continent of Mu was destroyed by a sudden cataclysmic change on the crust of the earth 50,000 years ago. There are a group of individuals who call themselves the 'Brotherhoods,' unobtrusively working to uplift mankind back to this ancient wisdom belief, and the Great Pyramid is indeed a monument to this particular Brotherhood.

Noone: Perhaps the truth is never

lost. Perhaps as we evolve towards a true understanding of essentials, we suddenly find ourselves faced with a question where we discover that we have really understood nothing at all, and consequently have to begin learning all over again on a new and higher level. Perhaps the memory of the destruction of Mu and other catastrophic events is contained in the collective unconsciousness of man. Perhaps some humans—direct genetic descendants of the survivors of these cataclysmic events—carry in their bloodline a genetic mutation. Perhaps this genetic mutation was deeply imprinted into the central nervous system (CNS) of some of our forebears, who actually experienced and survived a sudden slippage in the earth's tectonic plates or a supernova explosion. Such a genetic mutation, passed in genetic structures (DNA) from generation to generation, may explain why some of us today are more acutely sensitive to subtle earth tremors than our neighbors. In any case...this book, *The Ultimate Frontier,* started your mental processes working along these lines.

Valentine: Ah—they were already working along this line, just like many people's are without knowing about it. I had started into investigation of phenomena and mysticism on my own, because my religious convictions couldn't answer my questions. Going to different churches and checking them out I found didn't answer my question as to *why* I am. I've always wanted to know *why.* The human physiology is a remarkable thing. Why should it be? Why should we be different than the animals? Why should we have these philosophies when no other animal has philosophy? I studied many of the standard religions, but they couldn't answer my question to my satisfaction. I didn't like the idea of blind faith. To me blind faith is irresponsible and unreasonable. Then I got into science and became an atheist. I was working on a masters degree in anthropology and found that, just like the churches, the information from the scientific side fell short. They can't answer all the questions. In fact, the more we learn, the more anomalies we have, and we realize how little we know. Then my son—who at the time was four and a half years old—nearly drowned. In fact, he *did* drown. He was full of salt water and unconscious for 45 minutes. He should by all rights have died. The year was 1960. I was eating at a restaurant on the beach when I saw him floating face down in the water. I ran across the beach, jumped into the water, handed him to my brother, who handed him to a strange old man who appeared to be a derelict. Then this old man pumped out the water—I was in shock—out of my son for the next 45 minutes. He refused to give my son to the ambulance crew and the doctor who arrived and pronounced him dead. The old man looked into my eyes and said, 'This boy isn't dead. I'm going to bring him back.' I told the doctor, 'Let him keep trying,' and the old man kept working. Forty-five minutes is a long period of time to remain unconscious without breathing. However, my son not only recovered without brain damage from that episode, but he told us in the hospital exactly all of the events that took place—from me running out of the restaurant, jumping across the breakwater, diving into the water and getting him, handing him to my brother—he recalled all of this as if he had been watching it as a spectator, and yet he was unconscious. I mean, he wasn't Jean Dixon or anything. That personal experience was positive proof in my mind that the human mind is a lot greater than that body.

Noone: Did it reinforce a previous belief, or did it really serve to allow you to see for the first time that there are other realities?

Valentine: It made me relook at some of my own experiences. It made me stop and think about a lot of things. For instance, the first thing it made me think of is when I was studying anthropology, I was studying the theory of evolution, chance evolution, chemistry just providing a scenario for itself to keep procreating and surviving and improving and so on. If we accept evolution as the ultimate answer, we have to accept a ludicrous notion that atoms—all matter is made up of the atomic elements—can so arrange themselves as to be able to give themselves abstract qualities such as memory, desire, will, curiosity, consciousness, conscience, creativity, intuition, emotion, and reason. How can you get that chemically? You can't. It has to be something else that is endowed, and man is the only one that has it—a goat doesn't see the stars or know what's over the mountain or know anything about life and death, you see. But we do. These ideas were in my head, and intuitively I knew there was much more, but when that happened to my son then I realized that I too am a discrete bundle of mental energy—only I didn't have that phraseology for it. I didn't know about what life was all about as I feel I do now.

Noone: Were you able to determine the capability of the human being to deal with all these diverse areas of knowledge?

Valentine: Certainly. I'm doing it and I'm nothing extraordinary. I am dealing with all of these areas of knowledge in a relaxed and casual and fun way, and I feel that I am growing. I'm not impatient about my growth, because I know that someday, if I continue to try to improve myself, if I continue to use those qualities of mind that I have, then I will become as perfect as humanly possible. Now according to our basic beliefs in this country, human beings are created in the image of their creator. To me that means we have the same qualities of mind. We're certainly not the physical image, but the mental image. We have will, memory, desire, curiosity, consciousness, creativity, conscience—I've gone through those before—intuition, emotion, reason—those ten qualities of mind are the same qualities as the creator [has]. Perhaps we can never become absolute perfection as the creator, whatever it is, must have been. I cannot conceive of the creative force, not enough to verbalize it and make

sense to everyone, but I think we can obtain relative perfection and become one with the creator by improving ourselves based upon what we have to work with. There's no limit to human abilities, to what humans can do. We limit ourselves with our own conditioning.

Noone: Do you think that most people are really trying to find out about all these things?

Valentine: Many humans are. I would say there are millions of people who have an inner urging towards something better, especially in this day and age, because now there are more of them here. Out of the great majority, roughly 220,000,000 people today in the United States, only about two or three million are really interested in what makes them tick, what is involved in life, the purpose of it all, and in really growing and building on their character. The other two hundred and something million are merely living a conditioned response from their environment, and they don't think about it at all. Look, here we are in the city of Atlanta, a huge city. Look at the people walking back and forth. They're positive in many ways, and yet they never really give it a thought as to *why* they are, *why* they're capable of building these tremendous buildings and driving those tremendous vehicles they drive and where they got this great gift of mind and how really little they're using it—they don't give it a single thought.

Noone: Fundamental religion has been undergoing so many changes in the past few years. Catholicism has been losing quite a few members because those members say that their religion is not in tune with the times, and this is the case in many other religious bodies. Do you believe that formal religion is just not keeping in tune with the times, or has it ever been in tune with them?

Valentine: Oh, considerably in tune. Essentially it's this: the church for the last two thousand years has done a remarkable job with what it's had to work with. Remember, they're dealing with part of the truth. I've just finished this week a new book called *The Life and Death of Planet Earth.* Now, what it points out is that the absolute truth is what we're all trying to find out, and we prove this subjectively. We know it and nobody can change our minds, because we know it just like I know that fire burns my fingers because I've stuck them in there. You can tell me all you want, but I won't believe it until I do it. Knowledge is what we're seeking. The churches started off with a paradigm—a framework of understanding—and they had to work within that framework, and their framework was quite narrow. Then Jesus came along and broadened it tremendously. He *resurrected* the ideas of love and brotherhood and working *you-too*-can-do-as-I-do. He was showing by his lifestyle that you can be perfect, you can know yourself, you can know your creator, you can know what it's all about. All you have to do is get off the dime and stop being so lazy and pay attention. That's what he was saying. Human

beings have a tendency to want to put frameworks around things so they can be comfortable with them. So the early church put a framework around the truth. Theologians have translated and interpreted what has been said by all the great teachers until it's been quite distorted. However, even with all of the translations and misinterpretations of what was really said in the ancient times, they've done a remarkable job. They've done some bad things as well as good things in the eye of history, but the information is here. All you have to do is want it and dig for it. I found it. I found it for myself. There's more than one path. The reason I followed the path of the Great Pyramid is because I'm a doubter, a skeptic, and here's something made of stone, the world's largest stone structure. It can be checked and rechecked and measured and remeasured. It's been around for a very, very long time and there is no doubt it's there. However, the metaphysical idea—somebody going into a trance and some voice talking through him telling me he's Jesus—that doesn't prove anything to me. It could be, but I could never prove it. I can prove what the Great Pyramid does, and that turned me on. There are answers to everyone's questions. We each have progressed. You see, I accept we've lived many thousands of lifetimes. People say, 'Oh, reincarnation, I can't believe that.' Well, they probably didn't believe it in their last lifetime either. I probably didn't either. However, each time we live a life we learn something more towards this perfection. We're supposed to be growling until finally we reach a point where we choose our incarnation with such great care that we incarnate to two very sharp parents—at which point we grow with a tremendous rate of speed. *That's* the purpose of it all. Civilization's purpose is to provide the playground, the background, the environment that enhances soul growth, character growth. An environment which enhances the ability of humans to practice the virtues. By practicing these virtues (love, brotherhood, and working you-too-can-do-as-I-do) which are part of universal law—what you put out comes back to you—you set an example for others. By practicing patience, tolerance, forbearance, kindness, and charity in your everyday life, you grow. By your example you set off a multitude of self-sustaining series of events, a chain reaction which strengthens the truth. I found this for myself. This is the message in *all* of the esoteric teachings in all seven of the great religions. I think the key, the key thing that the present human civilization is missing, is that the idea has been lost that we're all responsible. Individual responsibility has been lost. We want some wizard to come along and do it for us. We want the preacher on Sunday to save us from our sins. We want the man in the confessional booth to cleanse us. We don't want to do it for ourselves. Well, there are no wizards. Every single ego, every single created individual or discrete bundle of mental energy, must do it for itself. This is part of the message of the Great Pyramid, and as soon as humans realize this and take responsibility for their

actions the problems of the planet earth will be diminished a thousand-fold.

Noone: I found it most fascinating, the fact you mentioned a moment ago, that the individual ego has a hand in the choice of his or her own incarnated person.

Valentine: This is esoteric information. I use the term 'esoteric' information, 'esoteric' meaning 'inside,' inside information, and it's only information that has been given to me. I have not proven it yet. Even if I did prove it, it would still be only information to you. So the difference between information and knowledge is clear. We need to make that clear. Now, my information is that each of us chooses our parents and our station and our situation, even our race. One of the individuals that I have been told about in this esoteric information was George Washington Carver, who deliberately incarnated into a race that was downtrodden to work on the idea of bringing them up. He was an ego of tremendous advancement, and when he did incarnate into that environment, which was a terrible environment, I understand he may have lost a few points because he became embittered near the end. Had he remained without bitterness, he would have gained. This is the story I have. We all take a chance incarnating into a civilization that can drag us down, because when you get inside of a physical body you become subject to the nuisances of that animal body and the conditioning and the responses, and it's up to *you* with those ten qualities of mind

9:16. *Napoleon's Artist's Impression of the Temple of Denderah in Operation.*

According to John Anthony West in his scholarly work *Serpent In the Sky: The High Wisdom of Ancient Egypt*:

The aim of all initiatic religions is the same the world over and has always been: to guide man from his natural state of consciousness (which is called 'illusion' or 'sleep') to a higher state. This higher state, (called 'illumination' or 'the Kingdom'), his destiny and birthright is, within the context of the natural world, 'unnatural'.

It is impossible to construct a rational argument to compel the unwilling and the immune into acknowledging either the existence or the importance of this higher state. It is impossible to 'prove' to the skeptic that this has any direct bearing upon hmself or his life. Initiatic writings are therefore comprehensible only to initiates, to those who have at least put one foot down upon the long road. And the further along the road, the greater and deeper the understanding.

to overcome those. That's why being well disciplined is vitally important, and permissiveness is not wise.

Noone: You talk of permissiveness. This is something that has become a part of the so-called 'modern' society, beginning with the decade of the 60's—at least it became prevalent then. Sociologists today are saying that it's caused some sort of decadence within society. Do you subscribe to that philosophy?

Valentine: Yes. It's terribly decadent, and I do not at all accept permissiveness. What you are saying is that there are no standards. Well, there *are* standards, and we should set them for ourselves—and if we don't set them for ourselves at least society, civilization, should say, 'These are the quality standards we want you to strive to meet.' That doesn't mean there's such a thing as blame. What we're trying to do is forgive ourselves by being permissive. There is no blame. If a person is lazy, don't blame him for being lazy—simply say, 'Okay, you were lazy on that last opportunity you had, try not to be lazy on the next opportunity presented to you,' and help him or her to make the decision not to be lazy. However, don't *permit* it. Don't say, 'Laziness is good for everybody, because you won't get uptight if you're lazy.' We have so many errors on the idea of human potential and what to do with it. I believe in being well disciplined, but not cruelly. I believe in responsibility. In the organization I belong to, the Stelle Group, we have a school which is our pride and joy. In order to have a civilization that promotes character growth, you must work with the children at a very early age. Those first four formative years are of the utmost importance. Our children start school at the age of two. At the age of two, three, or four, they are able to read. They have become decision-making and responsible little individuals with their mothers at a very early age. The children learn that this is a joyous thing—to make the right decision—and the children learn to accept responsibility and solve problems. They find that this is where joy comes from. The pats on the head—the 'stroking,' as the TA people like to say—our children find come from solving problems, making decisions, and being responsible for themselves. It doesn't take very long before our children have that habit pattern the rest of their lives. If we could just institute that into society—if we could institute it into society in America alone—we could effect tremendous changes on this planet right now. If we could do anything politically, and we don't believe in interfering with the environment of others—that is forbidden—we would only suggest that all of the people in the United States, from the inner cities to the farms, take their children from the ages of two through four with their mothers to a government-paid (if we must) institution where the children and their mothers are taught responsibility and decision-making and nothing more. You'd be amazed at the changes. Then here comes a teenager with that kind of idea, and look at the way his peer group can't influence him—he'd say, 'No, that's my decision.' How many children do you know that are taught that?

Noone: Not many.

Valentine: Okay!

Noone: So young people with parents who are out of tune with the times are placed at a great disadvantage when they're growing up.

Valentine: Yes. However, there are some very special genetic descendants of ours that intuitively know there's something better. These children overcome the so-called generation gap. They overcome the negative conditioning in any age and are never seduced by negative thinking—the dark side of the truth. Our direct genetic offspring in the 60's saw that the Vietnam War was insanity. Now whether their reaction to it was right or wrong in our eyes, our perception of reality, doesn't count. Why should the world be only as we perceive it? The point is, they were able to *see* insanity, at which point they took a step into a larger work, and we're getting closer to the point where we're seeing more of what man does to himself as insanity. This is part of the message a band of men at the dawning of the Age of Taurus, a more civilized age, embodied in the Great Pyramid's mathematical code to transmit to a generation of humans living in the Age of Aquarius, something they felt was vitally important. The age of Aquarius began 23 August 1953, and this is a new-age idea: the idea that we can perceive and try to improve. Of course there's still a larger majority of humans, even in the Age of Aquarius, that want to

drag people down and lower the standards. However, every single ego, every single human, has the capabilities of bringing himself up to the equal of his creator. It's just a matter of effort and patience and practicing the virtues.

Noone: As Jesus stood between the two columns Jackin and Boaz on the outer porch of King Solomon's temple (John 10:23) on 25 December—the celebration of the winter solstice—a large majority of the people did not understand him when he said, 'Ye are gods' (John 10:34). Some people in the crowd took up stones to kill him as a money-changer in the temple cocked his head away from his table to see what some in the crowd were yelling about. He heard Jesus say, 'Is it not written in your law, I said ye are gods,' as he saw a law-giver of the temple sit bolt upright to listen to this man speaking to the crowd. The money-changer wondered why such an important law-giver of the temple sat up to listen, as rigid as a rod of iron, remembering the law and his responsibility. As the law-giver remembered Psalm 82:6, he remembered a psalm of Asaph, in which God said, 'Ye are gods.' The man speaking to the crowd said, 'The Father is in me and I in him,' and what he meant could not have been other than what he said. As the crowd screamed 'Blasphemy!' and moved forward to kill Jesus, he simply disappeared. So when you say humans have the capability to bring themselves up to the equal of their creator, it would seem to me that this 'new age idea' is in reality a very, very

9:17. Jesus in the Temple.

295

ancient idea. However, you did say that this was part of the message of the Great Pyramid—but what about these ancient brotherhoods, these people who are responsible for all this secret type of teaching, which seems to be such a mystical notion—are they still around today?

Valentine: I think so, very much. In fact, I could say I know it—you could say it's information now. The 'brothers' are those individuals who have obtained a degree of advancement over other humans. They know a great deal more about the truth of existence than you and I do, and they naturally are compassionate toward us who are still struggling where they once struggled. They also know they can't do it for us—that is forbidden—they can't take us by the hand and lift us up in the rapture and give us God on a silver platter. We've got to strive for ourselves, make our own mistakes, make our own decisions and grow on our own—that is the rule. Now for some reason that rule has been overlooked, and that's the one big problem. The Brothers, unobtrusively rather than obtrusively, work among us today in the United States without disturbing our present culture. You may meet a person who seems to have tremendous control of his environment, he is always charitable, he is always kind, he is always patient, he is always forbearing, he is always understanding, he is just some kind (or she is just some kind) of an individual [that] you wonder how could I get to be like that? Yet that person never tries to force his beliefs off on any-

body, never tries to make waves, he or she just lives life in such a way that you say, 'I'd like to be like that.' That's probably a Brother.

Noone: And that person knows, of course, that he or she has those qualifications?

Valentine: Yes. Oh, yes. And he knows a great deal about metaphysics, but he won't go spouting off and say, 'I'm a psychic,' or, 'I want to give you a reading,' or 'I'm going to tune into Edgar Cayce down here,' or anything like that. He won't do that. However, if you ask the so-called psychics they'll volunteer all the time, because their mind has made a breakthrough and they've seen some part of the truth, and they suddenly think they've really got a lock on the future. So they say, 'I'm a psychic, give me thirty dollars and I'll tell you whether or not you're going to get married next week.' That's not where it's at! However, if you meet a Brother, and you get him alone and you say, 'I've noticed about you certain things, and I want to ask if you are familiar with the Rosicrucians or the Masons or the Stelle Group or the book *The Ultimate Frontier* or some of these metaphysical philosophies'—you, when you ask, are allowing him to interfere in your environment. This is the teacher appearing when the student is ready. But unless you ask, the Brothers won't help. However, when you ask, he will say to you whatever he believes is true, and he'll say, 'I believe I am mind inhabiting a body, and I've lived many lifetimes, and I've been waiting for you to ask these questions.' If I may, I'll explain what my philosophy says a *controlled* clairvoyant is. Let's assume that I practice the virtues and really make a habit of being kind, charitable, forbearing, and so on in my everyday life, until it's just second nature to me. Then when I'm in conversation with someone I'll begin to hear more than what is being said. I will begin to see more than what I can see with the physical light reflecting against the retina of my eye. I will begin to perceive reality on multiple levels of existence. I will begin to see answers to questions that the physicists will never find as long as they get big hammers and make smaller particles. I will see that there is a reality beyond the physical reality—the etheric, the astral, the mental, the angelic, all the way up to God. I will see at least three of these levels of existence, maybe four, and I will be able to function consciously on the astral level, where humans dwell when they're not in a body. When you die, you're not in your body. Your mind is dwelling on what is called the astral level. Now that's only information to you, but I say if you get out and work at it for the next sixteen years like I've done you can prove it to yourself.

Noone: Then it will be knowledge?

Valentine: Then it will be knowledge to you. Don't try to make it knowledge to anyone else—it doesn't work, all right? Then you will be able to function consciously on multiple levels of existence—the physical level, the mental level, the astral level—and you will understand the vital level. When you understand these levels,

you can do all kinds of things. You can read other people, you can see when a person's going to be very sick, you can see when they're going to be very healthy and well, you can see whether they're in love or when they're not—all because of these different...auras, shall we say, which some people claim they can see and so on. When you reach this level you will intuitively know that—that this new power is yours and that this new power is something you have earned through your behavior, and you can't give it to anyone else, because if you did...it's like many people have read the Carlos Castenada books [Carlos Castenada was a U.C.L.A. anthropologist who studied under Don Juan, a *brujo*—a sorcerer, curer, medicine man—in the Mexican desert], and you know Carlos would always ask Don Juan, 'Tell me what it's like, this astral projection, seeing this next level,' and Don Juan would keep saying, 'I can't tell you because what I perceive is mine and what you perceive is yours, and there are two different perceptions, and possibly two different realities. Stop bugging me.' Well, that's what it is, your perception you will know is yours, and it will be true, and it will be the ultimate truth—at which point you can now relax about a lot of things, so that when somebody else comes along and asks you, you may help him help himself. However, you can't go around giving them readings or playing psychic or anything like that.

Noone: That's a fantastic philosophy, but would you be able to say just how many people possibly contain—

297

nationwide—this ability?

Valentine: Hundreds of thousands.

Noone: Hundreds of thousands that have come to grips with reality in just this way?

Valentine: Yes. My feeling is that these people have gathered together at this particular time because we are indeed in the 'times of the end.' The people who wrote the *Holy Bible* were Brothers. They knew the truth and they also knew it would be distorted a certain way, but they also knew that some people would get the truth out of it, and they wrote it the way it was. In this latest book I've tried to explain this the best I can, and it's only my explanation. Good Lord, I try to make this point in my new book—that this is just my view. It's got to have my distortions. However, the hundreds of thousands of advanced egos who are here now are here for a purpose. They are here to help us bridge between these times of the end of the world as we know it and the coming nation of God. The Kingdom of God, as prophesied in the *Holy Bible*, in my opinion, is not some place in the sky where we're sitting around on clouds playing harps. The Kingdom of God is a civilization that practices these things I've been talking about—a civilization where everyone can do what is best for his or her character growth and can live in harmony and peace. Such a civilization could survive all the superficialities of the physical world, the physical reality, which includes many things—race, appearance—all of these things are superficial. I think the an-

gelic force built them in to help us learn to overcome them.

Noone: That's an interesting viewpoint.

Valentine: Oh yes. Why would there be subspecies of the species *Homo sapiens*? Why would there be black and yellow and red and caucasion white races of the same species? We all, obviously, have the same qualities of mind. So we're all identical in the mental respects. But physically—and it's only about 5% of the genes—there is a difference there. To me this was brought about by the creative forces, whatever they are, to give us something to overcome, to learn to overcome these very superficial petty differences. Yet—have we done it yet?

Noone: No.

Valentine: Of course not. If I may— I love to do this, I think it's the most underpublicized thing in the world— the idea of race is one of the most over-rated things there is. The blackest skin on earth belongs to the 'white' race: the darkest pigmentation of the skin belongs to the blue-black Melville Islanders of Australia. The Melville Islanders have red hair and blue eyes, and being an anthropologist I can tell you they are Caucasian and yet they have the blackest skin on this planet! The kinkiest hair on the planet belongs to the Laplanders of Finland. The difference between men of one race and another is less than 5% of the genes that make up the entire body. It's a superficial thing, and I just wish that humans would stop and think about that. We get so hung up on these physical things. All of the physical world is an arena for learning.

Noone: So in the beginning these creators knew that we would have to go through a period of evolution before we got to that final stage of readiness, and these are just tests?

Valentine: Yes.

Noone: But not everyone survives these tests.

Valentine: That's right. A lot of them aren't going to make it. A lot of them are going to have their memory wiped out, and it will be like the atheist says, 'There's nothing.' My philosophy has the creator, the creative Force, sitting up on the seventh level of existence. However, I can't conceive of the creative Force because my mind only goes to the fourth level of existence. The sixth level of existence is the archangelic level, and the archangelic level has worked—interworked or cooperatively coupled—with the physical level, the physical reality, on this planet in the form of what some humans call Christ—and has done so in other times in history and will do so again. The so-called Second Coming, in my philosophy, is actually the fourth coming. The angelic intelligence—

Noone: Is that the fifth level of existence?

Valentine: Yes.

Noone: Is that the angelic force?

Valentine: Yes. The fifth level of intelligence is responsible for the direct work with the planet, and they can make mistakes. The story of Lucifer and Jehovah is a tale of the mistake made by the angelic intelligence. The argument between the angelic forces on the fifth level of existence is that Jehovah, according to my philosophy, believed that humans could advance with a perfect environment, so at first humans were given the Edenic State. All they had to do was eat bananas, sleep, chase the girls, make love, swim, sun, and sleep. But they didn't grow in that Edenic State. They were lazy. All they wanted to do was eat, drink, make love, and sleep some more. They didn't want to grow, so Lucifer said, 'We should help mankind grow—and you know the rules, we can't go down and do it for them, so we'll give them problems to overcome.' And ZAP—like the thunderbolt of Zeus, Eden was gone and we now have winters in Chicago. And man has to overcome. The angelic intelligence even had problems to overcome. To me the difference between my creator on the seventh level and me down here on level one is that the creative Force never misses. It always makes the right decision.

Noone: This book that you've just completed—have you titled it yet?

Valentine: Yes. It's called *The Life and Death of Planet Earth*. It's a study of cataclysmology, geology, and the changes in the earth, and the idea that ancient advanced civilizations not only *could* have existed and been destroyed by cataclysms, but did so. The remnant from the early empire was split three ways. There was a group who believed in going back to

Eden, and they called themselves the Katholi—you'll read about this in *The Ultimate Frontier*—and a group who believed in practicality and not spirituality, who called themselves the Pfree. The Pfree went to Atlantis. The Katholi went to Rama, which is in India, and we still see the effects of that in India with the caste system and the power the priests had over them. Where did the balanced people go—the people who balance between spirituality and practicality because that's what life is really all about? The spiritual side of India is tremendous and their physical practicality is nil. They're starving in the streets, where over here our practicality is fantastic—yet we're living in a spiritual vacuum. It's to blend the two by using the mind, the mentality, is what the Brothers want us to get, and that's what they're seeking. Well, that's the third group that came out of the ancient early empire of Mu, and that third group built the Great Pyramid as their monument to mankind, to prove that such a thing exists. And the more anyone studies the Great Pyramid the more they'll realize that perfection is embodied there. Why embody perfection in stone if you're looking to argue...to me, it's to show perfection. Those balanced few are still working as the Brothers.

Noone: I've got to get a final thought in. We've been around for so long trying to progress to this period where we would be able to deal with all of these things. Do you have any idea when we will get to this point?

Valentine: That's up to the individ-

ual. You may grow in this one lifetime if you can make the effort and do it. But you'd give up a lot of things in relation to your environment. On my calendar the day May fifth 2000 is very important because that's house-cleaning day. The Christians call it 'doomsday.' There will have been a nuclear war, and the survivors of that nuclear war will be welcoming the big cataclysm that swallows them up and cleans up the mess. Doomsday is another cataclysmic change that's going to totally alter the face of the earth as humans know it today, and the survivors are going to be thrust back into a stone-age type of existence except for those that are prepared for it and have planned for it. Those survivors will, after the next cataclysmic change in the crust of the planet, use all of the positive aspects of the present human civilization—and there are many of them—to build the next civilization. I choose May the fifth of the year 2000 A.D. because it says so in *The Ultimate Frontier* and because of my own sixteen years of research and because of a particular alignment of the planets in this solar system that occurs on that day.

Valentine then explained in long and detailed mathematical terms how a sudden and devastating cataclysmic change is predicted in the Great Pyramid's mathematical message. David Davidson, in his book *The Great Pyramid: Its Divine Message*, after twenty-five years of researching the mathematical system of the Great Pyramid, presented proof that the Pyramid was a scale model of the earth's northern hemisphere. Davidson believed it was built to memorialize a tremendous cataclysm. Prof. Livio Catullo Stecchini, in the mathematical appendix to Peter Tompkin's book *Secrets of the Great Pyramid*, presents proof—in mathematical terms far beyond the comprehension of the average layman—that the Great Pyramid is a representation in scale of the earth's Northern Hemisphere.

Feeding Davidson's and Stecchini's information into a computer, I discovered with the help of Atlanta physicist Knox Robert Burnett that the message of the Great Pyramid with its truncated apex is this: When the earth's polar depression reaches the ratio of equatorial (or perhaps average) diameter versus the polar depression, then the polar mass is sufficient to begin the unstable dynamic condition that ends up as a careening cataclysm in which the earth's polar masses are suddenly displaced toward the equator.[20]

[20]See Appendix B.

The south becomes north and the Earth turns over.
Egyptian Magical Papyrus Harris

A little consideration reveals that, should the terrestrial axis be turned tomorrow into a new astronomical direction by *any* angle of inclination toward the ecliptic, the Great Pyramid would remain properly oriented to the north and south poles; there would be a new celestial pole and, if so positioned, a new polar star, but the pyramid would remain with two of its sides aligned with the geographical poles.

Immanuel Velikovsky,
commenting on the
Magical Papyrus Harris

The benefit of foreseeing catastrophe is the ability to take steps to avoid it, sacrificing short term for long-term benefits.

Dr. Carl Sagan
The Dragons of Eden

CHAPTER TEN
THE ULTIMATE DISASTER

Four years ago when I interviewed Tom Valentine, even the idea of a sudden and violent cataclysmic shifting of the tectonic plates that make up the crust of the planet Earth was considered preposterous. I remembered, however, that only ten years ago the idea of plate tectonics was discounted. In fact, most scientists discounted even the idea that earthquakes are caused by movement or slippage of gigantic plates on which entire continents ride as passive passengers. It is good to remember:

> The formulation of a problem is often more essential than its solution, which may be merely a matter of mathematical or experimental skill. To raise new questions, new possibilities, to regard old problems from a new angle, requires creative imagination and marks real advance in science.

Einstein and Infeld, *The Evolution of Physics.*

With these thoughts in mind, I was naturally curious as to whether or not the planet Earth could actually experience a sudden and violent shifting of all its tectonic plates. Little did I know that this quest would serve as the method of freeing my nervous system from conditioned perception! I imagined a few trips to the library and a few well chosen interviews with doctors and professors of geology would provide me with the answers as to whether or not a violent cataclysm could rearrange the "continental

plates" that make up the crust of the earth, sometime around the end of this century. What I discovered was unsettling.

After I interviewed Valentine he was kind enough to mail me a copy of his book *The Life and Death of Planet Earth.* Like Immanuel Velikovsky in *Worlds in Collision, Ages in Chaos,* and *Earth in Upheaval,* Valentine presents evidence and arguments for sudden and gigantic global geological changes in ancient times, submerging ancient civilizations beneath mud, boulders, lava, and oceans.

Back in the "seventies", the self-perpetuating dogma of the academic world scrowled, wrinkled its brow, and scoffed at such preposterous ideas.

This type of tunnel-vision thinking in the '70s by one's learned and respected teachers made it quite difficult psychologically to separate fact (accepted dogma, sometimes nonfact) from fiction (sometimes fiction, sometimes new possibilities). However, I knew that in the past 6,000 years of mankind's history new ideas have usually never been welcomed with open arms. I remembered the council commissioned by King Ferdinand and Queen Isabella in 1490, where shouts of "Preposterous!" and "Impossible!" were heard in reference to the voyage proposed by Columbus. I remembered that the *New York Times* had lampooned the idea of air travel a week before the Wright brothers lifted off an almost desolate beach at Kitty Hawk. I remembered Thomas Tredgold, a spokesman for the British Railroad Commission in 1835, who re-

10:1. *The 1883 Eruption of Krakatoa.* This engraving was made from a photograph taken in May 1883, at an early stage of the eruption. It was colored by an eyewitness and it is the only known contemporary picture of the volcano in progress.

ported that "any general system of conveying passengers—at a velocity exceeding 10 miles per hour, or thereabouts—is extremely improbable." I also remembered some advice Vannevar Bush, former head of the Carnegie Institute, offered Harry S. Truman in 1945—"Mr. President, the bomb will never go off, and I speak as an expert on explosives."

With the discovery of the ancient cosmic explosion now called Vela X, I thought of the immortal words of Robin Williams: "Wow! Reality—what a concept!" I remembered that in 1883 the volcano Krakatoa in Indonesia exploded in the center of the Sundra Strait with the force of a 100-150 megaton H-bomb, causing three huge waves. The wave at Anjer in Java was 118 feet high and the wave at Telukbetung in Sumatra reached a height of 131 feet.[1] Thirty towns were destroyed and 36,000 people were killed suddenly. The sound of the explosion was heard 2,250 miles to the southeast in Australia and 2,968 miles to the west in the Indian Ocean island of Rodriguez. The shockwave from the eruption smashed windows and cracked walls 100 miles away.[2] Prof. A.G. Galanopoulos, Director of the Seismological Institute of Athens, Greece, writes in his book *Atlantis: The Truth Behind the Legend* that:

> The sound waves travelled three times around the world.... The atmospheric waves generated by the Krakatoa eruption jumped over the land barriers and re-excited sea waves strong enough to break the anchor chains of ships moored in the port of Valparaiso, Chile.[3]

According to Lowell Ponte, former Pentagon consultant on environmental change and author of *The Cooling*, a study of the earth's changing climate that analyzes how volcanoes and industrial pollution influence our weather:

> Its [Krakatoa's] pillar of ash and smoke, 20 times larger than that of Mount St. Helens, blotted out the sun and blackened the sky more than 100 miles away. For two years thereafter, global temperature fell by almost one degree Fahrenheit as Krakatoa's smoke shrouded skies around the world.[4]

Ponte believes that the eruption of Mount St. Helens may signal the reawakening of at least fifteen other volcanoes in the Pacific Northwest, which are part of the "ring of fire"—a zone of high volcanic activity encircling the Pacific Ocean—mentioned earlier in this book by Manly P. Hall. Mount Shasta and Lassen Peak (which last erupted in 1917) in northern California, Mount Ranier and Mount Baker in Washington, and Crater Lake in Oregon are a few of the fifteen volcanoes Ponte believes may reawaken as we approach the year 2000.

The explosion of Krakatoa was huge and horrifying, and 26,000 men, women, and children died. Large quantities of ash fell on decks of ships at sea 1,600 miles away. Deep shipping lanes filled up with ash and were no longer navigable. Pumice covered the sea for 100 miles around the island, thirteen feet thick; men could walk atop the floating

---

[1]Galanopoulos and Bacon, pp. 108-22ff.

[2]Ibid.

[3]Ibid., pp. 108, 122.

[4]Lowell Ponte, *The Cooling*. Prof. Galanopoulos says the skies were darkened for 275 miles.

pumice. Volcanic dust rose to a height of fifty miles, well above the rains that cleanse the sky, and by filtering other colors out of the sun's rays changed sunrises and sunsets as far away as the United States to an eerie red glow that lasted for months. Krakatoa blew out eleven cubic *miles* of material and three cubic miles of gases. In 1950 the total consumption of electric energy on earth was 250 times *less* than the total thermal energy released at Krakatoa.[5] Prof. Galanopoulos states that the total energy of the 1883 eruption of Krakatoa was *two hundred million millions* of kilowatt hours.

It is extremely difficult psychologically for most humans to imagine or feel a deep personal sadness for the deaths of men, women, and children when the number is as large as 26,000. The number overwhelms us and becomes only a number, a statistic.

The volcanic eruption of Krakatoa was huge, awesome, sudden, and deadly. It *measurably* affected the earth's climate. We can only estimate today how many people died three to five years later of extensive lung damage from inhaling the silicon crystals in Krakatoa's volcanic ash. We can only estimate today how many people will die from inhaling into their lungs the silicon crystals Mount St. Helens cast into the air. The volcanic eruption of Krakatoa was awesome. Yet Prof. Galanopoulos points out that the volcanic eruption of the Greek island of Santorin around the time of the Exodus was *three times* as great as that of Krakatoa. Galanopoulos points out that the sound waves of Krakatoa travelled three times around the world, which means that the soundwaves of the volcanic eruption on the Greek island of Santorin would have been heard in Egypt with *great intensity*, and he concludes that the Santorin volcanic eruption may have lasted for as long as twenty-five years.[6] One remembers the writings of the Egyptian sage Ipuwer:

> Years of noise. There is no end to the noise. Oh, that the earth would cease from noise, and tumult be no more.... Lower Egypt [that part of Egypt nearest the Mediterranean Sea] weeps. ...the towns are destroyed. Upper Egypt has become waste...all is ruin.

The atmospheric waves generated by the Krakatoa eruption jumped over the land barriers and re-excited sea waves strong enough to break the anchor-chains of ships moored halfway around the world at Valparaiso, Chile. One can only shudder at the destruction the atmospheric waves generated by the Santorin eruption must have caused. The increase of volcanic activity since 1970[7] combined with increasing human pollution of the atmosphere today concerns scientists because by studying sediment layers from the bottoms of ancient oceans, they have found that *past ice ages have coincided with buildups of volcanic ash in the atmosphere.*

As horrible as volcanoes can be, Valentine's book *The Life and Death of Planet Earth* is about a far worse disaster—the ultimate disaster, if you will—pole-shift: the changing of the position of the earth's rotating axis in relation to other heavenly bodies, or a sudden relocation of the earth on its axis without changing position relative to the tilt from the solar orbit. The implications of the evidence Valentine

---

[5]Galanopoulos and Bacon, p. 115.

[6]Ibid., pp. 115-121.

[7]See Goodman, op. cit., and Ponte, op. cit. for details of this phenomenon.

presents point to a sudden and massive displacement of the earth's crust on 5 May 2000. A *very* simplified explanation of the large amount of evidence Valentine presents follows:

> The earth is like a round ball spinning in space. As the earth spins it also "wobbles." As the south polar ice mass grows, it becomes heavier and heavier. As the ice becomes heavier, the massive accumulation of ice creates an imbalance, with its enormous weight, in the earth's wobble. Year by year the ice grows heavier and heavier, until the tilt of the earth can no longer overcome the centrifugal force of the spinning earth. At this critical point the polar ice masses are thrown with devastating speed toward the earth's point of greatest spin—the equator. When this pole-shift takes place, most of civilization is destroyed in the same way other super-civilizations in the past have been obliterated.

Preposterous as the idea of a pole-shift sounds, we would do well to remember that in the past it has taken approximately 100 years for a new discovery to make its way from the laboratory into general public usage. However, the rate of change of knowledge to actual usage is increasing today at a very rapid rate. So it is very possible that the idea of a pole-shift will be completely accepted by orthodox science within the next ten years. Valentine believes that this pole-shift takes place about every 6,000 years. Meanwhile, the Stelle Group plans to airlift their people to an altitude of approximately 14 miles for a period of around two weeks in order to escape this pole-shift. However,

they may not be alone.

Dr. Gerard K. O'Neill, Professor of Physics at Princeton University and head of the Space Studies Institute,[8] plans to have people living in space in cylindrical modules divided into seven levels and rotated to provide Earth normal gravity by the late 1980's. Dr. O'Neill is author of *The High Frontier*, which won the Phi Beta Kappa award as the best science book of 1977. He specializes in high-energy particle physics.

In May 1977, newly installed President Carter asked the Council on Environmental Quality and the Department of State to make a study of the "probable changes in the world's population, natural resources, and environment through the end of the century." After three years the extraordinary 766-page document, the *Global 2000 Report to the President*, was issued. Richard Strout, long-time Washington correspondent for the *Christian Science Monitor*, wrote, "I defy anyone to read the summary of the report without a shudder." The report states that the world in the year 2000 will be more crowded, more polluted, less stable ecologically; the global food supply will not keep up with population, the population explosion in Mexico will force the U.S. to guard its borders (a possible 1,000,000 illegal immigrants *a year* now enter the U.S. despite 8.5% U.S. unemployment), Mexico City with 30 million people will be the largest city on earth. Again and again the report says time is running out. Barring revolutionary advances in technology (such as Dr. O'Neill's space program), life for most people on earth will be more precarious in 2000 than it is now unless the nations of the world act decisively to alter current trends.

Today, with our knowledge of plate tectonics, gigantic earthquakes and volcanoes,

---

[8]P.O. Box 82, Princeton, New Jersey 08540.

the cosmic supernova explosion of Vela X, and the discovery of submerged plateaus in the Pacific, we know that sudden and gigantic events *have* taken place in the past. What we do not know now with certainty is whether a future world-wide cataclysm will destroy our present civilization in the same manner as the mammoths of prehistoric times.

A few weeks after reading Valentine's book *The Life and Death of Planet Earth*, I found a book titled *The HAB Theory*, a chilling novel of global disaster by the bestselling author Allan W. Eckert. The book was copyrighted in 1976 (a year whose numbers, as we have noted, equal 23).

The novel begins with Herbert (H) Allen (A) Boardman (B) travelling at the age of 94 to Chicago with a gun in his pocket to stage an assassination of the President of the United States to gain publicity for his theory that the alarming accumulation and growth of the weight of the Antarctic Icecap is about to destroy our present civilization. As the fast-paced novel moves from start to finish, humans race desperately against time and terror to find a shockingly slim chance to survive.

At the start of his novel, in the Author's Note, Mr. Eckert says:

> Many of the scientists mentioned in this novel were actual people who lived in the past and who performed the work they are described as having accomplished. However, those characters who are portrayed in these pages in the story-line sense are entirely fictional and any resemblance they may bear to people living or

dead is purely coincidental.[9]

I wondered if the character named "Herbert Allen Boardman" in Mr. Eckert's novel was a "story-line" character or one of the actual scientists who lived in the past and performed the scientific research Eckert describes them as performing. Those who have read *The HAB Theory* may be shocked, as I was, to learn that this "novel" is based upon over fifty years of factual scientific research by Hugh (H) Auchincloss (A) Brown (B), HAB, author of *Cataclysms of the Earth*.

Cataclysms of the Earth was copyrighted in 1967, ten years before the newly installed President Carter asked for the *Global 2000 Report*. The numbers in the year 1967 again equal twenty-three, the number Robert Anton Wilson in his book *Cosmic Trigger* believes guided him to "a network of Adepts that extends far beyond our earth."

In the first 156 pages of *Cataclysms of the Earth*, Brown presents very valid evidence that the polar ice masses, when they grow oversize, cause a pole-shift, "each time that one or two polar icecaps grew to maturity; a recurrent event in global history."[10] Brown believes that this pole-shift happens about every 6,000 years. It was Hugh Auchincloss Brown who first stated:

> The enormous size of the South Pole Ice Cap is difficult to grasp. Were it centered in [the] United States with the South Pole [located] in North Dakota, its area would extend [east and west] to the Atlantic and Pacific Oceans, to Mexico [in the south] and [north] to the northern extremity of Canada.[11]

---

[9]Allan W. Eckert, *The HAB Theory*, (New York: Popular Library, 1977).

[10]Hugh Auchincloss Brown, *Cataclysms of the Earth* (New York: Twayne Publishers, 1967).

[11]Ibid., p. 8.

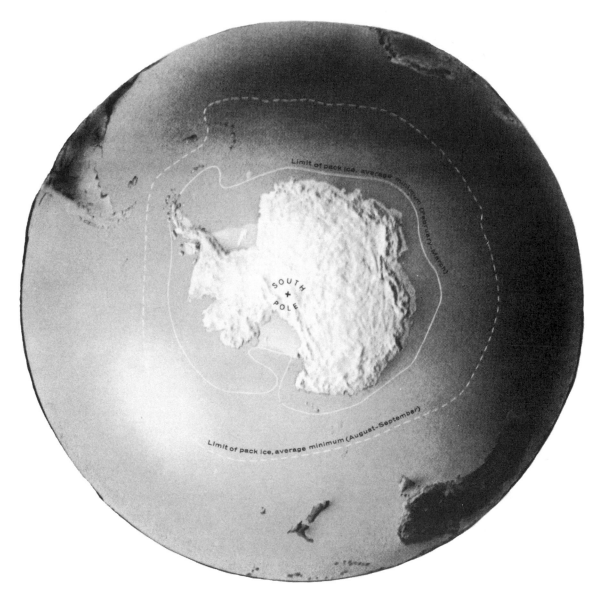

10:2. *A Continent of Ice.* (Reproduced from *Reader's Digest Great World Atlas* © 1963, The Reader's Digest Association, Inc. Used by permission.) In this drawing, the Southern Hemisphere, seen from a point over the South Pole, is dominated by a continent of ice larger than Europe. This ice sits atop and extends beyond the land it rests on, and is now over two miles high. The largest part of the enormous weight of the ice mass is considerably to one side of the polar center. According to Hugh Auchincloss Brown, all this ice on one side will have the same wobbling effect as that observed when heavy clothes get lumped together on one side of a rapidly spinning washing machine — the wobble increases, rips the bolts out of the floor, and the machine falls over.

Hugh Auchincloss Brown collected material for his theory of pole-shift for more than fifty years, spending years and years on investigating such things as:

—What immense force quick-froze hundreds of animals in Siberia[12] with grasses in their stomachs?

—By what process were entire tropical forests and volatile raindrops instantly arrested and fossilized?

—How could a soft jellyfish be quick-frozen along with oysters, clams, crabs, and starfish and turned to stone?

—How could a tree with fruit and leaves still on it be found in Siberia, quick-frozen?

—Why are there only but a few waterfalls on earth older than about 6,000 years?

These questions, one by one, Brown answers in his book. He eventually came to believe that a sudden and radical shift of the earth's axis is caused by a sudden and radical shift of one or both of the earth's ice-caps. When the pole-shift takes place, continents and sea areas are rearranged, so tropical regions suddenly become lands of ice and snow, and lands of ice and snow suddenly become tropical. Brown ends Part One of his book by saying:

People of education and initiative must become awakened to full awareness of the lurking danger represented by this wanton titanic power which is ready, able, and destined to end our civilization—if left uncontrolled by man.... An awakening to the danger among the people at large is the first requisite... It will indeed become a matter of great personal interest to many people...once we know that our lives are at stake![13]

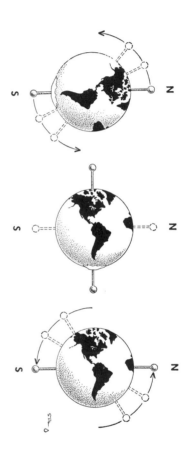

10:3. Pole shift according to Brown.

---

[12] On 23 June 1977 a bulldozer operator in NE Siberia struck a solid block of ice containing a perfectly preserved 9-month-old baby mammoth. Whisked to Leningrad's Zoological Institute, he was discovered to have been weaned, since there were traces of grass in the intestines. Radiocarbon tests indicate that he died around 6,000 or 7,000 years ago.

[13] Brown, p. 152ff.

Twelve years before Mr. Brown's book *Cataclysms of the Earth* was published, Albert Einstein was writing a Foreword to a book called *Earth's Shifting Crust*, by Prof. Charles H. Hapgood. Prof. Hapgood's book is about a pole-shift that took place around 6,000 years ago. Einstein wrote:

I frequently receive communications from people who wish to consult me concerning their unpublished ideas. It goes without saying that these ideas are very seldom possessed of scientific validity. The very first communication, however, that I received from Mr. Hapgood electrified me. His idea is original, of great simplicity, and—if it continues to prove itself—of great importance to everything that is related to the history of the earth's surface.

A great many empirical data indicate that at each point on the earth's surface that has been carefully studied, many climatic changes have taken place, apparently quite suddenly. This, according to Hapgood, is explicable if the virtually rigid outer crust of the earth undergoes, from time to time, extensive displacement over the viscous, plastic, possibly fluid inner layers. Such displacements may take place as the consequence of comparatively slight forces exerted on the crust, derived from the earth's momentum of rotation, which in turn will tend to alter the axis of rotation of the earth's crust.

In a polar region there is continual deposition of ice, which is not symmetrically distributed about the pole. The earth's rotation acts on these unsymmetrically deposited masses, and produces centrifugal momentum that is transmitted to the rigid crust of the earth. The constantly increasing centrifugal momentum produced in this way will, when it has reached a certain point, produce a movement of the earth's crust over the rest of the earth's body, and this will displace the polar regions toward the equator.

Without a doubt the earth's crust is strong enough not to give way proportionately as the ice is deposited. The only doubtful assumption is that the earth's crust can be moved easily enough over the inner layers.

The author has not confined himself to a simple presentation of this idea. He has also set forth, cautiously and comprehensively, the extraordinarily rich material that supports his displacement theory. I think that this rather astonishing, even fascinating, idea deserves the serious attention of anyone who concerns himself with the theory of the earth's development.

To close with an observation that has occurred to me while writing these lines: If the earth's crust is really so easily displaced over its substratum as this theory requires, then the rigid masses near the earth's surface must be distributed in such a way that they give rise to no other considerable centrifugal momentum, which would tend to displace the crust by centrifugal effect. I think that this deduction might be capable of verification, at least approximately. This centrifugal momentum should in any case be smaller than that produced by the masses of deposited ice.[14]

---

[14] Hapgood, *Earth's Shifting Crust,* foreword by Albert Einstein.

Einstein died a few weeks after writing this Foreword, with many unopened letters on his desk—including one from Prof. Hapgood. In his book, Hapgood says:

To understand what is involved in the idea of a movement or displacement of the entire crust of the earth, certain facts about the earth must be understood. The crust is very thin. Estimates of its thickness range from a minimum of about twenty to a maximum of about forty miles. The crust is made of comparatively rigid, crystalline rock, but it is fractured in many places and does not have great strength. Immediately under the crust is a layer that is thought to be extremely weak because it is, presumably, too hot to crystallize. Moreover, it is thought that pressure at that depth renders the rock extremely plastic, so that it will yield easily to pressures. The rock at that depth is supposed to have a high viscosity; that is, it is fluid but very stiff, as tar may be. It is known that a viscous material will yield easily to a comparatively slight pressure exerted over a long period of time, even though it may not act as a solid when subjected to a sudden pressure, such as an earthquake wave. If a gentle push is exerted horizontally on the earth's crust, to shove it in a given direction, and if the push is maintained steadily for a long time, it is highly probable that the crust will be displaced over this plastic and viscous lower layer. The crust, in this case, will move as a single unit, the whole crust at the same time.

This idea has nothing whatever to do with the much discussed theory of drifting continents, according to which the continents drifted separately, in different directions....

Prof. Hapgood makes his point quite clear when he states:

Let us visualize briefly the consequences of a displacement of the whole crustal shell of the earth. First, there will be the changes in latitude. Places on the earth's surface will change their distances from the equator. Some will be shifted nearer the equator and others farther away. Points on the opposite sides of the earth will move in opposite directions. For example, if New York should be moved 2,000 miles south, the Indian Ocean, diametrically opposite, would have to be shifted 2,000 miles north. All points on the earth's surface will not move an equal distance, however. To visualize this, the reader need only take a globe, mounted on its stand, and set it in rotation. He will see that while a point on its equator is moving fast, the points nearest the poles are moving slowly. In a given time, a point near the equator moves much farther than one near a pole. So, in a displacement of the crust, there is a meridian around the earth that represents the direction of the movement, and points on this circle will be moved the farthest. Two points, 90 degrees away from this line, will represent the 'pivot points' of the movement. All other points will be displaced proportionally to their distances from this meridian. Naturally, climatic changes will be more or less proportionate to changes in latitude, and because areas on opposite sides of the globe will be moving in opposite directions, some areas will be getting colder while others get hotter; some will be undergoing radical changes of climate, some mild changes of climate, and some no change at all.[15]

During a pole-shift, as trillions of tons of water and ice from the South Pole rush in a wave of destruction thousands of feet high north toward the equator, and as trillions of tons of water and ice from the North Pole sweep south toward the equator, the forces of nature, loosed from their equilibrium, will rage wildly in search of a new equilibrium. Volcanos will erupt, tidal waves will hurl themselves across many lands, global hurricanes of almost unimaginable size will roar around the globe, earthquakes ripping open nuclear power plants will create "dead zones," so it is quite clear that it will be only the survivors (those in space or those at one of the two "pivot points" Hapgood mentioned) who will be left to worry about climate changes.

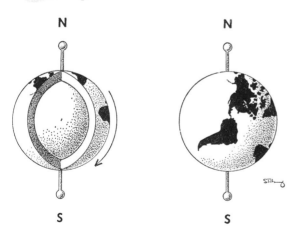

10:4. Pole shift according to Hapgood.

Climate change. What is it? What does it mean? What will it do? Is it going on now? In 1977 the Central Intelligence Agency released Document #ER76-10577U. The title of this CIA report is USSR: *The Impact of Recent Climate Change on Grain Production.* The CIA report states that climatic changes began in 1960, but were not noticed until the early 70's. The report says that the world's climate is cooling and will revert to conditions that prevailed between 1600 and 1850: "The change of climate is cooling some significant agricultural areas and causing drought in others." It goes on to say:

If, for example, there is a Northern Hemisphere drop of one degree centigrade it would mean that India will have a major drought every four years and can only support three-fourths of her present population.

The world reserve would have to supply 30 to 50 million metric tons of grain each year to prevent the death of 150 million Indians.

China, with a major famine every five years, would require a supply of 50 million metric tons of grain. The Soviet Union would lose Kazakhastan for grain production, thereby showing a yearly loss of 48 million metric tons of grain.

Canada, a major exporter, would lose over 50 percent of its production capability and 75 per cent of its exporting capabilities. Northern Europe will lose 25 to 30 per cent of its present production capability while the Common Market countries would zero their exports.[16]

---

[15]See *Earth's Shifting Crust*, New York: Pantheon, 1958.

[16]**Central Intelligence Agency, USSR: *The Impact of Recent Climate Change on Grain Production*, #ER76-10577U (1976). The Report may be obtained through the CIA.**

This report was basically concerned with possible political and economic threats to U.S. security as a result of such a drastic climate change (We all know what some people would do to feed their children). One entire section of the CIA report was kept secret. Under the section entitled "Recommendations" was only one word: "deleted."

This catastrophic climatic change means millions of men, women, and children will slowly die of starvation in India, China will suffer a major famine every five years, and Russia will lose a major wheat-growing area. As part of the world community the United States will be affected by these events. The report says, "The economic and political impact of major climatic shifts is almost beyond comprehension."

Moving into a colder climate also means the alarming accumulation of ice at the South Pole will increase more rapidly than Brown, Hapgood, and other investigators of pole-shift knew. Their books were published some time before the CIA report came out.

Brown wrote, back in the sixties, that Admiral Byrd erected two 70-foot-long steel radio towers at his camp at Little America. The towers projected upward into the air sixty feet. Byrd erected these towers in 1929. By 1934, only five years later, the towers projected only thirty feet into the air. By 1947, as the snow and ice crept higher, only eighteen feet remained above the ice shelf. By 1955 one tower extended eight feet and the other ten, above the ice itself. It would be interesting today (1982) to measure how far *under* the level of the ice shelf the tops of the sixty-foot towers are. That, however, is impossible, because as the ice grew it pushed a part of the Ross Ice Shelf, upon which Admiral Byrd's camp Little America sat, so far out to sea that it broke off and floated away. Brown points out that the same fate

befell the base camps used by the German Weddell Sea Expedition of 1911-12 and the Norwegian-British-Swedish Expedition of 1949-52. Brown presents evidence that the ice mass at the South Pole has grown to its present enormous size during the past 6,000 years—since the last pole-shift.

I remembered that the most ancient writings about the Great Pyramid state that it was built to memorialize a tremendous cataclysm in the earth's planetary system which affected the globe with fire and flood.

In 1966, eight years after Hapgood published *Earth's Shifting Crust*, he published a book entitled *Maps of the Ancient Sea Kings: Evidence of Advanced Civilization in the Ice Ages.* He worked with his students for seven years gathering evidence that produced concrete proof of an unknown civilization that existed long before ancient Egypt, a civilization much more advanced scientifically than Europe was in the sixteenth century. Hapgood and his students discovered that this early empire had mapmakers more advanced in the art of mapmaking than any people prior to the eighteenth century. In light of the facts Hapgood establishes in his book, ancient history must be rewritten and reopened and reexamined, or history may repeat itself on 5 May 2000. His research necessitates a worldwide revolution in our present concepts about the entire history of man, his science, and the evolution of human culture, most of which, at best, is enigmatical prior to 4699 B.C. Hapgood's seven years of research on ancient maps opens up entirely new vistas of man's life on this planet. In many beautiful ancient maps long known to scholars, the so-called Portolano charts of the Middle Ages, and in other maps—until now thought to have originated around the time of Columbus—Hapgood discovered that some ancient and unknown early empire employed mapmakers who mapped *all* the continents on earth around 6,000 years ago.

I wondered, since the mapmakers of the early empire had mapped "all" the continents on earth sometime around 6,000 years ago, what they had mapped at the position of Antarctica and the South Pole. Would the ancient maps of this early empire show the area of the Antarctic—excluding the offshore islands and ice shelves that today extend seaward around much of the continent—as a continent about 12,393,000 Km square, or would the maps of the early empire show something else? Today the Antarctic Continent contains about 90% of the glacier mass on this planet.[17] What do the ancient maps of this unknown early empire show us of today concerning what they saw 6,000 years ago? In Chapter Two of this book (written some years ago) it was clearly stated that the ancient maps of the Early Empire showed the Antarctic, the land mass today hidden below a shroud of ice two miles high, *without* ice. This is exactly what the ancient maps drawn six or seven thousand years ago show—the topography of the continent of Antarctica.

Now, for the mapmakers of some ancient and unknown early empire to have drawn maps of the topography of the Antarctic Continent, the land must not have been covered with the massive ice mass now covering the land. If the Antarctic *was* covered by ice two miles high 6,000 years ago, then the only way the ancient maps of the Early Empire could have been drawn is with the aid of highly sophisticated electronic sounding equipment. Take your choice! The authenticity of these ancient maps Hapgood has cautiously and comprehensively shown

to be beyond question.

In addition to the *Piri Re'is Map*, Professor Hapgood cites core samples of sediments taken from the bottom of the Ross Sea in 1949 by the Byrd Antarctic Expedition. These core samples were taken to the Carnegie Institute in Washington, D.C. for testing to determine the age of the sediments.

The first surprise came when the researchers found that a number of the layers were formed of fine-grained, well-assorted sediments such as are brought down to the sea by rivers flowing from *ice-free* lands. Hapgood writes in his book *Maps of the Ancient Sea Kings: Evidence of Advanced Civilization in the Ice Age* (p. 97):

> This discovery would indicate that the glacial history of Antarctica may have been roughly similar to that of North America, where we have had three or more ice ages in the last million years. Let us remember that, if most geologists cannot imagine how Antarctica could have had warm climates at short and relatively recent geological intervals, neither can they explain how North America could have had *Arctic conditions* at equally short intervals and just as equally recently. Ice ages remain for geologists an unsolved mystery...." (emphasis added)

When I first interviewed Professor Hapgood, one of the first questions I asked was as follows:

Noone: I was taught in school that ice ages were events that only took place millions of years ago.

Hapgood: Those who may be in-

---

[17] Colin Bull, *Snow Accumulation in Antartica*, p. 367.

THE PIRI RE'IS MAP OF 1513

IN ALL THE WORLD THERE IS NO OTHER MAP LIKE THIS MAP—PIRI RE'IS

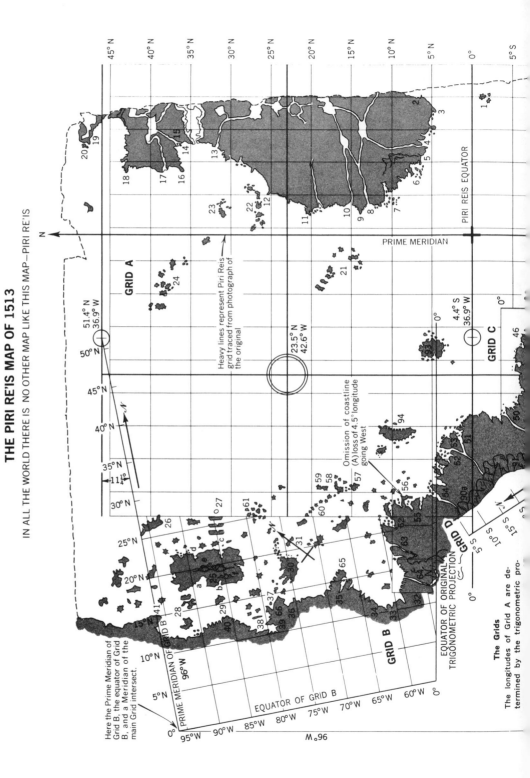

Here the Prime Meridian of Grid B, the equator of Grid B, and a Meridian of the main Grid intersect.

Heavy lines represent Piri Reis grid traced from photograph of the original

Omission of coastline (A) loss of 4.5° longitude going West

PRIME MERIDIAN

PIRI REIS EQUATOR

GRID A

GRID B

GRID C

GRID D

EQUATOR OF ORIGINAL TRIGONOMETRIC PROJECTION

EQUATOR OF GRID B

PRIME MERIDIAN OF GRID B

The Grids

The longitudes of Grid A are determined by the trigonometric pro-

316

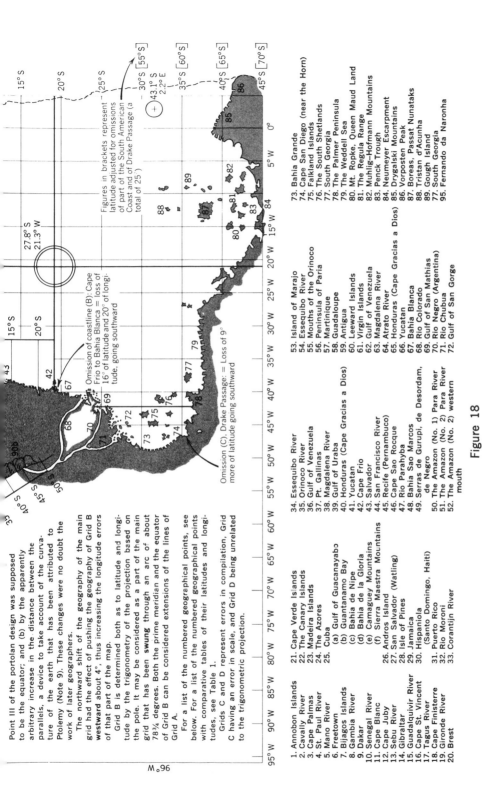

Point III of the portolan design was supposed to be the equator; and (b) by the apparently arbitrary increase in the distance between the parallels, a device to take account of the curvature of the earth that has been attributed to Ptolemy (Note 9). These changes were no doubt the work of later geographers.

The northward shift of the geography of the main grid had the effect of pushing the geography of Grid B **westward** about 4°, thus increasing the longitude errors of that part of the map.

Grid B is determined both as to latitude and longitude by the trigonometry of the projection based on the pole. It may be considered as a part of the main grid that has been **swung** through an arc of about 78¾ degrees. Both the prime meridian and the equator of Grid B can be considered extensions of the lines of Grid A.

For a list of the numbered geographical points, see below. For a list of the numbered geographical points with comparative tables of their latitudes and longitudes, see Table 1.

Grids C and D represent errors in compilation, Grid C having an error in scale, and Grid D being unrelated to the trigonometric projection.

Omission of coastline (B): Cape Frio to Bahia Blanca = loss of 16° of latitude and 20° of longitude, going southward

Omission (C), Drake Passage: = Loss of more of latitude going southward

Figures in brackets represent omissions of part of the South American Coast and of Drake Passage (a total of 25°)

1. Annobon Islands	21. Cape Verde Islands	34. Essequibo River	53. Island of Marajo	73. Bahia Grande
2. Cavally River	22. The Canary Islands	35. Orinoco River	54. Essequibo River	74. Cape San Diego (near the Horn)
3. Cape Palmas	23. Madeira Islands	36. Gulf of Venezuela	55. Mouths of the Orinoco	75. Falkland Islands
4. St. Paul River	24. The Azores	37. Pt. Gallinas	56. Peninsula of Paria	76. The South Shetlands
5. Mano River	25. Cuba	38. Magdalena River	57. Martinique	77. South Georgia
6. Freetown	(a) Gulf of Guacanayabo	39. Gulf of Uraba	58. Guadaloupe	78. The Palmer Peninsula
7. Bijagos Islands	(b) Guantanamo Bay	40. Honduras (Cape Gracias a Dios)	59. Antigua	79. The Weddell Sea
8. Gambia River	(c) Bahia de Nipe	41. Yucatan	60. Leeward Islands	80. Mt. Ropke, Queen Maud Land
9. Dakar	(d) Bahia de la Gloria	42. Cape Frio	61. Virgin Islands	81. The Regula Range
10. Senegal River	(e) Camaguey Mountains	43. Salvador	62. Gulf of Venezuela	82. Muhlig–Hofmann Mountains
11. Cape Blanc	(f) Sierra Maestra Mountains	44. San Francisco River	63. Magdalena River	83. Penck Trough
12. Cape Juby	26. Andros Island	45. Recife (Pernambuco)	64. Atrato River	84. Neumeyer Escarpment
13. Sebu River	27. San Salvador (Watling)	46. Cape Sao Rocque	65. Honduras (Cape Gracias a Dios)	85. Drygalski Mountains
14. Gibraltar	28. Isle of Pines	47. Rio Parahyba	66. Yucatan	86. Vorposten Peak
15. Guadalquivir River	29. Jamaica	48. Bahia Sao Marcos	67. Bahia Blanca	87. Boreas, Passat Nunataks
16. Cape St. Vincent	30. Hispaniola	49. Serras de Gurupi, de Desordam, de Negro	68. Rio Colorado	88. Tristan d'Acunha
17. Tagus River	(Santo Domingo, Haiti)	50. The Amazon (No. 1) Para River	69. Gulf of San Mathias	89. Gough Island
18. Cape Finisterre	31. Puerto Rico	51. The Amazon (No. 2) Para River	70. Rio Negro (Argentina)	77. South Georgia
19. Gironde River	32. Rio Moroni	52. The Amazon (No. 2) western mouth	71. Rio Chubua	95. Fernando da Naronha
20. Brest	33. Corantijn River		72. Gulf of San Gorge	

Figure 18

10.5. The *Piri Re'is Map* of 1513.

clined to disbelieve that Antarctica could have possessed a warm climate 10,000 years ago, [as suggested by the Hough cores], must be reminded of the evidence that Antarctica has many times possessed such a climate. So far as we know at present, the very first evidence of an ice age in Antarctica comes from the Eocene Epoch. That was about 60,000,000 years ago. Before that, for one-and-a-half billion years, there is no suggestion of polar conditions, though very much earlier ice ages existed in other parts of the world.

The second surprise the researchers discovered happened when they determined the age of the Hough core samples. The date found by Dr. Harold D. Urey for the end of the last warm period in Antarctica is of tremendous interest to us. Dr. Urey found all the core samples taken from the bottom of the Ross Sea agree that the last warm period in Antarctica ended about 6,000 years ago, or about 4,000 B.C.

The age of these core samples indicates that during 4,000 B.C. the coasts of Antarctica were *not* covered by the huge amount of ice now growing there. This is a very impressive piece of hard scientific evidence. The *Piri Re'is Map* and the core samples of the Ross Sea floor both indicate the coast of Antarctica were free of ice 6,000 years ago!

This evidence would tend to support Hugh Auchincloss Brown's evidence that approximately every 6,000 years one of the Earth's polar icecaps grows until it affects the Earth's wobble, triggering what modern science today terms a Pole Shift.

Perhaps all of the aforementioned information might explain why a band of men, who were survivors of a civilization destroyed by a sudden shift in the Earth's ter-

restrial axis, stood quietly while their eyes calmly scanned the heavens, noting, tracking, and plotting by nocturnal reckoning the Earth's wobble against their exact scale model of the Earth's Northern Hemisphere. Their scale model is today called The Great Pyramid.

Hugh Auchincloss Brown is not the only one to present evidence that the Antarctic ice mass might contribute to catastropic earth changes. In *The Ocean World of Jacques Cousteau: The White Caps* (Vol. 16, p. 38), Captain Cousteau writes that in 1964 J. Tuzo Wilson theorized that periodically, when the accumulation of ice on Antartica became large and heavy enough, the entire cap broke and slid into the ocean in a catastrophic manner that submerged the continents and sent enough ice to subtropical zones to cool the entire globe substantially.

This type of ice surge the engineer Brown shows is sudden. Brown computed that during a pole-shift the polar ice mass would be thrown toward the Earth's point of greatest spin (the Equator) at an approximate speed of 1600 miles per hour. In other words, the ice mass in Antarctica would be displaced to subtropical zones within 3 or 4 hours!

Cousteau also points out that before the Antarctic continent was buried beneath the shroud of ice now two-and-one-half miles high, it was first covered with a glacier before acquiring its present ice sheet.

In his book *Earth Changes Ahead* (released as this book went to press), Frank Don discussed Wilson's research:

> Although some of the ice cover on Antarctica creeps toward the coastal edges and breaks off from the continent as icebergs, the ice-surge theory contends that a massive build-up of ice cover on that polar continent could prevent the heat rising from

the earth's interior. The prevention of heat release then warms the bottom layers of the ice sheet, allowing it to slide relatively easily along the ground. This process eventually leads to the ice sheets breaking off into the ocean as large sections instead of as smaller icebergs. The immediate consequence of such an ice surge is the triggering of *tsunamis* and the raising of the level of the world's oceans by as much as 20 to 70 meters, thereby flooding many coastal areas around the world. In addition, it is asserted that an ice surge distorts the earth's radiational balance, for the huge block of floating ice increases the amount of solar radiation reflected back toward interstellar space. This condition in turn results in a dramatic lowering of surface temperatures, a cooling trend, and the beginning of another ice age.[18]

The effect of a sudden surge of the Antarctic ice sheet is perhaps captured best by Dr. Jeffrey Goodman in his book *We Are the Earthquake Generation*:

It is 5 p.m. in Boston and the people rushing home from work hardly notice how the setting sun seems to hang on the horizon. After several hours people start to wonder why darkness is not coming and they start to fear the faint dull roar they hear. Some also begin to feel light on their feet whether from giddiness induced by the prolonged twilight or from subtle gravitational and magnetic changes that the earth's shifting in space is creating. Some have that I-could-jump-over-anything feeling.

Animals act skittish and then suddenly all start to move or migrate in the same direction. Then the sky reddens as huge clouds of dust begin to blot out the sun. Next, a steady wind starts to blow. As the wind strengthens, the faint dull roar heard earlier grows even louder as if the source were moving closer. But just then, a temporary stillness sets in and the air seems like it is being sucked up by a giant vacuum cleaner. There is no sign of movement; all the animals are gone. After a few minutes, the winds are back even stronger. There are gusts up to 100 miles an hour. Trees are plucked out of the ground, and railroad trains are tumbled over and over and shuttled along like hockey pucks. As the wind jets up to 200 miles per hour, buildings and everything above ground are decimated. The air becomes a thick mixture of dirt and debris. Those fortunate enough to be tucked safely away below the ground find the air hard to breathe since it is being drawn by the holocaust above. The wind-chill factor has plummeted the temperature down to just above freezing, even though it is spring. There are almost continuous, grandiose electrical storms. Quakes and volcanoes are set off around the world and a rift opens up as the earth splits in several places to relieve the stress produced by the shift. This holocaust goes on and on as if it is never going to stop; ten hours, fifteen, twenty, forty, forty-eight. Then suddenly the winds subside and material from the sky starts to come crashing down. For a few

---

[18]From *Earth Changes Ahead*, Frank Don, Published by Destiny Books, New York, p. 183.

minutes it seems to be raining automobiles, boats, washing machines, and kitchen sinks. The temperature comes back to normal for this time of year, a pleasant 50° F. But this temperature rise continues. By the next day, the third since the start of the shift, the temperature has hit 103° F, just what one would expect in equatorial Africa for this time of year—not Boston. From Boston to St. Paul to Seattle to Anchorage, out come the Bermuda shorts. Layers of mud spread for thousands of miles as a grim reminder of the holocaust. The decaying bodies of animals of every size and shape are found in caves where they huddled together in their last moments.

Prof. Hapgood has not merely modified our existing ideas and concepts of the early history of man, he has (like the discoverer of the seven ancient cities of Troy, so long thought to be a myth) cast many false concepts out the window. If the coasts of Antarctica were free of ice around 6,000 years ago, then Hugh Auchincloss Brown was correct when he advanced the theory that the polar ice mass at the South Pole has grown and increased during the past 6,000 years to its present awesome size.

During a pole-shift, as the earth rolls over 80 degrees,[19] people at the 'pivot points' would see the sun *appear* to stand still and then move backward and set where it had risen. Brown presents evidence that Egypt escaped the inundation from the last pole-shift because it was one of the pivot points and was, therefore, not flooded. Every country on this planet has legendary records of a great flood—every country except Egypt, a country entirely without mythological and heroic ages, as if the country had never known youth.

The priests of Memphis told Herodotus that there had been 341 kings and 341 high priests in 341 generations during the past 11,000 years. And as if to corroborate their genealogy, the high priest of Memphis told Herodotus that "the sun had risen twice [in the past 11,000 years] where he [now] sat."[20] On the ceiling of the tomb of Queen Hatshepsut's [identified by Immanuel Velikovsky as the "Queen of the South" or "Queen of Sheba" who visited Solomon's Temple] chief architect's tomb, there is an astronomical ceiling panel showing the Orion-Sirius star group proceeding in the *reverse* direction from what they appear to move in today!

Masoudi, who died in A.D. 345, translated the Coptic language (an ancient Hamitic tongue used in Egypt until superseded as a living language by Arabic and tradition—M.S. #7503), and in his translation it is said:

> Surid, one of the Kings of Egypt...built the two great Pyramids following a dream in which the inhabitants [of earth] were laid prostrate [and] *the stars wandered confusedly from their courses.*[21]

Now, during a pole-shift of 80 degrees, anyone living at a pivot point, as the earth rolled over 80 degrees, would see the stars *appear to move from their regular courses,* when in fact the planet Earth was shifting or rolling over 80 degrees.

[19]Brown, p. 62.

[20]Herodotus, p. 131.

[21]Masoudi, quoted in Wake, p. 104.

320

In the old Hebrew records (Joshua 10:13) we read, "and the sun stood still, and the moon stayed." As if to echo this, we read in Isaiah 38:8, "Behold, I will bring again the shadow of the degrees, which is gone down in the sun-dial of Ahazten ten degrees backward. So the sun returned ten degrees by which degrees it was gone down."

H.A. Brown, in *Cataclysms of the Earth*, states that "all careening moves cover about 80 degrees of latitude."[22] This is a bold statement, as a "perfect" careen would be 90 degrees. However, the extra ten degrees might be estimated as those "lost" or absorbed in work such as pushing continents around to new positions, sloshing of ocean basins, heat from friction throughout the process, etc., subtracting from the perfect careen of a 90-degree displacement. Joshua 10:13 states, "So the sun stood still in the midst of heaven, and hasted not to go down about a whole day." Was this event in Joshua a pole-shift? I don't believe it was.

I remembered, however, that Velikovsky claimed that Venus originated as a comet in the second millennium B.C. (the time of the Exodus). It *twice* made a close approach to the earth and changed its cometary orbit. If a comet was for a short time "captured" by the earth's gravity, people would see the event described in Joshua. Today the tilt of the earth is 23 degrees. Has it always been so? Joshua 10:13 = 23.

Will a pole-shift ever be accepted by orthodox science? Will it be accepted before the year 2000 and make its way into general public usage? In the February 1979 issue of *Omni* magazine, an article was written about a scientist who thinks he knows why the earth has in the past reversed its polarity (meaning that compasses would have pointed south, rather than north), a fact discovered by British, Soviet, and American scientists aboard the research ship *Glomar Challenger* on the morning of 23 July 1979 (see Chapter Seven).[23] I remembered A. Pochan and his book *L'Enigme de la Grande Pyramide*, pointing out that:

> For the Egyptian of the Old Kingdom, the cardinal point was not

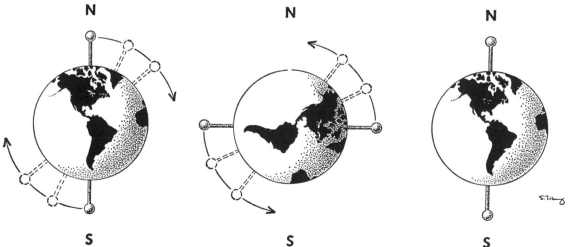

10:6. Pole shift according to Velikovsky.

---

[22]Brown, p. 62.

[23]See also Footnote 13, Chapter 10.

north, but south...during the Old Kingdom the guiding star was not in the Northern Hemisphere but in the Southern Hemisphere, and the cardinal point was south, not north...the guiding star chosen was of the first magnitude.[24]

What immense force or kinetic energy could bring a total reversal in the magnetic force fields of the planet?

The 1979 *Omni* article states that Peter Warlow, a scientist who published his findings in the *Journal of Physics*, thinks the earth occasionally flips end-over-end in space—so violently that the north and south poles change place. The earth spins relatively slowly, and Warlow thinks that makes the earth "flip-able," especially if a comet or asteroid were to approach too close to the earth. Warlow suggests that the shift could occur in one day and would cause massive upheavals; oceans would be drastically affected, the article states.

In his 23-page article Warlow uses six pages of mathematical and technical arguments to show the maximum value for the torque required to invert the earth—a motion which Warlow thinks:

> ...produces massive tidal waves carrying vast quantities of debris and sediment from the ocean floors and depositing them over the land. The inevitable severe storms as the atmosphere tries to adjust to the new positioning of surface features will be augmented by ash and gas ejected by the equally inevitable volcanic activity. The continental plates themselves would be set in motion, thus giving

rise to the volcanism at their boundaries, and with enough impetus to collide eventually and form new mountain chains. Some fauna, large or small, could be rendered extinct, others could survive; flora might have a somewhat better chance of survival. Indeed, of all the events that take place on such an occasion, the reversal of the magnetic field is probably the least significant. Only long after the event does it become important in that it has acted as a recorder of history.[25]

Will the idea of a pole-shift—which sounded so crazy back in the early 70's—ever be accepted by orthodox science? Back in the mid-seventies I intuitively felt that the time was approaching when this knowledge would, bit by bit, surface. However, I felt that when the idea of a pole-shift surfaced among the orthodox scientists, as it did in 1979 with the work of Peter Warlow, there would be many so-called experts who would rush forward shouting "Preposterous!" without even reading the research material. Perhaps I felt this way because I knew that new ideas, especially those whose time had come, have almost always been greeted with cat-calls and skepticism by those living only a conditioned response to their environment.

In any case, Peter Warlow's research surfaced in 1979. Almost as if to bear witness to an idea whose time has come, an important book was published a year later. It was massive in size and documented extremely well. The name of the book was *Pole Shift*.

Pole Shift is a 400-page, seven-year re-

[24]Pochan, pp. 150, 226.

[25]Peter Warlow, "Geographic Reversals Explain Geomagnetic Reversals," *Journal of Physics 11 (1979):* 2107, 436.

search work by John White. He holds degrees from Dartmouth and Yale and is an internationally recognized author and editor. Among his many books are *Future Science, Kundalini,* and *Evolution and Enlightenment.* In 1972 White joined the Masonic astronaut Edgar D. Mitchell to help found the *Institute of Noetic Sciences* for the study of human potential and its application to planetary problems. White worked with the Institute as Director of Education for two years, and is currently Director of Alpha Logics, a school in Bristol, Connecticut.

Drawing from the fields of archaeology, astronomy, and geology, White answers a question that concerns every person living on this planet. Have the north and south poles undergone sudden and massive changes in ancient times? Will the ultimate disaster—a pole-shift—happen at the end of this century? After seven years of research, John White has gathered massive and extremely well documented evidence that answers these questions, "Yes!"

White ends his book by saying:

> Here is a subject worthy, truly worthy, of the most concerted and full-scale investigation by the entire scientific and scholarly community. It represents a potential revolution in the earth sciences surpassing that which occurred through the concept of plate tectonics. It represents equally well a revolution in the biological sciences, in archaeology, and in intellectual history. Last of all, it

represents what may be the key to humanity's survival.... If we avoid or ignore the possibility of a pole shift, we will have only ourselves to blame should there be a cataclysmic repeat of the 'myth' of Atlantis.[26]

The words of Dr. David D. Zink, author of *The Ancient Stones Speak,* leaped into my mind:

> ...changes witnessed in the heavens and associated with these catastrophes led ancient man to precise observation of the skies...the beginning of astronomy was motivated by survival, not superstition.[27]

We read in the *Visud-dhi-Magga,* a book from ancient India:

> ...there are seven ages, each of which is separated from the previous one by a world catastrophe.[28]

In the *Sing-li-ta-tsiurn-chow,* an ancient Chinese enclyclopedia, we find:

> ...in a general convulsion of nature, the sea is carried out of its bed, mountains spring out of the ground, rivers change their course, human beings and everything are ruined, and the ancient traces effaced.[29]

In the writings of Ibrahim ben Ebn Wasuff Shah, we may read:

> The Giza Complex was built to memorialize a tremendous cataclysm in the Earth's planetary system which affected the globe with fire and flood.[30]

---

[26]*John White, Pole Shift,* p. 385.

[27]*Zink,* p. 178.

[28]*Quoted in Wake.*

[29]*Quoted in Wake.*

[30]*Quoted in Wake.*

I remembered a 1977 article in *Scientific American* by astronomer John A. Eddy, which concerned sunspots.[31] Scientists until recently believed that sunspots occurred in 11-year cycles. Eddie says the sun reached the high point of its 11-year cycle in 1969. Then began a decline in sunspots that should have reached a minimum in 1975. The period of minimum activity, however, extended almost two years longer than it should have. Eddy comments:

> This behavior is wholly unlike the modern behavior of the sun which we have come to accept as normal, and the consequences for solar terrestrial physics seem to be profound.... Whenever the sun loses its spots over a long period of time, the earth has gone into a very cold spell.[32]

This is bound to have some effect on the long Antarctic winters and the growth of ice thickness on the Antarctic Continent.

As the growth of ice thickness on the Antarctic Continent plays such an important part in a pole-shift, I thought it would be interesting to find out how large it is today, and at what rate it is growing. If I had some modern figures, I could compare them with H.A. Brown's earlier work. I called Georgia State University and asked to speak to someone who would know about ice in Antarctica. Information put me through to Dr. Bruce O'Connor, a geologist. He was as helpful as possible, but told me that as a geologist the Antarctic ice mass was "out of my field". He suggested that I talk to a geophysicist at Georgia Tech. "I'm sure they can give you some information," he said. "Try Dr. Long."

I was soon speaking with Dr. Leland T. Long, a geophysicist at the Georgia Institute of Technology. I asked Dr. Long about the ice mass on the Antarctic Continent, and he replied, "That really is a little bit out of my field...I would like to suggest that you check into the card catalog in the library."

Somewhat disgruntled and bewildered at being unable to locate someone who knew something about an ice mass bigger than Europe, I checked the card catalog. Nothing.

I did, however, run up against a book entitled *Climates of Hunger*, by Dr. Reid A. Bryson, a climatologist at the University of Wisconsin. Dr. Bryson's book deals with starvation based on the earth's climate's becoming cooler. I soon taped an interview with him.

Noone: After your years of research, do you think the earth's climate is cooling?

Bryson: I believe it *is*, but that doesn't mean it will.

Noone: I have a report by the Worldwatch Institute in Washington, D.C., and they are of the opinion that the "big melt" is coming. That is, they believe that by around the year 2000 temperatures will be way above normal.

Bryson: They don't know what they're talking about. You can get all the opinions you like—

At that point Dr. Bryson was kind enough to explain several technical points to me. I also learned that the Central Intelligence

---

[31] See "The Case of the Missing Sunspots," *Scientific American*, May 1977, Vol. 236 No. 5, pp. 80-92.

[32] John A. Eddy, in *Science*; 27 March 1977 *Atlanta Journal/Constitution* report, "Sun Changes its Spots."

Agency's report ER76-10577U was based on Dr. Bryson's research.

Noone: Where can I find some up-to-date information on snow and ice accumulation in Antarctica?

Bryson: At the Institute of Polar Studies at the Ohio State University.

Needless to say, I was soon on the phone talking to Information at the Institute of Polar Studies. Information put me in touch with a glaciologist, who told me many interesting things, but as snow and ice accumulations in Antarctica were "a bit out of his field," he suggested that I talk with the Director of the Institute, Colin Bull. "If anyone would know about *that*, he would," the glaciologist assured me.

Noone: If a large amount of ice built up at the south pole, could it—as more and more ice was added—be thrown or career toward the equator, where the earth's speed of spin is greatest, taking into account the spinning earth's centrifugal force?

Bull: Yes. But it would have to be a huge amount.

Noone: What is the present amount of snow and ice accumulation in Antarctica?

Bull: Well, that's pretty hard to say. The last work on that subject I did, but that's been some time ago and I imagine it needs to be updated.

Noone: May I please get a copy of your research?

Bull: Yes, I'll be happy to send you a copy.

He was true to his word. Within a few

days I had a copy of his book *Snow Accumulation in Antarctica* on my desk. Copyright 1971—just four years after H.A. Brown's book was published. On the first page I read:

> Estimates of the total volume of ice on the continent still vary widely, reflecting our inadequate knowledge of the ice thickness.

Further on there were similar statements, all of them frustrating:

> ...rates of accumulation or ablation that may be occurring at the bottom of the ice sheet and the ice shelves are not known....[Around the coasts of East Antarctica where the majority of the ice is offset from the south pole toward the east]...the pattern of snow annual balance is complex and not yet well defined.... The estimate of the mean balance will probably be used by others in assessments of the state of equilibrium of the ice mass.... At present no conclusion at all may be drawn on whether the ice sheet is decreasing or increasing in size.[33]

Bull writes in his book that from research performed by Giovinetto and Robinson in 1966 on the western part of the Ross Ice Shelf drainage system, the "total annual gain of mass exceeds the total loss by 4.8 x 10^{16} g." This means that each year *52,860,000,000 tons* of ice are added to the Ross Ice Shelf, which itself represents only between 4% and 5% of the total ice mass in Antarctica. It would take nine million men, each removing sixteen tons of ice a day, one full year to remove this ice to, as one might say, "keep the streets clean." And of course by that time an identical amount would already have accumulated and our nine mil-

[33]Bull, pp. 369, 402-407.

lion men would have to start all over again. Bull states that Giovinetto considers the accumulation of ice on the *interior* of the ice mass would be 40 x 10^16 g. per year.[34]

This means that in the year 1966 *444 billion tons* of ice were added to the interior of the South Pole's ice mass. Should this figure not have grown at all in the last 14 years, it would mean that between 1966 and 1980, 6,000,000,000,000 *tons* of ice would have been added to the unfortunately already off-axis placement of an ice mass that creates the eccentricity—the wobble—in the earth's rotation. How much more ice must be deposited before it will produce a movement of the earth's crust over the rest of the earth's body that will, as Einstein said, "displace the polar regions toward the equator?"

The CIA report stated that climatic changes began in 1960 but were not noticed until the early seventies. The report said the world's climate is cooling. Lowell Ponte, in *The Cooling,* states that the world's climate is cooling. This would mean ice deposited to the interior of the Antarctic ice mass might be far, far larger than the 6,000,000,000,000 tons mentioned above as estimated deposition of ice between 1966 and 1980.

On the last page of his book, Colin Bull sums it up:

> These may be the conditions necessary to produce, eventually, a surge of a major part of the Antarctic Ice Sheet, a rapid rise of sea level of perhaps 20 m, and the initiation of a major Northern Hemisphere glaciation (Hollin, 1965; Wilson, 1964).[35]

A rapid rise of sea level of 20 m (65 feet) means that the level of oceans would rise 65 feet from their present level—and it should be pointed out that the highest point in Florida is about 95 feet. And 99% of Florida is less than 65 feet above sea level! Goodbye, Florida.

Using Florida as an example, it can be seen that a rapid rise of sea level of 65 feet would change the coastline of every continent on this planet drastically, forcing abandonment of coastal cities and fertile coastal plains. When all this would happen is hard to predict with absolute certainty, because of our inadequate knowledge of the ice thickness in Antarctica.

During the third interview I taped with Dr. Colin Bull on 6 October 1980, I asked him if he had ever read *Cataclysms of the Earth* by Hugh Auchincloss Brown. He had not, but remembered the name because years before Brown had telephoned and written many times requesting research information from someone at the Institute about the snow accumulation in Antarctica.

Hugh Auchincloss Brown was not a prophet of doom. As a matter of fact, Brown was an optimist and a very practical engineer. He saw the south polar ice mass through the eyes of an engineer. He believed that the next pole-shift could be prevented by "bleeding off the ice and making it gravitate through newly made channels to the coasts."[36] Brown points out that icebergs drift away from the south pole—they drift north. Local southerly winds aid in starting the northward motion. After these southerly winds, which blow north toward the equator, abate their northward thrust, the icebergs continue to drift northward—towards the point of earth's greatest spin. To

---

[34]Bull, p. 408.

[35]Ibid.

[36]Brown, p. 117.

visualize this, take a globe and spin it. The equator spins faster than the north or south poles, so objects adrift on the ocean are drawn toward the equator. A very simple test will illustrate this. If one lives in the northern hemisphere, water will drain out of his sink clockwise. In the southern hemisphere it will go down the drain counter-clockwise.

I would gladly have taped an interview with Huge Auchincloss Brown, but he died in 1975, at the age of 96.

A scientific approach to any research work requires first reading, then thinking, and finally the formation and expression of an opinion. To prove every single idea advanced in this work beyond a shadow of a doubt would require writing a book on every idea advanced. For every fact or idea advanced in this work, twenty or more had to be omitted by necessity. Machiavelli once said, "All men have eyes, but few have the gift of penetration." By the weight of evidence presented from different ages over the past 6,000 years, it is hoped that the facts and ideas advanced will have opened the door to some new possibilities and perspectives.

Long ago, when I taped an interview with Manly P. Hall and asked him what the truth was, he answered, "The truth of a thing is the reality of it, and the realities are all more or less concealed in a world of causation, and all we get are their shadows in this world." A reality we can prove beyond a shadow of a doubt is that since Col. James Churchward wrote his research on the lost continent of Mu in the thirties—five books in which he presents evidence that Mu was *destroyed by a pole shift*—scientific evidence over the past 50 years has been growing toward proving him right. Another reality we can prove beyond a shadow of a doubt is that the earth's wobble is still as much a puzzle to scientists of today as it was to the scientists of Churchward's time.

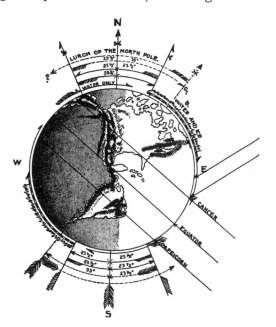

10:7. Pole shift according to Colonel James Churchward.

The pole's lurch

N. North pole at its mean position. S. South pole at its mean position. A. Normal western limit of the pole 23½° from mean. B. Normal eastern limit of the pole 23½° from mean. C. Point in east where pole was drawn before the lurch. D. The path of the pole to this eastern point. E. The path of the pole lurching to the west. F. The point west where the pole reached. 1 and 2. The normal variations from the equator. 3. The point reached with the sun vertical at D. X^1. Waves of water with mountains of ice rushing towards the south. X^2. Wave of water only rushing north. W^1. Waves of water with mountains of ice rushing towards the north. W^2. Wave of water only traveling southerly.

10:9. The South Wave.

As this book went to press I reread a book entitled *Egyptian Museum Cairo*. The book's Introduction was written by Mohammed Hassen Abdul Rahman, Director of that museum. My interest increased when I read on page twenty-one that in 4,000 B.C. "the potter's wheel came into use, there was a radical change in ceramics."

Is it just happenstance that the potter's wheel "came into use" around 6,000 years ago? Could a band of Hyksos (rulers of foreign countries) have introduced this device which suddenly altered forever the production of Egyptian ceramics? Is it just chance that the potter's wheel appeared at a time when the habits, customs and religious tenets of the people living in the Nile Valley were also to change rapidly? Is it just coincidence that the potter's wheel makes its appearance at a time when cannibalism was driven out of the Nile Valley; a time when the old practice of strangling servants to accompany their masters into the afterlife was abolished; a time when the old custom of tying up the bodies of the dead so they could not walk about at night was stopped; a time when women began to be treated with more respect and dignity; a time when human sacrifice was restrained?

Happenstance, chance, coincidence or Hyksos influence?

I remembered using an ancient Egyptian art work in this book's Introduction showing a potter's wheel (See Plate 1:3). This ancient stone carving (circa B.C. 4000) captures and freezes in stone the Hyksos religious tenet that Man was created out of clay by a supreme intelligence. This Plate shows the gods fashioning and nurturing Man. The focal point is the potter's wheel.

Basil Steward, author of *The Mystery of the Great Pyramid*, presented evidence in 1931 that the seeds of Egypt's evolution were "sown by a few colonists who entered the country peaceably and organized the carrying out of great construction works." Fifty years ago (in the "Thirties") little was known about ice accumulation at the Earth's South Pole. But, then, the ice was smaller.

As this book went to press new research studies like *Disaster Survival* by H.M. Conway and *Doomsday 1999 A.D.* by Charles Berlitz were published. These books reveal that certain geographic locations are far more vulnerable than others. *Disaster Survival* says that "by selecting the optimum location you may reduce or eliminate most major risks." *Disaster Survival* points out that the cold, harsh facts are that a superquake in California "would not be a surprise to seismologists."

Charles Berlitz in his book *Doomsday 1999 A.D.* leaves his readers wondering where (during a sudden shift in the Earth's terrestrial axis) the safe pivot points might be.

John White in his book *Pole Shift* points out that if the only safe pivot point was revealed to the undisciplined, then unscrupulous "land dealers" might fence that safe pivot point in and sell tickets to the highest bidder.

Can we prove a pole shift happened 6,000 years ago, beyond a shadow of a doubt? No. However, we can suggest that it may have, by presenting some evidence. The following time line may be helpful in giving a more graphic presentation of some of that evidence.

4500 B.C.— Robert K.G. Temple, fellow of the Royal Astronomical Society of England and author of *The Sirius Mystery*, after ten years of scientific research believes that an advanced race from a planet in the system of the double star Sirius visited earth in this year.

4266 B.C.— E.A. Wallis Budge presents evidence in his translation of the *Egyptian Book of the Dead* that the oldest chapter of these ancient writings was found in the "foundation deposit" of an ancient temple. Budge points out that the text was in use among Egyptians from about 4500 B.C., while the oldest existing chapter was found in this year, 4266 B.C.

4240 B.C.— John Anthony West, in *Serpent in the Sky: The high wisdom of Ancient Egypt*, presents evidence that the heliacal rising of the star Sirius established the ancient Egyptian new year and the founding of Egypt as a unified kingdom. The Supreme Being of the Egyptian religion was named *Osiris*.

and— The German Egyptologist Ludwig Borchardt believed that the establishment of the Egyptian calendar took place in this year, and because Sirius is the only fixed star with an unvaried cycle of 365.25 days it played an important part in the Egyptian calendar.

and— Schwaller de Lubicz, in *Le Temple de l'Homme*, presented evidence that the Egyptian calendar was established in this year. One may speculate, as the calendar was established a few years after the oldest chapter of the *Egyptian Book of the Dead* was found in the foundation deposit of an ancient temple, that perhaps star maps were

also in that deposit.

4000 B.C.— Sir Norman Lockyer, in *The Dawn of Astronomy*, mentions his belief that the Sphinx was built during the junction of the constellations Leo and Virgo, sometime before this date.

and— Duncan MacNaughton, in *A Scheme of Egyptian Chronology*, points out that the 41″ passage inside the Great Pyramid at the top of the Grand Gallery is in alignment with the trajectory of the star Sirius, which he says moved "between 26 degrees 18 minutes and 28 degrees 18 minutes" in the southern sky around this date. (Other astrophysicists believe that the heliacal rising of Sirius around this date had a trajectory of 23 degrees.)

and— The present writer has shown in this book that the supernova explosion of Vela X would have been observable through the Grand Gallery of the Great Pyramid during this year: a gigantic star explosion which decisively influenced western religious symbolism and star mythology, a supernova by which George Michanowsky, in *The Once and Future Star*, provides a startling explanation for the construction of ziggurats and pyramids.

and— Based on the research and calculations of Archbishop Ussher, it should be noted that the entire Christian world until the last century believed that the world was created in *4004 B.C.*

and—   Freemasonry uses two dating systems. The first is the regular A.D. system, and the second is the *Anno Lucis* ("Year of Light"), which memorializes the founding of Ancient Craft Masonry in this year. This dating system is thought of in terms of a 6,000-year cycle of star movements and gives us the year when the planets will align (A.D. 2000).

and—   Prof. Charles H. Hapgood presents evidence in *Earth's Shifting Crust* that a displacement of the entire crust of the earth may have taken place around 4000 B.C.

and—   Hugh A. Brown, in *Cataclysms of the Earth*, presents evidence that the ice mass in Antarctica has been steadily growing since around this date.

and—   Prof. Charles H. Hapgood, in *Maps of the Ancient Sea Kings: Evidence of Advanced Civilization in the Ice Age*, presents evidence that someone mapped Antarctica when its coasts were free of ice around this year. One may speculate that the supernova explosion of Vela X might have produced a surge of the Antarctic Ice Sheet, a rapid rise in sea level, and the initiation of a major northern hemispheric glaciation.

and—   Prof. A.G. Galanopoulos presents evidence in *Atlantis: The Truth Behind the Legend* that Crater Lake, Oregon, was formed by a cataclysmic eruption of Mount Mazama around this date. (Lowell Ponte, author of *The Cooling*, believes that the eruption of Mt. St. Helens may signal the reawakening of at least 15 other volcanos in the Pacific northwest which are part of the "ring of fire.")

and—   Prof. Charles H. Hapgood presents evidence in *Maps of the Ancient Sea Kings* that the Pyramid of Cuicuilco in the Valley of Mexico with its great elevated causeways was covered with lava around this date.

It seems, from the body of material I've examined, that some extraordinary activity took place on this planet between 4500 B.C. and 4000 B.C. In 1977, twenty-three years before 5 May 2000, a large number of books were published that were concerned with the future of the planet Earth. Many reports and research papers not generally available to the public were also published, expressing a grave concern with the future of the planet. It seems, from the body of material I've examined, that some extraordinary activity will take place on this planet around the end of this century.

People always ask me at lectures if I *really* believe that the polar regions will be displaced or careen toward the equator on 5 May 2000. Lately, as some scientists have noticed an increase in the earth's wobble (see, for instance, *Pole Shift*, by John White), I inevitably reply that should I be fortunate enough to live until then, and should I not be in space, I can foresee taking my family a week or two before the fifth of May for a vacation at one of the safe pivot points located at...

...deleted

10:10. *Death on the Pale Horse.*

EPILOGUE
August 1996

Sixteen years ago I wrote in this book's preface that the body of the text would intentionally remain unchanged. Why would I write that? To date, although there have been updates to the preface over the years as scientists made discoveries confirming parts of the text, not a single word in the text has been changed. Why was I so adamant that the evidence presented and conclusions drawn and published fourteen years ago would have to stand the acid test of time over the next eighteen years?

I knew, as any writer does, that most books published are out of print and forgotten after a year or two. "So why," someone asked me, "worry or care what people will think about what you wrote eighteen years from now?"

And yet I did care.

Had I been made privy by an ancient order to ongoing research that in the future would prove all of the text true?

I knew that for every piece of evidence put into this book demonstrating the existence of a technologically advanced civilization prior to the establishment of the first dynasty of ancient Egypt, a hundred other bits of evidence would have to be left out. The book had to be short enough to attract a publisher in the early eighties, a time when this subject had not yet escalated into the raging global debate now taking place.

In the 1980s the winds of discovery were starting to blow the dust of centuries from these other hundreds of bits of evidence. Would future analysis of the evidence be critical of or support the case for a technologically advanced pre-Egyptian empire? If the evidence supports the case, then it behooves us to explain *why* this advanced civilization suddenly vanished in a twinkling of the eye from the surface of our planet.

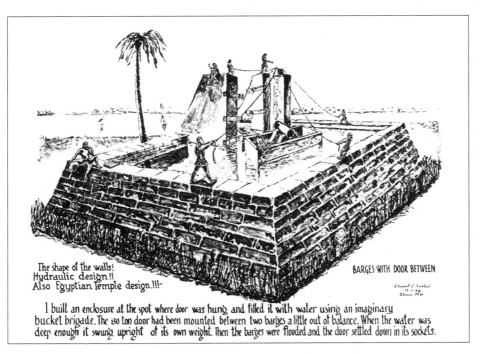

The shape of the walls!
Hydraulic design!!
Also Egyptian Temple design.!!!-

BARGES WITH DOOR BETWEEN

I built an enclosure at the spot where door was hung and filled it with water using an imaginary bucket brigade. The 80 ton door had been mounted between two barges a little out of balance. When the water was deep enough it swung upright of its own weight. Then the barges were flooded and the door settled down in its sockets.

1. From *Pharaoh's Pump* copyright © 1962 by Edward J. Kunkel. Used by permission.

Like the Sphinx in Egypt, I was to abide my time in patience for the next ten years. Then, in 1992, John Anthony West (see Plates 2:14, 7:2, and 9:16), author of *Serpent in the Sky: The High Wisdom of Ancient Egypt,* and Professor Robert M. Schoch, an American geologist and geophysicist at Boston University, made media headlines around the world with their discovery that the Sphinx in Egypt is thousands of years older than the beginning of Egyptian history—a startling revelation that simultaneously reveals the existence of a primeval and as yet unnamed civilization. Could this be the antediluvian empire discussed in Chapter Seven by Manly P. Hall?

In November 1993, NBC aired a one-hour television special, *The Mystery of the Sphinx,* hosted by Charlton Heston. Seen by some thirty million viewers, the show taught the public how the Sphinx had suffered erosion from rain in some remote period when Egypt was as lush and green as the Garden of Eden.

This television special was also the general public's first hint of a fierce battle between orthodox Egyptologists (who had managed, until the TV show, to keep this issue to themselves) and a new breed of investigators who have yanked this controversy out of the darkness and thrust it into the light for all to see. For an example of orthodox Egyptological thinking, see the interview with Dr. Edward Wente in Chapter Seven.

The Giza complex is the world's most mysterious site, and men of science have been drawn to it for over two thousand years. Herodotus wrote of it in 440 B.C. as did Strabo, Thales, and Diodorus Siculus.

Therefore, it is not surprising to find the site surrounded by more legends, rumors, myths, speculation, and lore than any other of antiquity. A persistent rumor is that during World War II, when American and Allied forces were driving the Nazis out of Egypt, two American servicemen were on furlough in Cairo. Allegedly they visited the Sphinx and were approached by a guide, who, for a large tip, showed them a secret passageway under the Sphinx, which they followed to a room where they saw something that drove them both insane.

Further speculation on what may lie hidden underground at the Giza complex can be directly attributed to one man, whose psychic "readings" are known to millions of his readers. Edgar Cayce (1877–1945), sometimes referred to as "the sleeping prophet," achieved acclaim in his lifetime by the remarkable accuracy of his medical diagnoses, suggested remedies, and curing of ailing clients while he was in a deep trance.

Perhaps his most quoted prophecy today, fifty-two years after his death, is that a hidden "hall of records" will be found beneath the Sphinx at Giza just before the year 2000. This "hall of records," Cayce said, will contain records of the destruction of a technologically advanced pre-Egyptian empire during a shifting of the earth's crust. He also warns that the crust of our earth will again shift around the year 2000.

No one had complied and edited Cayce's Egyptian "readings" until Mark Lehner published them in his book, *The Egyptian Heritage,* in 1974.

When I learned of the proposed West/Schoch expedition to scientifically establish the age of the Sphinx and conduct a seismographic mapping of the Giza plateau's underground, I was intrigued. I remembered my interview with Wilfred J. Gregson (see Chapter Five). He had expressed his view, both as an architect and Masonic scholar of ancient history, that the Great Pyramid had a connection with a very early civilization, that its purpose was to pass on to later generations what the builders had learned, and that "by following along the ancient principles of Mankind," we could expect to find four more chambers in or under the Great Pyramid.

Almost two years later, on August 23, 1978, I interviewed Dr. Lambert T. Dolphin, senior physicist in charge of the radio physics laboratory at Stanford Research Institute. The SRI team had been authorized by the Egyptian Antiquities Organization to hunt for secret chambers in the Great Pyramid. SRI's high-tech equipment located what Dr. Dolphin believed was a hidden chamber between the so-called King's and Queen's chambers (See Plate 5:15).

Now a small hole could be drilled down to the location and a fiber-optic camera run down the hole for a look into the void, but, instead, with perhaps the find of the century only a few feet away, the SRI team suddenly returned to America. Repeated attempts to discover more about this possible hidden chamber proved futile. Back in the 1970s, I had no idea what power the Egyptian Antiquities Organization had over scientists, nor of their own covert treasure hunt for the "hall of records."

What Dr. Dolphin and the SRI team did prove was the value of using seismographic equipment in the exploration of ancient sites. In all fairness to Dr. Dolphin, I do not know if he had any knowledge of a quest for a "hall of records." He did, however, five years later, write a letter to my publisher:

I like this book for two reasons. First, it is a useful collection of items concerning the Egyptian mystery religion, folklore, legends and stories that add to the knowledge conventional science and traditional Egyptology have accumulated.

More important, Mr. Noone presents evidence for past and future natural disasters—catastrophes on earth. Until a few years ago, science would not admit that any such interruptions of a uniform order ever occurred. Now, fortunately, it is acceptable to talk about these issues and, of course, there is lots of evidence to support the case of large catastrophes in the past. The Bible says more will come.

Before I return to the West/Schoch expedition, I would like to point out something interesting about the location of the SRI search.

I am looking at a letter dated March 3, 1934, addressed to Edward J. Kunkel from George Washington Carver of the Tuskegee Institute in Alabama. During the Great Depression, Kunkel read a newspaper story about Carver's efforts to revolutionize the agriculture of the southern United States (Carver had convinced Alabama farmers to, in place of cotton, grow peanuts, pecans, and sweet potatoes as part of his plan to restore economic stability to the region).

Kunkel realized that a hydraulic pump he had designed could help Carver transform the drought-stricken South into a lush green area criss-crossed with irrigation canals like those canals found today near monolithic buildings in Egypt, Mexico, South America, and the Pacific (See pages 198–202 and 236).

Kunkel had already tried to interest engineers, research institutes, Egyptologists, and technical departments of colleges and universities in the 1930s, with no luck. Every time he did get someone interested in learning how his pump could move so much water, he would take a pie pan, stand a candle in it, fill the pan with water, light the candle, and place a glass bottle upside down over the candle.

As the engineer watched the water being sucked up into the bottle, Kunkel would explain that the creation of a vacuum by this means involves three factors: the expansion and cooling of air, the consumption of oxygen, and the conversion of gases in the upper diagonal of his pump.

Usually about this time, the engineer would excitedly ask how he had come up with the idea. Kunkel would answer that he had copied the interior system of the Great Pyramid. Now a strange thing would happen. The engineer's excitement would vanish as his eyes glazed over, staring blankly. There would be an uncomfortable period of silence followed by much clearing of the throat, a furtive glance at the door for assurance it was still there providing escape should this madman become violent, a fumbling with papers, a glance at a watch, and a lame remark about being very busy, signaling the end of Kunkel's presentation.

A few days later, a letter arrived from the Tuskegee Institute. The letter was from a chemist whose research had won him more awards than I could list on this page, a chemist who in 1916 was elected a fellow in the Royal

TUSKEGEE NORMAL AND INDUSTRIAL INSTITUTE

FOUNDED BY BOOKER T. WASHINGTON

FOR THE TRAINING OF COLORED YOUNG MEN AND WOMEN

RESEARCH AND EXPERIMENT STATION
GEORGE W. CARVER, DIRECTOR

TUSKEGEE INSTITUTE, ALABAMA

3—3—34.

My dear, Mr. Kunkle:—

Your letter, drawings, Newspaper clipping, are all marvelously interesting to me.

Your explanation, I believe is the solution of one of the greatest mysteries of the ages.

Your drawings make it quite clear as to how it could be done.

To be sure I would like to have a book.

I am very certain that you got much joy and real satisfaction out of your search for truth which always enthuses and inspires the true scientist to go ahead.

You do not need to apologize for this picture at all I really like it, the eyes are very good and I can read so much character out of them. The contour of the face is strong

and expressive. It also shews strong creative power.

I hope our paths will meet some day.

I shall make a real study of your letter, drawings and the clipping, as you do indeed have something new.

Most sincerely yours,
G. W. Carver

2.

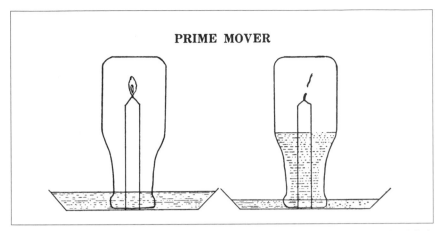

PRIME MOVER

3. The reaction from the candle flame is slow, because paraffin is the product of fossil fuel. Fossil fuels give off carbon monoxide, which is "very slightly soluble in water." But newsprint, which is made of wood pulp, when burned gives off carbon dioxide, which is soluble in water. The reaction is vigorous and fast. Try it in a wide-mouthed glass milk jug.

From *Pharaoh's Pump* copyright © 1962 by Edward J. Kunkel. Used by permission.

Society of Arts in London, an honor given few Americans. The letter from Carver, a *chemist*, who understood *the conversion of gases*, said: "Your letter, drawings, newspaper clippings, are all marvelously interesting to me. Your explanation, I believe is the solution of one of the greatest mysteries of the ages. Your drawings make it quite clear as to how it could be done"

Encouraged by Carver, Kunkel made another presentation, in which he played a little trick on the next engineer. He made a new drawing of the pump, eliminating any reference to the Great Pyramid, and made his presentation. "Young man, that will pump far more water than you think," the engineer exclaimed.

Encouraged, Kunkel built a scale model of the most complex pump ever built by ancient man. The pump was complex because it used the force of gravity twice in the same machine, that is, compounded, and together with this force, ancient engineers used another force, atmospheric pressure, twice, compounded also.

His model was built on a scale of one-half inch to the foot with a galvanized iron compression chamber only 23 inches long, its joints lapped, riveted, and soldered. Finished, his model of metal pipes and chambers duplicating the Great Pyramid's interior system looked like

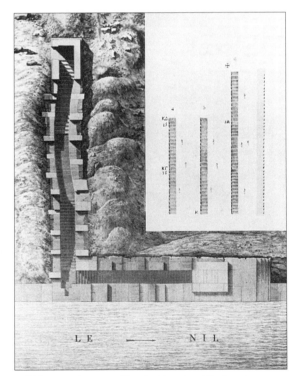

4. Nilometer discovered by the French at Elephantine, near Syene, used by the Egyptians for measuring the rise of the Nile at flood time, and marked in cubits very close to the royal cubit of Memphis.

From *Secrets of the Great Pyramid* copyright © 1971 by Peter Tompkins. Used by permission.

5A. I poured some water in the model. These photographs were taken November 1946. Kunkel's second pump.

Photos by M.E.L.

5B. Then I blew down the jet-bowl tube.

5C. A half gallon of water was discharged.

5D. Some traveled 22 feet.

a prop from the science fiction movie *Aliens*. Kunkel slowly filled the pump with water, and to start the water moving, like the flame of a candle does, he opened his mouth and blew down the jet-bowl tube. The moment of truth was at hand.

There came a deep rumble from within the pump. As the water moved through the system from pipe to chamber and from chamber to pipe, air was sucked into the pump. The water began to spin in a whirlpool motion. The spin of the water accelerated like a tornado as the rumble deepened and grew louder and louder. Six seconds passed, seven seconds, eight seconds, and then the pump blew up as a column of water shot out the discharge tube high into the sky like a just-tapped Texas oil well.

When I interviewed Kunkel in 1977, he said this: "Scared the living daylights out of me." He had never expected the violence of the reaction. He did tell me: "My next model was made of heavy-gauge steel which did not blow up." Over the ensuing years Kunkel fought battle after battle in the attempt to teach experts, "supposedly learned men in seats of power," what he had discovered—how the pump worked, and how it could "inexpensively provide an abundance of water to every governor of the western United States who has a shortage of water."

The fact that the pump had to be "new" to be granted a patent was a source of amusement to Kunkel, because it had been his insistence that the pump was a copy of an ancient pump that had caused him so much trouble in the first place. When I interviewed Kunkel in 1977, he told me that "the Sphinx was a smaller water pump which supplied, through underground tunnels, the pyramid pump by way of a well in front of the [Great] pyramid which you'll see in my book." In 1962 Kunkel published a book, *Pharaoh's Pump*, on his research .

For twenty-six years Kunkel battled the stupidity of Washington bureaucrats and the popular but erroneous belief of those years that our ancestors had infantile mentalities, until he *proved* the pump would work. In 1955 he applied for a patent on the pump and, after a four-year

battle with the United States Patent Office, he was granted U.S. Patent No. 2,887,956, Serial No. 479,428, on May 26, 1959, for a new type of pump.

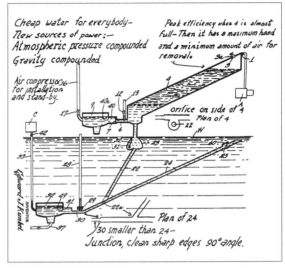

6. Cheap water for everybody. New sources of power: Atmospheric pressure compounded. Gravity compounded.

Before his book was published, Kunkel sent a copy of the manuscript to the Department of Egyptian Archeology at the Metropolitan Museum in New York. The manuscript painstakingly spelled out the mechanical details of how the pump could be made to build itself, the physical reason that it is constructed in the shape it is, and a copy of his new patent. The Egyptologist flipped through the manuscript, then smugly pronounced that there was no evidence for a cavity between the King's and Queen's chambers, nor do we have any evidence for tunnels under the Sphinx or that the Egyptians used hydraulic water pumps.

Apparently the certification by the United States Patent Office that the pump worked was lost on this Egyptologist. It takes, it seems, a long time for the penny to drop for some people. Kunkel's 1949 patent drawings of the water pump's interior and his drawings of the Great Pyramid's interior system both show a cavity exactly where, twenty-eight years later, Dr.

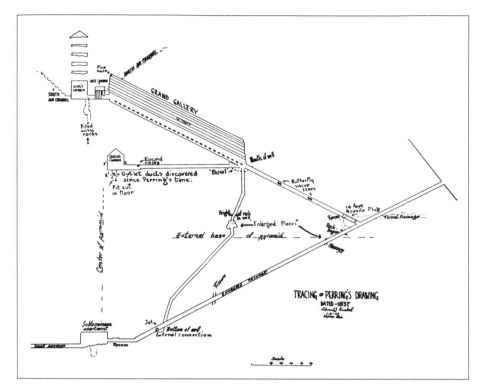

7. Perring made at least three drawings of the interior. All vary in detail. The above is a composite of drawings made over a period of two years, from 1837 to 1839.

In one the "firing hole" is not shown. In another the "masonry" on the lower diagonal is not shown, or mentioned, neither are the eight inch round holes shown or mentioned; however, Maspero shows drawings of them.

The part marked "bowl" varies in detail. Nothing is said or shown of the eight-inch-round holes in the long horizontal passage leading to the Queen's Chamber; however *Encyclopaedia Britannica* 9th ed., says they exist.

There is a variation of the drawing of the area marked "enlarged place." One drawing omits the well, shown at the bottom of the drawing; however, another shows its contours in detail.

The vents leading from the Queen's Chamber are not shown here. They were discovered since Perring's time.

From *Pharaoh's Pump* copyright © 1962 by Edward J. Kunkel. Used by permission.

Lambert T. Dolphin and the SRI team would find it (see pages 125–26)!

I should, however, before we rejoin the West/Schoch team on the Giza plateau, warn the reader that with the discovery of this cavity, this story will become as bizarre as the Bruce Willis film *12 Monkeys*.

How far beyond our modern technology the builders of the Great Pyramid were is a subject we are only now beginning to investigate, understand, and appreciate. A virtual flood of

new discoveries corroborating the existence of a pre-Egyptian empire are now erupting from scholars around the globe.

In 1994, for example, Robert Bauval and Adrian Gilbert wrote *The Orion Mystery*. The book leads the reader step-by-step through a secret astronomical master plan for the Giza complex, a plan designed by ancient astronomers thousands of years ago linking the Great Pyramid to a mysterious star clock in the heavens. Orthodox Egyptologists have always said

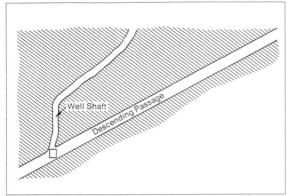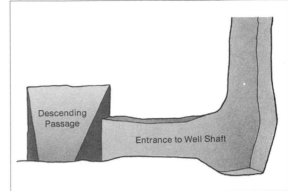

8 and 9. Kunkel's Lateral Connection

From *Secrets of the Great Pyramid* copyright © 1971 by Peter Tompkins. Used by permission.

that the builders of the Great Pyramid did not know how to make any metal stronger than copper. Bauval and Gilbert, however, report the discovery of copper, bronze, gold, and iron (not meteor iron) inside the Great Pyramid, which they show to be contemporaneous with its construction!

Who else had iron? What did they use it for? When was it mined? Where was it mined? Why was it made? May I here direct the reader's attention to pages 51, 235–36, and 136–37 for some evidence that sheds new light on these questions concerning the mysterious origins of mankind. In addition to all of the above, Kunkel mentions the finding of a brass chisel showing evidence of long usage in one of the pyramids. If hit against stone today, this chisel's edge will turn like that of soft brass. Kunkel told me that the ancient brass founders "mixed some compound of phosphorus in the brass, which gave it a degree of hardness sufficient to cut stones, and that through the ages, the phosphorus has slowly disappeared."

Solving the mystery of the Great Pyramid's construction creates a far greater challenge. I found this out a second later, when Kunkel told me something that caused me to drop my phone. Kunkel had just told me the location of a large stone door inside the Great Pyramid—a stone door that moved, a stone door that had a mechanical function, a stone door that after years of researching this building I didn't even

know existed, a stone door I have never seen in any book on the Great Pyramid, and a stone door never talked about by Egyptologists.

To say I was stunned would be an understatement. I checked the pyramid books in my library. A footnote on page 93 and a drawing on page 94 of Peter Tompkins's book, *Secrets of the Great Pyramid*, caught my eye and sent me to Piazzi Smyth's book, *Our Inheritance in the Great Pyramid*, published in 1877, and from there to *Operations Carried Out at the Pyramids of Gizeh* by Howard Vyse. To graphically record and measure in detail his discoveries, Vyse hired a civil engineer, John Shae Perring (1813–1869), who later published a book consisting mainly of his drawings, entitled *The Pyramids of Gizeh from Actual Survey and Measurements on the Spot*, in 1839.

Today, when one begins a descent into the Great Pyramid's lower diagonal, they descend for 130 feet through the core masonry of the building (see Plate 3:1). Here, one has arrived at a junction between the core masonry and the natural bedrock of the Giza plateau. To proceed, one must enter a square shaft that speaks volumes to the ancient builder's mining skill. Excavated by a method unexplainable by modern miners and engineers, this shaft, straight as an arrow, descends into the solid bedrock at the precise angle of 26 degrees, or a slope of about one in two, for 215 feet.

The total length of the Great Pyramid's

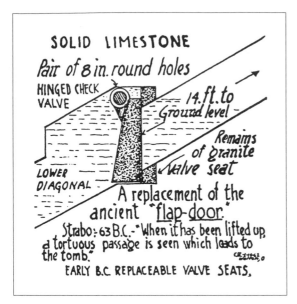

10. *Encyclopaedia Britannia* 9th ed., tells of eight-inch-round holes here. Maspero's drawings show them. Perring's drawings show masonry here. Holes have been plastered over, masonry has been removed, and the whole area covered with dark red gloss paint.

From *Pharaoh's Pump* copyright © 1962 by Edward J. Kunkel. Used by permission.

rounded corners following an irregular course must join these two with the surface above, resulting in the formation of a bastard U tube. The so-called "well shaft" joins these two (see Plate 3:1). The junction can be defined as a lateral connection.

Kunkel's pump requires the installation of a "check valve," sometimes termed "flap door" by hydraulic engineers. To withstand tremendous water pressure, this flap door should be made of granite for strength, it should be set in granite (valve seat) for a tight seal, and it must be hinged to open and close to control the flow of a liquid, gas, etc. Since this ancient pump was complex, because it used the force of gravity twice in the same machine, that is, compounded and that together with this force, ancient engineers used another force, atmospheric pressure, twice, compounded also. Kunkel deduced that the flap door/check valve, for stability in repeated usage, should be built into the bedrock and positioned underground.

Before Kunkel ever built his first pump, he knew that if his idea was correct, there should be two underground check valves, one in the lower diagonal and one in the so-called well shaft. He needed to see detail of the Great Pyramid's interior. He went to the library and asked for Perring's large folio of drawings. Kunkel wrote in his autobiography *One Bright Day*: "I turned to the drawing of the interior of the Great Pyramid and within five minutes located the two valve chambers cut in limestone." Kunkel had seen an

lower diagonal is 345 feet, then it levels out for twenty-five feet before it enters an oddly cut subterranean pit. The lower diagonal of Kunkel's pump duplicates the Great Pyramid's lower diagonal. The compression chamber of Kunkel's pump duplicates this oddly cut pit. Kunkel's pump requires that a vertical shaft with

11. From *Pharaoh's Pump* copyright © 1962 by Edward J. Kunkel. Used by permission.

Kunkel's Calculations from *Pharaoh's Pump*

Four beveled base casing stones that once covered the building can be seen today. They are fitted with matchless workmanship practically as true as modern work by optical instrument makers. . . . The joints, almost invisible, are 35 square feet in area, and not thicker than a silver paper, yet they include between the polished surfaces an extraordinary fine film of white cement. They are more than 5 feet high and weigh some 16 tons.

This simple quotation hit me right between the eyes, because it disclosed a phase of pyramid construction that other observers seem to have missed, or ignored. Think of it: one joint, 35 square feet in area.

These casing stones are precision-cut in five planes: bottom, top, two sides, and facing, which adds up to about 168 square feet of precision cutting of each stone.

Each base length of the pyramid is 764 square feet. The slant sides are 720 feet, and the height is 480 feet.

The total length of the four bases is 3,056 feet, a distance of more than a half mile.

Assuming that each casing block was four feet in width, it would require 764 blocks to complete the first course around the base and 764 times 168 is 128,352, which represents the square feet of cutting, in the first course.

Very elementary mathematics revealed that millions and millions of square feet were precision-cut, which in any man's language is a bewildering, nightmarish job of precision production.

I'll guess out loud that it was done with remarkable ease, and remarkable speed, and involved very little heavy manual labor, and comparatively light handwork.

I'll guess, too, that it was done with water, in a special pool that was quite shallow at one end and of considerable depth on the other. Also, that the floor had a steep pitch, and attached to the floor were diamond-cutting members.

The procedure would be to float the blocks on a barge and deposit them at the shallow end, then drain the pool. The heavy blocks would slide down the steep bottom, and during this sliding-down action the great weight of the blocks would bear against the cutting members with tremendous pressure and cut their bottom faces.

If a water lock were at the deep end of the pool, the casing blocks could easily be removed by a barge and floated away.

enlarged section of the Great Pyramid's lower diagonal 14 feet down from the junction between the core masonry and the natural bedrock. The other one was just below ground in the grotto of the well shaft.

The oldest drawing I had access to when I put this book together was a drawing from C. Staniland Wake's book, *The Origin and Significance of the Great Pyramid*, published in 1882. That drawing is Plate 3:1 in this book, which shows these two locations. Fourteen feet down the shaft cut into the bedrock, the builders of the Great Pyramid enlarged it to install large granite lintels, worked masonry, and two eight-inch-round holes identical to the eight-inch-round holes opposite each other in the walls at the Queen's Chamber entrance.

Kunkel explains: "A short distance down in the solid rock of the Lower Diagonal is a tiny offset, 'wherein,' says Petrie, 'hung a door that swung inward.' A pair of eight-inch-round holes are found here, one in the east and the other in the west wall. Adjacent to these round holes is granite masonry. Giving this mechanical element an interpretation in hydraulics, is, check valve. The holes support a round shaft, and the granite masonry is the valve seat." The shaft measures three feet five inches wide and is one-half inch short of four feet high, which gives us an approximate size of the door. When a sufficient amount of water came down this shaft, the weight of the water and the pull of gravity would cause the door/check valve to swing open, allowing water to rush downward toward the pit which, in Kunkel's pump, is the compression chamber. In the operation of Kunkel's pump, water attempting to escape back up this diagonal would force the door/check valve closed.

How many thousands of years ago the granite door was smashed and broken is impossible to say. Perhaps some early explorer pushed it open while exploring the shaft. Once inside, the granite check valve would swing closed into the granite valve seats. With no way to open it from the inside, the check valve had become a trapdoor of death, entombing the intruder forever. Perhaps, because of this danger, it was smashed to pieces.

The duty of many Egyptologists is to pre-serve, protect, and restore ancient Egyptian relics and architecture. Now, however, it becomes their duty to explain why the worked masonry was removed from this area, why the whole area was plastered over, and, in Kunkel's time, painted over with dark red gloss paint. This is not the only incident of evidence being plastered over or of evidence being conveniently "lost," as we will soon see.

Today, two open shafts in the Queen's Chamber run upward into the building. In *The Orion Mystery*, Bauval and Gilbert write that in 1872, Waynman Dixon and Dr. J.A.S. Grant, suspecting that the Queen's Chamber might have shafts like the King's Chamber, probed a crack with a wire for some length, then hammered through five inches of stone, opening the shaft in the south wall, and then a similar shaft in the north wall was hammered open. Reading an account of this in Piazzi Smyth's book, they were surprised to learn that in the northern shaft a gray granite or green stone ball weighing one pound three ounces, a piece of cedarlike wood, and a bronze thing which Smyth called "a grapnel hook" had been found (see *Nature*, December 26, 1872).

Waynman Dixon, a high-degree Freemason and engineer, returned these three ancient relics to England, as well as a sample of white mortar from within the shaft. This mortar, which exuded from the joints of the just-opened shaft, was analyzed. Smyth wrote that this mortar was, "composed not of *carbonate*, as generally used in Europe for mason's mortar, but *sulphate* of lime, or what is popularly known as 'plaster of paris' in this country." A bigger mystery to Bauval and Gilbert was "why no Egyptologist had thought it important to inform us of Dixon's amazing find." Bauval telephoned a world-renowned Egyptologist, Dr. I.E.S. Edwards (see page 13 in *5/5/2000*). Dr. Edwards, former keeper of Egyptian antiquities in the British Museum (1954–74), is the author of the book *The Pyramids of Egypt*, published in 1949. When Bauval asked Dr. Edwards about this amazing find, the eminent Dr. Edwards replied that he didn't know anything about it. How could he have *not* known about it?

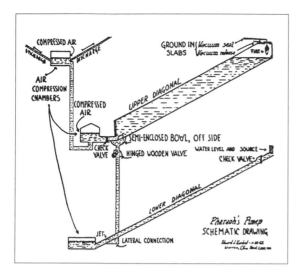

12. The above schematic drawing is an effort to simplify the hydraulic principles involved in the pyramid pump.

The position of the upper diagonal has been reversed. However, the shape of the pyramid will not permit such an arrangement of the various mechanical elements.

A movement of water, caused by a vacuum and its release, causes a downward movement in the lower diagonal, which compresses air in the subterranean rock-hewn chamber.

The compressed air pushes water up and into the upper diagonal, thereby supplying it with water.

A downward movement of water in the upper diagonal compresses the air in the two compression chambers.

The lower compression chamber supplies the upper one, while the upper one discharges water to the outside.

In the pyramid pump, the lower diagonal holds 88 tons of water, while the upper diagonal has a capacity of 300 tons of water. The pump itself, when full, holds about 600 tons of water.

A search for these ancient relics from the Great Pyramid at the British Museum proved fruitless. Bauval and Gilbert searched diligently, but nobody knew what had become of them. They did find at the British Library at Colindale newspaper accounts, complete with drawings, of the three relics. This was a big news story, with plenty of coverage. The bronze relic was especially important because, as Bauval and Gilbert correctly point out, the discovery of bronze "means that the Bronze Age had already started in Egypt" centuries before Egyptologists had *assumed*. Before the discovery of this bronze relic, Egyptologists reported that the ancient Egyptians did not know how to make any metal but copper.

A good newspaper editor will recognize, no matter how good the story, when it has run its course, and the coverage of the discovery will cease. This fact was, of course, known by Egyptologists as well. Eventually, newspaper coverage of the discovery of *bronze*, hammered and chiseled out of a *sealed* shaft within the Great Pyramid, ceased. With the disappearance of press coverage and the disappearance of the relics, Egyptologists continued to write in textbooks that the ancient Egyptians did not know how to make any metal but copper. And that's what you and I grew up being taught! Was every Egyptologist in England out of the country when newspapers were running this story? In addition to the newspaper accounts, the Astronomer Royal for Scotland, Piazzi Smyth, F.R.S.E., F.R.A.S., described these relics and their discovery in his book, *Our Inheritance in the Great Pyramid*. For the careful measurements he had taken in Egypt, Smyth received a gold medal from the Royal Society of Edinburgh (see *Secrets of the Great Pyramid* by Peter Tompkins, also his interview in Chapter Three of this book).

Bauval and Gilbert were again surprised when two Egyptologists at the British Museum told them that two vessels previously assumed to be copper had just been checked and were found to be bronze. This would have been big news thirty-four years earlier, when Kunkel published his book, but in light of the fact that these Egyptologists had realized that Bauval and Gilbert's book would let the whole world know that the British Museum had had in its possession, for over a hundred years, a piece of man-made iron a foot long from the Great Pyramid, seems a lifeless gesture reeking of cover-up. As the authors state: "It means that the Iron Age too began many centuries before Egyptologists had thought!" After an interesting intellectual game of "relics, relics, who's got the relics" between the authors and Egyptologists, the authors wrote: "As yet, the Dixon relics have not been found." The Dixon brothers, however, were soon back in newspaper headlines around the world when a group of British Freemasons had them bring one of the obelisks of Thothmes III to London (its twin now stands in New

York's Central Park, see pages 17–19 in this book). Peter Tompkins points out in the 1981 edition of his book *The Magic of Obelisks* that in the foundation deposit of the obelisk taken to New York, "embedded in the mortar were also a mason's trowel of iron or steel."

The same year *The Orion Mystery* was published in England, on the other side of the Atlantic, New Millennium Productions in Glencoe, Illinois, released a documentary film entitled *Enter Darkness: Enter Light*. The different theories of how the Great Pyramid was constructed extolled by Egyptologists—the slave, whip, single ramp, spiral ramp, roller, lubricated rollers, men harnessed together pulling in cadence to shouted directions one, two, three, heave "which poor beast of the field cannot be trained to do"—disintegrates under scrutiny as fast as their "the ancient Egyptians did not know how to make any metal but copper" theory.

Two architects are interviewed in this documentary; both are construction specialists in the erection of large structures, both have designed large and expensive structures in the United States, both have, at the request of foreign governments, assisted in the design, development, and completion of large architectonic projects around the world, and both know that the fantasies of construction ventured by Egyptologists are like so much pabulum spooned up and fed to children.

The first architect is Wilfred J. Gregson, now ninety-six years young. Gregson is as fascinating to listen to on film as he was when I interviewed him in 1977 (see Chapter Five). He talks about shafts in the Great Pyramid in alignment with ancient stars, modern and ancient Freemasonry, and who really built the Great Pyramid and why. Professor Livio Catullo Stecchini, professor of the history of science, who wrote the hundred-page mathematical appendix in Peter Tompkins's book *Secrets of the Great Pyramid*, wrote me a letter in 1977. He and Tompkins had been kind enough to answer many questions I had at the time, and I had mailed Stecchini a copy of my interview with Gregson for review. Stecchini, characterized by Professor Giorgio de Santillana of MIT as a

"Copernicus of the twentieth century," wrote: "Mr. Gregson raised an entire series of problems of engineering that are of great interest to me. Keep working on your project. I believe that the interview with Gregson not only is valuable to specialists like me, but would be exciting to the general public."

Then the film interviews Atlanta astronomer James E. Summers (see Preface). He discusses the planetary alignment coming on May 5, 2000, and states that if you were to make a record of this unique alignment, "astronomers one hundred thousand years from now could use this information and come back and identify the date of this particular alignment." Quite true, but the record must *survive*. That the Great Pyramid incorporates advanced astronomical data there is no question. Then something happened and the knowledge was lost and it has taken thousands of years for mankind to regain that once-known astronomical knowledge. The astronomical data built into the Great Pyramid was not known when Washington took the oath of office. It was not known when Columbus crossed the Atlantic. It was not known when Cleopatra rolled out of a rug in front of Caesar. Why?

Graham Hancock, in his 1995 book *Fingerprints of the Gods*, presents astonishing new evidence of a technologically advanced early empire. This civilization flourished during the Pleistocene period, the last Ice Age, until a terrible cataclysm that afflicts our planet in great cycles at irregular intervals brought the last Ice Age to a screeching halt. Can we imagine ourselves living at the end of the Pleistocene? What if we were now back in time, side by side with our ancient ancestors. What would it be like? Professor Frank C. Hibben, author of *The Lost Americans*, can help us imagine. He begins his book with a description of Alaska:

> The Alaskan muck is like a fine, dark gray sand. . . . Within this mass, frozen solid, lie the twisted parts of animals and trees intermingled with lenses of ice and layers of peat and mosses. It looks as though in

the midst of some cataclysmic catastrophe of ten thousand years ago the whole Alaskan world of living animals and plants was suddenly frozen in midmotion in a grim charade.

In a later chapter Hibben writes:

The Pleistocene period ended in death. This is no ordinary extinction of a vague geological period which fizzled to an uncertain end. This death was catastrophic and all-inclusive. . . . The large animals that had given their name to the period became extinct. Their death marked the end of an era.

When Professor Hibben wrote this in 1949, Professor Hapgood's first book, *Earth's Shifting Crust,* lay nine years in the future. Is it any wonder, then, that Hibben, witnessing the sudden death of millions of plants, animals, and, of course, any humans who might also have lived in the area, was puzzled by what looked like a geological Armageddon. He wrote:

But how did they die? What caused the extinction of forty million animals?

The end of the Ice Age was marked by death, death on a worldwide scale as Alaska, Canada, the United States, Mexico, and Central and South America were shifting south, while continents on the opposite side of the earth were shifting north. Where might we find more evidence of the sudden extinction of Pleistocene animals? Hibben writes:

Their bones lie bleaching on the sands of Florida and in the gravels of New Jersey. They weather out of the dry terraces of Texas and protrude from the sticky ooze of the tar pits of Wilshire Boulevard in Los Angeles. Thousands of these remains have been encountered in Mexico and even in South America. It might at first appear that many of these great animals died natural deaths. . . . However . . . whole herds of animals were apparently

killed together, overcome by some common power.

Everywhere Hibben looked, he was appalled by evidence of universal death and destruction. The evidences of violence were, he wrote:

. . . as obvious as in the horror camps of Germany. Such piles of bodies of animals or men simply do not occur by any ordinary means.

As Dr. Einstein commented in Chapter Ten: "At each point on the earth's surface that has been carefully studied, many climatic changes have taken place, apparently quite suddenly." Hibben soon found more disturbing evidence. In the Alaskan and Siberian grave pits he discovered interspersed between the bones and the mammoth tusks, volcanic ash of such magnitude that it compelled him to write that the end of the Pleistocene had been accompanied by "earthshaking volcanic eruptions of catastrophic violence."

While it's true that toxic clouds of volcanic gas could have killed whole herds of animals or groups of humans in their tracks or by covering them with volcanic ash, causing death by heat or suffocation or by molten lava *floods* as much as a mile deep covering hundreds of thousands of square miles (see *The Path of the Pole*, p. 227) or by massive earthquakes resulting from the eruptions, Hibben had found an additional agent of death at work. He had discovered evidence for atmospheric disturbances of unparalleled violence in which mammoths, which weighed two tons, and bisons were plucked from the ground, torn and twisted apart as though by a cosmic hand in universal rage, and scattered over the landscape like confetti. He found no evidence on the *corpus delicti* of the deceased of a knife or cutting instrument having been used. He wrote:

The animals were simply torn apart. . . .

And then the animals, the humans, and the green plants were *frozen.* . . . (See pages 3 and 311–313 in this book). In South America we see the upheaval of half a continent in which the death of millions more of our ancient brethren resulted from extensive volcanic eruptions, earthquakes, vast floods, and atmospheric disturbances. What emerges is a picture of quick extinction as the earth's crust shifted. The only reason mankind, too, did not become extinct was because it was widely dispersed around the planet. After the major shifting halted, survivors, those not driven mad by three days of ear-splitting, continuous noise, terrifying thumps, and tremendous shaking as the earth rolled to and fro, came out of their hiding places exhausted from lack of sleep and thirsty, to find their world ripped asunder, their food supply gone, which eventually bred cannibalism, "and man fled from his own kind."

Is it any wonder, then, that Graham Hancock writes in his best-selling book, *Fingerprints of the Gods*:

> As we have seen, this testimony appears to be trying to tell us that a hideous calamity has indeed descended upon mankind from time to time, that on each occasion it has afflicted us suddenly, without warning and without mercy, like a thief in the night, and that it will certainly recur at some point in the future, obliging us—unless we are well prepared—to begin again like orphaned children in complete ignorance of our true heritage.

I recalled that Plato, in his *Timaeus*, describes Solon's visit to ancient Egypt. Solon is given an account of what, let us hope, we don't see on the night of 5/5/2000. Solon was given a description of the heavens, as viewed from the earth, during a shifting of its crust (see pages 36 and 50–51). I also remembered the writings in the Papyrus Ipuwer:

> The sky is in confusion . . . Earth turned upside down . . . The residence is over-turned in a minute . . . The towns are destroyed . . . Upper Egypt has become waste . . . All is ruin . . . Blood is every-where . . . Human beings thirst after water . . . Egyptians dug round about the river for water to drink . . . No fruits nor herbs are found . . . Trees are destroyed. Grain has perished on every side . . . Men flee . . . Hunger. . . .

Any written astronomical records seem to have been lost during these exciting years since the last Ice Age. The only way we know that the ancients had an enormous body of astronomical data is because we find that astronomical data as part of those ponderous buildings that have survived from very ancient times. In the case of the Great Pyramid, that astronomical data is now being "read" (see *The Orion Mystery*). Hancock also informs his readers that a German robotics engineer, Rudolf Gantenbrink, in March 1993, was "maneuvering a $250,000 robot up the narrow southern shaft of the Queen's Chamber" and found "a solid limestone door complete with metal fittings" some 200 feet up this small shaft.

Gantenbrink and his team of engineers had planned to open that door with another high-tech robot later that year, but then something happened. Millions of people have seen Gantenbrink's robot, *Upuaut*, on television; they saw it maneuvering up the shaft and they saw the door with its metal fittings. Everyone wondered what Gantenbrink and his team would find behind that door when they returned to open it. The "something" that happened was that Egyptologists with the Egyptian Antiquities Organization in Cairo stopped Gantenbrink and his team from opening that door or gate or check valve in 1993. That was almost four years ago! What could be behind it? Why have Egyptologists gypped us from knowing? If Egyptologists ever do open that door and show the opening on television, one may wonder if the opening shown is actually its *first* opening. There has already been sufficient time for the door to have been opened, objects removed or inserted, and the door closed.

This chamber is where the "Dixon relics" were found in 1872. The relics Bauval and Gilbert had searched for. The relics that caused them to wonder "why no Egyptologist had thought it important to inform us of." The relics that Egyptologists at the British Museum had

13. Causeway to the pyramid of Kephren.

From *Secrets of the Great Pyramid*, copyright 1971 by Peter Tompkins. Used by permission.

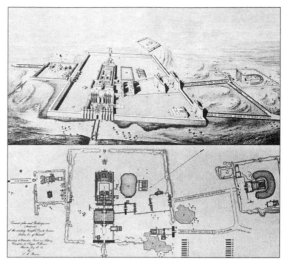

14. Reconstruction of the temple compound at Karnak, showing the variation in axis of different buildings and colonnades.

From *Secrets of the Great Pyramid*, copyright 1971 by Peter Tompkins. Used by permission.

disavowed any knowledge of. The relics that they had telephoned the world authority on pyramids [sic], Dr. I.E.S. Edwards, about, who also had disavowed any knowledge of them. The relics that were donated to the Egyptian Antiquities Department in 1972. The relics that Bauval and Hancock in their own new book, *The Message of the Sphinx*, found had been signed for "in the meticulous hand of the Keeper himself—Dr. I.E.S. Edwards."

"For," as news personality Paul Harvey says, "the rest of the story," see *The Orion Mystery, Fingerprints of the Gods, The Message of the Sphinx*, and Peter Tompkins's comments on a similar incident of men being caught *in flagrante*, on pages 64–65 of this book. Perhaps this scandal is why Dr. Edwards, whose theories, taught to our children as fact, admitted on a recent television documentary entitled *The Great Pyramid*, aired on the Arts and Entertainment network, that "pyramids in general are not very popular with Egyptologists because I think they're too pitiful."

Let us, then, in light of the above, separate our thinking from orthodox Egyptological thinking, forever stuck in time to the mummy like Joel Chandler Harris's Br'er Bear stuck to the Tar Baby, and return to the other documentary *Enter Darkness: Enter Light*. The second architect interviewed in this documentary is James M. Hagan (see Plate 3:2, pages 113–14 and Appendix C). He, like Wilfred Gregson, finds nothing "pitiful" about the Great Pyramid's construction. When asked to account why the old slave-ramp-roller theories, little more than an exercise in sophistry, are still pushed by Egyptologists, he replied, "Information management," then adds it's a "Nilegate scandal." Commenting on the structure, Hagan states: "My theory is that it is a machine. It has none of the items that you would find in what we call a building. It has those things that you find in a machine, like a battery or an engine."

Could the vanished engineers who built the Great Pyramid have used an engine, located nearly in the exact center of their building, offset by 286.1 inches, to *build* their astronomical observatory, still the largest observatory on earth? Was it a chemical engine? Kunkel states: "It is the chemistry of fire consuming the oxygen that does the job." Is that why Carver, a *chemist* who understood the *conversion of gases*, wrote: "Your drawings make it quite clear as to how it could be done." And Carver ends his letter: "You do indeed have something new."

Hancock, in *Fingerprints of the Gods*, takes his readers with him as he visits ancient and mysterious construction sites around the world. In that book he uses words like *ancient, water, interlocking polygonal blocks, walls that taper upwards, zig-zagging stone canals, served to sluice water, a moat that the entire site, plumbing, hydraulic system, basalt-lined troughs, reflecting pools, a series of locks, vast hydraulic system, construction of capacitors, thermal and electric insulator, drainage system, rock pipes, whirlpool, machine-age standards of precision, downward step, salty emanation, canals, with flood gates and regulators, Strabo's well, well shaft* [in center of Great Pyramid], *builders had done* nothing *by chance. . . .* Hancock's wonderful words bring Plate 7:4 to life.

I reread Dr. J. C. McCoan's description of his excursion to the Great Pyramid in 1882, to see through his eyes what the site looked like 114 years ago (also shown on page 236):

The excursion to the Pyramids, which was once almost formidable from the inconvenience of crossing the Nile by a ferry and then riding on donkey-back for seven or eight miles along a tortuous track, broken at frequent intervals by *ruinous* canals [emphasis added] or patches of submerged ground, is now a pleasant carriage drive of an hour and a half over the fine iron bridge from Kasren-Nil to Ghizeh.

Herodotus wrote in 440 B.C., 2,322 years before Dr. McCoan did so, a description of his excursion to the Great Pyramid. I wanted to see through the eyes of Herodotus the physical condition of the "ruinous canals" seen by Dr. McCoan.

It [the 2nd largest pyramid] has no subterraneous apartments, nor any canal from the Nile to supply it with water as the other pyramid [the Great Pyramid] has. [See Plate 7:4.]

Herodotus wrote that the Great Pyramid was built "on a sort of island . . ." The word *island* is as clear today as when Herodotus used it. Kunkel writes that during the Great Pyramid's construction, the entire building site was surrounded by water, contained by a moat encircling the construction site.

Herodotus wrote that the water "was introduced from the Nile by a canal."

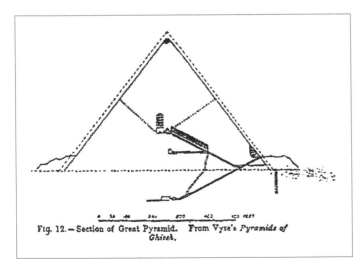

Fig. 12.—Section of Great Pyramid. From Vyse's *Pyramids of Ghizeh.*

15. Section of Great Pyramid from Vyse's *Pyramids of Gizeh*, 1839, showing well in front of entrance.

16. Colonel (afterward General) Howard Vyse in 1830.
From *Secrets of the Great Pyramid*, copyright 1971 by Peter Tompkins. Used by permission.

When the construction specialists arrived to build the Great Pyramid, a large rocky plateau stood before them. This plateau sits at the center of the earth's land masses. A thirteen-and-a-half acre building site was leveled, leaving a hill of bedrock at the center of the site, atop the plateau. Sightings were made by ancient astronomers, and an angle was established to drill the Great Pyramid's lower diagonal. At the same time, another shaft was cut down through the rock hill left at the center of the construction site. When the two met, this resulted in the formation of a bastard U tube. The junction can be defined as a lateral connection. This was done, Kunkel wrote, so that water could be brought to the center of the building site and used as the lifting medium. Canals were built from the Nile to the construction site as tons of water would be utilized to build this ancient observatory.

How could a pump be used to a build a pyramid?

Kunkel explains:

"Let us imagine the Great Pyramid in the process of construction, say to a height of 275 feet. Here is the working level. At this level a shallow pool is formed. Water is supplied to it by two fountains, one on the north side of the pool and the other on the south side.

"On the northern face of the building is a series of locks, which ascend in a zigzag pattern, back and forth up to the pool. As the pumped water flows down through these locks, stone-laden barges are floated up through them, and then into the pool. Here they are unloaded somewhat in the same manner that the door was hung in the Temple of Karnak, that is, by letting the water out of the pool so that the barges sink and leave their cargoes high and dry on a special type of dock. From this dock they could be taken by a special type of setting barge and be placed in position. Thus, by raising and lowering the water level in the pool, the blocks can be picked up, moved, and set with remarkable ease. By using water and barges, varying the sizes of the locks, weight is rendered irrelevant."

On the northern face, to this day, can be traced "the remains of an old carriage road,"

which was filled in with small stones and "debris" as the pyramid neared completion. The logical conclusion, then, is that as the pyramid neared completion, the Egyptians could not use the locks anymore, and thus were forced to fill these cavities by hand (see plate 7:4).

In 1962, when Kunkel could afford to, he self-published an eighty-four-page book on his research. Kunkel mailed his book to research institutes, colleges, universities, and senior Egyptologists in New York, London, and Cairo. Kunkel wrote in his autobiography, *One Bright Day:*

One of the world's most famous Egyptologists who has written books on the subject of ancient Egypt, and who also was a believer in the ramp theory of construction, replied to a letter I had written to him on this subject that his commitments "did not permit him to go into this subject at this time"! It always seemed odd

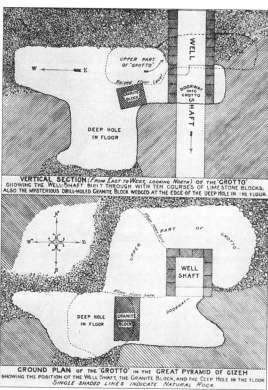

17. From *Secrets of the Great Pyramid,* copyright 1971 by Peter Tompkins. Used by permission.

18. Lower end of the well shaft.

From *Secrets of the Great Pyramid* copyright 1971 by Peter Tompkins. Used by permission.

19. Grotto showing walls of the well shaft built out of masonry from the level of the grotto to the first course of masonry of the pyramid.

From *Secrets of the Great Pyramid* ©1971 by Peter Tompkins. Used by permission.

20. Kunkel, left, in front of North Face of Great Pyramid.

21. Kunkel, left, at Sphinx.

to me that a person . . . could not spare a few fleeting moments to examine a subject such as this, when from a moral and ethical standpoint, he was obliged to do so.

Egyptologists who did flip through Kunkel's book dismissed it as the work of a crank. I remembered Mark Twain's definition of a crank: A person with a new idea is a crank until the idea succeeds. Kunkel said that water was brought "to" the Great Pyramid by "underground canals" and that a "well" in front of the Great Pyramid supplied water to the lower diagonal and Egyptologists laughed at Kunkel's missing parts. Kunkel said that there were "tunnels" under the Sphinx and they laughed even harder. I went looking for the missing parts. In Vyse's book, *Operations Carried Out at the Pyramids of Gizeh,* I found a 159-year-old drawing that shows this *well* right where Kunkel said it would be. Today this well has been plastered over.

In 1991, the West/Schoch team of American scientists, educated in the disciplines of geology and geophysics and armed with sensitive space-age electronic equipment that can detect underground rooms, tunnels, and objects in underground rooms, arrived in Egypt. The team had written permission from the president of the Egyptian Antiquities Organization to do geological research on the Giza plateau; however, when Dr. Zahi Hawass, an Egyptologist with the Egyptian Antiquities Organization in charge of the Giza plateau, found out they had arrived, he sprang into action to revoke their permission. Five days passed before their permission was revoked, but during those five days the American team had discovered the great age of the Sphinx, an underground room with stuff in it, and two *tunnels under the Sphinx.* One tunnel runs up and one tunnel runs down, kind of like a pump.

In his book, Kunkel also shows how butterfly valves were used to control the flow of water that lifted the blocks used to build the Great Pyramid. A butterfly valve is a stone with a hole drilled through it, or, as Kunkel says:

A door with an axis in the middle. It is opened and closed by turning the axis with a handle. Butter-fly valves are the easiest of all valves to open and close.

I had found a 159-year-old drawing of the well in front of the Great Pyramid, which is now paved over for parking. In their quest for Edgar Cayce's "hall of records," the Egyptologists Dr. Zahi Hawass and Dr. Mark Lehner, who compiled and edited Edgar Cayce's Egyptian "readings," had found a wizened old man who had been a guide at the Sphinx for a long time. In 1980 he showed Hawass and Lehner a secret passageway under the Sphinx, where one tunnel runs up and the other runs down, as Kunkel wrote. But where could I find an ancient butterfly valve thousands and thousands of years old with so much already smashed and dynamited to bits inside the Great Pyramid? The odds against finding even a fragment of one that could be shown to be contemporaneous with the Great Pyramid's construction seemed wildly implausible. Then I remembered something the architect Wilfred J. Gregson had taught me.

I began to follow the flow of water down the Great Pyramid's lower diagonal, made square because water will flow faster with less friction through a square tube than that of any other shape. I saw the water, momentarily stopped, by the heavy granite-hinged check valve, fourteen feet below ground, but, as the weight of the backed-up water increased, the downward pull of gravity caused the check valve to swing open, releasing a measured amount of water into the subterranean pit. In this way, water rose in the subterranean pit, trapping air against its ceiling. Water seeks its own level. As more water was introduced in this manner, water rose up the well shaft toward the center of the construction site. As the water rose up to a level equal to the height it had come from, I found not a fragment of a smashed butterfly valve, but a completely undamaged one!

I jumped on the phone and called Peter Tompkins, because I had found in his book *Secrets of the Great Pyramid,* among its 350 illustrations from the most disparate medieval, Renaissance, Romantic, and modern sources, from the four hundred engravers of Napoleon's twenty-volume *Description de l'Egypte* to the most recent archeological journals at the time his book was published, an old drawing of a butterfly valve wedged at the edge of a deep hole in the floor of the "grotto" below the intake of the Grand Gallery (see Illustration 17). Tompkins's book has the first photographs of the inside of the Great Pyramid, taken by Professor Piazzi Smyth in 1865. From the grotto upward, the walls of the well shaft are lined and built with blocks of limestone. Smyth wrote in his *Our Inheritance in the Great Pyramid*, "Had not Pliny duly written that there was a *water-well* in the Great Pyramid, 80 cubits deep [Smyth's italics]"? And, he writes, this would be "at or just inside the lower end of the gallery, and in, or beneath,

the floor thereof, a more extensive trap-door, which concealed the access to the Queen's Chamber and the horizontal passage leading to it."

Secrets, secrets, and more secrets surround this ancient building. Perhaps we should just go ahead and change its name from the Great Pyramid to the Great Secret. On July 27, 1996, I interviewed Professor Robert M. Schoch to see if, after all this time, the Egyptologist Dr. Zahi Hawass, now director-general of the Giza pyramids, might have changed his mind. I thought it would be professional courtesy for one academician to assist another academician. Professor Schoch told me that he and his team of American scientists were still prohibited from doing any more geological research on the Giza

---

HYDRAULIC RAM PUMPS

EDWARD J. KUNKEL

295 WEST MARKET STREET   WARREN, OHIO
Telephone EXpress 3-3487

October, 1977

[handwritten note:] Dear Richard: We sent 15 books to various profs at Universities in Tokyo and regret I have not heard from one. That they are studying or giving guess that they are studying me. In haste sincerely Edward J Kunkel

N. Hozumi
Professor of Architectural Planning
Waseda University
Shinjuku-Ku, Tokyo 160

Dear Sir:

I recently read with interest of Waseda University's planned Pyramid-Building Project. It was very exciting to me since I have spent 45 of my 80 years developing my own theory on How the Pyramids were built.

I claim that the Egyptians were past-masters of the complicated science of Hydraulics! The inside structure of tunnels and chambers was the Actual Machine that "Built" the pyramid; not a burial tomb for kings.

Stone blocks were quarried, loaded, shipped to the site, raised by a series of locks and set into place with a Bare Minimum of Human Labor. The Egyptians used water, atmospheric pressure and the laws of nature as their "Working Force."

I have enclosed *[handwritten: mailed]* a copy of my book, Pharaoh's Pump, which I hope you will read and study. After much thought, it is my hope that you will come to the same conclusion that the famous American Scientist, Dr. George Washington Carver, reached. He wrote in a letter that appears in the Book: "...Your Explanation, I believe, is the Solution to one of the Greatest Mysteries of the Ages..."

Enclosed is also a list of people to whom this letter and book are being sent, as well as a post card. Please fill out the postcard and return at your earliest convenience. Thank you very much.

Sincerely,

Edward J Kunkel
Edward J. Kunkel
Author: Pharaoh's Pump

50-VI-33

HYDRAULIC RAM PUMP — SIC 3561:
Patented (C1. 103-77)

This ram pump is for handling large volumes of water. Two connected diagonal tubes have air compression chambers at the bottom of each. Two diagonal water columns are balanced by the air cushion in the lower chamber. A vacuum release upsets this balance, which actuates a downward flow in both diagonals. The lower diagonal is the intake, the upper the discharge. Gravity pumps the water. Since little vacuum is required to cause this balance upset, operating costs are low. After installation, compressed air forces water from the lower chamber into the upper part, making it vacuum tight and ready for operation. Claims the simple valves are not damaged by silt or aquatic life.

U.S. Patent 2,887,956

Cheap water for Irrigation, Rice culture, Steel Mills, Blast Furnaces, Paper Mills,

New Source of Power. New Economic Use of Fire.

22.

plateau. I asked Professor Schoch if he had asked permission to examine the tunnels under the Sphinx. He said yes, but had not been allowed to. In Hancock and Bauval's book, *The Message of the Sphinx*, Rudolf Gantenbrink and his team of engineers had not been allowed, after spending $250,000 of his own money, to return and have the honor of opening the door. The authors write: "Our informant also said that he had been invited by 'Zahi' to be amongst the select group of witnesses present inside the Pyramid when this moment comes. . . ."

I read that in 1986 the same fate befell two French architects, Gilles Dormion and Jean Patrice Goidin, and in 1988, Professor Sakuji Yoshimura and his team of scientists from Waseda University in Japan (see Chapter Seven, footnotes 1 and 2 in *The Message of the Sphinx*). I knew Professor Yoshimura's name so well that it leaped from the page at me. Hancock and Bauval write that Professor Yoshimura and his team of scientists had, with high-tech equipment, detected a "cavity," like the French architects, behind the northwest wall of the Queen's Chamber and never returned to complete their work there. I would

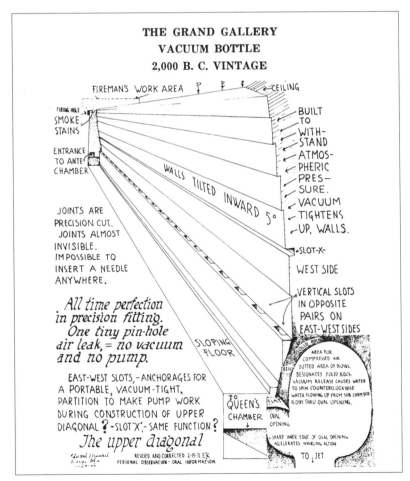

23. A partition made of short slabs may have been installed in slot X, forming two diagonals, the lower one for water, and the upper one for air. This pump uses plenty of air. A down flow activated a valve mechanism, which diverted water to the Queen's Chamber.

From *Pharaoh's Pump* copyright © 1962 by Edward J. Kunkel. Used by permission.

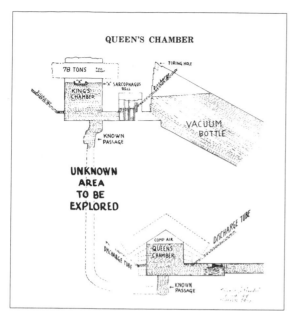

QUEEN'S CHAMBER

24. Guides say smoke will pass upward from the Queen's Chamber through an "unknown area to be explored" to the King's Chamber, indicating this area is filled with loose rock.

It is a good bet that Al Mamoon's wrecking crew filled it with broken slabs, broken valve parts, round granite shafts, and parts of a float mechanism.

Note the location of the firing hole in relation to the ceiling of the King's Chamber. A water level near the firing hole will fill the King's Chamber.

The interior of the Great Pyramid is perhaps the strangest ever built by man. It consists of two diagonal tubes, one below the ground cut in the solid limestone, and the other above the ground made of ponderous masonry. Each diagonal has an air compression chamber at the bottom of it. The lower chamber in the solid rock is a cavernous room of very unusual shape, while the upper chamber, the Queen's Chamber, is made of enormous slabs. The blocks that compose the north and south walls are wedge-shaped, with the thickest part of the wedge to the inside. "It has a pointed roof of great blocks of stone, inclined upwards and meeting in the middle." (*Encyclopaedia Britannica*, 9th ed.). This chamber is designed to withstand pressure from within. Inside pressure will tighten up the wedge-shaped blocks that compose the walls.

From *Pharaoh's Pump* copyright © 1962 by Edward J. Kunkel. Used by permission.

suggest that perhaps in this case Professor Yoshimura's fact-finding journey to the Giza plateau had been accomplished, much to the delight of Professors T. Kawase and E. Ota, in the fluid engineering department of Waseda University.

I am looking at a letter Kunkel sent to sixteen professors, including Yoshimura, Kawase, and Ota, at Waseda University in October 1977 along with copies of his book. After forty years of trying to interest American engineers and scientists, he spoke to Japanese engineers, who are practical and very clever people, about using his pump for irrigation, rice culture, steel mills, blast furnaces, and paper mills. This "cavity" is the same "cavity" looked at by Dr. Lambert T. Dolphin and the SRI team, and it is the same "cavity" that appears on page 47 of Kunkel's book published in 1962, and it is the same "cavity" that is shown on Kunkel's 1949 patent drawings! Maybe people were starting to listen to him. Maybe, somewhere in Japan, rice is being irrigated by a strange-looking pump of very ancient design. If so, I know Ed Kunkel would be happy.

Kunkel wanted no child to go to bed hungry. How many times he explained to me how this ancient pump worked before I understood, I can't say. Ah, but once I did. I, too, saw how this ancient knowledge could transform deserts into irrigated fields groaning with produce to feed the world. Someone would have to tell Kunkel's story. I remembered a statement made in the film *Enter Darkness: Enter Light* by Dr. Jean Houston: "If not now when, if not you who?"

When King Tut's grave was discovered in Egypt, members of the world press were invited to report on its opening. If the discovery of tunnels under the Sphinx, made in 1980 by Dr. Zahi Hawass and Professor Mark Lehner, had been made public in 1980, I could have told Kunkel's story much earlier. The tunnels looked the same, if not identical, to me, as the well shaft inside the Great Pyramid when I saw them in 1988. The corners of the shafts are rounded, as in the well shaft in the Great Pyramid, with cuttings for hand- and foot-holds. Why Professor Schoch was not extended a bit of professional courtesy and allowed to see these shafts is all part of "information management" in what the architect James M. Hagan has termed a "Nilegate" scandal. The reason the well shaft in the Great Pyramid follows such a tortuous track up to the Great Pyramid's Grand Gallery is so that Bernoulli's theorem of fluid dynamics would take place in this shaft (see *Pharaoh's Pump*, page 30). In 1914 P.D. Ouspensky, author of *A New Model of the Universe* (see pages 147–48 and 166–67 in this book), visited the Giza plateau. He described the Grand Gallery:

> This corridor is the key to the whole pyramid. What strikes you first is that everything in this corridor is of very exact and fine workmanship. The lines are straight, the angles are correct. At the same time there is no doubt that this corridor was not made for walking along. Then for what was it made? And suddenly it becomes clear to you that up and down this "corridor," some kind of stone or metal plate must have moved. . . .

Hancock wrote in *Fingerprints of the Gods* that when he was inside the Grand Gallery he felt as if he were inside an enormous instrument and the feeling "was of intense and overwhelming *compression*."

Bauval and Gilbert wrote in *The Orion Mystery* that:

> There is a quasi-inhuman quality about the Grand Gallery that is hard to explain, as though it were not intended for people to walk up and down but to serve some other specialized or specific function. Many have remarked that the Grand Gallery looks like part of a machine whose function is beyond us.

The Grand Gallery is *a part* of a very ancient machine, an ancient machine that allowed ancient architects to design square, rectangular, or pyramidal structures to be built of ponderous stone blocks providing there was water near the construction site or if water could be conveyed to the site in canals, like those

THE SPHINX

FACT:
Sphinx built first.
W = Pools of water on photo.

25. "Fifty years ago," said a guide, "flood waters rose within a foot of the paws of the Sphinx."

The body, exposed to the hot summer sun, attains a high temperature. I have long believed it to be hollow. If cold water is introduced into the hot body, the expansion of both air and water would be tremendous.

The Sphinx has had a face-lifting job, also some body work. It is being covered with square buff-colored tiles. The top of the head is about level with the pavement of the pyramid.

canals seen near monolithic buildings in Mexico, South America, the Pacific, and Egypt.

To understand better the mechanics of what took place in the Grand Gallery, I highly recommend the reader try Kunkel's example of water in a pan with a burning candle, and watching, as a wide-mouthed glass jug is put over the candle, the movement of water as it is sucked seeming effortlessly upward into the jug. Now, if you change your *fuel* to newsprint made of wood pulp (which I did by sticking a small wadded-up ball of newspaper atop the unlit candle) and light the ball and place the jug over this *fuel*, you will see a dramatic increase in the volume of water sucked upward into the jug. In July 1765 Nathaniel Davison discovered a short shaft at the top of the Grand Gallery that led to the chamber over the King's Chamber. Kunkel calls this chamber the "firing hole."

Kunkel demonstrates that the ancient builders constructed the Grand Gallery "to withstand pressure from without, that is, atmospheric pressure." He writes that when a wood fire was lit in the "firing hole" at the top of the Grand Gallery, the granite slabs in the antechamber were lowered, and the burning wood created a *vacuum* in the Grand Gallery

that caused water in the well shaft to *move* upward! He explains:

> It is MOTION that makes this pump work. Water is sucked up, and dropped—Sucked up, and dropped—Sucked up and dropped—at will.

This machine (a pump is a machine) must have water; it needs water, it feeds on water, tons of water utilized to raise and lower the water level in the work pools. When the water was in motion in this system, the Great Pyramid's lower diagonal held more than 80 tons of water, the upper diagonal 300 tons, and the pump, when full, held about 600 tons of water, a very powerful lifting force. Kunkel wrote that water was brought from the Nile "to" the construction site by underground canals. Egyptologists ridiculed him.

On October 28, 1995, the Associated Press ran a story about the discovery of an underground canal in front of the Sphinx. Zahi Hawass of the Egyptian Antiquities Authority informed the press that the canal had been found accidentally. When reporters arrived at the site, over 149 feet of this underground canal had been excavated by pickax and shovel. The

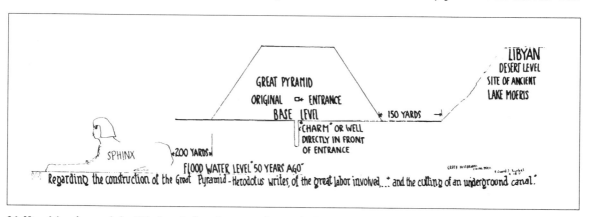

26. King Men dammed the Nile long before the pyramids were built. The backed-up water flowed through the Hawara Gap and formed Lake Moeris. Geologists have traced its ancient beaches. The elevation of Lake Moeris, being higher than the pavement of the pyramid, could have supplied the pump with water by gravity, water coming up through the charm, which is situated directly in front of the intake.

As late as A.D. 1250, a governor of this lake area complained that the lake was disappearing, and that it covered an area of only 80 square miles (*Encyclopaedia Britannica*, 9th ed.).

"When it runs outward it returns a talent of silver daily to the royal treasury from the fish that are taken, but when the current is the other way, the return sinks to one third that sum." (*Herodotus, Book II*).

From *Pharaoh's Pump* copyright © 1962 by Edward J. Kunkel. Used by permission.

article states that the canal's walls are lined with limestone and, judging from the AP photograph, looks to be about eight feet wide and four feet tall. A canal that size would be capable of transporting a huge amount of water from the Nile to the construction site. Hawass, however, tells reporters that this canal was "probably" used to carry water from the Nile to wash the dead body of the Pharaoh Chephren. This Chephren must have been one hell of a big fellow if that much water was required to wash his body. I wondered if this underground canal might have fed water into the thirty-by-forty-foot chamber below the paws of the Sphinx, discovered in 1991 by the West/Schoch team before Hawass canceled their permit, forcing them to leave. I believe Hawass was worried that the sensitive electronic equipment the American scientists had brought with them would detect the vast labyrinth under the Giza plateau that he and Dr. Mark Lehner had gained access to sometime around 1980.

The AP story also states that a tunnel had also been discovered which runs under the Valley Temple. Excavators also found small holes and a basin in front of the Valley Temple. The article states that Egyptologists have theorized that canals may have been used in a mummy burial ritual, then quotes Hawass as saying this canal "is the first physical evidence for the theory," forgetting to mention what he and Lehner have been finding *under* the Giza plateau during the past fifteen years.

Kunkel wrote that the Sphinx was a smaller pump that pumped water, brought from the Nile, underground to the well in front of the Great Pyramid. He wrote: "Consistent hydraulic engineering practice demands two pumps. One below to pump it up from the catch basin, and the other to pump it up the pyramid. . . . Considering the Sphinx as a functional mechanical unit, the logical conclusion is that it was built first for a functional purpose." This would explain why Perring found so much "Nile

27. Herodotus speaks of a palace complex of 3,500 chambers half above and half below ground at Moeris. The Egyptians called it "the temple at the entrance to the lake." Herodotus called it a "labyrinth," and considered that it outranked the pyramids as a wonder.

From *Secrets of the Great Pyramids* copyright 1971 by Peter Tompkins. Used by permission.

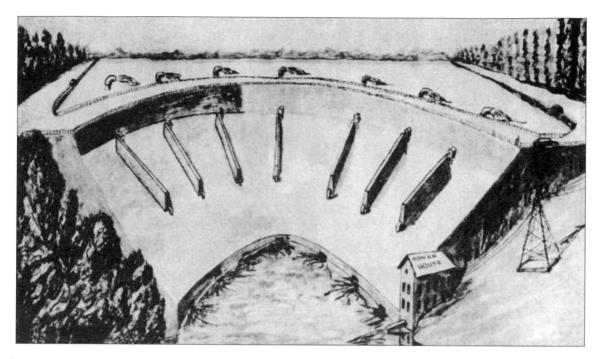

28. Power for all. Flat, inland cities may have cheap power and heat. Northern countries may have greatest benefits. The little shed is control station. In actual practice, the long, narrow tanks would be embedded in the concrete.

The drawing shown above was suggested by the late Robert Lee Spencer, dean of the School of Engineering of the University of Delaware. (May 2, 1933).

He said, "Engineers feed on new ideas. Give them a new idea, and they will equip it with so many gadgets, that even YOU will not know what they are for. They will develop an automatic ignition system, special fuels, use inert gases, and all sorts of pressure and vacuum gauges. Tubes could be made big enough to run a boxcar through, with everything else in proportion—enough power to throw a stream over the top. A bushel of wood should operate it for a day." Thanks, Dean Spencer.

From *Pharaoh's Pump* copyright © 1962 by Edward J. Kunkel. Used by permission.

Earth" in the lime mortar of the Great Pyramid. Kunkel writes: "Nile earth adds nothing to structural strength of mortar, but rather does it weaken it. For this reason, I believe that it was not mixed with the mortar, but rather, it was forced in during pumping operations. . . ."

Kunkel writes quite a bit about the Sphinx, including the rear of the Sphinx. The last time I saw the rear end of the Sphinx, about ten minutes ago, Lehner was going through a hole in it. This was on a videotape entitled *Mysteries of the Pyramids . . . Live* and hosted by Omar Sharif. This two-hour show was originally broadcast on television in 1988 and later the videotape was sold. On this tape we see Lehner as he climbs to the top of one shaft inside the Sphinx and then we see him climb a little way down another shaft. Then the camera cuts to Sharif and Hawass talking outside the Sphinx. This is odd. I had read on page 99 of Hancock and Bauval's book *The Message of the Sphinx* that in December 1995 Hawass was interviewed for a possible television documentary about the Sphinx and is quoted telling the interviewer that this tunnel has never been opened before!

The 1988 production states that Lehner and Hawass were shown this tunnel in 1980. Sharif asks Hawass if such a thing as reincarnation exists, and who did Hawass think he was in a previous lifetime? Without batting an eye, the director-general of the Giza pyramids for the Egyptian Antiquities Authority replied: "Cheops." This may help explain why Hawass restricts access to scientists like Professor

Schoch. Cheops is Greek for Khufu, and every Egyptologist will tell you that Khufu built the Great Pyramid and that the mummy of Khufu has never been found. Since the mummy of Khufu has never been found and every Egyptologist would be thrilled to discover it, can we assume, then, that Hawass is searching for his own mummified body from a previous lifetime? I supposed that would give him a little extra incentive.

The show does not mention Kunkel's book by name, but Sharif does mention Kunkel's theory of construction when he says "hydraulic pump." I wondered if Lehner and Hawass had read one of Kunkel's books that he had mailed to the Egyptian Antiquities Organization in 1977. Sharif talks about an ancient and secret hall of records, Atlantis, pyramid power, and it's mentioned that the viewer will see an ancient *water tunnel* under the Giza plateau. The only missing piece to Kunkel's pump is a shaft or tunnel that would bring water to the well in front of the Great Pyramid's entrance, and again I wondered why Professor Schoch was not allowed to go down the shafts inside the Sphinx. Do the shafts go down to a tunnel that runs to the hundred-foot-deep well in front of the Great Pyramid? Why all this secretiveness? Why can't the world press see and film this vast complex under the Giza plateau? Lehner and Hawass have had it all to themselves for sixteen years. What are they doing down there?

Lehner comes on camera and is asked by Sharif how the pyramids were built. Lehner drags out the timeworn ramp theory, both single and spiral. I don't know anybody who believes that story anymore. He says they measured with string, which the architect Gregson (in Chapter Five in this volume) shows to be ludicrous. He picks up a wooden mallet and says the Great Pyramid was built with wooden hammers and cooper chisels because they had no metal but copper. Then Lehner says something chilling. He tells Sharif that his good friend Hawass and the Egyptian authorities are looking at a plan to make the Giza plateau into some kind of national park which would restrict access to the area! What have they found under that plateau?

I had a telephone call last year about a small mummy being found in Giza's underground complex. The caller said a U.S. military team had flown to Cairo to perform an autopsy on the body because the body was that of a "human-looking" alien. I didn't believe the story then, and I don't now. And yet . . . if an Egyptologist who believes he's Khufu has the power to keep highly respected scientists away from perhaps the most important archeological site on earth, and if plans are under way, as Lehner says on the video, to further restrict access to the entire plateau, one must wonder why.

Throughout history, almost every new breakthrough in our understanding of this ancient building has been made by mavericks who, in their own time, were ridiculed. I present here in this short epilogue only a faint glimpse of Kunkel's thirty years of research. I am working to see that Kunkel's work, more an instruction manual than a book, is reprinted and made available especially to those fellow investigators of the Great Pyramid, which continues to spew out data as fast as we can assimilate it and understand it, even when the information does not seem to fit neatly into our present understanding of it. I harbor no ill will against Dr. Hawass or Professor Lehner; point in fact, they are perhaps in a better position to see that the remarkable data discovered by Kunkel is put into use. With this hydraulic principle Hawass and Lehner have in their hands the knowledge to push back the advancing sands of the Sahara Desert, and by irrigating the land they can attract rain, and by attracting rain clouds they can change the climate over Egypt and make Egypt once again the breadbasket of the world. And for that, history will remember them as heroes.

Now, as we are inexorably moving closer to May 5, 2000, a virtual flood of new and amazing discoveries collaborating the existence of this pre-Egyptian empire are now erupting from scholars around the world. It is as if we are on some ancient astronomical timetable, prepared millennia ago, whereby here, at the eleventh hour, something incredible about our past is about to be revealed to us.

From a book by G.P. Flannigan the following
measurements are given for the great pyramid.

Table 1

i.   Original height (5,813")

ii.   Base measurement one face (9,131")

iii.   Edge, face, corner to apex (8,684")

iv.   Apothem center of base of face and to apex (7,387")

v.   Apex interfocial angle (76° 17' 32")

vi.   Edge to ground level (41° 59' 50")

vii.   Dihedral angle face to face edge (106° 54' _?_)

viii.   Apex edge to edge (96° _?_ _?_)

ix.   Circuit of base (36,524.24")

At this point it is well to note that the inch that is used may or may not be the pyramid inch, and there was ambiguity on this point in reading the text. In addition to this it is well to note that a number of significant figures and stated accuracies are not in keeping with accepted scientific format. The angular measurements are especially poor. As an exercise:

Since there are 2.54 cm /in and 10^{-2} m /cm

$\therefore$ (2.54 cm/in) $(10^{-2}$ m/cm$)$ = 2.54 x 10^{-2} m/in

and as a length conversion one has for some lengths on page

___56 ___:

i.	5,813"	$(2.54 \times 10^{-2}$ m/in)	(i") = 1.477×10^2m
ii.	9,131"	("	) (ii") = 2.319×10^2m
iii.	8,684	("	) (iii") = 2.206×10^2m
ix.	36,524.24"	("	) (ix") = 9.277×10^2m

Starting with the base one has the following given measurement:

$$2.319 \times 10^2 \text{ m}$$

and for the circuit around the base one has the following given measurement:

$$9.277 \times 10^2 \text{ m}$$

yielding an average base measurement of

$$\frac{9.277 \times 10^2 \text{ m}}{4} = 2.319 \times 10^2 \text{ m}$$

As a matter of interest I am going to carry out the given and average measurements to two more decimal places. So one has

$$(2.31927 \times 10^2 \text{ m}) \text{ (ii)}$$

and

$$(9.27716 \times 10^2 \text{ m}) \text{ (ix)}$$

and obtaining an average for (ix) generates

$$2.31929 \times 10^2 \text{ m as opposed to}$$

$$2.31927 \times 10^2 \text{ m as a given for base measurement}$$

If one accepts as a standard, the average of the permiter, then one can calculate a % deviation from this value. Then one can say that the measured side deviates by 2 mm or

$$\frac{2 \times 10^{-3}}{2.31927 \times 10^2} \times 100$$

or $+8.623 \times 10^{-4}$ %

Using another source (Secrets of the Great Pyramid by Peter

364

Tompkins, Appendix 287 by Livio Catullo Stecchini, page 320):

3 values for the Royal cubit:

524.1483 mm

525.0000 mm

526.3231 mm

From page 364 one has measurements for the sides as follows:

Table 2

Side		Est. Error
W	230.357 m	30 mm
N	230.293 m	6 m
E	230.391 m	6 m
S	230.454 m	10 mm 30 mm

It will be assumed that this series of measurements was taken with sufficiently accurate instruments. Let us just assume that these past measurements are completely accurate and take an average, then generating

230.374 m

Now let's calculate some deviations and % from the average.

		%	
W	− 0.017 m	7.38×10^{-3}	
N	− 0.081 m	3.52×10^{-2}	
E	+ 0.017 m	7.38×10^{-3}	
S	+ 0.08− m	3.47×10^{-2}	

(Assuming all positive, then the average deviation is just 4.9×10^{-2} m.)

Let us now take an average of these % of (all positive) deviances, which is

$$2.12 \times 10^{-2} \%$$

This seems to be somewhat of a standard of accuracy for the building or structure. It is well to note that this is just an <u>average</u> % error.

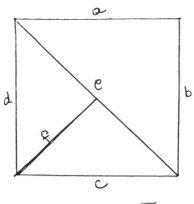

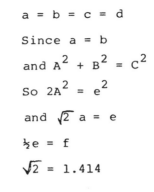

$a = b = c = d$

Since $a = b$

and $A^2 + B^2 = C^2$

So $2A^2 = e^2$

and $\sqrt{2}\, a = e$

$\frac{1}{2}e = f$

$\sqrt{2} = 1.414$

So then $\dfrac{\sqrt{2}}{2}\, a = f$

if $a = 230.374$ m

then $e = 325.798$

then $f = 162.899$

If one takes a coordinate system and imposes this upon a pyramid, then one can generate a means of calculating the volume of this solid.

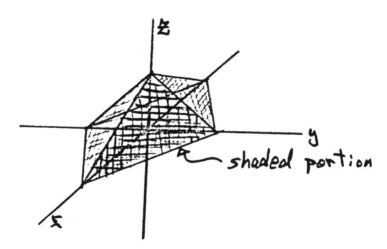

shaded portion

Though this is a poor drawing, one can visualize this and extrapolate from the shaded portion the idea that this really represents $\frac{1}{2}$ the volume of the pyramid.

In view of this, one can redraw the figure as

366

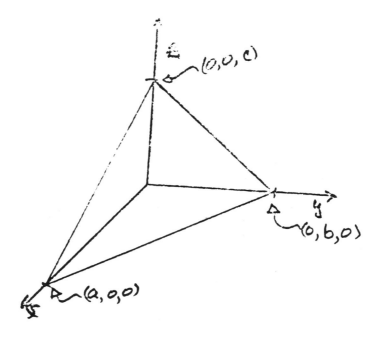

One can view this as a plane intersecting each one of the coordinate axes. It is not hard to extrapolate a slope intercept equation of the form:

$$\frac{z}{c} + \frac{x}{b} + \frac{y}{b} = 1$$ where the plane intersects the axes at x = a, y = b, z = c. For a check assume that z,y = 0 and solve for x = a, and this can be verified by setting the other two = 0 and find y = b, etc.

Once can write the generalized volume of a solid

$$V = \underset{S}{\int \int \int} \, dx \ dy \ dz$$

where S is over the surface of the volume.

as x ranges from 0 to a

    y ranges from 0 to b $(1-\frac{x}{a})$

    z ranges from 0 to c $(1-\frac{x}{a} - \frac{y}{b})$

hence three inequalities

$$0 \le x \le a$$

$$0 \le y \le b \ (1 - \frac{x}{a})$$

$$0 \le z \le c \ (1 - \frac{x}{a} - \frac{y}{b})$$

and one can rewrite the following

$$V = \int_0^a \int_0^{b(1-\frac{x}{a})} \int_0^{c(1-\frac{x}{a} - \frac{y}{b})} dz \ dy \ dx$$

$$V = c \int_0^a \int_0^{b(1-\frac{x}{a})} \left[1 - \frac{x}{a} - \frac{y}{b} \right] dy \ dx$$

$$V = c \int_0^a \left. y - \frac{xy}{a} - \frac{y^2}{2b} \right|_0^{b(1 - \frac{x}{a})} dx$$

$$V = c \int_0^a b(1 - \frac{x}{a}) - \frac{x}{a}(b - \frac{xb}{a} - \frac{1}{2b}(b^2 - \frac{2xb^2}{a} + \frac{x^2 b^2}{a^2}) \ dx$$

$$V = c \int_0^a \left[b - \frac{2xb}{a} + \frac{x^2 b}{a^2} - \frac{b}{2} + \frac{2xb^2}{2ab} - \frac{x^2 b^2}{2b a^2} \right] dx$$

$$= c \int_0^a \left[\tfrac{1}{2}b + \frac{xb}{a} - \frac{2xb}{a} + \frac{x^2 b}{2a^2} \right] dx$$

$$= c \left[\tfrac{1}{2} bx + \frac{x^2 b}{2a} - x^2 b + \frac{x^3 b}{6a^2} \right]_0^a$$

$$= c \left[\tfrac{1}{2}ba + \frac{a^2 b}{a} - \frac{a^2 b}{a} + \frac{a^3 b}{6a^2} \right]$$

$$V = c \left[\tfrac{1}{2}ba - ab + \frac{ab}{6} + \frac{ab}{2} \right]$$

$$= c \left[-\frac{ab}{2} + \frac{ab}{6} + \frac{ab}{2} \right] = \tfrac{1}{6} \ cab$$

368

And having generated this as the volume of the tetrahedron,
let us check this in a limiting case. Let there be a cube
with side A, then

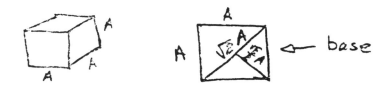

then for the tetrahedron one has

$a = \frac{\sqrt{2}}{2} A$ then $V = \frac{cab}{6} = \frac{1}{24} A^3$

$b = \frac{\sqrt{2}}{2} A$ and there are 4 tetrahedrons to each
                              one of these pyramids, so the volume

$c = \frac{1}{2}A$ of one pyramid is just $4V = \frac{1}{6} A^3$ for

the pyramid. And the volume of the cube is just $V = A^3$ since
there are six pyramids to this cube. This is in keeping with
what is actually observed. For use in the pyramid formula
one can modify this only partially, so one generates the
volume of an equal pyramid, i.e., square base center of
square perpendicular to the base.

So $V = \frac{2}{3} cab$

The above may be confirmed by a triple scalar product
using vector calculus. Now it seems somewhat extreme to go
to all of this trouble to calculate the theoretical volume;
this is basically as an exercise and to see if there is a
possibility that this could cause a gravitational deflection
of a plumb used in surveying.

The density of limestone (59th Handbook of Chemistry and Physics, page F1) is

$$167 - 171 \text{ lbs/cu.ft.}$$

$$169 \text{ lbs/cu.ft.} \qquad \text{slugs} \times a = w$$

$$5.28 \text{ slugs/cu.ft.}$$

$$5.28 \text{ slugs/cu.ft.} \qquad \frac{1}{0.02832} \qquad \frac{\text{cu.ft.}}{\text{cu. m.}}$$

$$186.44 \text{ slugs/cu.m.} = \text{avg density limestone}$$

(MASS)

$$1 \text{ ft}^3 = 12^3 \text{ in}^3$$

$$2.54 \times 10^{-2} \text{m/in}$$

$$(2.54 \times 10^{-2})^3 \text{ m}^3/\text{in}^3$$

$$1\text{ft}^3 = (12^3 \text{in}^3)(2.54 \times 10^{-2} \text{ m}^3/\text{in}^3)^3$$

$$1\text{ft}^3 = 2.832 \times 10^{-2} \text{m}^3$$

$$1 \text{ kg} = 0.0685 \text{ slug mass}$$

Now if one goes back to the volume formula one can substitute the following:

$$V = \frac{2}{3} cab$$

$$V = \frac{2}{3} (162.9)(162.9)(c)$$

The only unknown dimension at this time is (c) using the following angular measurements to two decimal places and the average of 230.37

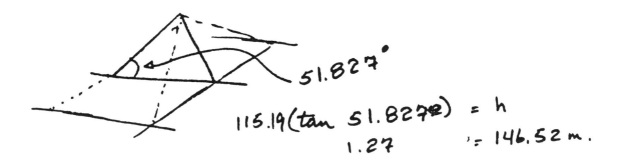

$$51.827°$$

$$\frac{115.19(\tan 51.827°)}{1.27} = h$$

$$= 146.52 \text{ m}.$$

370

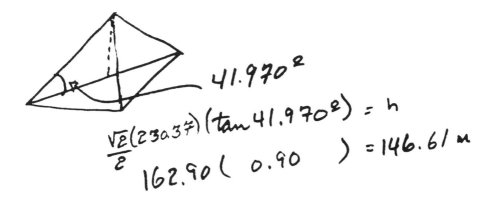

$$\frac{\sqrt{2}(230.37)}{2}(\tan 41.970^\circ) = h$$

$$162.90(\quad 0.90\quad) = 146.61 m$$

Taking an average, one generates 146.57 m. as the height of an ideal pyramid. So now one can calculate

$$V = \frac{2}{3} (162.9)^2 (146.6) m^3$$

$$V = 2593491.8 \ m^3$$

$$V = 2.593 \times 10^6 m^3$$

$$V = 9.158 \times 10^7 ft^3$$

Note: An ideal pyramid would be completely solid and symmetrically constructed, i.e., theoretically ideal. Since limestone has a density (weight) of an average of 169 lbs/c.ft., one has the weight assuming $32 f/s^2$ gravitational acceleration on the average:

$$W = (9.158 \times 10^7 ft^3) \ (169 \ lbs/cuft)$$

$$W = 1.548 \times 10^{10} \ lbs$$

$$= 1.548 \times 10^{10} \ lbs \times \frac{1}{20000} \ ton/lb$$

$$= 7.738 \times 10^6 \ tons$$

$$Mass = \frac{1.548 \times 10^{10} \ lbs}{32 \ f/s^2} \quad = 4.838 \times 10^8 \ slugs$$

62.427 grms/cc. = 1 lb/cu.ft. density of earth $\fallingdotseq$ 5.431 g/cc

$$\fallingdotseq 339.1 \ lbs/cu.ft$$

Average radius of the earth

$$6371.32 \text{ km.}$$

$$\text{Volume} = \frac{4}{3}\pi (6371.32 \times 10^3)^3 = 1.083 \times 10^{21} \text{m}^3$$

$$= 1.083 \times 10^{21} \text{m}^3 \quad 35.31 \text{ cu.ft/m}^3$$

$$= 3.825 \times 10^{22} \text{ cu.ft.}$$

Mass kg of earth $= 5.98 \times 10^{24}$ kg

$$\cong 5.98 \times 10^{24} \text{ kg} \times 6.85 \times 10^{-2} \text{ slugs/kg}$$

$$\cong 4.096 \times 10^{23} \text{ slugs}$$

20% error in weight

$$F_{Grav} = \frac{M_1 M_2}{r^2} \quad G$$

$$G = 6.67 \times 10^{-11} \frac{N \cdot m^2}{Kg^2} = 3.44 \times 10^{-8} \frac{lb.ft^2}{slug^2}$$

Consider the mass of the pyramid to be a point mass on the ground the closest one could get to the center would be just

$$\frac{230.37 m.}{2} \quad \text{or} \quad \frac{3.28 \text{ ft/m.} \times 230.37 \text{ m.}}{2} = 377.81 \text{ ft.}$$

The mass of the pyramid $= 4.838 \times 10^8$ slugs

Assume a mass of the surveyor's plumb of

A.) $\frac{1}{32}$ slug $\cong$ 1 lb.

B.) $\frac{5}{32}$ slug $\cong$ 5 lbs.

C.) $\frac{10}{32}$ slug $\cong$ 10 lbs

Then $G (M_1 M_2) =$

For A. $= 5.20 \times 10^{-1}$ lb ft^2

B. $= 2.60$ lb ft^2

C. $= 5.20$ lb ft^2

Since 377.81 ft. is the closest distance that one can get, let us incorporate this into the formula to find the gravitational attraction for each case:

$$F_A = \frac{Gm \cdot m_2}{r^2} = 3.64 \times 10^{-6} \text{ lbs}$$

$$F_B = 1.82 \times 10^{-5} \text{ lbs}$$

$$F_C = 3.64 \times 10^{-5} \text{ lbs}$$

Now suppose that this plumb is suspended by a mass-less string, one would see

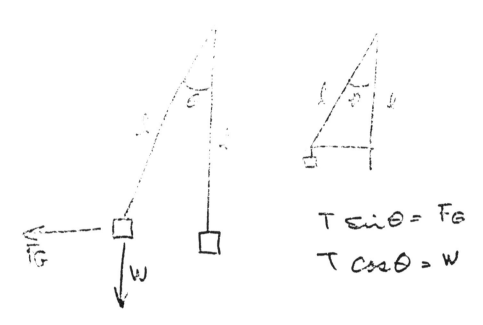

$$T \sin\theta = F_G$$
$$T \cos\theta = W$$

So one can now write $\tan\theta = \dfrac{F_G}{W}$

and arc $\tan \dfrac{F_G}{W} = \theta$

So one can write for each one:

A.)   arc $\tan \dfrac{3.64 \times 10^{-6} \text{ lbs}}{1 \text{ lb}} = \theta_A = 2.09 \times 10^{-4} \dfrac{\text{deg}}{}$

B.)   arc $\tan \dfrac{1.82 \times 10^{-5} \text{ lbs}}{5 \text{ lbs}} = \theta_B = $ "

C.)   arc $\tan \dfrac{3.64 \times 10^{-5} \text{ lbs}}{10 \text{ lbs}} = \theta_C = $ "

but $2.09 \times 10^{-4} \dfrac{\text{deg}}{} = 0.75$ sec.

APPENDIX B
by
Knox Robert Burnett
Computer Consultant
P.O. Box 450227
Atlanta, Georgia 30345

September 9, 1981

Mr. Richard Noone
Atlanta, Georgia 30338

Dear Richard:

There are three places where a force may be applied to the earth which might cause a "pole shift" or change in the location of the axis of rotation: 1) under the surface, 2) on the surface, and 3) above the surface of the earth.

You have given your readers a very good evaluation of what the effect on the surface of the earth would be should we live to the beginning moments of such an event as a pole shift. Further, you have described the possibility of the ice mass as a force of imbalance to tumble the earth as the most plausible of the "on the surface" possibilities. Let me address for a moment the other two places as possibilities for some of the cause of a "pole shift."

One piece of evidence has caught my attention. In the 1957 geophysical year, a mathematical model was created which described the "pear" shape of our planet Earth. The process involved comparing the satellite measurements with the mathematical model. The researchers described a "flat spot" which I recall was in the Atlantic Ocean off the southeastern coast of South America. Using simple logic and a certain amount of trust in the theories of Isaac Newton, I conclude that the core of our planet Earth is not perfectly symmetrical

about the present axis of rotation. At least this one spot is different. The effect on the water is such that the Earth appears "heavier," such that the water is attracted toward the center of the Earth more in the one area than in the surrounding neighborhood. Because of this greater "attraction" the water appears to have a "flat spot". The evidence indicates to me that the core of our planet Earth is different from place to place. The point of all of this is: that where there are physical differences, that is where forces may be applied which can change the location of the spin axis of our planet Earth. All of this suggests an irregularity in the mass-centroid of the earth. The wobble of the earth about the "pole star" is further evidence of such an irregularity.

The only external force which comes to my mind which could possibly have any chance of influencing the location of the spin axis on the planet is our star, the Sun. The local astroids called "Apollo objects" are too small to change the spin and too large to be ignored if one hits us. The astroid belt is too far, too small and too disorganized. The other planets and our moon have effects which may or may not cause earthquakes. Taken singly these objects of our Solar System are known to have low

374

magnitude effects on the crust of the Earth.

Take the Solar System collectively and the Sun particularly and there is an improbable but possible combination which could cause a change in the orientation of the Earth's "spin axis" with respect to the Sun, but which would not significantly change the location of the spin axis to the magnetic poles.

The influence of the heat and light of our Sun are obvious. The output of our Sun also includes properties such as magnetic flares. When the planets line up on one side of our Sun nearly in a straight line, the local activity of the surface of the sun closest to that line could change. The questions I pose are: Could that change in our Sun include a magnetic flare of rare occurrence, huge size, great magnetic force and for a significant duration? Would that huge force be enough to have an effect on the planet Earth? If so, how much? Could it "tumble" our planet? What more?

Let us suppose the Sun's magnetic field was applied to the Earth's magnetic field in a different direction and at the same time the Sun's magnetic flux density increased by some large amount. The axis of spin of Earth does not significantly change location. The Earth's orientation to the Sun changes by an amount which depends on the Sun's magnetic field, its strength and duration. Once changed, Earth's inertia tends to hold the new rotational orientation to the Sun, while the "hystresis" of the Earth's magnet keeps it oriented near the old location relative to the spin axis. Being near the old location, the Earth's magnet tends to change the Earth's rotational axis back toward the current orientation of our "Pole Star" which takes a long time under normal levels and orientation of the Sun's magnetic field.

In my opinion, the three places where a force might be applied to the Earth mentioned at the beginning of this letter are all possibilities, but unequal in probability. For example, suppose the volume below our surface crust is very fluid and can allow the crust to slide to a new orientation. The coefficient of friction once exceeded would permit the catastrophe you describe to occur. The magnetic evidence is very much against this possibility. The Earth's magnet could spontaneously change polarity, but that evidence shows itself to be very infrequent (twice). The inside and surface of our planet Earth show evidence of staying together except for plate shifts which are too slow for kinetic catastrophe. Therefore, I have looked for a different internal possibility. The irregular nature of our core is real, but how important?

Information is newly available from a scientific research satellite which is dedicated to measuring the output of our Sun. One report alleges that the sun lowered its output for a period of several hours an average of 0.2%. The effect is such that millions of tons of water did not rise in temperature the same as that of the oceans nearby, namely in an area 30 degrees out of 360 degrees around our Earth on that one special day. That report being true, we must consider our Sun as a "variable" source of heat, light and magnetic properties! Now, what could influence our Sun to change its output?

The evidence of different areas of the earth's being covered with ice is very real. In my opinion, the heat of our Sun has been much less for most of planet Earth's history. I give in evidence to support this last idea: the long lines of cliffs which border the "continental shelves". Cliffs form for several reasons. One reason is the action of water at the boundary of ocean and land. I assert that the contiguous cliffs interrupted by river valleys are proof that the land of the continental shelves once and many times were above the oceans and, therefore, dry land. The river systems cut through the cliffs because the water did not cover the cliffs. The cliffs exist because the oceans washed away the more gentle undulations of the earth's surface. Therefore, your idea of watching the polar caps is very correct. The ocean waters move through the air-surface cycle only in the amount available. Frozen water is trapped. The economic results are the same as any "pole shift". The tremendous forces that tore the earth's surface at such places as Patagonia, Terra Del Fuego and Chili could be massive ice such as a frozen surface contiguous at those latitudes. Part of the deep trenches could be the accumulation of ice at the boundary of earth and ice. Perhaps the "continental drift" is in part the push and shove of contiguous ice.

The ice theories do not require the magnetic pole to shift and neither does the sun's magnetic influence require the location of the magnetic pole to drastically change. The evidence of many different magnetic pole locations supports the theory that something changed internal to the earth, whether the cause was internal or external. The cluster of magnetic pole locations near the current axis of rotation supports the theory that the core of the earth and the crust have been well bonded together. Evidence abounds that cold as well as tropical climates occurred over all parts of the planet Earth. This suggests that the Sun has changed its magnitude of output such that the Earth's general climate has been drastically altered from time to time. The current state of the Sheppard Islands and the age of the waterfalls all over the Earth suggest the last thaw released water long captured in the polar icecaps. The studies of the coral growth give strong evidence of the relative strength of the annual output of the Sun over a long period of time or else of gross changes in latitude of specific coral formations with respect to time. The strongest evidence for or against the "tumble" of the earth should be in the ancient to recent coral growth patterns.

The ideas shared in this letter are offered in the spirit of good fellowship and the sense that we are all responsible for understanding the universe about us to the best of our combined capabilities. I wish you good fortune in your book.

Warm personal regards,

Knox Robert Burnett

APPENDIX C

The following is unedited correspondence from Jim Hagan, a construction specialist, who led the design team for such major projects as the Sanford Stadium at the University of Georgia and the Marta Five Points Station in Atlanta.

To: Richard Noone
From: Jim Hagan
Date: August 5, 1996
Subject: The Great Pyramid at Giza

Our field of study is the built environment and the relevant construction techniques.

The analyzing and verbalizing of any building program commences with the architectural concept and methodology, while always establishing "the knowns."

In the African portion of the study of architecture, the inquisitive student senses a pyramid anomaly.

The curriculum of thirty plus years ago ended the detailed inventory of the Egyptian era, thus "and pyramids."

From the first mention to every evidence-gathering expedition, the pyramid distinguishes itself from its neighbors.

In philosophy, concept, and technique, we are seeing two dissimilar construction types.

The temple at Karnak, typical for the period, is constructed of repetitive columns and beams, highly decorated, with caryatids, and sheathed with small blocks.

All of the building examples in this era have flat roofs, which would suggest dry conditions.

If Dr. Schock says "torrential rain," I'll say, "the pyramid with the skin of fitted, polished stone and filled joints is very effective in the rain."

These two building types are too divergent for one culture.

The people who did the hypostyle hall did not do the pyramid.

In architectural lineage African, Greek, Roman, French, English, Early American, the Pyramid is not in any of these.

It's somewhere between the Eiffel Tower and Hoover Dam.

Mankind has never invented out of whole cloth. Mankind's earliest trait was to find, study, and use.

This continues today and is especially true in architecture.

Being inspired to be creative means conceptualizing something seen.

Occasionally a methodology of architecture is developed as a manifestation of the culture. The tepee is a good example. The pyramid is not this to any Egyptian era.

We do know where it is. We don't know the who or when. The facts, old and new, are better at telling us what it is.

The builders of the pyramid were gifted enough to build anything they wanted.

They designed and constructed it for a specific reason to accomplish a given task.

It could be used as a Pharaoh's tomb, pump, or cleaners. It could be used to impress initiates or to store pennies. It sounds like a handy gadget. I can use a Ferrari engine as a boat anchor, but that's not its highest and best use.

The evidence continues to mount.

1. Shape
2. Mass
3. Isolation
4. Insulation
5. Thermal activity in the ascending passage
6. Salt deposits in the Queen's Chamber
7. Melted box in the King's Chamber

The newer generation of information aligns thusly:

The eight-inch-diameter shafts are conduit for conductor or tempering matter.

The iron/gold piece is an electrode that appears to have eroded in an arid land.

Gantenbrink's fabulous camera revealed a valve (door) and copper electrodes.

The body of knowledge on this subject is accumulating.

The only thing we know "for sure" is that the most documented building of our time is a "works project" for authors and academicians.

For every fact revealed, you get a load of fiction and speculation.

Great designers seek equilibrium in the resolution of forces and resources.

This building, in the abstract, demonstrates this more than any built example.

The net generated material is void in the architectural discipline, but is organizing about fire, water, rain, equilibrium, connection, site planning, and cosmic alignment. Prominently mentioned are hydrogen, sky link, zep tepi, big bang, "the first time," subterranean, downward, the lower part, causeway, and stars within circles.

The Kunkel Brief

I just received and studied Edward J. Kunkel's book. For at least forty-five years I have heard of his rendition of the pharaoh's pump as discussed by hobbyists of mechanical things. I had no need for such, so that ended my interest. Now that I have read his 84 page book, I formed these opinions.

1. Kunkel's writing represents the most thoughty information on the Giza pyramid.

2. Kunkel's is the most plausible construction methodology. Of the existing theories:

   a. His is the only quarrying theory I accept.
   b. His is the only surfacing theory I accept.
   c. His is the only transport theory I accept.
   d. His is the only erection theory I accept.
   e. His is the only scheduling rationale I accept.

The fault I find with Kunkel is not in his multidisciplined thesis, but rather his innocent attempt to capitalize on it. I'm sorry he did not comprehend the steadfast denial of his efforts by the *accepted* knowledge institutions. His place in history is indelible, and the dissemination of his information is right on schedule. Now that he is defeated, tired, and deceased, the measured rate of his impact will become more evident.

Bibliography of Articles

1923

"Talks on the Great Pyramid: A Series of Special Articles" by David Davidson. Reprinted from *The Morning Post*, Leeds, England, 1923.

1962

"Whiz Kid, Hands Down", *Life*, September 14, 1962.

1965

"Early Formative Period of Coastal Ecuador: The Valdavia and Machalilla Phases" by Betty J. Meggers, Clifford Evans, and Emilio Estrad. *The Smithsonian Institution*, 1965.

"The Composition of the Earth's Interior" by Taro Takahashi and William A. Bassett. *Scientific America*, June 1965, Vol. 212, No. 6.

1966

"Earth Getting Colder as Ice Age Nears", *Science News*, Nov. 26, 1966, Vol. 90, No. 22.

1967

"Position of Planets Linked to Solar Flare Prediction" by Rex Pay. *Technology Week*, May 15, 1967.

1968

"Earthquakes and the Earth's Wobble" by L. Mansinha and D. E. Smylie. *Science*, Sept. 13, 1968, Vol. 161, No. 3846.

1969

"Seismic Activity and Faulting Associates with a Large Underground Nuclear Explosion" by R. M. Hamilton, F. A. McKeown, and J. H. Healy. *Science*, October 31, 1969, Vol. 166, No. 3905.

"Australarctica," *Scientific American*, August 1969, Vol. 221, No. 2.

"Earth's Cooling Climate" by Kendrick Frazier. *Science News*, November 15, 1969, Vol. 96, No. 20.

"The Upper Mantle of the Earth" by L. Knopoff. *Science*, March 21, 1969, Vol. 163, No. 3873.

"The Origin of the Oceanic Ridges" by Egon Orowan. *Scientific American*, Nov. 1969, pp. 102-119.

1970

"Transcontinental Tidal Gravity Profile Across the United States" by J. T. Kuo, R. C. Jachens, M. Ewing and G. White. *Science*, May 22, 1970, Vol. 168, No. 3934.

"Polar Ice and the Global Climate Machine" by Joseph O. Fletcher. *Bulletin of the Atomic Scientists*, Dec. 1970.

"Nuclear Explosions and Distant Earthquakes: A Search for Correlations" by J. H. Healy and P. Anthony Marshall. *Science*, July 10, 1970, Vol. 169, No. 3941.

"Hunting Clues to an Ancient Supercontinent" by Daniel Behrman. *UNESCO Courier*, July 1970.

1971

"Magnetic Reversal 12,500 Years Ago", *Nature*, Number 234, 1971.

"Man's Impact on Climate: What is Ahead?", *Science News* July 31, 1971, Vol. 100, No. 5.

"The Rotation of the Earth" by D. E. Smylie and L. Mansinha. *Scientific American*, December 1971.

"The Wobbling Earth", *Science News*, August 14, 1971, Vol. 100, No. 7.

1972

"Antarctic Fossils and the Reconstruction of Gondwanaland" by Edwin H. Colbert. *Natural History*, January 1972, Vol. LXXI, No. 1.

"Love Among the Cabbages: Sense and Sensibility in the Realm of Plants" by Peter Tompkins and Christopher Bird. *Harper's* Magazine, November 1972, pp. 90-96.

"Probing the Earth's Inner Core" by Louise Purrett. *Science News*, March 11, 1972, Vol. 101, No. 11.

"Rainmaking: Rumored Use Over Laos Alarms Arms Experts, Scientists" by Deborah Shapley. *Science*, July 16, 1972, Vol. 176, No. 4040.

"Science Officials Bow to Military on Weather Modification" by Deborah Shapley. *Science*, August 4, 1972, Vol. 177, No. 4047.

1973

"The Ice Age Cometh" by James D. Hays. *Saturday Review of the Sciences*, April 1973, Vol. I, No. 3.

1974

"Weather Warfare: Pentagon Concedes 7-Year Vietnam Effort" by Deborah Shapley. *Science*, June 7, 1974, Vol. 184, No. 4191.

"Senate Bans Use of Weather, Fire as Weapons" by DOD. *Science*, June 7, 1974, Vol. 177, No. 4048.

"Soviets in U.S. Decry Weather Warfare." *Science News*, November 2, 1974, Vol. 106, No. 18.

" 'Jupiter Effect': Mixed Reaction." *Science News*, April 1974, Vol. 106, No. 13.

1975

"Atmospheric Dust Increase Could Lower Earth's Temperature" by Gloria B. Lubkin. *Physics Today*, September 1975, Vol. 24, No. 10.

"The Caracol Tower at Chichen Itza: An Ancient Astronomical Observatory?" by Anthony F. Aveni, Sharon L. Gibbs, and Horst Hartung. *Science*, 6 June 1975, Vol. 188, Number 4192.

"How I Became the First Person to Sleep in the Great Pyramid" by John Sack. *Esquire*, April 1975.

1976

"How Climate Might Shift in Next 1,000 Years" by Douglas Starr. *The Christian Science Monitor*, Wed., February 14, 1976, p. 17.

"Ice Ages Attributed to Orbit Changes". *Science News*, December 4, 1976, Vol. 110, No. 23.

"Maya Lowland Hydraulic Systems" by Ray T. Matheny. *Science*, 20 August 1976, Vol. 193, No. 4254.

"The Paluxy River Tracks" by John D. Morris, B.S. *ICR Impact Series*, May 1976, No. 35.

"The Pyramid and its Relation to Biocosmic Energy" by G. Patrick Flanagan, Ph.D., 1976.

"Pyramid Power" by Jerry C. Dunn, Jr., *Coronet*, April 1976.

"Pyramid Power." *Oui*, January 1976.

"Searching the Great Ruins of the World." *Argosy; Adventure Annual*, 1976.

"The Secret of the Pyramids" by Marvin Grosswirth. *Science Digest*, February 1976.

"Variations in the Earth's Orbit: Pacemake of the Ice Ages" by J. D. Hays, John Imbrie, and N. J. Shackleton. *Science*, December 10, 1976, Vol. 194, No. 4270.

1977

"California's Shifting Crust: Slip Sliding Away". *Science News*, December 17, 1977, Vol. 112, No. 25.

"Can Animals Anticipate Earthquakes?" by Evelyn Shaw. *Natural History*, November 1977, Vol. LXXXVI, No. 9.

"The Flow of Heat from the Earth's Interior" by Henry N. Pollack and David S. Chapman. *Scientific American*, August 1977, Vol. 237, No. 2.

"I Held the Regius Manuscript" by H. Raymond Lowe. *The New Age Magazine*, September 1977, Vol. LXXXV, No. 9.

"The Oldest Rocks and the Growth of Continents" by Stephen Moorbath, *Scientific American*, March 1977, Vo. 236, No. 3.

"Probing the Mystery of the Medicine Wheels" by John A. Eddy. *National Geographic*, January 1977, Vol. 151, No. 1, pp. 140-146.

"Retort to the Vatican" by Henry Clausan. *The New Age* Magazine, November 1977, Vol. LXXX, No. 17.

"The Strange Truth About Pyramid Power" by Bill D. Miller, *Mechanix Illustrated*, April 1977.

"Sun Changes Its Spots" by Charles Seabrook. *The Atlanta Journal and Constitution*, Sunday, March 27, 1977.

"Upsetting the Climatic Balance". *Chemistry*, October 1977, Vol. 50, No. 8.

"What's Behind This Winter...and What's Ahead." *Science News*, February 12, 1977, Vol. III, No. 7.

"Wisconsin's Case Against Nuclear Energy" by Douglas LaFollette. *The Christian Science Monitor*, Wednesday, December 20, 1978.

1978

"Atlantis: Fact or Fiction" by Thomas Fleming. *The Atlanta Journal and Constitution*, Sunday, August 13, 1978.

"The Big Blast at Santorini" by Stephen Sparks and Haraldur Sigurdson. *Natural History*, April 1978, Vol. LXXXVII, No. 4.

"Earthquakes, Faults, and Nuclear Power Plants in Southern New York and Northern New Jersey" by Yash P. Aggarwal and Lynn R. Sykes. *Science*, April 28, 1978, Vol. 200, No. 4340.

"An Epic Find". *Time*, June 26, 1978, p. 64.

"Foundation of Templars in the Old World" by Joe W. and Karl J. Krayer, *Knight Templar Magazine*, 1978, Vol. XXIV, No. 1.

"Freemasonry in Ancient Egypt — New York's Silent Sentinel" by Ralph W. Lichty. *Knight Templar Magazine*, Vol. XXIV, No. 7, July 1978.

"Templar on the Moon" by J. E. Behrens, Assistant Editor. *Knight Templar — The Magazine for York Rite Masons*, Vol. XXIV, November 1978, Number 11.

"Tracking the Fault". *Newsweek*, July 1978, p. 62.

"Through Mexico" by James A. Frank. *Diversion Magazine*, June 1978, p. 29.

"Air Samples Reveal New Threat to Ozone". *Science News*, September 23, 1978, Vol. 114, No. 13.

"Measuring Volcanic Particle Production". *Science News*, September 16, 1978, Vol. 114, No. 12.

"San Andreas Fault Found Shifting at Rapid Rate". *The New York Times*, June 19, 1978, p. 12.

"Coast Power Company Plagued Since 1958 by Earthquake Faults" by Gladwin Hill. *The New York Times*, December 17, 1978.

1979

"Acid Rains and Poison Snows". *The Futurist*, April 1979, Vol. 13, No. II.

"Antarctic Sea Ice May Herald Ice Age". *Science News*, January 13, 1979. Vol. 115, No. 2.

"Brave New Worlds: Space Colonies" by Steve Oney. *Atlanta Journal and Constitution*, July 15, 1979.

"Five Atomic Plants Ordered Shut Down" by Richard Halloran. *The New York Times*, March 14, 1979.

"How Old Is It? — The Elegant Science of Dating Ancient Objects" by Robert Gannon. *Popular Science*, November 1979.

"The Iron King" by Druon. *Knight Templar Magazine*, Vol. XXV, No. 1, January 1979.

"Science Team Preparing to Release Data Covering Research on Shroud of Turin". *Atlanta Journal and Constitution*, Sunday, October 14, 1979.

"Sensing Quakes". *Time* Magazine, January 29, 1979, p. 73.

"The Source of the Earth's Magnetic Field" by Charles R. Carrigan and David Gubbins. *Scientific American*, February, 1979, Vol. LXXXI, No. 1.

"Soviet Scientist Says He Has Solved England's Stonehenge Mystery", The Associated Press, Moscow. *The Atlanta Journal*, Thursday, September 20, 1979.

"The Year Without a Summer" by Henry Stommel and Elizabeth Stommel. *Scientific American*, June 1979, Vol. 240, No. 6.

1980

"The Shroud of Turin". *National Geographic*, June 1980, Vol. 157.

Bibliography of Works Cited

Bailey, James. *The God-Kings and the Titans.* New York: St. Martin's Press, 1973.

Berlitz, Charles. *Mysteries from Forgotten Worlds.* New York: Dell Publications, 1972.

The Book of Mormon. Independence, Missouri: Reorganized Church of Jesus Christ of the Latter-Day Saints, 1974.

Brachet, J. *Nouvelles Recherches sur la Grande Pyramide.* Aix-en-Provence: La Pensee Universitaire, 1965.

Breasted, James Henry. *The Conquest of Civilization.* New York: Harper & Breothers, 1938.

Brown, Hugh Auchincloss. *Cataclysms of the Earth.* New York: Twayne Publishers, 1967.

Brown, J.P. *The Dervishes.* Philadelphia, 1868.

Budge, E.A. Wallis, trans. *The Egyptian Book of the Dead.* 1895; reprint ed., New York: Dover Books, 1967.

Bull, Colin. *Snow Accumulation in Antartica.* Columbus: Institute of Polar Studies, 1971.

Careri, Giovanni. *Giro del Mundo.* Venice: G. Malachin, 1719.

Castaneda, Carlos. *The Teachings of Don Juan: A Yaqui Way of Knowledge.* New York: Simon and Schuster, 1974.

Churchward, James. *The Lost Continent of Mu.* 1931. Reprint ed., New York: Paperback Library, 1968.

Central Intelligence Agency. *USSR: The Impact of Recent Climate Change on Grain Production.* Document # ER76-105776, 1971.

Clausen, Henry C. *Commentaries on Morals and Dogma.* San Diego: Neyenesch Printers, 1974.

Council on Environmental Quality/Department of State. *Global 2000 Report to the President.* Washington: U.S. Government Printing Office, 1980.

Custance, Arthur C. *Fossil Man in the Light of the Record in Genesis.* Creation Research Society Annual, 1968.

Davidson, David. *Coptic Christiantity.*

_____. *The Great Pyramid: Its Divine Message.* 9th ed. London: Williams & Norgate Ltd., 1941.

Duncan, Andrew. *Money Rush.* New York: Doubleday, 1979.

Eckert, Allan W. *The HAB Theory.* New York: Paperback Library, 1977.

The Editors of Pensee. *Velikovsky Reconsidered.* New York: Warner Books, 1977.

Edwards, I.E.S. *The Pyramids of Egypt.* 1947. Reprint ed., Baltimore: Penguine, 1975.

Fell, Barry. *America B.C.* New York: Pocket Books, 1978.

Fix, William R. *Pyramid Odyssey.* New York: Mayflower, 1978.

Flanagan, Patrick G. *Beyond Pyramid Power.* Marina del Rey, California: DeVorss and Company, 1975.

_____. *Pyramid Power.* Santa Monica: DeVorss and Company, 1975.

Galanopoulos, Angelo G. and Bacon, Edward. *Atlantis: The Truth Behind the Legend.* New York: Bobbs-Merril, 1969.

Garnett, Lucy J.J. *Mysticism and Magic in Turkey.* London, 1912.

Goodman, Jeffery. *We Are the Earthquake Generation.* New York: Berkeley Books, 1979.

Gribben, John and Plageman, Stephen. *The Jupiter Effect.* New York: Walker Books, 1974.

Hall, Manly P. *An Encyclopedic Outline of Masonic, Hermetic, Qabbalistic and Rosicrucian Symbolical Philosophy.* 1925. Golden Anniversary Edition, Los Angeles, 1975.

_____. *Lost Keys of Freemasonry.* 1923. Reprint ed., Richmond: McCoy, 1968.

Hapgood, Charles H. *Earth's Shifting Crust.* Introduction by Albert Einstein. New York: Pantheon, 1958.

Hawkins, Gerald S. *Stonehenge Decoded.* Garden City, New York: Doubleday, 1965.

Herodotus. *History.* Trans. George Rawlinson. New York: Tudor, 1941.

Kieninger, Richard. *The Ultimate Frontier.* Steele, Illinois: The Stelle Group, 1963.

Kunkle, Edward. *Pharoah's Pump.* Columbus: Kunkel, 1962.

Lauer, Jean Philippe. *Fouilles a Saggarah.* Cairo: Institute Francais, 1935.

Lockyer, Norman. *The Dawn of Astronomy.* London: Macmillan, 1894.

The Lost Books of the Bible and the Forgotten Books of Eden. New York: New American LIbrary, 1974.

McCoan, J.C. *Egypt.* New York: Peter Fenelon Collier and Son, 1882.

Mcad, G.R.S. *Fragments of a Faith Forgotten: The Gnostics.*

Mertz, Henriette. *Gods from the Far East: How the Chinese Discovered America.* 1953. Reprint ed., New York: Ballantine, 1975.

Michanowsky, George. *The Once and Future Star.* New York: Hawthorne Books, 1977.

Mulfinger, George. *The Flood and the Fossils.* Pamphlet. Greenville, South Carolina: Bob Jones University Press, n.d.

Nelson, Byron C. *After Its Kind.* Minneapolis: Bethany Fellowship, 1967.

Nelson, D.J. and Coville, David H. *Life Force from the Great Pyramid.* California: DeVorss & Co., 1977.

Ouspensky, P.D. *A New Model of the Universe.* 1931. Reprint ed., New York: Vantage Books, 1971.

Pike, Albert. *Moals and Dogma.* 1871. Revised reprint ed., Richmond: L.H. Jenkins, 1950.

LePlongeon. *Maya/Atlantis Queen Moo and the Egyptian*

Sphinx. 1896. Reprint ed., Blauvelt, N.Y.: Rudolph Steiner Publicatons, 1973.

_____. *Secret Mysteries Among the Mayas and Quiches*. 1886. Reprint ed., Savage, Minnesota: Wizard's Bookshelf, 1973.

Pochan, A. *L'enigme de la Grande Pyramide*. 1971. Trans., New York: Avon Books, 1978.

Ponte, Lowell. *The Cooling*. Englewood Cliffs: Prentice-Hall, 1976.

Raup, David M. "The Revolution in Evolution." *World Book Science Annual*. Chicago, 1980.

Redding, M.W. *The Scarlet Book of Freemasonry*. New York: Redding & Co., 1889.

de Santillana, Giorgio and von Dechend, Hertha. *Hamlet's Mill: An Essay on Myth and the Frame of Time*. Boston: MIT, 1969.

Steiger, Brad. *Worlds Before Our Own*. New York: Berkeley Boks, 1978.

Suares, Carlo. *The Cipher of Genesis: The Original Code of the Qabala as Applied to the Scriptures*. London: Shambhala Publications, 1978.

Temple, Robert K.G. *The Sirius Mystery*. London: Sidgwich and Jackson Ltd., 1976.

Tompkins, Peter. *Mysteries of the Mexican Pyramids*. New York: Harper & Row, 1976.

_____. *Secrets of the Great Pyramid*. New York: Harper & Row, 1971.

Valentine, Tom. *The Great Pyramid: Man's Monument to Man*. New York: Pinnacle Books, 1975.

_____. *The Life and Death of Planet Earth*. New York: Pinnacle Books, 1977.

Velikovsky, Immanuel. *Ages in Chaos*. New York: Doubleday, 1952.

_____. *Earth in Upheaval*. Garden City, N.Y.: Doubleday, 1955.

_____. *Peoples of the Sea*. New York: Doubleday, 1977.

_____. *Worlds in Collision*. New York: Doubleday, 1950.

Wake, C.S. *The Origin and Significance of the Great Pyramid*. 1882. Facsimile reprint ed., Savage, Minnesota: Wizard's Bookshelf, 1975.

West, John Anthony. *Serpent in the Sky: The High Wisdom of Ancient Egypt*. Foreword by Peter Tompkins. New York: Harper & Row, 1979.

White, John. *Pole Shift*. New York: Doubleday, 1980.

Wilson, Robert Anton. *The Cosmic Trigger: The Final Secret of the Illuminati*. New York: Pocket Books, 1977.

Zink, David D. *The Ancient Stones Speak*. New York: E.P. Dutton, 1979.

Bibliography

Abbott, Jacob. *Alexander the Great*. Akron, Ohio: The Superior Printing Company, 1901.

———. *Cleopatra*. Akron, Ohio: The Superior Printing Company, 1901.

———. *Caesar*. Akron, Ohio: The Superior Printing Company, 1901.

———. *Hernando Cortez*. Akron, Ohio: The Superior Printing Company, 1901.

Adams, Walter: Marshal. *The Book of the Master*. New York: Putnam, 1898.

Aldred, Cyril. *Development of Ancient Egyptian Art, 3200-1315 B.C.* London: Tiranti, 1952.

Alpert, Richard. *Remember, Be Here Now*. Lama Foundation, Albuquerque, New Mexico: Modern Press, 1971.

Applications of Modern Sensing Techniques to Egyptology. A report of the 1977 Field Experiments by a joint team: Ali Helmi Moussa, Chairman, Department of Physics, Ain Shams University, Cairo, A.R.E., and Lambert T. Dolphin, Senior Physicist, SRI International, Menlo Park, Calif. Menlo Park: SRI International Radio Physics Laboratory, 94025.

Archaeological Institute of America, Compilers. *Archaeological Discoveries in the Holy Land*. New York: Bonanza Books, 1967.

Bailey, Foster. *The Spirit of Masonry*. London: Lucis Press Limited, 1957.

Bailey, James. *The God-Kings and the Titans*. New York: St. Martin's Press, 1973.

Balfour, Michael. *Stonehenge and Its Mysteries*. New York: Charles Scribner's Sons, 1979.

Batres, Leopoldo. *Explorations of Mount Alban, Oaxaca*. Mexico City: Gante St. Press, 1902.

Benavides, R. *Dramatic Prophecies of the Great Pyramid*. Mexico City: Editores Mexicanos Unidos, 1970.

Bennett, J. G. *Gurdjieff: Making a New World*. London: Turnstone Books, 1973.

Bergier, Jacques. *Extraterrestrial Visitations from Prehistoric Times to the Present*. New York: Signet, 1974.

Berlitz, Charles. *Doomsday 1999*. Garden City, New York: Doubleday and Company, 1981.

———. *Mysteries from Forgotten Worlds*. New York: Dell Publications, 1972.

———. *Without a Trace*. New York: Ballantine Books, 1978.

Blavatsky, Helene P. *The Secret Doctrine*. Two Vols. Los Angeles, California: Theosophy, 1930.

Boadella, David. *Wilhelm Reich: The Evolution of His Work*. London: Vision Press, 1972.

Boland, Charles Michael. *They All Discovered America*. New York: Doubleday, 1961.

The Book of Mormon. Independence, Missouri: Reorganized Church of Jesus Christ of the Latter-Day Saints, 1974.

Boulanger, Robert. *Egyptian Printing and the Ancient East*. New York: Funk and Wagnalls, 1965.

Bramwell, James. *Lost Atlantis*. New York: Freeway Press, Inc., 1973.

Brauchet, J. *Nouvelles Recherches sur la Grande Pyramide*. Aix-en-Provence: La Pensee Universitaire, 1965.

Breasted, James Henry. *The Conquest of Civilization*. New York: Harper & Brothers, 1938.

Brown, Hugh Auchincloss. *Cataclysms of the Earth*. New York: Twayne Publishers, 1967.

Brown, J. MacMillan. *The Riddle of the Pacific*. New York: A.M.S. Press, 1924.

Brown, J. P. *The Dervishes*. Philadelphia: 1868.

Budge, E. A. Wallis. *Egyptian Language: Easy Lessons in Egyptian Hieroglyphics with Sign List*. London: Routledge & Kegan Paul Ltd., 1951.

———. *Egyptian Magic*. Evanston, Ill.: University Books, 1958.

———. *Egyptian Religion*. New Hyde Park, New York: University Books, 1959.

———. *History of Egypt*. London: Keagan, Paul Trench, Trubner, 1928.

———. *Osiris: The Egyptian Religion of Resurrection*. New Hyde Park, New York: University Books, Inc., 1961.

———. trans. *The Egyptian Book of the Dead*. 1895; reprint ed., New York: Dover Books, 1967.

———. *The Gods of the Egyptians*. 2 vols. New York: Dover Publishers, 1969.

Bull, Colin. *Snow Accumulation in Antarctica*. Columbus: Institute of Polar Studies, 1971.

Buhler, Georg, Trans. *The Laws of Manu*, Vol. XXV of *Sacred Books of the East*. Ed. by F. Max Muller. Oxford: The Clarendon Press, 1886.

Burckhardt, Titus. *Alchemy*. London: Vincent Stuart & John M. Watkins Ltd., 1967.

Burtt, Edwin A., Ed. *The Teachings of the Compassionate Buddha*. New York: New American Library, 1955.

Capra, Fritjof. *The Tao of Physics*. Berkeley: Shambhalla, 1975.

Careri, Giovanni. *Giro del Mundo*. Venice: G. Malachin, 1719.

Carson, Rachel. *Silent Spring*. Boston: Houghton Mifflin, 1962.

Castanada, Carlos. *A Separate Reality*. New York: Simon and Schuster, 1973.

———. *Journey to Ixtlan*. New York: Simon and Schuster, 1972.

———. *Tales of Power*. New York: Simon and Schuster, 1974.

———. *The Eagle's Gift*. New York: Simon and Schuster, 1981.

———. *The Second Ring of Power*. New York: Simon and Schuster, 1977.

———. *The Teachings of Don Juan: A Yaqui Way of Knowledge*. New York: Simon and Schuster, 1974.

Castells, The Rev. F. de P., A.K.C. *Our Ancient Breth-*

ren: *The Originators of Freemasonry*. London: A. Lewis (Masonic Publishers) Limited, no date given.

Cayce, Edgar. *Edgar Cayce on Atlantis*. New York: Paperback Library.

_____. *Readings on Atlantis*. Selected by the A.R.E. Foundation. Virginia Beach: 1975.

Central Intelligence Agency. *USSR: The Impact of Recent Climate Change on Grain Production*. Document #ER76-105776, 1971.

Charroux, Robert. *One Hundred Thousand Years of Man's Unknown History*. Berkeley: Medallion Books, 1971.

_____. *The Gods Unknown*. New York and Berkeley: Medallion Books, 1974.

Chatelain, Maurice. *Our Ancestors Came From Outer Space*. New York: Dell Publishing Co., Inc., 1979.

Churchward, James. *The Children of Mu*. 1931. Reprint Ed., New York: Paperback Library, 1968.

_____. *The Cosmic Forces of Mu*. 1934. Reprint Ed., New York: Paperback Library, 1968.

_____. *The Lost Continent of Mu*. 1931. Reprint Ed., New York: Paperback Library, 1968.

_____. *The Sacred Symbols of Mu*. 1933. Reprint Ed., New York: Paperback Library, 1968.

_____. *The Second Book of the Cosmic Forces of Mu*. 1935. Reprint Ed., New York: Paperback Library, 1968.

Clark, Glenn. *The Man Who Tapped the Secrets of the Universe*. Waynesboro, Virginia: University of Science and Philosophy, 1946.

Clark, I. Edward. *The Royal Secret*. Louisville, Kentucky: John P. Morton & Company, Inc., 1923.

Clausen, Henry C. *Commentaries on Morals and Dogma*. San Diego: Neyenesch Printers, 1974.

Coleman, Henry R. *Light from the East: Travels and Researchers in Bible Lands in Pursuit of More Light in Masonry*. Louisville, Kentucky: The Grand Lodge of Masons in Kentucky, 1911.

Corliss, William R. *Ancient Man: A Handbook of Puzzling Artifacts*. Glen Marm, Maryland: The Sourcebook Project, 1978.

Costain, Edward E. *Pyramid Power*. New York: Dell Publishing Company, 1977.

Cottrell, Leonard. *The Horizon Book of Lost Worlds*. New York: American Heritage, 1962.

_____. *The Lost Pharaohs*. London: Pan Books Ltd., 1956.

Council on Environmental Quality/Department of State. *Global 2000 Report to the President*. Washington, D.C.: U. S. Government Printing Office, 1980.

Cousteau, Jacques-Yves. *The Ocean World of Jacques Cousteau: The White Caps*, Vol. 16. Danbury, Connecticut: The Danbury Press, 1973.

Custance, Arthur C. *Fossil Man in the Light of the Record in Genesis*. Creation Research Society Annual, 1968.

Daraul, Arron. *History of Secret Societies*. New York: Pocket Books, 1961.

Darwin, Charles. *A Library of Universal Literature*. 4 Vols. New York: P. F. Collier and Son, 1859.

Davidson, David. *The Great Pyramid: Its Divine Message*. 9th Ed. London: Williams & Norgate Ltd., 1941.

Davies, Nina. *Egyptian Tomb Painting*. London: 1953.

DeCamp, L. Sprague. *The Ancient Engineers*. New York: Ballantine Books, 1974.

DeCamp, L. Sprague and Catherine C. DeCamp. *Citadels of Mystery*. New York: Ballantine Books, 1973.

DeGrazia, Alfred, Ralph Juergens, and Livio Stecchini, Editors. *The Velikovsky Affair: Scientism Vs. Science*. New Hyde Park, New York: University Books, 1966.

De Mille, Richard. *Castaneda's Journey*. Santa Barbara, Calif.: Capra Press, 1976.

De Lubicz, Isha Schwaller. *Her-Bak: The Living Face of Ancient Egypt*. London: Hodder and Stoughton Ltd., 1954.

Don, Frank. *Earth Changes Ahead*. New York: Destiny Books, 1981.

Donnelly, Ignatius. *Atlantis: The Antedeluvian World*. New York: 1949.

Driolon, Etienne. *Egyptian Art*. New York: Golden Griffen Books, 1950.

Duncan, Andrew. *Money Rush*. New York: Doubleday, 1979.

Earil, Tony. *Mu Revealed*. New York: Warner Paperback, 1975.

Ebon, Martin, Ed. *Mysterious Pyramid Power*. New York: Signet Books, 1976.

Eckert, Allan W. *The HAB Theory*. New York: Paperback Library, 1977.

The Editors of Pensee. *Velikovsky Reconsidered*. New York: Warner Books, 1977.

The Editors of Scholastic Book Services. *The Middle East*. New York: Scholastic Book Services.

The Editors of The World Almanac. *The World Almanac Book of the Strange*. New York: Signet, 1977.

Edwards, I. E. S. *The Pyramids of Egypt*. 1947. Reprint ed., Baltimore: Penguine, 1975.

Egyptian Museum Cairo. New York: Newsweek, Inc. and Arnoldo Mondadori Editore, 1969.

El Inca. *Royal Commentaries of the Incas*. University of Texas: 1966.

Ernsting, Walter. *The Day the Gods Died*. New York: Bantam Books, Inc., 1976.

Evans, J. D. *The Prehistoric Antiquities of the Maltese Islands*.

Evans-Wentz, Walter Y. *The Tibetan Book of the Dead*. London: The Oxford University Press, 1957.

Fairservis, Jr., Walter A. *The Ancient Kingdoms of the Nile*. New York: Thomas Y. Crowell Company, 1962.

Fakhry, Ahmed. *The Pyramids*. Chicago: University of Chicago Press, 1961.

Fell, Barry. *America B.C.* New York: Pocket Books,

1978.

Fix, William R. *Pyramid Odyssey*. New York: Mayflower, 1978.

Flanagan, G. Patrick. *Beyond Pyramid Power*. Marina del Rey, Calif.: DeVorss and Company, 1975.

_____. *Pyramid Power*. Santa Monica, Calif.: DeVorss and Company, 1975.

_____. *Pyramid Power II*. Tucson: Innergy Publications, 1981.

Fort, Charles. *The Book of the Damned*. 1919. Reprint ed., New York: Holt, Rinehart and Winston, Inc., 1941.

Fortune, Dion. *Sane Occultism*. London: Inner Light Publishing Society, 1938.

Frankfort, H. *The Art and Architecture of the Ancient Orient*. Harmondsworth, Middlesex, England: Penguin Books, Pelican History of Art, 1954.

Fuller, R. Buckminster. *Intuition*. Garden City, New York: Anchor Books, 1973.

Galanopoulos, Angelo G. and Edward Bacon. *Atlantis: The Truth Behind the Legend*. New York: Bobbs-Merrill Company, 1969.

Garbini, Giovanni. *The Ancient World*. London: Paul Hamlyn Limited - Drury House, 1966.

Garnett, Lucy J. J. *Mysticism and Magic in Turkey*. London: 1912.

Garvin, Richard. *The Crystal Skull*. New York: Doubleday, 1973.

Goodman, Jeffrey. *Psychic Archaeology*. New York: G. P. Putnam's Sons, 1977.

_____. *We Are the Earthquake Generation*. New York: Berkeley Books, 1979.

Green, John Richard. *England*. 4 Vols. New York: Peter Fenelon Collier & Son, 1868.

Gregson, Wilfred J. *Evidences of Masonry in Ancient Civilization*. Atlanta: Privately published, 1962.

Gribben, John, and Stephen Plageman. *The Jupiter Effect*. New York: Walker Books, 1974.

Guizot, M., and Madam Guizot DeWitt. *France*. 8 Vols. Trans. by Robert Black. New York: Peter Fenelon Collier & Son, 1860.

Hall, Angus. *Signs of Things to Come*. London: Aldus Books Limited, 1975.

Hall, Manly P. *An Encyclopedic Outline of Masonic, Hermetic, Qabbalistic and Rosicrucian Symbolical Philosophy*. 1925. Golden Anniversary Edition. Los Angeles: The Philosophical Research Society, 1975.

_____. *Freemasonry of the Ancient Egyptians*. Los Angeles: The Philosophical Research Society, Inc.

_____. *Lost Keys of Freemasonry*. 1923. Reprint ed., Richmond: McCoy, 1968.

_____. *The Mystical and Medical Philosophy of Paraceisus*. Los Angeles: The Philosophical Research Society, Inc., 1969.

_____. *The Phoenix*. Los Angeles: The Philosophical Research Society, Inc., 1931.

_____. Other Works.

Hammerton, Sir J. A. *Wonders of the Past*. New York: Wise and Company, 1937.

Hapgood, Charles H. *Earth's Shifting Crust*. Introduction by Albert Einstein. New York: Pantheon, 1958.

_____. *Maps of the Ancient Sea-Kings*. Philadelphia: Chilton, 1966.

_____. *Mystery in Acambaro*. Winchester, N.H.: Privately published, 1973.

_____. *The Path of the Pole*. Philadelphia: Chilton, 1970.

Hawkins, Gerald S. *Beyond Stonehenge*. New York: Harper and Row, 1973.

_____. *Stonehenge Decoded*. Garden City, N.Y.: Doubleday, 1965.

Herodotus. *History*. Trans. George Rawlinson. New York: Tudor, 1941.

Hesse, Hermann. *Siddhartha*. 1922. Reprint ed., New York: Bantam Books, Inc., 1951.

Heyerdahl, Thor. *Aku-Aku: The Secret of Easter Island*. London: George Allen and Unwin, 1958.

Hieronimus, Robert. *The Two Great Seals of America*. Baltimore: Savitriaum.

Hitching, Francis. *Earth Magic*. New York: Pocket Books, 1978.

_____. *The Mysterious World: An Atlas of the Unexplained*. New York: Holt, Rinehart and Winston, 1979.

Homer. *The Odyssey*. E. V. Rieu, Trans. London: Penguin, 1945.

Huxley, Aldous. *Doors of Perception*. New York: Harper and Row, 1954.

Imbrie, John, and Katherine P. Imbrie. *Ice Ages: Solving the Mystery*. New Jersey: Enslow Publishers.

The Impact Team. *The Weather Conspiracy: The Coming of the New Ice Age*. New York: Ballantine Books, 1977.

Indiana Limestone Institute of America, Inc. *Indiana Limestone Handbook*. 1977.

Irwin, Constance. *Fair Gods and Stone Faces*. New York: St. Martin's Press, 1965.

Jung, C. G. *VII Sermones and Mortuos*. London: Vincent Stuart and John M. Watkins Ltd., 1967.

Keen, Martin L. *The How and Why Wonder Book of Magnets and Magnetism*. New York: Wonder Books, Inc., 1963.

Kieninger, Richard. *The Ultimate Frontier*. Stelle, Illinois: The Stelle Group, 1963.

King, Francis. *Secret Rituals of the O.T.O.* New York: Weiser, 1975.

Krippner, Stanley, and Daniel Rubin, Eds. *Galaxies of Life: The Human Aura in Acupuncture and Kirlian Photography*. New York: Interface, 1973.

Krupp, E. C., Ed. *In Search of Ancient Astronomies*. Garden City, New York: Doubleday and Company, 1977.

Kunkel, Edward J. *One Bright Day*. Published by Edward J. Kunkel, 295 West Market Street, Warren,

Ohio 44481, 1978.

_____. *Pharoah's Pump*. Columbus: Published by Kunkel, 295 West Market Street, Warren, Ohio 44481, 1962.

LaBarre, Weston. *Ghost Dance: Origins of Religion*. New York: Doubleday and Company, 1970.

Landsbury, Alan. *In Search of Lost Civilizations*. New York: Ballantine Books, 1976.

Landsbury, Alan, and Sally Landsbury. *The Outer Space Connection*. New York: Bantam Books, 1975.

Lange, Kurt, and Max Hirmer. *Egypt: Architecture, Sculpture, Painting in Three Thousand Years*. New York: Phaidon, 1968.

Lauer, Jean Philippe. *Fouilles a Saggarah*. Cairo: Institute Francais, 1935.

Leadbeater, 33°, C. W. *The Hidden Life of Freemasonry*. Madras, India: The Theosophical Publishing House, 1955.

Lemurian Fellowship. *Into the Sun*. Ramona, Calif.

LePlongeon. *Maya/Atlantis Queen Moo and the Egyptian Sphinx*. 1896. Reprint ed., Blauvelt, N.Y.: Rudolph Steiner Publications, 1973.

_____. *Secret Mysteries Among the Mayas and Quiches*. 1886. Reprint ed., Savage, Minn.: Wizard's Bookshelf, 1973.

Lewis, C. S. *The Screwtape Letters*. New York: The Macmillan Company, 1962.

Lewis, L. M. *Footprints on the Sands of Time*. New York: The New American Library, 1975.

Lilly, John. *The Center of the Cyclone*. New York: Bantam Books, 1972.

Lindsey, Hal. *The Late Great Planet Earth*. London: Zondervan, 1970.

Lockyer, Norman. *The Dawn of Astronomy*. London: Macmillan, 1894.

The Lost Books of the Bible and the Forgotten Books of Eden. 1926. Reprint ed., New York: New American Library, 1974.

Macaulay, David. *Pyramid*. Boston: Houghton-Mifflin Company, 1975.

Macquitty, William. *Abu Simbel*. New York: G. P. Putnam's Sons, 1965.

Mann, W. Edward. *Orgone, Reich and Eros*. New York: Simon and Schuster, 1973.

Martineau, LaVan. *The Rocks Begin to Speak*. Las Vegas, Nevada: K C Publications, 1973.

Masonic Code of The Grand Lodge of Free and Accepted Masons for the State of Georgia. Ninth Edition. Atlanta, Georgia: Published by The Grand Lodge of Free and Accepted Masons of Georgia, 1973.

Masonic Manual of the Grand Lodge of Georgia. Ninth Edition. Atlanta, Georgia: Published by The Grand Lodge of Free and Accepted Masons of Georgia, 1973.

McCoan, J. C. *Egypt*. New York: Peter Fenelon Collier and Son, 1882.

Mead, G. R. S. *Fragments of a Faith Forgotten: The Gnostics*. England: University Books, 1960.

_____. *Thrice-Greatest Hermes, Studies in Hellenistic Theosophy and Gnosis*. 3 Vols. London: John M. Watkins, 1906.

Mendelssohn, Kurt. *The Riddle of the Pyramids*. United Kingdom: Thames and Hudson, 1975.

Mertz, Henriette. *Gods from the Far East: How the Chinese Discovered America*. 1953. Reprint ed., New York: Ballantine Books, 1975.

Mesmer, Franz Anton. *Le Magnetisme Animal*. Paris: R. Laffont, 1972.

Michanowsky, George. *The Once and Future Star*. New York: Hawthorne Books, 1977.

Michell, John F. *City of Revelation*. New York: Ballantine Books, Inc., 1972.

_____. *The View Over Atlantis*. New York: Ballantine Books, Inc., 1973.

Morley, Sylvanus G. *The Ancient Maya*. Stanford University, Calif.: Stanford University Press, 1947.

Morrill, Sibley S. *Ponape*. San Francisco: Cadleon Press, 1970.

Muck, Otto. *The Secret of Atlantis*. Introduction by Peter Tompkins. New York: Times Books, 1978.

Mulfinger, George. *The Flood and the Fossils*. Pamphlet. Greenville, South Carolina: Bob Jones University Press, n.d.

Needham, Joseph. *Science and Civilization in China*. 4 Vols. New York: Cambridge University Press, 1962.

Nelson, Byron C. *After Its Kind*. Minneapolis, Minn.: Bethany Fellowship, 1967.

Nelson, D. J., and David H. Coville. *Life Force in the Great Pyramids*. California: DeVorss and Company, 1977.

Noone, Charles Ashton. *Christmas Letters of Charles A. Noone*. Privately published, 1959.

Noorbergen, Rene. *Secrets of the Lost Races*. New York: The Bobbs-Merrill Company, Inc., 1977.

Ostrander, Sheila, and Lynn Schroeder. *Psychic Discoveries Behind the Iron Curtain*. New York: Bantam Books, 1970.

Ott, John N. *Health and Light*. New York: Pocket Books, 1976.

Ouspensky, P. D. *A New Model of the Universe*. 1931. Reprint ed., New York: Vantage Books, 1971.

_____. Other Works.

Pauwels, Louis, and Jacques Bergier. *The Morning of the Magicians*. Trans. by Rollo Myers. London: Gibbs and Phillips, 1963. Reprint ed., New York: Avon Books, 1968.

Petrie, W. M. F. *The Arts and Crafts of Ancient Egypt*. London: 1923.

Pike, Albert. *Morals and Dogma*. 1871. Revised reprint ed., Richmond, Va.: L. H. Jenkins, 1950.

Plato. *Dialogues*. Trans. by Jowell. 1871. Out-of-print.

Pochan, A. *L'enigme de la Grande Pyramide*. 1971. Trans., New York: Avon Books, 1978.

Ponte, Lowell. *The Cooling*. Englewood Cliffs, N.J.:

Prentice-Hall, 1976.

Pope, Maurice. *The Story of Archaeological Decipherment.* New York: Scribner, 1975.

Prabhavananda, Swami, and Christopher Isherwood, Trans. *The Song of God: Bhagavad-Gita.* Introduction by Aldous Huxley. New York: New American Library, 1972.

Pranhavananda, Swami, and Frederick Manchester. *The Upanishads.* New York: The New American Library, 1957.

Pritchard, James. *The Ancient Near East in Pictures.* Princeton: Princeton University Press, 1954.

Raknes, Ola. *Wilhelm Reich and Orgonomy.* Baltimore, Md.: Penguin Books, 1971.

Rasputin, Maria and Patte Barham. *Rasputin: The Man Behind the Myth.* New York: Warner Books, Inc., 1981.

Raup, David M. "The Revolution in Evolution." *World Book Science Annual.* Chicago, 1980.

Redding, M. W. *The Scarlet Book of Freemasonry.* New York: Redding & Company, 1889.

Reich, Wilhelm. *Ether, God and Devil/Cosmic Superimposition.* New York: Noonday Books, 1972.

_____. *The Discovery of the Orgone: Volume I, The Function of the Orgasm, Sex-Economic Problems of Biological Energy.* New York: Orgone Inst. Press, 1942.

Reichenbach, Karl L. F. Freiherr von. *The Odic Force; Letters on Od and Magnetism.* New Hyde Park, New York: University Books, 1968.

_____. *Physico-Physiological Research on the Dynamics of Magnetism, Heat, Light, Electricity and Chemism, in Their Relations to Vital Force.* New York: 1851.

Robinson, Lytle. *Edgar Cayce's Story of the Origin and Destiny of Man.* New York: Berkley Medallion Books, 1973.

Rutherford, Adam. *Pyramidology.* 3rd Edition, 5 Vols. Harpenden, United Kingdom: Institute of Pyramidology, 1968.

Sagan, Carl. *The Dragons of Eden.* New York: Ballantine Books, 1977.

_____. *The Cosmic Connection.* New York: Dell Publishing Co., Inc., 1975.

Sampson, Holden Edward. *The Bhagavad-Gita Interpreted.* London: William Rider & Son, Limited, 1923.

Santesson, Hans Stefan. *Understanding Mu.* New York: Paperback Library, 1970.

de Santillana, Giorgio and Hertha von Dechend. *Hamlet's Mill: An Essay on Myth and the Frame of Time.* Boston: Mass. Institute of Technology, 1969.

Schul, Bill, and Ed Pettit. *The Psychic Power of Pyramids.* Greenwich, Conn.: Fawcett Publications, Inc., 1976.

_____. *The Secret Power of Pyramids.* Greenwich, Conn.: Fawcett Publications, Inc., 1975.

Seiss, Joseph A. *The Great Pyramid: A Miracle in Stone.* 1877. Reprint ed., New York: Rudolf Steiner Publi-

cations, 1973.

Shah, Idries. *The Sufis.* London: Jonathan Cape, 1969.

Shea, Robert J., and Robert Anton Wilson. *The Eye in the Pyramid.* New York: Dell, 1975.

Smith, Warren. *The Secret Forces of the Pyramids.* New York: Zebra Books, 1975.

Smith, William S. *The Art and Architecture of Ancient Egypt.* London: Penguin Books, 1966.

Smyth, Piazzi. *Our Inheritance in the Great Pyramid.* 1877. Reprint ed., Blauvelt, N.Y.: Steinerbooks, 1977.

Steiger, Brad. *Worlds Before Our Own.* New York: Berkeley Books, 1978.

Stelle, Robert D. *The Sun Rises.* Ramona, Calif.: The Lemurian Fellowship, 1952.

Stewart, Basil. *The Great Pyramid: Its Construction, Symbolism and Chronology.* London: The Covenant Publishing Company, Ltd., 1931.

Suares, Carlo. *The Cipher of Genesis: The Original Code of the Qabala as Applied to the Scriptures.* London: Shambhala Publications, 1978.

Temple, Robert K. G. *The Sirius Mystery.* London: Sidgwich and Jackson Ltd., 1976.

Tiller, William A. "On Devices for Monitoring Non-Physical Energies." (Unpublished paper).

Toffler, Alvin. *Future Shock.* New York: Bantam Books, 1970.

Tomas, Andrew. *We Are Not the First.* New York: Bantam Books, 1973.

Tompkins, Peter. *A Spy in Rome.* New York: Simon and Schuster.

_____. *Italy Betrayed.* New York: Simon and Schuster.

_____. *The Magic of Obelisks.* New York: Harper and Row, 1981.

_____. *The Murder of Admiral Darlan.* New York: Simon and Schuster.

_____. *Mysteries of the Mexican Pyramids.* New York: Harper and Row, 1976.

_____. *Secrets of the Great Pyramid.* New York: Harper & Row, 1971.

_____. *Shaw and Molly Tompkins.* New York: Simon and Schuster.

Tompkins, Peter, and Christopher Bird. *The Secret Life of Plants.* New York: Avon Books, 1974.

Toth, Max, and G. Nielsen. *Pyramid Power.* New York: Freeway Press, 1974.

Umland, Eric, and Craig Umland. *Mystery of the Ancients.* New York: Signet Books, 1975.

Valentine, Tom. *The Great Pyramid: Man's Monument to Man.* New York: Pinnacle Books, 1975.

_____. *The Life and Death of Planet Earth.* New York: Pinnacle Books, 1977.

_____. *Psychic Surgery.* 1973. Reprint Ed., Chicago, Pocket Books, 1975.

Vandenberg, Philipp. *The Curse of the Pharaohs.* New York: Pocket Books, 1977. (Originally published in German under the title Der Fluch der Pharaonen.)

Velikovsky, Immanuel. *Ages in Chaos*. New York: Doubleday, 1952.

_____. *Earth in Unheaval*. Garden City, New York: Doubleday, 1955.

_____. *Oedipus and Akhnaton: Myth and History*. Garden City, New York: Doubleday and Company, 1960.

_____. *Peoples of the Sea*. New York: Doubleday and Company, 1977.

_____. *Ramses II and His Time*. Garden City, New York: Doubleday and Company, 1978.

_____. *Worlds in Collision*. New York: Doubleday and Company, 1950.

Van, Selm. *The Hyksos*. New Haven, Conn.: Yale University Press, 1966.

Voltaire. *The Complete Romances of Voltaire*. 8 Vols. New York: Walter J. Black, Inc. 1927.

von Daniken, Erich. *Chariots of the Gods?* New York: G. P. Putnam's Sons, 1970. Reprint ed., New York: Bantam Books, 1971.

_____. *Gods from Outer Space*. New York: G. P. Putnam's Sons, 1971. Reprint ed., New York: Bantam Books, 1972.

_____. *The Gold of the Gods*. New York: G. P. Putnam's Sons, 1973. Reprint ed., New York: Bantam Books, 1974.

_____. *Von Daniken's Proof*. Trans. by Michael Heron. New York: Bantam Books, 1978.

Vyse, H. and J. S. Perring. *Operations Carried Out on the Pyramid's of Gizeh*. 3 Vols. London: 1840-42.

Wake, C. S. *The Origin and Significance of the Great Pyramid*. 1882. Facsimile reprint ed., Savage, Minnesota: Wizard's Bookshelf, 1975.

Ward, J. S. M., B.A., F.R. Econ.S., F.S.S. *Freemasonry and the Ancient Gods*. London: Simpkin, Marshall, Hamilton, Kent and Co., Ltd., 1921.

_____. *The Sign Language of the Mysteries*. 2 Vols. Cambridge: The Baskerville Press, Ltd., 1928. (Limited edition — 1000 sets)

Wasson, Gordon R. "The Hallucinogenic Fungi of Mexico," *Harvard University Botanical Museum Leaflets*. Feb. 17. 19(7), 19(7), 137-162, 1961.

Watkins, Alfred. *The Old Straight Track*. London: Garnstone Press, 1970.

Webre, Alfred L., and Phillip H. Liss. *The Age of Cataclysm*. New York: Berkley Books, 1974.

West, John Anthony. *Serpent in the Sky: The High Wisdom of Ancient Egypt*. Foreword by Peter Tompkins. New York: Harper & Row, 1979.

White, John. *Pole Shift*. New York: Doubleday and Company, 1980.

Wilcox, Elizabeth G. *Mu — Fact or Fiction*. New York: Pageant, 1963.

Wilcox, Robert K. *Shroud*. New York: Macmillan Publishing Company, Inc., 1977.

Wilgus, Neal. *The Illuminoids*. New York: Pocket Books, 1979.

Williams, Gertrude Marvin. *Madame Blavatsky: Priestess of the Occult*. New York: Lancer Books, Inc., 1946.

Wilmhurst, W. L., P.M. *The Ceremony of Passing*. London: Privately published by The Lodge of Living Stones, No 4957.

Wilson, Clifford. *Crash Go the Chariots*. Australia: Word of Truth Productions, Ltd. Reprint ed., New York: Lancer Books, n.d.

_____. *The Chariots Still Crash*. New York: New American Library, 1976.

Wilson, Colin. *Mysterious Powers*. London: Aldus Books Limited. 1975.

Wilson, Robert Anton. *The Cosmic Trigger: The Final Secret of the Illuminati*. New York: Pocket Books, 1977.

Woldering, Irmgard. *The Art of Egypt: The Time of the Pharaohs*. New York: Crown Publishers, 1965.

Zink, David D. *The Ancient Stones Speak*. New York: E.P. Dutton, 1979.

_____. *The Stones of Atlantis*. Englewood Cliffs, N.J.: Prentice-Hall, 1978.

Credits

The illustrations not listed here are either from the author's collection or in the public domain.

Chapter One

1:1 1:6 1:12 1:20 *Secrets of the Great Pyramid* by Peter Tompkins. Copyright © 1971 by Peter Tompkins. Reprinted by permission of Peter Tompkins.
1:8 Collection of The Library of Congress. Reprinted by permission of The Library of Congress.
1:13 1:19 *Serpent in the Sky* by John Anthony West. Copyright © 1979 by John Anthony West. Reprinted by permission of John Anthony West.
1:18 *Stonehenge and Its Mysteries* by Michael Balfour. Copyright © 1979 by Michael Balfour. Reprinted by permission of Charles Scribner's Sons.

Chapter Two

2:2 *The Physical World* by Paul D. Lowman, Jr. Copyright © 1975 by the National Geographic Society. Reprinted by permission of the National Geographic Society.
2:4 "*Chinese Earthquakes: The Maoist Approach to Seismology*" by Shapley, D., *Science*, Vol. 193, pp. 656–657. August 1976. Reprinted by permission of *Science* magazine.
2:11 2:12 2:13 2:14 *Secrets of the Great Pyramid* by Peter Tompkins. Copyright © 1971 by Peter Tompkins. Reprinted by permission of Peter Tompkins.

Chapter Three

3:7 3:8 3:9 3:10 3:12 *Mysteries of the Mexican Pyramids* by Peter Tompkins. Copyright © 1976 by Peter Tompkins. Reprinted by permission of Peter Tompkins.
3:11 "*The Caracol Tower at Chichen Itza: An Ancient Astronomical Observatory?*" by Anthony, F., et al., *Science*, Vol. 188, pp. 977–978. Fig. 1, 6 June 1975. Reprinted by permission of *Science* magazine.
3:13 From Peter Tompkins' private collection. Reprinted by permission of Peter Tompkins.

Chapter Four

4:1 Photograph by A. Y. Owen, *Life Magazine*. Copyright © 1962 by Time Inc. Reprinted by permission of Time Inc.
4:2 4:7 4:9 4:10 4:11 4:12 4:13 4:14 4:15 4:16 4:18 4:24 *Secrets of the Great Pyramid* by Peter Tompkins. Copyright © 1971 by Peter Tompkins. Reprinted by permission of Peter Tompkins.
4:4 *The How and Why Wonder Book* by Martin L. Keen. Copyright © 1963 by Martin L. Keen. Reprinted by permission of Wonder Books Publishing.
4:17 4:19 4:21 From the private collection of The Institute of Pyramidology. Reprinted by permission of The Institute of Pyramidology.
4:20 From Tom Valentine's private collection. Reprinted by permission of Tom Valentine.
4:22 4:23 From G. Patrick Flanagan's private collection. Reprinted by permission of G. Patrick Flanagan.

Chapter Five

5:1 Reproduced by permission of the Indiana Limestone Institute of America, Inc.
5:4 From Peter Tompkins' private collection. Reprinted by permission of Peter Tompkins.
5:7 5:21 *The Great Pyramid: Man's Monument to Man* by Tom Valentine. Copyright © 1975 by Tom Valentine. Reprinted by permission of Pinnacle Books.
5:8 5:9 5:12 *Secrets of the Great Pyramid* by Peter Tompkins. Copyright © 1971 by Peter Tompkins. Reprinted by permission of Peter Tompkins.
5:15 Reproduced by permission of Stanford Research Institute International (Menlo Park, California).
5:16 *Top:* Reproduced by permission of the Library of Egyptian Museum (Cairo, Egypt). *Bottom:* From William R. Fix's private collection. Reprinted by permission of William R. Fix.
5:17 *Serpent in the Sky* by John Anthony West. Copyright © 1979 by John Anthony West. Reprinted by permission of John Anthony West.

Chapter Six

6:1 Photograph by Vern Miller, Brooks Institute, Chief Photographer, STURP. Copyright © 1978. Reproduced by permission of the Brooks Institute.
6:2 6:4 6:5 6:7 6:8 6:9 6:10 6:14 (*Photo*) *Secrets of the Great Pyramid* by Peter Tompkins. Copyright © 1971 by Peter Tompkins. Reprinted by permission of Peter Tompkins.

6:11 6:12 *The Once and Future Star* by George Michanowsky. Copyright © 1977 by George Michanowsky. Reprinted by permission of George Michanowsky.

6:13 Reproduced by permission of the Library of Egyptian Museum (Cairo, Egypt).

6:14 (*Drawing*) *The Pyramids of Egypt* by I.E.S. Edwards. Copyright 1947 by I.E.S. Edwards. Reprinted by permission of Pelican Books Ltd., Publisher.

6:15 *Stonehenge and Its Mysteries* by Michael Balfour. Copyright © 1979 by Michael Balfour. Reprinted by permission of Charles Scribner's Sons.

6:16 6:22 *Secrets of the Lost Races* by Rene Noorbergen. Copyright © 1977 by Rene Noorbergen. Reprinted by permission of Macmillan Publishing Company.

6:17 6:18 *Mystery in Acambero* by Charles Hapgood. Copyright © 1973 by Charles Hapgood. Reprinted by permission of Charles Hapgood.

6:19 *The Ancient Stones Speak* by David D. Zink. Copyright © 1979 by David D. Zink. Reprinted by permission of David D. Zink.

6:23 *The Great Pyramid: Man's Monument to Man* by Tom Valentine. Copyright © 1975 by Tom Valentine. Reprinted by permission of Pinnacle Books, Inc.

Chapter Seven

7:2 *Serpent in the Sky* by John Anthony West. Copyright © 1979 by John Anthony West. Reprinted by permission of John Anthony West.

7:3 7:4 *Pharaoh's Pump* by Edward J. Kunkel. Copyright © 1962 by Edward J. Kunkel. Reprinted by permission of Edward J. Kunkel, Publisher.

7:6 *The Phoenix* by Manly P. Hall. Published by the Philosophical Research Society, Inc. Reprinted by permission of Manly P. Hall.

7:7 7:8 7:19 *The Secret of Atlantis* by Otto Muck. Copyright © 1978 by William Collins & Co. Ltd. and Quadrangle/The New York Times. Reprinted by permission of Times Books, a division of Random House, Inc.

7:10 7:17 *The Ancient Stones Speak* by David D. Zink. Copyright © 1979 by David D. Zink. Reprinted by permission of David D. Zink.

7:11 *Earth Changes Ahead* by Frank Don. Copyright © 1971 by Frank Don. Reprinted by permission of Destiny Books, New York.

7:12 7:13 Reproduced by permission of the Bishop Museum, Hawaii.

Chapter Eight

8:6 *Life Force in the Great Pyramid* by Dee Jay Nelson and David H. Coville. Copyright © 1977 by Nelson and Coville. Reprinted by permission of DeVorss & Company.

8:8 *The Phoenix* by Manly P. Hall. Published by the Philosophical Research Society, Inc. Reprinted by permission of Manly P. Hall.

Chapter Nine

9:8 9:9 *Stonehenge and Its Mysteries*. Copyright © 1979 by Michael Balfour. Reprinted by permission of Charles Scribner's Sons.

9:10 Reproduced by permission of The Stelle Group (Stelle, Illinois).

9:12 From Tom Valentine's private collection. Reprinted by permission of Tom Valentine.

9:13 Collection of The Library of Congress. Reprinted by permission of The Library of Congress.

9:16 9:18 *Serpent in the Sky* by John Anthony West. Copyright © 1979 by John Anthony West. Reprinted by permission of John Anthony West.

Chapter Ten

10:1 *Atlantis: The Truth Behind the Legend* by A. G. Galanapoulos and Edward Bacon. Copyright © 1969 by Galanapoulos and Bacon. Reprinted by permission of BBC Hulton Picture Library.

10:2 *Reader's Digest Great World Atlas*. Copyright © 1963 by The Reader's Digest Association, Inc. Reprinted by permission of The Reader's Digest Association, Inc.

0:3 10:4 10:6 *Pole Shift* by John White. Copyright © 1980 by John White. Reprinted by permission of Doubleday & mpany, Inc.

Maps of the Ancient Sea Kings by Charles H. Hapgood. Copyright © 1966 by Charles H. Hapgood. Reprinted by sion of Charles H. Hapgood.